i

ORION RESURGENT
RENÉ CHAR: POET OF PRESENCE

Orion Resurgent
René Char: Poet of
Presence

BY
MECHTHILD CRANSTON

studia humanitatis

PUBLISHER, PRINTER AND DISTRIBUTOR
José Porrúa Turanzas, S. A.
Cea Bermúdez, 10 - Madrid-3
España

Dep. legal M. 22.188.-1979

I. S. B. N. 84-7317-082-2

IMPRESO EN ESPAÑA
PRINTED IN SPAIN

Ediciones José Porrúa Turanzas, S. A.
Cea Bermúdez, 10 - Madrid-3

TALLERES GRÁFICOS PORRÚA, S. A.
JOSÉ, 10 - MADRID-29

In memoriam Betty Magin
1901-1976

TABLE OF CONTENTS

APPENDIX

ACKNOWLEDGMENTS

Many have helped in the preparation of this book begun aeons ago under the direction of Warren Ramsey, and recently completed with a fellowship from the American Council of Learned Societies.

Numerous colleagues have offered their generous criticism of the original essays, some of which first appeared in *Forum for Modern Language Studies, French Review, Kentucky Romance Quarterly, The Modern Language Review, PMLA,* and *Rivista di Letterature Moderne e Comparate.*

We thank Corti, G.L.M., and Gallimard for their kind permission to reprint Char's texts, and the Bibliothèque Littéraire Jacques Doucet, Paris, for making available to us rare editions and original manuscripts.

The poet himself corrected and refined the critic's vision, bestowing on us gifts both material and intangible.

We gratefully acknowledge the encouragement and support of all those mentioned above, as of those who will remain unnamed.

Berkeley, Summer 1975

MECHTHILD CRANSTON

RENÉ CHAR

Ce siècle a décidé de l'existence de nos deux espaces immémoriaux: le premier, l'espace intime où jouaient notre imagination et nos sentiments; le second, l'espace circulaire, celui du monde concret. Les deux étaient inséparables. Subvertir l'un, c'était bouleverser l'autre. Les premiers effets de cette violence peuvent être surpris nettement. Mais quelles sont les lois qui corrigent et redressent ce que les lois qui infestent et ruinent ont laissé inachevé? Et sont-ce des lois? Y a-t-il des dérogations? Comment s'opère le signal? Est-il un troisième espace en chemin, hors du trajet des deux connus? Révolution d'Orion resurgi parmi nous.

Aromates chasseurs, 1975

INTRODUCTION

In his Preface to a critical edition of Rimbaud's *Œuvres*, René Char speaks as follows of the aims —and limitations—of literary criticism:

> L'observation et les commentaires d'un poème peuvent être profonds, singuliers, brillants ou vraisemblabes, ils ne peuvent éviter de réduire à une signification et à un projet un phénomène qui n'a d'autre raison que d'*être*. La richesse d'un poème si elle doit s'évaluer au nombre des interprétations qu'il suscite, pour les ruiner bientôt, mais en les maintenant dans nos tissus, cette mesure est acceptable (1).

No critical method, old or new, can explain the artistic phenomenon. Therefore, the most difficult decision faced by any critic concerns, I believe, his choice of perspective and approach. For those dealing with a living author this difficulty is compounded by two factors. First, the artist behind the work is known to us in all his human complexity. Unless we carefully screen subjective contact from objective analysis, we either assume the role of *raconteur*, relating fascinating and irrelevant anecdotes, or, having established

---

(1) «Arthur Rimbaud,» reprinted in *Recherche de la Base et du Sommet* (Paris: Gallimard, 1965), p. 126.

human bonds, we no longer speak freely—without personal interference and inference—of the artist's work. Second, in attempting to deal, in finite form, with an unfinished product, we run—and must accept —the risk that one word, still unwritten, may at any moment redirect the course of our examination.

I first met René Char in 1970, after the publication of my *Enfance, mon amour...* (2). Char had read the work and commented generously. *Enfance, mon amour...* is an investigation along Bachelardian lines of the functioning of the poetic imagination. In Char's dream narrative, «Eaux-mères» (*Abondance viendra*, 1934), I try to decipher the interaction of psychological event and material reality. Some chapters of the first book, revised and abridged, have been incorporated here into the section called «Intimate Space: Imagination's Way,» as «The Dream: *Eaux-mères.*»

Though it deals with an early work, the chapter appears in the second part of the book, at the very heart of the present essay. For in the dream lies the *materia prima* of the poem. There is nothing more artificial, to my mind, than the arbitrary division, along chronological lines, of an artistic whole (3). If a work of criticism is to have any intrinsic merit, it must itself be a work of art, verifiable on its own grounds as structurally sound and aesthetically pleasing. While the three parts of the present essay roughly respect

---

(2) *Enfance, mon amour... La Rêverie vers l'enfance dans l'œuvre de Guillaume Apollinaire, Saint-John Perse et René Char* (Paris: Debresse, 1970).

(3) The first book in English attempting to study *The Poetics and the Poetry of René Char* (Virginia A. La Charité, Chapel Hill: The Univ. of North Carolina Press, 1968) divides the poet's work as follows: «I. 1907-1930: A Poetics of the Act of Poetry; II. 1930-1936: A Poetics of Creative Activity; III. 1936-1947: A Poetics of Moral Responsibility; IV. 1947-1952: A Poetics of Interdependency; V. 1952-1961: A Poetics of Fusion; VI. Conclusion: 1962-1966: A Poetics of Renewal.»

Char's dates of composition, chronology was not the primary structural concern.

The present *étude* takes its compositional cue from the opening text of *Aromates chasseurs* as published in 1975. The first part of the book deals with the circular space of the concrete world; the second, with the «espace intime où jouaient notre imagination et nos sentiments.» I have reversed Char's order to facilitate access to a difficult road. Both parts are, of course, closely intertwined: «Les deux étaient inséparables. Subvertir l'un, c'était bouleverser l'autre.» Both lead to the third dimension, «Space in Motion,» Orion's land.

«Vous ne faites pas une autopsie,» wrote Char. «Vous allumez une lampe» (4). I read his remark as an exhortation to remain «dans le cercle de la bougie,» to follow the circular paths of the poem in preference to the prevailing linear roads of criticism. In the organization of the present study, I have tried to retrace Char's progress from surrealism to phenomenology, from Bachelard to Heidegger. I have applied to each of the poet's collections the method best suited to illuminating what I take to be the work's most interesting facet. The broader issues raised along the way include the questions of collective poetry, poetry of socio-political *engagement*, literary influence and artistic cross-fertilization, and the relationship of poetry, philosophy, and art.

In recent years, the work of René Char has attracted increasing attention among scholars and poets on both sides of the Atlantic. Yet we have no systematic study in English of the poet's complete work to date (5). The

---

(4) In a letter to the author dated 21 January, 1974.

(5) This study was completed before publication of Mary Ann Caws' *The Presence of René Char* (Princeton: Princeton University Press, 1976). However, whenever appropriate and possible, I have

present book surveys more than fifty years (1923-1975) of Char's literary activity. Many texts are given in their entirety, and while some aspects of the poet's work (his theater, for example) receive only passing attention, others are subjected to detailed and repeated critical analysis.

It is difficult to situate Char in any poetic tradition. No pigeonhole can contain the bird in flight. Even formal lineage is hard to establish. The aphorism —characteristic of Char—is essentially alien to French poetry. Practiced by the *moralistes* of the seventeenth and eighteenth centuries, the aphoristic form is generally reserved for social and moral commentary. Outside of France, only Heraclitus, Hölderlin, and Nietzsche have been suggested as presumed literary ancestors.

Ideologically speaking, Char may be closer to recent American poets than to the French writers of his generation. W. C. Williams writes of him:

> ... I think
> of the poetry
> of René Char
> and all he must have seen
> and suffered
> that has brought him
> to speak only of
> sedgy rivers,
> of daffodils and tulips
> whose roots they water,

---

referred to Professor Caws' beautiful book in footnotes. Unfortunately, her 1977 Twayne study of Char reached me when this book had already gone to press. I am happy to learn that James Lawler is also publishing a Char volume with Princeton University Press. It can, therefore, no longer be said that Char is suffering from neglect in the Anglo-American world. It seems, rather, that in recent years his poetry has received more attention in America than in France itself.

even to the free-flowing river
that laves the rootlets
of those sweet-scented flowers
that people the
milky
way
...
René Char
you are a poet who believes
in the power of beauty
to right all wrongs.
I believe it also.
With invention and courage
we shall surpass
the pitiful dumb beasts,
let all men believe it,
as you have taught me also
to believe it.
            (*The Desert Music and Other
            Poems*, 1954).

More immediately, perhaps, than Williams, Wallace
Stevens and Howard Nemerov come to mind as kindred
spirits. Denise Levertov—turning from Supervielle to
Char—may be progressing in a similar direction. Yet,
except for two translations of Theodore Roethke (6),
Char has had little direct contact with the Anglo-Saxon
world.

Though seemingly linked, in his earliest period, to
both the romantic tradition of visionary poetry and
to the Mallarméan ideal, Char quickly moves from
allegory, myth, and symbol, from a mind-reflected and
conceptual world, to the awareness of an outer reality
destroyed, defended, loved and reborn. Mallarmé's cry
of «L'Azur! l'Azur! l'Azur! l'Azur!» is answered in *Les*

---

(6) «*Le Réveil* et *Les Orchidées*, poèmes de Theodore Roethke.
Paris, revue *Preuves*, juin 1959.» Listed in *L'Herne*, special issue,
1971.

Cloches sur le cœur, 1928, by «peur peur peur peur» («Tenailles»).

During the Paris surrealist years, 1929-34, the world bursts in upon the poet. The confrontation with reality comes, at first, in the form of outrage, provocation, and revolt. Lautréamont and Rimbaud—as well as Breton and surrealism—lead Char to systematized violence practiced indiscriminately upon an established natural, social, and political order seen to be hostile or absurd, arbitrary and morally unsound (*Le Marteau sans maître*, 1934). By taking a nominalistic inventory of the world not subject to preordained significance, by fracturing that which is whole and reducing it to its elemental parts, Char hopes to reach ultimate revelation of truth.

Shattered illusion and fragmented reality are the rubble on which *Fureur et Mystère*, 1948, the poet's first postwar collection, must build. Patience and humility, acquired in the service of the *maquis*, make Char attentive to the call of the world. Social commitment is but one aspect of the poet's new awareness of his task.

In *Le Poème pulvérisé*, 1947, Char reaches a first halt on his journey beyond destruction and decay. The *mystery* of life emerging intact from the *fury* of war is safeguarded in the Heraclitean universe of cyclical evolution which guarantees permanence in change. The conflicts of movement and stability are resolved. The whirlwind comes to rest in the circle, the perfect harmony to which «Le Requin et la Mouette» testify. The poet recognizes—and accepts—destruction as an integral part of creation, in which he participates. From the fragments of the past, from the pulverized stone, Char creates a new existence which both includes and transcends reality. But that reality *excludes* the poet, and individual man. Whether he seek an invisible *azur* or impose upon the world a shape and color already perceived and defined, the poet is caught. Whether virtual or actual, conceived or observed, reality eludes the detached onlooker and passerby. The permanence of art—*aere perennius*—will prove, in the end, as illusory as the permanence of the world, death-ridden and sterile.

The collaboration with Braque, begun in 1947, and the meeting with Heidegger in 1955 may have marked Char's most recent evolution. In *Les Matinaux*, 1950, and—more particularly—in «Le Bois de l'Epte,» he breaks out of the circle and begins anew his journey into the void. He does not now, however, seek to fill that void with any established socio-political platform. Content to walk through the emptiness of space and time while remaining in the true presence of existence, the poet dismisses both history and science, which his early work sought to rival. The tool, once a destructive force operating independently of man (*Le Marteau sans maître*), is, at first, subjugated to human will in the service of clearly defined goals (*Feuillets d'Hypnos*), but finally seen as participating with man in the mutual transformation of matter and mind. Poetry is perceived, in the end, as provocation in its original sense, as a call that «disturbs the universe.» Char does not remain fixed in Prufrock's «formulated phrase,» nor caught in Eliot's seaweed. Proceeding along the road of language, *Le Nu perdu*, 1971, leads not to any predetermined goal, but toward the discovery of ever new *rapports* between word and world.

The poet overcomes both «reductive realism» and «reductive essentialism,» and the linguistic positivism that would refuse «any system of exchange between language and the world» (7). From his early pes-

---

(7) Jacques Garelli, «The Search for the Place of Poetry. Artaud's 'Invocation de la momie,' in *About French Poetry from Dada to «Tel Quel»; Text and Theory* (Detroit: Wayne State University Press, 1974), p. 174.

simism, his «héritage intellectuel,» Char moves on to an acceptance of life not as it was or will be, but as it is experienced, each day anew, by the traveler in the house of language, Heidegger's «Haus des Seins.» In the process, he puts man the creator, Orion resurgent, back into the contemporary scene. And that—by whatever yardstick we measure human accomplishment— will guarantee to the poetry of René Char a notable place in the humanistic tradition.

No critical study can comprehend all the material it surveys. Nor can any commentary, however sensible or sensitive, substitute for the poem. Martin Heidegger writes:

> Die Erörterung des Gedichtes ist eine denkende Zwiesprache mit dem Dichten. Sie stellt weder die Weltansicht eines Dichters dar, noch mustert sie seine Werkstatt. Eine Erörterung des Gedichtes kann vor allem nie das Hören der Dichtungen ersetzen, nicht einmal leiten. Die denkende Erörterung kann das Hören höchstens fragwürdig und im günstigsten Fall besinnlicher machen (8).

And a fellow-poet, Jacques Garelli, reminds us that

> the interrogation of the poem should be carried out neither as a study of objectified signs nor as meanings fossilized into a series of objective themes, nor as an intellectual structure to be built abstractly from a global reading of the signifieds of the work and its signifiers considered as material things to be observed, but rather in the temporal unveiling of the text conceived as an operation which renders visible («donne à voir») one which, according to

---

(8) Martin Heidegger, *Unterwegs zur Sprache* (Pfullingen: Verlag Günther Neske, 1971), p. 39. I quote from the new edition of the work first published in 1959.

Roue à aube

its success or its failure, leads the way to *being* or to disappearing (9).

The pages that follow seek not to prove, but to suggest readings and interpretations of Char texts. They should serve as an introduction to the poem, an introduction which is, furthermore, a personal statement, subject to blindness and error. I realize, of course, that the intercourse of text and sense is never innocent, and that the «unmediated vision» (*pace*, Geoffrey Hartman) must forever remain a sublime fiction.

Yet it is hoped that from this study there will emerge—despite the limitations—a poet seen in all his complexity, a poet who—torn by all the conflicts of his age—yet keeps inviolable and intact «sa vérité personnelle,» respecting, in turn, the freedom and true being of every man and all things that are.

In a commentary on Yves Battistini, the translator of Heraclitus, René Char defines the poet of our time... and his own vision:

> Le poète vaut mieux que la leçon de ses pères.
> La plaie qui brille où la phrase s'efface, voilà sa signification. Le poète du xxᵉ siècle a pu rejoindre la révolte de son temps, mais il sait encore mourir pour le frisson le plus avancé de la nuit orageuse, ou, mieux, vivre dans l'attente des prochaines combustions auxquelles il viendra indéfiniment s'ajouter (10).

In the pages that follow, I have tried to let the poem—and the poet—*be*.

---

(9) Jacques Garelli, *op. cit.*, p. 175.
(10) «Feuillet de garde,» 1947, in *Recherche de la Base et du Sommet.*

I

CIRCULAR SPACE: THE CONCRETE WORLD

1

EARLY LANDSCAPES:

MOUNTAIN, RIVER, AND FIELD

> La poésie moderne a un arrière-pays dont seule la
> clôture est sombre. Nul pavillon ne flotte longtemps
> sur cette banquise qui, au gré de son caprice, se
> donne à nous et se reprend. Mais elle indique à nos
> yeux l'éclair et ses ressources vierges...
> «Arthur Rimbaud,» 1956.

René-Emile Char was born on 14 June, 1907, in L'Isle-sur-la-Sorgue, a small Provençal town of the Vaucluse, «one of the least eccentric *départements* of France» (1). This *département* stretches from the fertile plains of the Rhône and Durance rivers to the barren pinnacle of Mount Ventoux—the giant of Provence—visible, on clear days, from the outskirts of L'Isle. In the imagination of the young Char, this giant harbored some secret and unfathomable treasure, «la chimère d'un âge perdu,» which the poetry of the man will try to rediscover:

> Dans le sentier aux herbes engourdies où nous
> nous étonnions, enfants, que la nuit se risquât à
> passer, les guêpes n'allaient plus aux ronces et les
> oiseaux aux branches. L'air ouvrait aux hôtes de la
> matinée sa turbulente immensité. Ce n'étaient que

---

(1) Lawrence Wylie, *Village in the Vaucluse* (New York: Harper and Row, 1964), p. xii.

filaments d'ailes, tentation de crier, voltige entre
lumière et transparence. Le Thor s'exaltait sur la
lyre de ses pierres. Le mont Ventoux, miroir des
aigles, était en vue.
Dans le sentier aux herbes engourdies, la chimère
d'un âge perdu souriait à nos jeunes larmes.
(«Le Thor,» *Fureur et Mystère*, 1948) (2).

L'Isle-sur-la-Sorgue, a rectangle eight kilometers long and
six kilometers wide, lies about 21 kilometers east of Avignon,
the capital of the Vaucluse. The town, like so many of its
Provençal neighbors, is approached via an avenue of fine old
plane trees. It is surrounded by water and rush; tall reed
barriers protect the many small fields against the ever threatening blow of the mistral. *Borïs* (3), broom, olives, and the
curious configurations of the *chêne vert* stand out against the
sky; lavender, rosemary, sage and thyme cover the gentle slopes
with an aromatic fragrance familiar to any Mediterranean
traveler. Rising in the distance—and closing in the valley on
all sides—are the mountain ranges of the Alpilles to the south,
the Luberon mountains to the southeast, and to the north, the
Plateau de Vaucluse with Mount Ventoux, facing onto the
lace-like outlines of Montmirail, evoked by the poet in a series
of sketches, *Les Dentelles de Montmirail,* 1960:

L'écriture d'un bleu fanal, pressée, dentelée, in-
trépide, du Ventoux alors enfant, courait toujours
sur l'horizon de Montmirail qu'à tout moment notre
amour m'apportait, m'enlevait.

The Montagnette chain completes the *vallis clausa* on the west.
Surrounding L'Isle-sur-la-Sorgue are the ancient rock-
perched, half deserted cities of Saumane, Gordes, Ménerbes,

---

(2) Throughout this study, I quote Char's poems in their latest
definitive version (unless otherwise specified).
(3) *Borïs* are low huts of rough native stone. Once used by
shepherds, and recently bought by tourists, many of these huts
still provide shelter from the *mistral*.

Oppède, Lagnes, with their ruins of ramparts, churches, and castles—alleged or real—of the Marquis de Sade. These were the favorite sites of boyhood excursions, where the child René-Emile sought his first companions among foresters and hunters, free and «natural» men for whom poetry was an integral part of existence: men like Francis Curel, who, when asked by the surrealists to name twenty poems that had influenced his life, made the following reply:

> Je suis tailleur d'arbres de mon métier. Je n'ai pas peur du vent (jusquà ce qu'il casse la branche où je suis perché, ce n'est pas encore arrivé). Il m'arrive souvent de me réciter là-haut un des poèmes que je vous indique sur l'air de ma scie ou de ma hache. Tout cela se marie très bien, la Poésie et mon travail, ça m'est même indispensable. La nuit souvent je pêche. Ainsi j'ai remarqué que les poèmes que j'aime me tiennent plus volontiers compagnie quand je suis occupé que quand je suis désœuvré. Peut-être que je suis un original, ici les camarades le disent. Mais vingt poèmes pour moi c'est beaucoup: Villon, Hugo, Apollinaire, Reverdy, Char: *Artine* (4).

In the Luberon mountains lie dead today many of Char's friends: poets and partisans who fought by his side in the *maquis*. Over there, says Char, pointing to the hills, «là sont toutes mes joies et toutes mes tristesses» (5). Not far from Céreste, where the Resistance was centered, and on the road to the village of Oppedette, there stands a memorial to Roger Bernard, one of Char's closest companions: poet, husband, father, shot down by the enemy at the age of twenty-three. Char remembers his friend in a text of *Le Poème pulvérisé*, 1947, entitled «Affres détonation silence»:

> Roger Bernard:• l'horizon des monstres était trop proche de sa terre.

(4) *Cahiers* G. L. M., 8e cahier, oct. 1938, p. 56.
(5) In a private interview, April 1970.

> Ne cherchez pas dans la montagne; mais si, à quelques kilomètres de là, dans les gorges d'Oppedette, vous rencontrez la foudre au visage d'écolier, allez à elle, oh, allez à elle et souriez-lui car elle doit avoir faim, faim d'amitié.

At the southern tip of the plateau, dividing the Grand and the Petit Luberon, lies the city of Lourmarin where stands the rosemary-covered grave of Albert Camus, one of Char's late companions and collaborators. «L'Eternité à Lourmarin,» first published in May 1960, is Char's tribute to the dead friend:

> A l'heure de nouveau contenue où nous questionnons tout le poids d'énigme, soudain commence la douleur, celle de compagnon à compagnon, que l'archer, cette fois, ne transperce pas.

Char had read *L'Etranger* in the *maquis*. He also knew some of Camus' articles written for the paper *Combat*. After the Liberation, Camus—then director of the Gallimard collection *Espoir*—asked Char to send him the manuscript of *Feuillets d'Hypnos,* the poet's war journal. The two men subsequently met at the Gallimard office in Paris. In an interesting passage which also makes a statement about the poet's relationship to and appreciation of the modern novel, René Char has recorded his first meeting with Albert Camus:

> Il me donna rendez-vous chez Gallimard. Je le rencontrai, je sus que nous aurions un chemin à faire ensemble. Un certain temps passa que je mis à profit pour lire Camus, découvrir sa voix d'homme et sa main d'écrivain. Je suis mal disposé à l'égard du roman contemporain,—les récits de Blanchot mis à part—; je ne sais pas *désirer* son sujet ou épouser ses intrigues, ses fonds et son enclos. Toute chose dont il traite est posée autrement qu'il ne le prétend (6).

---

(6) «Naissance et jour levant d'une amitié,» identified in the text.

In the fall of 1946 the two writers met again, this time near the poet's home, in Avignon. Char tells of the encounter:

> Nous nous rencontrâmes dans un vieil hôtel d'Avignon, qui jouxte les remparts, l'Hôtel d'Europe. J'avais là plusieurs camarades. Je présentai Camus à chacun, et tout de suite il fut de plain-pied avec eux, sachant dire et écouter avec l'enjouement ailé ou réfléchi qui était le sien. Il ne faisait pas effort pour briller ou pour capter l'attention. Beauté et bonté de son silence qui ne contrariait point le côté excessif des récits que ces grands adultes répétaient pour la centième fois...

The novelist then accompanied Char to L'Isle-sur-la-Sorgue where, according to Char, Camus immediately felt at home. Did the Vaucluse remind him of his native Algeria? The poet writes:

> Le repas achevé, nous partîmes pour l'Isle. Je sentis à la vue de ces montagnes: le Luberon, les Alpilles, le Ventoux, qui entourent la plaine de l'Isle-sur-Sorgue, je compris à l'expression des yeux de Camus, à l'exubérance qui les éclaira, qu'il touchait à une terre et à des êtres aux soleils jumeaux qui prolongeaient avec plus de verdure, de coloris et d'humidité, la terre d'Algérie à laquelle il était si attaché.

For three years, Camus rented a house near Char, before moving to Lourmarin. In his *Carnets* (vol. II, January 1942-March 1951), he remembers: «L'Isle-sur-Sorgue. Grande chambre ouverte sur l'automne. Automnale elle-même avec ses meubles aux arborescences contournées et les feuilles mortes des platanes qui glissent dans la chambre, poussées par le vent sous les fenêtres aux rideaux couverts de fougères brodées... Char. Calme bloc ici-bas chu d'un désastre obscur.»
During this time of close contact, a lasting friendship was

sealed between novelist and poet. Char describes the early years together at L'Isle:

> Plusieurs personnes l'accueillirent, le reçurent, le fêtèrent; et moi qui l'observais, avec quelque méfiance—lorsqu'on partage avec autrui de récentes sympathies—je m'aperçus que ce qui m'avait prévenu favorablement, dès l'abord, vraiment ici prenait tout son sens: une simplicité tantôt ironique et grave, le geste délié sans excès, une mesure non recherchée, une discrétion subite dans les échanges, au seuil d'une confiance prématurée, faisaient que cet homme n'était jamais un étranger parmi les autres, un importun à peine dessiné. Etranger, celui qui se présente, sans parler le premier, à des êtres qui ignorent tout de lui et désirent apprendre, et qui saura tout sans souhaiter trop savoir.

On their many walks and hikes, Char and Camus explored together the «closed valley» so dear to the poet. A young photographer, Henriette Grindat, had captured the hidden mystery, «l'aspect mental» of the region in pictures that both writers admired. They decided that each of them would furnish a series of texts to accompany the photographs. But when Camus presented Char with his contributions (lyrical sketches that are closer to prose poems than to prose), the poet decided not to add anything. The words of Camus could stand by themselves. Char did, however, promise an introductory note, first published as «Pourquoi ce chemin» in March 1949. The title was changed to «De moment en moment,» and the text was included in *Poèmes et Prose choisis,* 1957:

> Pourquoi ce chemin plutôt que cet autre? Où mène-t-il pour nous solliciter si fort? Quels arbres et quels amis sont vivants derrière l'horizon de ses pierres, dans le lointain miracle de la chaleur? Nous sommes venus jusqu'ici car là où nous étions ce n'était plus possible. On nous tourmentait et on

allait nous asservir. Le monde, de nos jours, est hostile aux Transparents. Une fois de plus, il a fallu partir... Et ce chemin, qui ressemblait à un long squelette, nous a conduit à un pays qui n'avait que son souffle pour escalader l'avenir. Comment montrer, sans les trahir, les choses simples dessinées entre le crépuscule et le ciel? Par la vertu de la vie obstinée, dans la boucle du Temps artiste, entre la mort et la beauté.

When the photographs and the accompanying texts finally appeared after the death of Camus (*La Postérite du Soleil,* Genève: Edwin Engelberts, 1965), René Char also wrote a «Postface,» «Naissance et jour levant d'une amitié,» which ends:

> Camus qui *nomma* «La Peste,» en porte le poids de malédiction. Quand l'état de siège ne serait qu'une superstition, une angoisse contenue et stridente, l'oasis de *l'ailleurs* n'en demeurerait pas moins le météore, la lampe qui traversa le ciel et toucha notre cœur derrière son carreau.

What attracted Char to Camus was perhaps the same «natural» quality he admired in the simple men of the Vaucluse: the attachment to the earth, the closeness to nature, the alliance of poetry and life. In a text entitled «Je veux parler d'un ami,» dated 1957, Char had noted:

> Depuis plus de dix ans que je suis lié avec Camus, bien souvent à son sujet la grande phrase de Nietzsche réapparaît dans ma mémoire: «J'ai toujours mis dans mes écrits toute ma vie et toute ma personne. J'ignore ce que peuvent être des problèmes purement intellectuels.»... De l'œuvre de Camus je crois pouvoir dire: «Ici, sur les champs malheureux, une charrue fervente ouvre la terre, malgré les défenses et malgré la peur.» Qu'on me passe ce coup d'aile; je veux parler d'un ami.
> (*Recherche de la Base et du Sommet,* 1965).

* * *

Through and around L'Isle-sur-la-Sorgue (advertised by
the local Chamber of Commerce as «La Venise Comtadine,»
another Venice!) wind the many little branches of the Sorgue,
a tributary of the Rhône, originating in the Fontaine de
Vaucluse, where a coin-operated multilingual guide still tells
the story of Laura and Petrarch, whose hymn to the Fountain
(«Chiare, fresche e dolci acque») is hewn into the rock. On
summer evenings, tourists flock to the performances of «Lumière, Son et Poésie, un spectacle unique dans un cadre unique.»

> Dans cet asile, point de citoyen insolent qui nous
> brave, point de langue mordante qui nous déchire.
> Ni querelles, ni clameurs, ni procès, ni bruits de
> guerre: on n'y connaît pas l'avarice, l'ambition, ni
> l'envie. Il n'y a point de seigneur orgueilleux à qui
> l'on doive s'adresser en tremblant; tout y respire la
> joie, la simplicité, la liberté; c'est un état moyen
> entre la pauvreté et les richesses; je mène une vie
> douce, modeste et sobre. Le peuple est bon, facile,
> sans armes; le seigneur populaire est affable... A
> Vaucluse, l'air est sain, les vents tempérés, les sour-
> ces claires, la rivière poissonneuse (7).

Char uses these quotations from a letter by Petrarch to
introduce his play *Le Soleil des eaux,* first published in 1949
and staged in Paris in 1967-68 by the Studio des Champs-
Elysées (8). The play, an *acte d'accusation* against water
pollution, is based, in part, on actual fact. Even during the
poet's childhood, the establishment of factories along the banks
of the Sorgue threatened to kill the river-fish and the fishermen, once the backbone of the island's economic strength and
stability:

_____

(7) «Pétrarque. Manuscrit de la Bibliothèque Nationale. Livre XVI. Lettre 6.» Char's plays have been gathered under the
title, *Trois coups sous les arbres* (Gallimard, 1967). My quotations
are taken from this edition.
(8) A television film was made of the play in 1969.

> A la grande époque des pêcheurs, il y avait à l'Isle-sur-Sorgue trois cents familles qui vivaient de la pêche. On pouvait voir le long des quais de la Sorgue les femmes et les jeunes filles travailler à réparer les filets... Il faut vivre avec le poisson. Vous parler des pêcheurs, c'est vous parler de disparus. J'étais le dernier. Je ne pêche plus.
>
> («Pourquoi du *Soleil des eaux*. Témoignages et documents») (9).

In the play, the fishermen of Saint-Laurent (which is the presumed original name of L'Isle) rise in revolt against the changed order of things. When the owner and the chief engineer of the newly constructed paper factory allow drainage of chemical waste products into the river, the fishermen, in unison (they have killed off the only traitor among them) draw up their boats and dynamite the establishment.

Factories, air- and water-pollution have today reached alarming proportions in and around L'Isle, despite the fishermen's revolt, despite the recently begun «travaux d'assainissement,» and in spite of the poet's continued protest voiced in texts like *Le Soleil des eaux* and «Aux riverains de la Sorgue,» a bulletin posted on the walls and trees of L'Isle-sur-la-Sorgue in September 1959, after the launching of the first satellite in the region:

> L'homme de l'espace dont c'est le jour natal sera un milliard de fois moins lumineux et révélera un milliard de fois moins de choses cachées que l'homme granité, reclus et recouché de Lascaux, au dur membre débourbé de la mort.

In his poetic universe, Char seeks to return to the pure and peaceful landscape sung by the Italian master. The spirit of Petrarch's prose, introducing *Le Soleil des eaux*, is curiously

---

(9) This text was added to the 1951 edition of the play.

recaptured and poetically transformed in a prose poem of *Les Matinaux,* 1950, entitled simply «Qu'il vive!»

Dans mon pays, les tendres preuves du printemps et les oiseaux mal habillés sont préférés aux buts lointains.

La vérité attend l'aurore à côté d'une bougie. Le verre de fenêtre est négligé. Qu'importe à l'attentif.

Dans mon pays, on ne questionne pas un homme ému.

Il n'y a pas d'ombre maligne sur la barque chavirée.

Bonjour à peine, est inconnu dans mon pays.

On n'emprunte que ce qui peut se rendre augmenté.

Il y a des feuilles, beaucoup de feuilles sur les arbres de mon pays. Les branches sont libres de n'avoir pas de fruits.

On ne croit pas à la bonne foi du vainqueur.

Dans mon pays, on remercie.

The poem is, however, prefaced by the epigraph: «Ce pays n'est qu'un vœu de l'esprit, un contre-sépulcre.» The bucolic setting is but a vision of the inner eye.

Traditionally, the inhabitants of L'Isle-sur-la-Sorgue looked to the river and to the field for sustenance. Like the fisherman, the farmer played an important role in the life of the island. In Char's childhood days, wheat was one of the major products of the fertile valley. The mill and the grain acquired symbolic significance in the works of the poet from *Moulin premier,* 1936, to *Le Poème pulvérisé,* 1947, and beyond.

Le poète vivifie puis court au dénouement.
Au soir, malgré sur sa joue plusieurs fossettes d'apprenti, c'est un passant courtois qui brusque les adieux pour être là quand le pain sort du four.
(«Pourquoi la journée vole,» *La Parole en archipel*, 1961).

Today, here as elsewhere in southern France, Spaniards and Portuguese are hired as seasonal workers to pick the fruit and vegetables now cultivated in the region: apples, peaches, melons, tomatoes. L'Isle-sur-la-Sorgue today boasts close to 12,000 inhabitants, and while it maintains some agricultural importance—small individual farms hold out against the more ambitious *coopératives*—the town's chief interests are, at present, tourism and industry. L'Isle was proposed, not long ago, as a «station climatique,» and Avon projected the construction of an industrial park. Both projects failed, but prospecting continues in these and similar areas.

The old established trades of tawing, tanning, weaving, silk- and wool-spinning miraculously survive in the region. The well-known «tapis d'Avignon» are still made in L'Isle. Some mills are operative to this day, though cultivation of grain and processing of wool are no longer the prime occupations of the villagers, some of whom have taken employment in small-scale industries outside the city. The once famous «écrevisses» have all but disappeared from the waters of the Sorgue, and the trout served at table are the «truites d'élevage.» Factories and camp-grounds flourish along the banks of the river. The clear, fresh and sweet waters hailed by Petrarch are largely a thing of the past.

Not far from L'Isle are the atomic centers of Marcoule, Pierrelatte and Cadarache. When Apte, a town close to the Fountain of Vaucluse, was chosen as an atomic missile site, René Char published (November 1965), at his own expense, the little brochure *La Provence Point Oméga,* in which he asks:

Qui se moque du danger de tarir la Fontaine de Vaucluse ou d'infecter de poison ses eaux?

The booklet is reprinted in February 1966 with a drawing by Picasso. The poet takes a stand against the established political authority and calls upon the citizens of Apt to oppose their mayor:

APTÉSIENS

Vous avez un maire à tête thermonucléaire.
Lui ne risque rien. Mais vous?

The brochure concludes with the proud assertion that

Tout finit par mourir, excepté la conscience qui témoigne pour la Vie.

In April 1966, *Fusées en Provence,* a six page dittoed leaflet is published, followed in June by a protest rally staged by Char and many of his friends in Fontaine-de-Vaucluse, where banners reading «Non aux Fusées atomiques en Haute Provence» are flown. In July, *Terres mutilées,* a series of Char texts, is recited during the Festival d'Avignon, to the accompaniment of guitars. In February 1967 there follows another tract, *Non aux Fusées atomiques!*

Truffes du Ventoux, vignes de partout, champignons sauvages, pommes d'aujourd'hui, primeurs accourcies, pêches de Provence, blessé à mort serait le sol qui vous produit.

(*La Provence Point Oméga*).

Thus, long before it became a marketable and commercially profitable «product,» ecology was one of the poet's major concerns. Char has fought with the pen and with the sword for the protection and the preservation of the land of his childhood, for the mountains, rivers, and fields of the Vaucluse. But progress has steamrolled over much of the ancient beauty of Provence. Under the banner of urban renewal, many of the ancient ruins dear to the poet have been leveled to make room for low cost housing. Forests and streams have been commercially exploited. «Tout ce que je touche, meurt.» These must be the saddest words I ever heard René Char speak (10). L'Isle-sur-la-Sorgue itself has undergone considerable changes since the poet's boyhood. About the only remnants of the past worth mentioning are the *roues à aube,* the large wooden wheels that once operated wool-, oil-, and grain-mills. The three or four wheels still turning in the waters of the Sorgue have no more than folklore significance now. But once there were more than forty water-mills operative in L'Isle. The wheel is an important element in Char's poetic universe. Of the child turning ten, near the end of World War I, the poet asks:

> Mais quelle roue dans le cœur de l'enfant aux aguets tournait plus fort, tournait plus vite que celle du moulin dans son incendie blanc?
> («Déclarer son nom,» *La Parole en archipel*).

In 1941, René Char, who has joined the Resistance movement organized in Céreste, writes to his friend Francis Curel:

> Je te recommande la prudence, la distance. Méfie-toi des fourmis satisfaites. Prends garde à ceux qui s'affirment rassurés parce qu'ils pactisent. Ce n'est pas toujours facile d'être intelligent et muet, contenu et révolté. Tu le sais mieux que personne. Regarde, en attendant, tourner les dernières roues sur la Sorgue. Mesure la longueur chantante de leur mousse. Calcule la résistance délabrée de leurs planches. Confie-toi à voix basse aux eaux sauvages que nous aimons. Ainsi tu seras préparé à la brutalité, notre brutalité qui va commencer à s'afficher hardiment. Est-ce la porte de notre fin obscu-

_____
(10) In a private interview, April 1970.

re, demandais-tu? Non. Nous sommes dans l'in-
concevable, mais avec des repères éblouissants.
(«Billets à F. C.» *Recherche de la Base et du
Sommet,* 1965).

One of the original *roues à aubes* can still be seen turning
in front of the local Caisse d'Epargne, perhaps the most impos-
ing building of L'Isle. The tourist's attention is further drawn
to the fourteenth century church, richly decorated, in the
seventeenth century, in Italian baroque style. The local hos-
pital boasts a fine wrought iron gate and a monumental seventeenth century fountain. In a brochure advertising the Hôtel-
Dieu and commending those connected with its preservation
and restauration, Char wrote in 1965:

> Peu d'hôpitaux auront autant sollicité la faveur,
> l'intérêt profond et la conservation que l'Hôpital
> historique de L'Isle-sur-la-Sorgue. Son origine est
> antérieure au XVIIme siècle, en un temps où notre
> ville devait être, en hiver, une île visible de loin,
> un archipel d'îlots derrière ses remparts, dans une
> plaine exposée, où voies et chemins serpentaient à
> travers des marais bordés de roseaux, sous la garde
> des collines voisines (11).

A few sixteenth and seventeenth century houses and *hôtels
particuliers* still stand in the narrow, dimly lit streets of the
old town. But on the outskirts, housing developments flourish,
one of them on the grounds of the Névons, Char's boyhood
home.

When, on my first visit to the «island,» I asked for directions to the Névons estate, the natives almost invariably began
their reflections with: «Ah, le château Char!» The house is

---

(11) «L'Hôtel-Dieu de L'Isle-sur-Sorgue.» A copy of the brochure
is preserved in the Bibliothèque Littéraire Jacques Doucet, Paris.
It is interesting to see in the prose text the probable *material* origin
of Char's title: *La Parole en archipel.*

clearly marked as such on the city map, which also shows a Rue Emile Char to the north, a Place E. Char to the south, and a Cité Char, the housing development on the grounds of the Névons.

At the end of the Cité stands—rather forlorn—the solidly bourgeois three storey «château,» surrounded by a wall. This was the private domain of Emile Char, the boy's father, who for seventeen years (and right up to his death in January 1918) exercised the functions of town mayor (while pursuing, at the same time, a successful career in industry). The most attractive part of the original estate was its large garden shaded by fine old trees: poplars, planes, and chestnuts. The property was bordered by meadows and fields, and by two rivers: the Sorgue, and the Névons (a name presumably derived from the Provençal word *nive,* meaning cloud. The river is very shallow and fills with water only when it rains.)

The boy René-Emile grew up in the family «castle» and the man always returned to it until 1952, the year of his mother's death, following which the property was divided. The two older children, Albert and Emilienne Char, opted in favor of subdividing and selling the estate, which quickly fell prey to the entrepreneurs. Two poems, «Le Deuil des Névons» from *La Parole en archipel,* and «Sept parcelles de Luberon,» first published in *Commune Présence,* 1964, tell of the poet's loss:

> Le bien qu'on se partage,
> Volonté d'un défunt,
> A broyé et détruit
> La pelouse et les arbres,
> La paresse endormie,
> L'espace ténébreux
> De mon parc des Névons.
>
> Puisqu'il faut renoncer
> A ce qu'on ne peut retenir,
> Qui devient autre chose
> Contre ou avec le cœur, —
> L'oublier rondement,

Puis battre les buissons
Pour chercher sans trouver
Ce qui doit nous guérir
De nos maux inconnus
Que nous portons partout.
(«Le Deuil des Névons»).

C'était près. En pays heureux.
Elevant sa plainte au délice,
Je frottai le trait de ses hanches
Contre les ergots de tes branches,
Romarin, lande butinée.

De mon logis, pierre après pierre,
J'endure la démolition.
Seul sut l'exacte dimension
Le dévot, d'un soir, de la mort.
(«Sept parcelles de Luberon»).

Char then left the Névons for his new home, «Les Busclats»
(a Provençal word meaning *broussailles,* brush) situated on a
slope just outside the town, on the road to Saumane. He has
not revisited Les Névons, hacked to pieces by the greed of
developers.

The poet has always remembered his childhood in tender
and laconic verses, in texts like «Le Deuil des Névons,»
«L'Adolescent souffleté,» and «Jouvence des Névons,» which
begins:

Dans le parc des Névons
Ceinturé de prairies,
Un ruisseau sans talus,
Un enfant sans ami
Nuancent leur tristesse
Et vivent mieux ainsi.

In this poem of *Les Matinaux,* the speaker presents himself
as a lonely and melancholy child. Though he did not grow up
as an *enfant unique* (René-Emile was the youngest of four
children), Char excludes from his private world everything but

the river and the cricket that saves the child from the *ennui* of summer:

> Mortel serait l'été
> Sans la voix d'un grillon
> Qui, par instant, se tait.

The word *ennui* appears quite early in Char's poetry and may be more than a literary borrowing from Baudelaire. A poem of *Les Cloches sur le cœur,* Char's earliest collection of verse, begins:

> Jadis j'hébergeais en ma maison
> L'ennui croissance de raison
> («Echafaud d'adolescence»).

It would seem, at first glance, that the young Char spent a lonely yet privileged childhood in simulated aristocratic conditions. The Névons castle was guarded by an iron gate. The trees and flowers growing within that gate do not form a simple garden, but a park:

> Dans le parc des Névons...
> Un enfant sans ami...

This park was, of course, tended by a gardener, and the «castle» served by maids (as told in «Le Fantôme de Lola Abat,» a text of *L'Action de la Justice est éteinte,* 1931) (11a). No material comfort was lacking to members of the mayor's family.

Yet, as «Le Deuil des Névons» shows, the boy was not happy in his seclusion. The early version of «Lola Abat» spoke of «le risque réel que courent les existences provisoires dans les

---

(11a) The title of the text was changed to «La Manne de Lola Abba» in the poem's final version, given in the second edition of *Le Marteau sans maître,* 1945. The symbolism of the girl's name is made less immediately apparent.

jardins des propriétés privées.» In a much later text, the poet recounts:

> Dans un bel arbre sans essaim,
> Vous languissez de communion,
> Vous éclatez de division,
> Jeunesse, voyante nuée.
> («Sept parcelles de Luberon,» *Retour amont*, 1966).

Another poem of *Retour amont* marks the distance between the Névons and the outer world:

> Entre eux et moi il y eut longtemps comme une haie sauvage dont il nous était loisible de recueillir les aubépines en fleurs, et de nous les offrir. Jamais plus loin que la main et le bras. Ils m'aimaient et je les aimais...
>
> («Lenteur de l'avenir»).

Whenever possible, the young Char joined the more «ordinary» village children in their escapades through meadow and brush:

> L'heure entre classe et nuit,
> La ronce les serrant,
> Des garnements confus
> Couraient, cruels et sourds.
> La brume les sautait,
> De glace et maternelle.
> Sur le bambou des jungles
> Ils s'étaient modelés,
> Chers roseaux voltigeants!
> («Le Deuil des Névons»).

«Echafaud d'adolescence,» the poem quoted earlier from *Les Cloches sur le cœur*, 1928, already expressed the same desire for escape:

> Exotiques mes peines le sont
> De poudre sont bourrées les larmes

> Et l'explosion a tant de charme
> Subtil qu'il m'isole de la destruction.

Field, meadow, rush and reed, symbols of the free world, are the favorite hiding-places of the young «prince.» Looking back at his childhood, Char remembers (in a letter to the author, 1974): «Je n'étais pas un enfant sage, mais pas du tout! Le parc des Névons n'était pas grille fermée. Avec les garnements de mon âge, j'étais mêlé—et rudement là—insupportable! Le parc des Névons, et les prairies attenantes ont subi nos assauts conjugués... Plutôt chef de bande votre ami, malgré ses tendresses et mélancolies soudaines...»

Among the child's early heroes there is the nameless «Suzerain» of *Le Poème pulvérisé,* «l'homme violet» who—persecuted and imprisoned—finally escapes from his bourgeois existence and teaches the young Char to «voler au-dessus de la nuit des mots, loin de l'hébétude des navires à l'ancre.» The description would fit Rimbaud, whom the young poet had read. But Char dedicates the poem to the hunters and fishermen of the Vaucluse, to Francis and Louis Curel de la Sorgue, to Apollon and to the Armurier of *Le Soleil des eaux,* men for whom sheer physical strength and beauty are at least as important as the aesthetic qualities of a poem. In a text entitled «Les Quatre Frères Roux» (Cahiers G. L. M., 8e cahier, octobre 1938), Char describes some of his early poet-friends: «...quatre indigènes d'un îlot de Pâques au versant provençal des Alpes, se passant impeccablement de la compagnie dramatique des livres captent—ces ruraux—et rédigent de leurs mains de figues sauvages la très pure espérance de la Poésie» (12). Later on, the poacher-partisans of the Resistance inspire in Char an almost Gidean sense of pleasure and admiration:

> Je remercie la chance qui a permis que les braconniers de Provence se battent dans notre camp.

---

(12) This text is later printed as a preface to *Quand le soir menace,* a collection of poetry by the Brothers Roux (G. L. M., 1939).

La mémoire sylvestre de ces primitifs, leur aptitude
pour le calcul, leur flair aigu par tous les temps,
je serais surpris qu'une défaillance survînt de ce
côté. Je veillerai à ce qu'ils soient chaussés comme
des dieux!

(Feuillets d'Hypnos, no. 79).

«Le Deuil des Névons» evokes the people that shared with
the child René-Emile the life of the «château,» gathering at
night under the poplars, to listen to the sound of guitars:

> Tous ses dons répandus,
> La rivière chérie
> Subvenait aux besoins.
> Peupliers et guitares
> Ressuscitaient au soir
> Pour fêter ce prodige
> Où le ciel n'avait part.

The poem mentions «un pas de jeune fille,» perhaps Char's
sister Julia, or her best friend, Marthe, who died in adolescence.   It speaks of the «jardinier invalide» and of an older
(unidentified) female figure:

> Quand le lit se fermait
> Sur tout mon corps fourbu,
> De beaux yeux s'en allaient
> De l'ouvrage vers moi.

> L'aiguille scintillait;
> Et je sentais le fil
> Dans le trésor des doigts
> Qui brodaient la batiste.

> Ah! lointain est cet âge.

This tender portrait of a woman bent over her embroidery
by the boy's bedside does not match the picture Char usually
draws of his mother. «S'il faut distinguer plusieurs qualités
dans l'amour maternel,» he once wrote, «il y a lieu d'établir

une hiérarchie dans la pourriture» (13). In a note to the prose poem «Jacquemard et Julia,» published after her death, Char explains that his mother had always been good to him, «bien que maladroite parfois» (*Arrière-Histoire du Poème pulvérisé*, 1953). René-Emile was regarded as the revolutionary, the young rebel in a staunchly bourgeois family. In an early prose text, «Le jour et la nuit de la liberté,» Char clearly marks the distance separating him from his mother:

> Voici ceux qui ne souffrant pas le péril dans leur demeure, s'appliquent à parler correctement 'comme les livres.' La facilité de ces gens déconcerte. Ma mère se range dans cette catégorie. L'avenir en lui donnant raison lui a laissé le choix des armes. Incontestablement, «elle s'attend à tout» de ma part, mais l'assurance de faire triompher la Morale sur le monstre prête encore à son imagination des ressources insoupçonnées. Charmante mère. Au temps des guerres de religions on réussissait rarement à mettre de son côté un nombre d'atouts aussi appréciable! (14).

In *Aromates chasseurs*, 1975, the poet writes:

> «Ton fils sera spectre. Il attendra la délivrance des chemins sur une terre décédée.»
> Tel le peintre Poussin, je me lavais au vent qui durcissait mes ailes sans un regret pour ma mère disparue.

The portrait of the poet's mother is particularly unflattering when set against that of Emile Char, the boy's father. The «Frontispice» of *La Nuit talismanique*, 1972, paints the couple as follows:

---

(13) «L'Esprit poétique,» in *Le Surréalisme au Service de la Révolution*, no. 3. The text is dedicated to Aragon.
(14) *Le Surréalisme au Service de la Révolution*, no. 1, June 1930.

Mon père avait les yeux brillants, courtois, peu possessifs et bons. Ses colères étaient énormes et soudaines. Ma mère semblait toucher à tout et n'atteindre rien, à la fois affairée, indolente et sûre d'elle. Les lignes fortes de leurs natures contrastées se heurtaient sur un point d'intersection qui s'enflammait. Ma mère alors se retirait, ne répondait plus aux paroles. Excuses et tendre appel la laissaient de marbre. Seul un rêve qu'elle avait fortuné, fortuné comme fut impériale Théodora de Byzance—rêves de riches heures dont elle était le théâtre—mettait fin à leur mésentente. Elle en énonçait les péripéties en famille...

The woman portrayed in «Le Deuil des Névons» is probably not Char's mother, but his maternal grandmother whom the poet remembers, in conversation, as a free, beautiful, and generous spirit, so different from his mother. It was his grandmother who, secretly, gave the boy the 600F that paid for the publication of *Les Cloches sur le cœur,* then died before the work appeared. Char still remembers the loving vigil he and his sister kept by her deathbed.

«Le Deuil des Névons» evokes Char's father in the exclamation:

Que d'années à grandir,
Sans père pour mon bras!

René-Emile was only ten years old when Emile Char died. The poet recounts the last days of his father's suffering in *La Nuit talismanique*:

Les jours de mes dix ans n'ont pas manqué d'espace. Il arrivait que mon père, qui commençait à souffrir, posât, comme improvisant, sa main sur mon épaule gauche. Ses lèvres tremblaient sans que je sache pourquoi. Chaque soir il rentrait de l'usine, les habits saupoudrés de plâtre, avec sa fatigue de moins en moins bien cachée. Ma mère l'embrassait longuement. Il s'alita à plusieurs reprises. Une forêt de chênes passa dans la cheminée. Puis le mal qui le rongeait se lassa. Il mourut.

Un peintre nommé Hierle a fait de lui un vivant portrait. Si ressemblant que je découvre dans le présent de son regard un rêve qui ne lui appartient pas mais dont nous sommes ensemble l'Ecoutant.

The young boy laments the death of his father in «Présence chère qui n'est plus,» a poem of *Les Cloches sur le cœur*:

> L'essoufflement d'une vipère
> Juste au-dessous de ce hallier
> Fait toutes les tiges vibrer
> Et moi j'appelle en vain mon père
>
> Père n'est plus trace le jour
> En caractères perméables
> Ainsi les hommes admirables
> Ont leur nom gravé sur un mur
>
> Mon regard incline à la tombe
> Jusqu'à ce qu'une palombe
> Gicle de la nue titubante
> D'avoir roulé seule la pente
>
> Alors dans un éclat de rire
> J'ouvre à la vie et c'est le pire

Despite the Apollinairian echo («Mon verre s'est brisé comme un éclat de rire,» «Nuit rhénane,» *Alcools*), the poet here makes a personal statement of grief. In the play *Claire,* 1948, the title-heroine declares: «Mon père demeure en toute saison ce géant dont la lointaine présence trouble et incite à agir.»

His father's death coincided with the boy's first separation from home. Char remembers that moment in the «Frontispice» to *La Nuit talismanique,* given above, and in a prose poem of *La Parole en archipel,* «Déclarer son nom,» later chosen as the liminary text of *Commune Présence*:

J'avais dix ans. La Sorgue m'enchâssait. Le soleil chantait sur le sage cadran des eaux. L'insouciance et la douleur avaient scellé le coq de fer sur le toit des maisons et se supportaient ensemble. Mais quelle roue dans le cœur de l'enfant aux aguets tournait plus fort, tournait plus vite que celle du moulin dans son incendie blanc?

The prose poem suggests again the privileged nature of Char's childhood: «La Sorgue *m'enchâssait*.» Like a religious relic, the boy is enshrined by the river. His world is orderly («le sage cadran des eaux»), secure («le coq scellé») and peaceful («le soleil chantait... l'insouciance»). But as the poem ends, something is about to happen: «Mais quelle roue dans le cœur de l'enfant aux aguets tournait plus fort...»

The child is about to step out of «le sage cadran des eaux.» The year is 1917-18, the time of the last German offensives in the north of France, the time of the battle of the Marne. History is about to take a turn, and with it—though independent of it—the life of the young Char who, having completed his studies at the *école communale* of L'Isle-sur-la-Sorgue, is sent off to a lycée in Avignon.

This is the moment of farewell to the carefree life of the castle. The years that follow, spent behind the four walls of the big city school, are not particularly happy times for the young poet. Char tells of his new life in a prose poem of *Premières alluvions*, 1946, entitled «Un fils naturel»:

Cet enfant qui observe de la route la bâtisse du collège à l'heure où la ruche fonctionne dans tous ses compartiments, me sourit lorsque, arrivé à sa hauteur, j'exprime à haute voix, et pour moi seul, le sentiment de gêne irréductible que la rencontre de ce bâillon de ciment inflige à mon insouciance. L'enfant me désigne malicieusement les livres de poèmes dont je viens de faire l'emplette et que je serre affectueusement sous mon bras. En guise d'excuse je raconte: «Ceux-là sont des livres migrateurs comme ces étourneaux que tu vois là-haut

dans la tombée de la nuit qui nous les propose.»
Alors l'enfant: «Sifflons ensemble et vivent les
oiseaux.»

I think the title of the poem has a double meaning. «Un
fils naturel» describes the «natural» child who prefers the
birds of the «école buissonnière» to dusty books, but it also
refers to the boy René-Emile feeling like an outcast in a new
and strange environment.

This is a significant text, as it contains one of the key-
words of Char's poetry, the word *gêne*. Shyness, awkward-
ness, embarrassment to a point of torture, these are the young
boy's first reactions to his new surroundings, and they are
feelings that remain with Char throughout his life (15). I
believe that this *gêne* has, first of all, physiological roots.
Char is over six feet tall, indeed a giant by French stand-
ards (16). Even as a boy he must have towered uncomfortably
over the schoolchildren of his age. This simple physiological
fact—compounded, perhaps, by the knowledge that his grandfather had been a foundling—caused a deep sense of uneasiness in the sensitive child.

> L'aimant baigné de tendresse est un levier mort
> Faute d'hérédité
>
> («Leçon sévère,» *Arsenal*, 1934.) (16a).

---

(15) Char's expression of *gêne* is well caught in many of the
photographs we know of him, but best expressed in the picture
taken of him by his friend, P.-A. Benoit, at the Busclats, autumn
1970. It was published in the special issue of *L'Herne*, 1971.

(16) The word *géant* figures prominently in Char's poetry, and
is used, as in the key text of *Le Poème pulvérisé*, to describe the
poet himself: «Plus tard, on t'identifiera à quelque géant désagrégé,
seigneur de l'impossible» («J'habite une douleur»). Or else, as in
the play *Claire* (v. *supra*, p. 25), the *géant* is identified as the poet's
father.

(16a) The second line quoted here was deleted from the 1945
(and all subsequent) editions of *Le Marteau sans maître*.

But there were other differences as well between the young Char and the «fils naturels.» This is the time when René-Emile writes his first verse, under the sign of Rimbaud, Baudelaire, and Mallarmé. Like the latter, the young Char is searching to reconcile poetry and life, books and birds. Does he succeed? Char destroyed most of the poems of *Les Cloches sur le cœur,* written during adolescence. And the first dialogue recorded between the young poet and the «natural» child clearly marks the distance separating the two. The pose, the flowery, highly literary language is the boy's defense against an *Umwelt* which he presumes to be hostile: «L'enfant me désigne *malicieusement* les livres de poèmes...» The budding poet does not understand the simple but irrefutable categorical imperative of the ordinary youngster: «Sifflons ensemble et vivent les oiseaux.»

As he entered his new school, the boy from the Vaucluse exchanged one prison for another, the ramparts of a castle for the walls of a *collège,* referred to as «ce bâillon de ciment.» «This cement gag,» an unusual description of a school, but one which captures percisely the fears and embarrassments of the child from the village. The feeling of being gagged, of being reduced to *mutisme,* is evident throughout Char's work. «L'Egalité,» a poem from the second edition of *Arsenal,* 1930, puts it this way:

> La bouche en chant
> Sous les verrous
> Comme à l'école
> La première tête qui tombe

In the copy of the work sent to Eluard in 1931, Char changes the opening lines to read:

> La bouche en chant
> Dans un carcan

And in the definitive version, the title of the poem is changed to: «Un levain barbare.» The poet's voice is choked, his neck caught in an iron collar. This seems very strong and direct commentary on the schooldays in Avignon.

No doubt the new classmates brought to their studies much more worldly wisdom and moral freedom than that tolerated in the house of Madame Char. Asked about his occupation after leaving school, Char once jokingly remarked that, in rebellion, he set off to sell whiskey in the brothels of Marseille. «Probable,» a poem first published in *Méridiens,* the literary magazine edited by Char, and included in the 1930 edition of *Arsenal,* seems to tell the same story:

> Pour faire l'Amour et le pire
> une dernière fois MARSEILLE
> La maison-lanterne
> Et son ange
> Au deuxième étage.

A variant reading, again in the copy sent to Eluard, shows the barred version:

> La maison-lanterne
> Et sa vierge

Char complains of the restrictions that governed his boyhood in a text published by Breton in *Le Surréalisme au Service de la Révolution,* no. 1, June 1930:

> Les terres incultes, mon solide désespoir, la vision fugitive d'une épave au fond de la mer, n'arrivent pas à distance, à rendre supportables à la mémoire ceux qui, au nom de la société, m'ont tenu, à l'âge de la puberté, longuement, les yeux grands ouverts devant le soleil de midi. C'est ce souci des *justes proportions* qui devait me permettre, un peu plus tard, de prendre place dans un foyer où les crachoirs remplaçaient les meubles et les cache-sexes les ciels-de-lit. Dans l'immense parapluie rouge que je tiens à la main, chaque soir le soleil vient se coucher, soleil de plomb, heureusement.

The poet takes leave of his adolescence in a series of diary notations dated 1927-29, first published as «Profession de foi du Sujet» in *La Révolution Surréaliste,* no. 12, December 1929, and subsequently included in the 1930 edition of *Arsenal.* These notes, retitled «Le Sujet,» accompany the different months of the year. In January, Char writes:

> Je touche enfin à cette Liberté, entrevue,—combien impérieusement—sur le déclin d'une adolescence en haillons et fort peu méritoire.
> Les objets familiers que l'on a harmonieusement dressés autour de moi restent muets là-dessus à l'encontre de mes plus secrètes espérances: cette grande lueur mobile qui a supplanté dans mon cœur l'imbécile soleil...

And in February:

> Cette épreuve futile en somme ne m'a apporté aucun acquis nouveau. Si, celui d'une certaine gravité non déplaisante: la terre n'est plus dans le prolongement de mes chaussures et n'importe quel ciel, le ciel.

Outwardly, the years 1918-1928 seem uneventful. There is a trip to Tunisia in 1924. In 1925, Char enters—without much enthusiasm—the Ecole de Commerce of Marseille. From 1927-28 he does his military service in Nîmes. He returns to L'Isle and works as editor of the literary review *Méridiens,* which has its third and final publication in December 1929.

Meanwhile, Char keeps writing poetry and sends a copy of *Arsenal* to Eluard. Eluard likes the poems, goes to see Char in the Vaucluse and invites him to Paris in 1929. Here the young poet from the provinces is introduced to the prominent figures of the second wave of surrealism: Aragon, Breton, Crevel, Dali, and Buñuel. This «escape» from the Névons represents his first prolonged absence from home.

Char's stay in Paris is interrupted by trips to England, Switzerland, and Spain (with Eluard and Nusch), and visits to his family. In 1936, the poet is called upon to head the Société Anonyme des Plâtrières de Vaucluse, a company founded by his grandfather and developed by his father. He resigns from the post a year later, for reasons of incompatibility.

The same year, 1936, Char contracts a case of blood poisoning and spends several months recuperating in L'Isle and near the Mediterranean coast, where Eluard and Man Ray are among his visitors. In 1939, he is mobilized and sent to fight in Alsace. Texts like «Les Parages d'Alsace,» «Sur la paume de Dabo,» «Chaume des Vosges,» speak of this region which Char came to love. He returns to L'Isle in 1940, but has to leave his mother's home again very shortly, when a warrant is issued for his arrest. The Vichy government argued that he had been a surrealist, hence, a communist. In fact, Char had never been a member of the party. However, the new provisional government did not distinguish between poetic theory and political belief. No doubt, Char's marriage, in 1933, to Georgette Goldstein, an Israelite, did not simplify matters (17).

«Je suis, en quelque sorte, devenu réfractaire malgré moi,» Char remembers in conversation, calling himself by the same name he had previously given to Rimbaud («Tu as bien fait de partir, Arthur Rimbaud!»). Char could not, like so many of his friends, pack up and take the ship to America or other *havres de grâce*. He could not leave home, but neither could he continue to live in the house of his mother, the only *foyer* he had ever known. And so he takes refuge with friends in the little mountain village of Céreste, not far from L'Isle. He assumes the name of «Capitaine Alexandre» and eventually heads the *Section Atterrissage Parachutage Région 2* of the F. F. C. (Forces Françaises Combattantes) in the Basses-Alpes.

---

(17) A poem dedicated to Georgette Char was part of the original edition of *Le Marteau sans maître*, 1934, but deleted from the 1945 and all subsequent editions. In a letter to Francis Curel (May 1943) Char had voiced his concern over the «rafles d'Israélites» (*Recherche de la Base et du Sommet*, 1965).

In July 1944, he is called to Algiers as a liaison officer, a change of station not much to his liking:

> A la mi-juillet 1944, l'ordre me parvint d'Alger, dans le maquis de Céreste, de me tenir prêt à m'envoler par la plus proche opération d'atterrissage clandestin... Cette perspective de départ au lieu de me séduire me contraria.»
> («La Lune d'Hypnos,» *Recherche de la Base et du Sommet,* 1965).

In his *Carnets* (II), Camus evokes the landing in North Africa:

> Lorsque R. C. quitte le maquis en mai 44 pour rejoindre l'Afrique du Nord, un avion quitte les Basses-Alpes et survole la Durance dans la nuit. Et il aperçoit alors tout le long des montagnes les feux allumés par ses hommes pour le saluer une dernière fois.
> A Calvi il se couche (irruption des rêves). Le matin il se réveille et voit une terrasse jonchée de grands mégots de cigarettes américaines. Au bout de quatre ans de luttes et de dents serrées, les larmes jaillissent, et il pleure, une heure durant, devant les mégots.

Char is not a good tourist and does not really feel at home anywhere outside his native Isle. He returned to it in 1946 and has lived in L'Isle-sur-la-Sorgue ever since, with only occasional trips to the capital. Though he once proclaimed that the big city had adopted him («Paris est aujourd'hui achevé. J'y vivrai. Mon bras ne lance plus mon âme au loin. J'appartiens,» *Neuf merci pour Vieira da Silva*: I, 1957), Char now goes to Paris (where he keeps an apartment) primarily for medical reasons, and, by his own account, only «quand je ne peux pas faire autrement.»

The men and women about whom Char writes can be found, for the most part, among the farmers, fishermen, foresters and artisans of L'Isle-sur-la-Sorgue, and among the partisans of Céreste. The geographic references in his work are, with few exceptions, to villages, mountains, and rivers of the Vaucluse. The sites sung in *Retour amont* have been beautifully photographed and accompany a private edition of the work.

Does this make of René Char a *poète du terroir?* Only in the sense that all poetry is intimately related to the soil that nurtured it. The *Fontaine narrative* springs from the *arrière-pays* of collective civilizations and private experience. For René Char, that hinterland was made up of the Vaucluse, the valley closed in by mountain and stream. «Nulle poésie,» writes Pierre Guerre, «n'embrasse plus totalement l'homme et l'univers, n'est plus éloignée d'une restriction, fût-elle géographique. Mais cette terre natale, toujours présente à ses mots, semble le témoin invisible et permanent de sa création. Jouant souvent le rôle d'un contrepoids à la condensation de sa pensée, elle a peut-être permis à Char de créer la matière poétique si dense qui est la sienne. Elle est le domaine inépuisable, le garant de vérité des mots... Sans doute a-t-il mis dans ses poèmes d'autres terres, les Vosges, l'Ile-de-France, les Pyrénées, la Grèce même, mais c'est à l'Isle-sur-Sorgue, au 'soleil des eaux,' que sa poésie se *voit* le mieux» (18).

In a recent study, Jacques Sojcher comments: «Pour qui ne se souvient pas du pays de l'enfant lointain qu'il était, la fontaine ne parle plus sous les arbres, le retour, la rencontre sont perdus, le présent ne peut s'assembler autour des premiers pas, les ruines ne sont pas 'doués d'avenir'» (19). Those who have followed the poet's itinerary uphill (*Retour amont*) from the «nuit gouvernée» to *La Nuit talismanique* know that for Char the return to the source continues. And despite commercial exploitation and chemical poisoning that source will remain, for the poet, ever fresh and pure:

---

(18) Pierre Guerre, *René Char* (Paris: Seghers, 1961), p. 10.
(19) Jacques Sojcher, *La Démarche poétique* (Paris: Editions Rencontre, 1969).

Nous commençons toujours notre vie sur un crépuscule admirable. Tout ce qui nous aidera, plus tard, à nous dégager de nos déconvenues s'assemble autour de nos premiers pas.

La conduite des hommes de mon enfance avait l'apparence d'un sourire du ciel adressé à la charité terrestre. On y saluait le mal comme une incartade du soir. Le passage d'un météore attendrissait. Je me rends compte que l'enfant que je fus, prompt à s'éprendre comme à se blesser, a eu beaucoup de chance. J'ai marché sur le miroir d'une rivière pleine d'anneaux de couleuvre et de danses de papillons. J'ai joué dans des vergers dont la robuste vieillesse donnait des fruits. Je me suis tapi dans des roseaux, sous la garde d'êtres forts comme des chênes et sensibles comme des oiseaux...

(«Suzerain,» *Le Poème pulvérisé*).

The poetry of René Char, drawn from the unfathomable Fontaine de Vaucluse, is dedicated to the preservation of mountain, river, and field, bird and tree; to the restoration of health, and to the rediscovery of «la chimère d'un âge perdu.»

2

EARLY MENTORS:

BRETON, ELUARD, AND CHAR: *RALENTIR TRAVAUX.* ELECTIVE AFFINITIES?

> Et la vérité, il ne faut pas craindre de se répéter,
> est personnelle, stupéfiante et personnelle.
> (René Char, Letter to Henri Peyre, 1963).

Recently, José Corti republished *Ralentir Travaux* (1), the little volume of thirty poems written jointly by Breton, Eluard and Char «en automobile, un soir, de l'Isle-sur-Sorgue à Avignon» (2), or, more precisely, between 25-30 March, 1930. The title and occasional lines in the book refer directly to this *situation* of the poems.

Ralentir Travaux is dedicated to Benjamin Péret with whom Eluard had writen, in 1925, the *152 Proverbes mis au goût du jour.* The most notable example of collective writing had, of course, been furnished by Breton and Soupault in *Les Champs magnétiques,* published in 1919. While these works have been amply discussed by literary historians, *Ralentir Travaux* has been all but ignored by the critics (3). And yet,

---

(1) André Breton, René Char, Paul Eluard: *Ralentir Travaux* (Paris: José Corti, 1968). All page indications refer to this edition.

(2) A manuscript note following the poem «L'Ecole buissonnière.»

(3) I have seen only one recent review which compares *Les Champs magnétiques,* republished by Gallimard in 1969, and *Ralentir*

as the joint effort of three major poets, this work has no equal in twentieth century French poetry. It affords many insights into the nature of all three collaborators and into their relationship to each other. It is an interesting defense and illustration of a surrealist doctrine even if it proves—as I think it does—the ultimate failure of collective poetry.

René Char, nearly ten years the junior of both Breton and Eluard, was a newcomer to the surrealist group, and *Ralentir Travaux* represents his first recorded attempt at collective writing. Eluard had adhered to the movement as early as 1920. He is mentioned in the first *Manifeste du Surréalisme*, 1924, and his definitive break with Breton does not come until the end of 1938, when he chooses communism in preference to the *Fédération internationale de l'art révolutionnaire indépendant*.

By 1930, Eluard had published some of his major poetry: *Répétitions* in 1922, *Mourir de ne pas mourir,* 1924, *Capitale de la douleur,* 1926, and *L'Amour la poésie,* 1929. Breton, on the other hand, had been engaged chiefly in polemics and —with the exception of his poetic novel *Nadja,* 1928— concentrated on theoretical writings, such as the two surrealist manifestoes, 1924, 1929, the *Légitime Défense,* 1926, and *Le Surréalisme et la peinture,* 1928.

Travaux, stating: «*Ralentir Travaux* se déroule en vers plus courts, en aphorismes concis, en éclairs brefs, pris dans la coulée d'une langue fluide qu'ils sertissent d'étincelles: un tel mélange porte à la fois les empreintes de René Char et de Paul Eluard, l'une brillante et claire, l'autre souple et précieuse, tandis que les deux livres sont étoffés par la phrase d'André Breton... Une telle expérimentation —fût-elle de laboratoire—qui s'obstine à défricher, retourner et ensemencer les terres de la parole trouve sa solution dans la parfaite unité et dans la scrupuleuse exactitude d'une mise en mots qui se proposait alors '*d'exprimer, soit verbalement, soit par écrit, soit de toute autre manière le fonctionnement réel de la pensée.*' Nombre de tentatives et d'essais qui mettent de nos jours en lumière les nécessités d'une expression totale... pourraient s'appuyer avec bonheur sur de tels textes et leur restituer leur valeur historique en même temps que leur rôle d'avant-garde...» Christian Audejean, *Esprit,* no. 388, janvier 1970, p. 243.

It was natural, therefore, that the young Char—interested in poetry more than in poetics—should have sent the poems of *Arsenal,* 1929, to Eluard rather than to Breton. *Arsenal,* we remember, was Char's second published work, written in his Provençal seclusion «dans l'ignorance du surréalisme.» The young poet's *opusculum* was favorably received by Eluard, who paid Char a visit in the Vaucluse and, in turn, invited him to Paris in October 1929. Here he was introduced to Breton and Aragon, the veterans of surrealism, and to Dali and Buñuel, newcomers, like himself, to the second phase of the movement. In December 1929, Char signed the *Second Manifeste du Surréalisme* as it appeared in *La Révolution Surréaliste.*

Char contributed to Breton's publications *La Révolution Surréaliste,* 1929-1930, and *Le Surréalisme au Service de la Révolution,* 1932. Six months after *Ralentir Travaux,* he published his first work with the *Editions surréalistes,* the long prose poem *Artine,* reminiscent of Breton's *Nadja.* In 1931, *L'Action de la justice est éteinte* is published under the same auspices. The third and last of Char's works to be sponsored by the *Editions surréalistes* is *Le Marteau sans maître,* 1934. Here his formal adherence to the movement—never wholehearted—ends. While Char politely offers some of his works to the acknowledged leader of surrealism, his true admiration and friendship will be reserved, from the beginning, for Paul Eluard, of whom he writes, in 1933:

> A hauteur d'Eluard les nuages invisibles deviennent des fleuves visibles. C'est simple comme la croissance du charbon. De la même époque la perfection du poète et l'humanité primitive. L'anneau de la terre est passé dans la grande Classe des Sommeils.
> Les yeux ouverts regardent les yeux fermés et se persuadent de souffrir jusqu'au néant de cet inquiétant mystère. C'est ainsi que l'amour, de son vivant, s'afflige volontiers de ses propres larmes.
> (*Recherche de la Base et du Sommet,* 1965).

Char will share with Eluard most of the significant events

of his life. In 1930, the two men are engaged, with Breton, in the writing of *Ralentir Travaux,* when Eluard learns that Gala will not return. He meets Nusch in the company of Char, and again the young friend is at his side for the burial of Nusch, in 1946, in the Père Lachaise cemetery. Eluard tells of these events in a letter to Alain Trutat, dated 15 July, 1947:

> René Char n'était que depuis quelques mois mon ami quand, avec lui, un jour de mai 1930, j'ai rencontré, dans la rue, la petite Nusch.
>
> A ces débuts de mon amour, il m'a encouragé, il m'a soutenu, il a surtout étayé la fragile et déconcertée Nusch. A sa mort, il l'a veillée avec moi trois nuits qui m'ont caché depuis les couleurs du monde, de la vie (3a).

Char had accompanied Nusch and Eluard on several trips to Spain. Little is publicly known of their life together on the Butte Montmartre, but it is certain that at least from 1930 until Char's marriage to Georgette Goldstein in 1933 and Eluard's marriage to Nusch, a year later, the two poets shared much of the colorful life of Montmartre and Montparnasse (4). In the letter quoted above, Eluard states that their intimate friendship lasted until 1947. Char writes, on the occasion of Eluard's death in 1952:

> Pourquoi m'interrogez-vous «à présent» sur Paul Eluard? Sa vraie mobilité, sa course glorieuse, durant laquelle, rare et merveilleux poète, il va enfin pouvoir distancer par le seul verbe ses bons frères de partout, vient de commencer depuis ce matin

---

(3a) Eluard's letter is reproduced in the *Album Eluard* published by Robert D. Valette (Paris: Tchou, 1967), p. 212.

(4) It was during a manifestation staged by the surrealists in the Bar Maldoror of Montparnasse that Char received a knife wound in the groin, shortly after the publication of *Ralentir Travaux.* The knife will play an important part in Char's later poetry.

neuf heures. Nous ne pouvons plus rien pour lui et il pourra encore beaucoup pour nous. Mais il ne peut plus rien contre les dieux libres de son berceau revenus et le visage en flamme de son amour.

Durant des dizaines d'années nous nous sommes rencontrés presque chaque jour avec le même impatient entrain. Puis nous avons cessé de nous retrouver. Nous nous adressions dérisoirement des livres, comme d'anciens jumeaux fendus, mais qui s'estiment, savent et communiquent doucement... Misère!

(«A la mort d'Eluard,» *Recherche de la Base et du Sommet*).

Eluard remembers Char in many of his poems. The first title of «L'Age de la vie,» a poem of *Poésie ininterrompue I,* 1946, was a salute to Char: «A René Char.» In 1931, Eluard writes the prose poem «Dors,» in which he relates his encounter with Nusch in the company of Char, December 1929. In 1932, Eluard dedicates to his young friend the poem «Pour un moment de lucidité,» from *La Vie immédiate.* In the same collection, «A peine défigurée» is dedicated to Char, as is «Le Pont brisé» of *Les Yeux fertiles,* 1936. The poem «Le Soir et la fatigue,» published in *Cours naturel,* 1938, is first found in a letter that Eluard sent to Char from Cornwall in July 1937. Another text of *Les Yeux fertiles,* «La tête contre les murs,» is sent to Char the same year. *Capitale de la douleur* is inscribed «A René Char qui n'a pas hésité une seconde à affirmer, au péril de sa vie, que j'existais, à René Char, que j'aime au péril de ma vie» (*Album Eluard*). *La Rose publique,* 1934 (poems attacked by Breton for being «totalement dénués d'agressivité») was offered «à mon compagnon de vie René Char distributeur de la lumière des plus grands mystères, ce livre encore inédit mon meilleur livre...» And to Char, serving in the Resistance, Eluard sends *Poésie et Vérité,* with the inscription: «Au capitaine Alexandre premier chevalier poète de ce temps désarmé» (*ibid.*).

Char also receives mention in Eluard's theoretical writings. Two of the younger poet's *images* figure in the French manuscript of *Poetry's evidence,* published in 1932 in the English surrealist journal *This Quarter. Poetry's evidence* is a first draft of «L'Evidence poétique,» the talk given by Eluard in London in 1936. In the early version, the poet noted: «Voici les images qui, entre tant d'autres, m'obsèdent, images fulgurantes qui m'inquiètent et qui me rassurent, qui me font admettre qu'il n'y a rien d'incompréhensible et que rien n'est perdu pour l'esprit.» Among these *images,* drawn primarily from the writings of Lautréamont and Rimbaud, Eluard cites the following lines from *L'Action de la Justice est éteinte,* 1931: «Les soleils fainéants se nourrissent de méningite» («Les Messagers délirants de la poésie frénétique»), and «le poète solitaire / Grande brouette des marécages («Poètes») (4a). Again in 1942, in the essay *Poésie involontaire et poésie intentionnelle,* Eluard cites two texts by Char. From *Artine,* he quotes the passage: «Offrir au passage un verre d'eau à un cavalier lancé à bride abattue sur un hippodrome envahi par la foule suppose, de part et d'autre, un manque absolu d'adresse; Artine apportait aux esprits qu'elle visitait cette sécheresse monumentale.» This quote is followed by a line from «Domaine»: «Ma maîtresse mouillée, écorchée insultante, je te plante dans mon cri» (in *Abondance viendra,* 1933, dedicated to Eluard).

While Eluard will collaborate with Breton in other collective writing, right up to the time of their break in 1938 (*L'Immaculée Conception,* 1930; *Notes sur la Poésie,* 1936; *Dictionnaire abrégé du surréalisme,* 1938), Char did not co-

---

(4a) The same definition of the poet is given, less explicitly, in «Le Cheval de corrida,» a text contained in the original version of *Poèmes militants,* 1931-1933. The poem ends:

> Et que la brouette
> Expose à travers les marécages
> Le cerveau de ce même amour
> Courtisé par les tessons de bouteilles
> Application du cercle rouge.

operate further with Breton in matters of poetry. With Eluard, he wrote two poems, «Neuve» and «Paliers,» in January 1937, while Nusch and Eluard were guests of Char—recuperating from a case of blood poisoning—in Le Cannet, near Cannes. In 1960, eight years after Eluard's death, Jean Hugues published the manuscripts of *Deux poèmes,* and the living poet took the opportunity to improve on some of Eluard's original lines. In conversation, Char jokingly referred to the incident as a «collaboration posthume.» The 1930 edition of *Artine* had announced another collaborative work by Char and Eluard, *Chemin des sources,* a title never published (4b).

While in 1930 the relationship between Eluard and Breton was and will be of long standing—both had already belonged to «le groupe Dada»—, Char's creative cooperation with Breton began and ended with *Ralentir Travaux,* the poems written by the three on the occasion of a visit by Eluard and Breton to L'Isle-sur-la-Sorgue. Char's junior position in the triumvirate is reflected in the distribution of lines. The thirty poems of *Ralentir Travaux* come to a total of 335 lines; 134 by Breton, 123 by Eluard, and 78 by Char. Only 14 poems represent a collaboration of all three poets: 176 lines, almost evenly distributed (Breton: 66, Eluard: 57, Char: 53).

With Eluard alone, Char writes five poems, a total of 35 lines, of which 13 are by Char and 22 by Eluard. With Breton, Char shares four poems, totaling 29 lines, 12 by Char, 17 by Breton. The lion share of the volume goes to Eluard and Breton, who divide among them six poems or 92 lines: 51 by Breton, 41 by Eluard. The shortest poem written jointly by Eluard and Breton has 11 lines, the longest—which is also the longest in the collection—comes to 25 lines. The

---

(4b) In her *René Char* (Twayne, 1977), Mary Ann Caws writes that «A poetic portrait of Eluard is to be found in 'Convergence des multiples',» a text of *Retour amont.* I do not know the source of her information, but even as a speculation, it would be interesting. The poem ends: «Un soleil qui n'était point pour nous s'en échappa comme un père en faute ou mal gratifié.»

average length of the poems written by the two is 15 lines.

With Char, Eluard writes poems varying in length from three to ten lines, with an average of seven lines per poem. The pieces that Char writes with Breton are somewhat longer, ranging from five to 12 lines. The shortest poems in the book are one of three lines by Eluard, and another three line poem shared by Eluard and Char. The longest poems in the volume are divided between Eluard and Breton.

Although quantitatively Char is the last of the contributors to *Ralentir Travaux,* supplying less than a fourth of the total volume, he does write nearly a third of the lines for the poems to which he contributes. Furthermore, his verses stand in key positions. Char writes the opening lines for ten poems and the closing lines for thirteen. For «Isolée à ravir,» which stands almost at the center of the book, Char supplies both the opening and the closing verses. By volume, his contributions to *Ralentir Travaux* are nearly the equivalent of *Arsenal.*

The copy of *Ralentir Travaux* presented to Eluard's first wife, Gala, contains a 27 line dedication also written jointly by Breton, Eluard and Char. It might be of interest to quote it here. The initials preceding the lines indicate the author:

B Corridor obscur
B Pavé d'amorces en forme de cœurs
B (Il faut marcher sur les raies)
C L'escalier
C La lumière tombe des pierres sous le vent
C alors une empreinte de caresse
C une chevelure a poussé
B 1re chambre les neiges éternelles
B Ce sont des épaules nues
E La tête se renverse en arrière traversée par
     l'ombre d'un rapace
E On ne sait pas que les mains se referment
E Sur de doux vêtements abandonnés depuis long-
     temps
C Des vêtements chanteurs
C Un nom est sur toutes les bouches

```
E    2e chambre aux miroirs enfumés
B    Cave centrale liqueurs spectrales
B    Toiles d'araignées jusqu'au fond des lampes
E    Toutes les parties claires des corps sont indivi-
        sibles
C    On tousse un peu à cause du soufre
C    3e chambre les papillons gigantesques
C              Automne ou idée fixe?
C              une petite hutte
C              un amour de soleil
E    Il faut subir les plus absurdes volontés
E    Les robes les plus longues les caresses les plus
        ignorantes
C    4e chambre le calendrier perpétuel
E    Les pièges sont tendus
```

It seems natural that Breton, who shared much of his intellectual experiences with Eluard but kept fairly aloof in personal matters, should take last place in this private *dédicace* to Gala, and it is equally natural that Char, who already in 1930 was so well acquainted with Eluard's inner life, should here take the lead (12 lines). This dedication is much more structured than its authors would admit. The «1ᵉ chambre» is described by Breton, the second by Eluard, the third and fourth by Char. The fourth room, «le calendrier perpétuel,» leads back to the first of «neiges éternelles.» The whole poem describes a circle from winter to autumn, from «neiges éter-nelles» to «un amour de soleil.»

Like the *dédicace,* all of *Ralentir Travaux* is a rationally structured entity, quite the opposite of the «frénésie» alleged in *La Quinzaine Critique,* which published one of the early reviews of the work (25 July, 1930):

A. Breton, R. Char et Paul Eluard mettent en ruines, selon le dogme de leur école, les monuments du verbe, éparpillent au vent ce qui garnissait les magasins de décors poétiques. Dans ces frénésies, dans le parti pris de heurter l'individualisme romantique par des publications plutôt grégaires qu'anonymes,

certains peuvent goûter un vandalisme momentanément salubre.

The astute reviewer apparently caught Breton's deliberate
persiflages of Hugo, Char's imitations of Apollinaire and
Rimbaud, without, however, making specific mention of them.
He further saw—and that, to my mind, is the more important
observation—that the verses of *Ralentir Travaux* are *grégaires*
rather than *anonymes,* for each poem, each line clearly bears
the unwritten signature of its author. The work brings
together three independent minds, each elaborating—in the
others' company—his favorite themes to his accustomed tune.
Eluard, Char and Breton do not reach here the «affranchisse-
ment de la personnalité» that Lautréamont predicted for
collective writing and that A. Rolland de Renéville spoke of
in another early review of *Ralentir Travaux* (*N. R. F.,* 1 January, 1932), stating that:

> Puisque le but du poète doit être l'affranchissement
> de la personnalité au profit d'une conscience cosmi-
> que, rien ne s'oppose, en principe, à ce qu'un poème
> soit composé par plusieurs auteurs. La feuille de
> papier blanc deviendra le lieu de rencontre de mul-
> tiples consciences, qui ne sont en réalité que les
> aspects d'une conscience unique...

Even in its outer structure, *Ralentir Travaux* is the work
of the calculating intellect and has nothing to do with
surrealist dream-recitals or games of the *cadavre exquis* type.
Most of the texts are evenly—and often mathematically—
divided among the authors. The second poem, for example,
has six lines, of which Char, Breton and Eluard each write
two. In the twelfth poem, «Commencement et fin,» five
lines go to Breton and Eluard, four to Char. «Autour de
l'amour,» the text that follows, is justly divided between Char
and Breton (three lines each). «Un Sort rejeté,» poem 17, is
written in equal parts (5 + 5) by Eluard and Char. «Histoire
naturelle» counts three lines each by Breton, Eluard and Char.

While Breton and Eluard nearly always divide fairly between them the poems they write together and usually have an equal share in poems written by all three men, Char is sometimes at a disadvantage. Thus he gets only two lines in the 14 line poem «L'Ecole buissonnière,» and one line of the nine in «Toujours les mêmes,» the text that follows. If Breton and Eluard emerge as the dominant figures of *Ralentir Travaux,* it is no doubt because they have enjoyed a long acquaintance as men and previous experience in collective writing, which Char lacked. In theory, therefore, Breton and Eluard should be able to come closer to the «conscience unique» of which Rolland de Renéville spoke. It remains for us to examine whether they do in fact write *one* poem.

Breton must be regarded as either the most versatile or the least authentic of the three authors. He follows with equal ease lines by Eluard (15 times) and Char (11 times). Eluard, on the other hand, follows Breton 20 times, but Char only four times. Char follows Breton three times, Eluard, 12 times. It can be deduced from these figures that in *Ralentir Travaux* Eluard remains in the role of the disciple vis-à-vis Breton, a role which he had assumed as early as 1920, and against which he finally rebels in 1938, when he declares:

> J'ai rompu *définitivement* avec Breton, à la suite d'une discussion relativement calme, au café... Le surréalisme ne devait pas devenir une école, une chapelle littéraire où l'enthousiasme et je ne sais quelle misérable action devaient répondre à la commande... Ma vie en changera sûrement... Au bout de 18 ans, tout cela devenait une habitude, un ordre... (5).

Eluard plays the opposite role with respect to Char. In *Ralentir Travaux,* he takes the attitude proper to the older man: he often points the way, but rarely follows. A small

---

(5) Eluard's letter to «H,» dated «De Paris, 1938.»

detail throws additional light on the image of Eluard as the teacher or father figure. In the Saint-Denis manuscript of *Ralentir Travaux,* he takes the liberty of correcting a line by Char. In the poem «Ordre du jour,» the latter had written: «Il y aura davantage de manchots que d'aveugles,» which Eluard corrects to: «Il y aura plus de manchots...»

Eluard's role of the disciple vis-à-vis Breton is evident already in the second poem of *Ralentir Travaux,* «L'Usage de la force.» Breton begins:

> Ne secoue pas ainsi tes cheveux on ne s'y voit plus
> C'est tout de suite plein d'ouvriers

Eluard continues, taking his entire first sentence from Breton, but giving it an ironic twist:

> Ne secoue pas ainsi tes cheveux ou bien celui qui
> part pour le Nord
> Déçu se retrouvera dans le Sud

Eluard's lines, besides suggesting a pun (on the expression «perdre le nord») may refer to the poets' projected journey northward from l'Isle to Paris, whence Char, several years later, did return South, *déçu.*

While keeping to the pattern set by Breton, Char ends the poem above with images of a more personal nature:

> Mais apprends plutôt à rouler tes cheveux
> Pour que les pierres y trouvent leur compte

From the beginning, Char demonstrates an independent turn of mind. In the sixth poem, «En retour,» Eluard and Breton write a piece of social criticism which Char ends with a five line stanza unrelated to the rest. It reads like verses modeled on Apollinaire (who was, we remember, one of Char's earliest and greatest admirations). Here the concluding stanza:

> On dépasse le temps cahin-caha dans sa brouette
> Alors un étranger s'avise que les couples n'ont
>   plus leur raison d'être
>
> Qu'ils chantent faux
> C'est une bande de brigands
> Les têtes ont quitté les épaules

We are reminded of Schinderhannes or of «La Maison des morts» from *Alcools*. The stanza above is reduced to one image in «Poètes,» the poem already quoted from Char's *L'Action de la Justice est éteinte,* published one year after *Ralentir Travaux*: «le poète solitaire / Grande brouette des marécages.»

Char shows the same attitude of aloofness in «Le Mauvais Sujet,» the next poem of *Ralentir Travaux,* to which he adds overtones of Rimbaud and Lautréamont. He answers Eluard's «Je te ferai savoir comment je me nomme» with these lines, which conclude the poem:

> Tu vas voir de quel bois je me chauffe les idées
> Je ne me gratte plus le cuir chevelu avec les ongles
> Mais avec le fœtus viager
> Serré dans le bocal de mes ancêtres
> Maintenant de la famille
> Je suis la coqueluche du vingtième siècle

The provocative tone and some of the vocabulary here point to Rimbaud, who permeated much of *Les Cloches sur le cœur,* as well as to Lautréamont, with whose work Char had just become acquainted, at the suggestion of Eluard.

In the ninth poem, «Toujours les mêmes,» Breton and Eluard voice their disdain of bourgeois morality:

> ...le courage alors s'en prend aux autres vertus
> Calme la mauvaise humeur flatte le risque
>   corrompt la méfiance

And Char ends the poem with one short line, set off from the rest and an ironic commentary on it:

Le jeu de société

On the surface at least, Eluard is in a much more dependent position with respect to Breton. In the poem «Commencement et fin,» he once again repeats the pattern set by Breton, who begins:

> Seulement l'ombre d'une larme sur un visage perdu

which Eluard takes up in the beginning of the second stanza:

> Seulement l'ombre d'une larme l'enjeu du souvenir

Char gets the last four verses of the text, not set off this time as a separate stanza:

> Des ruines difficiles
> Un horizon inespéré qui monte comme une brûlure
> La tête renversée se livre émouvante à la
>   première mer qui passe
> On la nomme sans la reconnaître

These verses may be reminiscent of Baudelaire, but they also express Char's own inner world, the tension he feels between *horizon* and *mer* seen as early as 1923-25 in the «Jouvence» poem of *Premières Alluvions*. Char does not pay much attention to the lines preceding his. No one in «Commencement et fin» had mentioned the sea or the horizon, nor the *brûlures,* for that matter. Breton in the first stanza spoke only of «deux chenêts à tête de lion [qui] étincellent devant le soleil presque mort.» There are no references to fire in Eluard's lines which precede Char's. However, in the poem just before «Commencement et fin,» Eluard ended Char's two line stanza:

> Si j'ai peine à te suivre
> Je mets le feu aux lèvres

with one verse which might well have given Char the cue for the next poem:

Je brûle le silence

All of *Ralentir Travaux* is to be read as one long conversation, where divisions between poems are really arbitrary stops and, perhaps, an involuntary concession to convention.

In «Autour de l'amour,» the poem which follows, Char continues the image on which he had concluded «Commencement et fin»:

> Je t'enfouirai dans le sable
> Pour que la marée te délivre
>
> La liberté pour l'ombre

Lines which the more earthy Breton ends with: «Je te ferai sécher au soleil...» Despite Breton's deviation, Char stays with the image that obsesses him and writes what for him is the most significant text of the collection, «Isolée à ravir,» the only poem of *Ralentir Travaux* for which he provides both the beginning and the end:

> Elle a jeté un pont de soupirs
> Sur la mer inhabitable
> Elle a quitté ses habits de terre
> Mis ses habits de sable
> Elle parle une langue de liège
> Epuise le temps en une saison

Breton gives a humorous twist to the poem by adding to it the pseudo-realistic details that are his specialty:

> Elle danse pour des parterres de galets
> Sous des lustres de larmes
>
> Un jour elle est revenue d'un étrange voyage
> Tous ses bagages étaient couverts d'étiquettes
> orangées
> Les porteurs l'un après l'autre se trouvaient mal

And Eluard, who follows, stays in the slightly burlesque tone of Breton:

4

> Accablés par le point-du-jour qu'elle avait
>   enveloppé dans ses dessous tourbillonnants
> Elle est revenue pour distraire la fraîcheur de
>   son ennui brûlant
> Pour ne plus être seule à maudire le feu

Char adds one more line to the poem, the last, consisting of one word:

> Originale

I am not sure whether this is a matter-of-fact commentary on his own creation or a snide remark about Breton's and Eluard's deformation thereof.

«Ordre du jour,» the twentieth poem, is the one in which Eluard takes the liberty of correcting Char. At the same time, however, he pays a hidden compliment to his younger colleague by mentioning the latter's *Arsenal*. Char starts the poem:

> Pour peu qu'on serre encore des mains
> Il y aura davantage de manchots que d'aveugles
> Je ne parle pas du bon sens de nos mères
> Qui tirent à hue et à dia le fil de la conversation

Eluard continues:

> Sans se douter qu'elles ont couvé tout un arsenal

The lines read like a direct reference to Char's mother, unaware of her rebel son's early collection, *Arsenal*. There follow five verses by Breton which have little to do with Char's. The final line of the poem is written by Eluard, who continues his earlier reference to *Arsenal*:

> Nous en acceptons les salutations distinguées

In 1929, when Char first sent his work to Eluard, it no doubt bore the customary inscription of «salutations distinguées.» (The 1931 version sent to the poet shows the dedication:

«Poèmes pour un ami qui m'obligea.») There can be no doubt about the conscious biographical reference in Eluard's lines.

Breton gives more room to Char than does Eluard, but Char finds it difficult to associate, poetically, with the newly acquired master. He follows Breton's verses only three times, once in an independent stanza («Le Mauvais Sujet»), once with a single line (the last of «Découverte de la terre»), and once with a direct continuation of a verse started by Breton («Le Lierre»). Only the last instance presents an example of true collaboration between Breton and Char. The latter feels much closer to Eluard, whose lines he follows twelve times, taking from him, now and then, his cues regarding vocabulary, atmosphere, and rhythm. Thus, in «L'Ecole buissonnière,» Char continues these verses by Eluard:

> L'amour le premier enseignait
> Aux amants à bien se tenir

with

> Les pierres suivaient leur ombre douce-amère

which continues the theme introduced by Char in «L'Usage de la force»:

> Mais apprends plutôt à rouler tes cheveux
> Pour que les pierres y trouvent leur compte

For «Un Sort rejeté,» Eluard writes the first five lines, Char the next five, and the break is barely perceptible:

> Ce grand orage qui rompt d'éclairs
> La main réduite à son destin
> Et ses rayons aux fûts des routes
> Tu règnes sur ce miroir brisé
> Sur ces oiseaux que tu massacres
> Tu serres la dernière cartouche

— 51 —

Dans une cave de salpêtre
Avec l'oreille de l'amour
Ton écho dans le cœur

L'habitude de montrer les dents

Char and Eluard write a simple poem, made up primarily of octosyllables, a favorite metre of both. They move in the realm of an inner reality projected upon an outer landscape. Except for the last line, Char stays in the mood set by the older poet, although from the beginning, his tone is more virile than Eluard's.

The longest poem of the collection, «A la promenade,» serves to demonstrate how despite structural and other superficial similarities, there is really no «communion en profondeur» even between Eluard and Breton. In this poem, each one paints his own inner world, his own obsession. Breton begins, speaking of a woman who sings to a wounded man, while the rest of the crowd looks on unmoved:

          ...
      On apportait un blessé
      Et dans le rassemblement il y avait une femme
          qui chantait

Immediately, Eluard tries to detract from the woman's beauty:

      Un bouquet fané sur l'oreille
      Son visage était une grande place déserte
      Que l'ivresse murait...

Breton continues his praise of the singing woman, ignoring Eluard's insertion:

      Sa chanson nous apportait les bribes de notre vie
      A venir
      Il flottait une terrible odeur de foin coupé
      Mais les autres n'entendaient rien ne sentaient rien

Later, Eluard speaks of tears of blood which Breton, remembering the earlier «foin coupé,» quickly transforms into tears that are «de l'avoine.» While Breton insists on the beauty, the mystery, and the healing power of woman, Eluard—perhaps because of his own precarious relationship to Gala at this time—ends the poem:

La femme crache sur le blessé
Des buissons d'amoureux jettent au feu leurs
    fleurs d'amour

Insoumission du déjà-vu

From the beginning, Eluard had struck up in *Ralentir Travaux* a note of rebellion and remorse, anger and shame. Here, for example, is the ending he supplies for the third text, «Page blanche»:

Parce que le corps et l'âme se compromettent
    ensemble
Parce qu'ils se servent d'excuse l'un à l'autre

In the next poem, «Ainsi de suite,» his message comes even clearer:

Ils sont fous
Ils sont morts
Ils ont la tête au fond du corps

Nous ne les connaissons pas

Elles sont folles
Elles sont mortes
Leur tête n'est plus en nous

Char writes one line, the last of this poem, and a comment on Eluard's predicament:

L'obsession bouteille vide

The fifth piece, «L'Air se charge,» has these lines by Eluard:

> J'ai déjà provoqué en toi la peur la méchanceté
> Je serai cette fois celui que tu n'as pas connu
> Et qui n'aime qu'à te surprendre

And the following text, «En retour,» continues in the same vein:

> Le cynisme ne suffit point ni la ceinture
>   des deux mains
> Autour du corps qui s'isole

Then follow, in «Le Mauvais Sujet,» these lines by Eluard:

> Je te ferai savoir comment je me nomme
> Quelles étaient mes vertus et le nombre des
>   années que je n'ai pas volé

From «Je brûle le silence,» Eluard progresses to:

> Mes paroles les plus dures
> L'insolence

and the

> Insoumission du déjà-vu

already quoted.

When we consider that all thirty poems of *Ralentir Travaux* were written within a span of five days, it is hardly surprising to note that each poet stays so close to one central obsession which, no matter what the subject matter set before him, he reiterates with varying degrees of intensity. Thus, despite Breton's praise of *das ewig Weibliche* («l'éternelle femme sur un banc de square,» p. 53), Eluard continues his theme of woman's infidelity (and his own). Char, who starts out the volume with

> Le regard qui jettera sur mes épaules
> Le filet indéchiffrable de la nuit

will come back again and again to the theme of the dead or dying woman, to the theme of suicide through drowning:

> La tête renversée se livre émouvante à
>   la première mer qui passe (p. 32)

> Je t'enfouirai dans le sable
> Pour que la marée te délivre (p. 33)

> Elle a jeté un pont de soupirs
> Sur la mer inhabitable (p. 34)

> Les mauvaises herbes ont gagné la route-
>   chevelure
> La parole a changé de bouche
> L'ombre a mouché une à une les chandelles
> Qui célébraient les accidents mortels
> Dans les tournants dangereux... (p. 39)

> On gagne le soleil par enchantement
> L'amour a un goût de verre très prononcé
>   (p. 52)

> Ce mur d'où se détache chaque nuit ton
>   portrait
> S'écroule dans la mer que tu aimais
> Les veines s'éteignent dans ta nuque... (p. 55)

Ralentir Travaux does not end «accidentally» after a five days' excursion into the outer world. It is not the physical journey that comes to an end on 30 March, 1930 for Breton, Eluard and Char. It is an inner world which crumbles and dies in «Je m'écoute encore parler,» the last poem of the collection:

> C Fou comme je suis
> C Je ne suis pas à toute extrémité
> C J'arrache les arbustes qui retiennent le suicide
>   au bord des précipices
> C Les animaux pris à mes pièges se corrompent
>   sur place

C Il n'y a guère que le crépuscule qui les évente
C Le crépuscule criblé de plomb que mes chiens
  épuisés ne peuvent atteindre
B Je serre dans mes bras les femmes qui ne
  veulent être qu'à un autre
B Celles qui dans l'amour entendent le vent passer
  sur les peupliers
B Celles qui dans la haine sont plus élancées que
  les mantes religieuses
B C'est pour moi qu'on a inventé la boîte de
  destruction
B Mille fois plus belle que le jeu de cartes

E Je m'en suis pris aussi à l'absence
E Sous toutes ses formes
E Et j'ai serré dans mes bras des apparitions sous
  le signe
E De la cendre et d'amours plus nouveaux que le
  premier
E Qui m'a fermé les yeux l'espoir la jalousie

Nowhere in *Ralentir Travaux* do the three poets write a more unified poem: «Je serre dans mes bras les femmes qui ne veulent être qu'à un autre,» ... «Et j'ai serré dans mes bras des apparitions...» For the first time, Breton the strong and healthy man, the unfailing optimist of vast appetites, he who sang the omnipotence and omnipresence of woman, Breton who believed in the eternal feminine, in Nadja and «une femme qui chantait,» Breton, like Eluard, sings the infidelity, the destructive force of woman. This is a farewell by Eluard and Breton, a cry of outrage by Char, who looks on helplessly, and hints at suicide. By an extraordinary coincidence, 30 March, 1930 signaled the end of an era for both Breton and Eluard. The former learns that he has been excluded from «L'Union libre,» and Eluard suddenly knows that Gala will not return.

With the exception of «Je m'écoute encore parler,» where «communion en profondeur» is brought about by personal circumstance, the texts of *Ralentir Travaux* do not achieve this unity. Despite frequent structural similarities, the three collaborators are distinguished not only by the very personal obsessions which each one subsumes under a general theme, but also by the expression given to that theme. Each poet has his own *écriture* which distinguishes him from the other two. Thus, for example, one easily recognizes the conversational tone of Breton and is always reminded that from 1917-18 he was one of the «cercle Apollinaire.» Throughout *Ralentir Travaux,* it is Breton who writes the longest lines, the longest uninterrupted insertions, the longest poems. We remember that in 1930, Breton had distinguished himself chiefly as a novelist and journalist. It is easier for him to write prose than poetry, and prose is more agile than verse, better suited to the art of *enchaînement.* And so it is Breton who emerges as the mediator of the group. He begins only seven of the thirty poems in the collection, and he ends eight. He is, it seems, most at home in the central sections, embroideries on given themes to which he usually contributes humorous or pseudo-realistic details. Breton is good at imitation and persiflage. Lines like:

> Tiens il neige
> Mais non c'est un rayon de soleil un peu plus
>   pâle que les autres
> Encore un qui va être passé à tabac (p. 40)

remind us both of the *poèmes-conversations* of the later Apollinaire and of the early somewhat whimsical pieces, like «Merlin et la vieille femme.» Bits like «Le pli du ciel est pris pour toujours» (p. 22) and «Les pis de la vache d'ombre / Donnent un lait d'incendie» (p. 24) recall the surrealists' general disdain for much of Hugo.

Breton's are the only learned references in the work. His scientific background is visible in words like «la pharmacie madréporique» (p. 46), «l'anthropométrie,» and «l'agate-œillet» (p. 47). Breton is best at the surrealist litanies. His gradation: «C'est le corail... c'est le parfum... c'est la transparence... c'est toujours» is an interesting development of a theme given by Char: «L'amour a un goût de verre très prononcé» (p. 52).

It is Breton who makes the most direct references to social commitment, another item on the surrealist agenda. Only he writes the word *ouvriers* and lines such as:

> Les porteurs l'un après l'autre se trouvaient mal
> (p. 35)

> Chaque fois que nous passons à côté de quelqu'un
> Son visage est remplacé par l'inscription Secours
> aux noyés (pp. 42-43)

> Sur la terre la terre qu'on n'habite plus la terre du
> déracinement
> Du déboisement et de la dénidification par la base
> (p. 53)

and finally:

> Le monde renversé serait charmant
> Dans les yeux de l'anti-homme... (p. 56)

Of Char's late-romantic «pont de soupirs» (p. 34) Breton —remembering his Apollinaire—quickly makes «Le pont sur tout le monde c'est un cri que vous entendrez» and writes, with Eluard, a piece of social criticism («L'Enjeu inutile»).

I said earlier that Breton must be regarded as either the most versatile or the least authentic of the three poets, since it is he who can spread his lines most comfortably between those of Eluard and Char. He can handle any given subject with humor and irony, with detachment and... a good literary memory. However, his contributions to *Ralentir Travaux,* although the most frequent and the longest, yet do not set the tone of the work. It is Eluard who emerges as the real pace-maker, and who draws to him the young Char. While apparently agreeing, on occasion, with Breton's whimsical or ironic interpolations, he clearly takes his distance in the majority of cases: «Le cynisme ne suffit point ni la ceinture des deux mains / Autour du corps qui s'isole» (p. 22).

It is Eluard who writes the most musical lines of *Ralentir*

Travaux. End and internal rhyme and the frequently repeated rhythm of the octosyllable give his verses the songlike quality to which his readers, in 1930, were already accustomed:

> L'amour le premier enseignait
> Aux amants à bien se tenir... (p. 26)

> Le feu réduit au vent des sables
> Mes yeux devant n'importe qui (p. 36)

> Ce grand orage qui rompt d'éclairs
> La main réduite à son destin... (p. 38)

Despite their private message, Eluard's lines have a popular ring. His sentences are of the simplest kind, unelliptical and without any special syntactical complications. His vocabulary keeps to that of the common man, but without falling into the banality of a *poème-conversation.* When it does not take on the rhythm of a popular song, (6) Eluard's simplicity reminds us of French classical verse: (6a)

> A l'heure exacte que marquent sans cesse les doigts
>   de la femme désolée
> Tu passes par les portes condamnées
> En ne prenant pas garde aux émois des rencontres
>   (p. 54)

Even when he seems to follow directly in Breton's line of

---

(6) See, for example, the *comptine*-like quality of the poem «Ainsi de suite,» quoted earlier.

(6a) Anna Balakian has commented on the «radical difference» of language between Breton and Eluard, stating that: «Even in his prime as a surrealist poet, Eluard prolongs the tradition of Racine, whereas the language of Breton, raucous, irregular in its breathing span, rich in its multiplicity of rare words culled from all areas of usage, and possessing multicontextual significations, abandoned at the same time rimed verse and the prose poem, to follow the model of Apollinaire...» Anna Balakian, «Breton in the Light of Apollinaire,» in *About French Poetry from Dada to «Tel Quel»; Text and Theory* (Detroit: Wayne State University Press, 1974), pp. 51-52.

social protest, Eluard is really talking about a private conflict and speaks, finally only for himself in lines like:

> Le monde entier s'est dégradé les éléments n'y
>   pouvaient rien
> S'est dégradé par la constance et l'ordre l'idée
>   d'homme
> Ne valait rien... (pp. 56-57)

He, Eluard, the inconstant man, caught between Gala and Nusch, full of outrage and shame, guilt and rebellion, he sees himself «dégradé par la constance et l'ordre.» Of the three poets of *Ralentir Travaux,* Eluard is the most personal, the most delicate and the most vulnerable. «Eluard, jamais sur ses gardes» (Francis Ponge) lays himself bare before the reader. Everything in his poetry is open and direct and reads like a confession. Eluard is without the defenses of irony or allegory in the face of his own predicament. This makes him perhaps the most endearing of the three poets.

Char often intervenes in the poems of *Ralentir Travaux* with only one line, but that one placed, as we have seen, in key positions. It could be construed as a gesture of courtesy on the part of Breton and Eluard to have left to their host, René Char, the role of the initiator. But I think the young poet naturally assumed the place best suited to him. It was not for Char, the youngest and newest collaborator in the group, to act as mediator between Breton and Eluard. And so his lines—with only two exceptions—stand either at the beginning or at the end of the poems to which he contributes. He is still, in a way, the outsider. Throughout his poetic career, Char will remain the man of morning, the singer of *Les Matinaux* and of eternal beginnings. Some of his opening lines have the power and the grandeur of the magnificent first lines of a Stefan George and are in themselves a poem.

As we have seen, Char's contributions to *Ralentir Travaux* are short and often limited to one verse. By 1930, he had already learned the art of the aphorism. When he is not, like

Breton, writing imitations of Apollinaire or of his other mentor, Rimbaud, Char's lines already have the terseness and the poignancy which will become characteristic of his verse (among the densest and swiftest in twentieth century French letters). There are in Char no detours, no explanations, no «belle conjointure,» nothing but «le raccourci fascinateur» (*Poèmes militants,* 1932).

> Ce qui suit ressemble à ce qui part
> Raison valable
> («Réussite,» *Ralentir Travaux*).

Char favors the short poem and line, which he can write more readily in conjunction with Eluard than with Breton. His verses are often elliptical, tracing the bare skeleton of his thought. His vocabulary, though simple, tends towards the abstract and never has about it the down-to-earth quality of Eluard. Nor does Char lay himself bare before the reader as does Eluard. His poem is never a personal confession, but aphorism, allegory, or myth. His are the most memorable single lines of *Ralentir Travaux,* lines that whole systems of philosophy will be drawn upon to explain. For «Découverte de la terre,» for example, Char supplies the final line, which captures, in capsule form, the discoveries of Einstein:

> La belle inconnue-limite (7)

«Le Lierre,» another poem for which Char furnishes the ending, leaves us with

> La Beauté dont on ignore l'histoire

a favorite image with Char and one which, down to his last published verse, contains in its most condensed form all of

---

(7) The line «La belle inconnue-limite» is used again to end a variant reading of «L'Illusion imitée,» a poem of *Le Tombeau des secrets,* in the version sent to Eluard in February 1931.

his essentially a-historic thought, marked more by Heraclitus and Heidegger than by the *engagement* of the 1940's.

***

«La poésie doit être faite par tous, non par un.»
—Lautréamont.

Ralentir Travaux should be of great interest to literary historians. It preserves for us some of the early verses of Breton and Char. It allows us to observe three major poets at work together and thus tells us much more than mere biographies about their relationship to each other. I think, however, that as an experiment in collective writing, *Ralentir Travaux* is a failure, if the purpose of such writing is to be the emergence of a «conscience unique» discernible in the work. With one possible exception, the verses of *Ralentir Travaux* belong to their separate and identifiable authors.

In his *Préface* to the work, Eluard writes: «Il faut effacer le reflet de la personnalité pour que l'inspiration bondisse à tout jamais du miroir. Laissez les influences jouer librement...» But even Eluard knows that ultimately each poet writes only one authentic poem, the expression of his inner world, his «seule vision, variée à l'infini» (*ibid.*). Like Eluard, Breton also knows of the intimate and intricate nature of the poetic word which cannot be reduced to any common denominator. In his preface he writes: «Tout le monde a vu une table mais quand nous disons une table *le malheur* est que cette table à ce moment pour M. Breton est une table de café (car il boit), pour M. Char une table de jeu (car il ne joue pas), pour M. Eluard une table d'opération (car il est passé ce matin place de l'Opéra).» Despite the facile word-play (*opération-Opéra*), despite Breton's usual attempt at humor, the seriousness of his message comes clear (8). Communication in depth is not

_____
(8) In a 1932 letter to Rolland de Renéville—who had questioned the authenticity of Eluard's automatic writing—Breton flatly states

possible on the level of the word.   Apparent similarities are superficial.   One and the same form is receptive to different contents, one object can assume different contours, the same word, different affective connotations, depending on every individual's personal experience of the world.

René Char writes the longest and, at first glance, most affirmative of the three prefaces to *Ralentir Travaux*: «L'utilité collective fait taire les reproches et fondre les hésitations. Dans la tête étroite comme l'espace les coudes n'ont pas place, les mains sont à niveau, l'horizon est vertical et au-dessous de tout.   C'est alors qu'on entend la parole en liberté mais au supplice.»   It is not until some thirty years later, however, that Char can solve, in *La Parole en archipel,* the contradiction inherent in «la parole en liberté mais au supplice.»

As poets, Breton, Eluard and Char will each go his own way, in the full awareness that despite the exhortations of Lautréamont, despite all the high ideals of surrealism aspiring to a *conscience unique* and *utilité collective,* poetry will always remain the personal expression of an inner reality which is different for every man.   «Et la vérité, il ne faut pas craindre de se répéter, est personnelle, stupéfiante et personnelle» (9).

---

that the surrealists had never claimed to present «le moindre texte... comme exemple parfait d'automatisme verbal.»

(9) The original version of this chapter appeared in the *Rivista di Letteratura Moderne e Comparate,* vol. 24, no. 2, Florence, July 1971.

THE CIRCLE EXPLODED:

FUREUR ET MYSTÈRE: POÉSIE ENGAGÉE? (1)

> Le poète passe par tous les degrés solitaires d'une
> gloire collective dont il est, de bonne guerre, exclu...
> Il ajoute de la noblesse à son cas lorsqu'il est
> hésitant dans son diagnostic et le traitement des
> maux de l'homme de son temps, lorsqu'il formule
> des réserves sur la meilleure façon d'appliquer la
> connaissance et la justice dans le labyrinthe du
> politique et du social...
> *Fureur et mystère* est, les temps le veulent, un
> recueil de poèmes, et, sur la vague du drame et du
> revers inéluctable d'où resurgit la tentation, un dire
> de notre affection ténue pour le nuage et pour
> l'oiseau.
>
> (*Bandeau de Fureur et Mystère*, 1948).

During his years of military engagement (2), René Char
wrote most of the poems and prose now contained in the
collective volume entitled *Fureur et Mystère,* first published
in 1948, and reprinted, with variants, in 1962. In the second

---

(1) Char objects to the very term *engagée.* In a letter to the
author (28 February, 1974) he comments on the title of this chapter:
«*Conviée à, invitée à,* me paraît mieux convenir. *Conviée à* ou
invitée à marque un état passager, libre-arbitre gardé; *engagée* c'est
se rendre à l'ordre. En ma poésie s'est réfléchie la part impérieuse
de l'essentiel menacé par un événement totalitaire, par conséquent,
mental.»

(2) I had originally spoken of the poet's *political* engagement.

5

edition, *Fureur et Mystère* consists of five sections: *Seuls demeurent*, 1938-1944; *Feuillets d'Hypnos*, 1943-1944; *Les Loyaux Adversaires*, 1946; *Le Poème pulvérisé*, 1945-1947, and *La Fontaine narrative*, 1947. In 1948, the collection further included *La Conjuration*, a «Ballet» in five strophes dated 1946 and moved, in 1967, to Char's collected theater, *Trois coups sous les arbres*.

It was *Feuillets d'Hypnos*, published separately in 1946, which revealed Char to the people, many of whom thought that this was his first work. To this day some critics continue to see in Char first and foremost a political thinker and a poet of social protest (3). Char's social awareness came, as I tried to show in the last chapter, during his years of close contact with the surrealists and with Breton and Eluard in particular. A few verses contributed by Char to *Ralentir Travaux* show the poet at the crossroads indicated by Breton. On the one hand, there are lines that a Lautréamont could have written:

> Fou comme je suis
> Je ne suis pas à toute extrémité
> J'arrache les arbustes qui retiennent le suicide au
>   bord des précipices
> Les animaux pris à mes pièges se corrompent sur
>   place...
> («Je m'écoute encore parler»).

This is the young, rebellious surrealist speaking, the would-be anarchist, the advocate of violence for whom *L'Action de la Justice est éteinte*. But there are also in *Ralentir Travaux* first hints at the awakening of a social conscience. To the poem «Histoire naturelle,» Char supplies this ending:

Again, Char objects. In the letter quoted above he writes: «L'engagement n'était pas politique mais militaire. Pour être efficace. Et il le fut. La poésie, elle, n'était pas pour autant 'engagée'.»

(3) Georges Mounin says of Char: «... ce poète aura été aussi le plus grand de nos poètes politiques,» *op. cit.*, p. 31. Raymond Jean published an article entitled: «La Politique de René Char» (Paris, *Politique d'aujourd'hui*, novembre 1969).

Le spectacle déchirant du chien qui lève la patte
dans la cour d'honneur de la caserne
Fait penser aux vieillards tenus en laisse par les
uniformes

La bonne soupe pour le joli monde de l'abattoir

These lines are interesting because here for the first time
the poet's attention is drawn away from himself and towards
a specific animal (in contrast to the mythical *Animal* of «Sosie,»
a poem of 1928). Most of Char's early verse (*Les Cloches sur
le cœur, Le Tombeau des secrets*) had consisted of self-centered
and self-directed meditations of the *Spleen et Idéal* type, of
confessional verse as it was brought over into the twentieth
century by Apollinaire. «Histoire naturelle» adds a new dimension of social realism.

In *Ralentir Travaux,* Char tries the two roads indicated in
the first surrealist manifesto: on the one hand, the way of
violence, madness, suicide—a path traced by Lautréamont, «en
dehors de toute préoccupation esthétique ou morale.» And on
the other, the narrow road of *Le devoir et l'inquiétude* that
Eluard had taken as early as 1917:

Le devoir et l'inquiétude
Partagent ma vie rude.
(C'est une grande peine
De vous l'avouer.)

Which route will Char follow? Neither one, I believe.
His home, his childhood had formed the man who was to
assume, at every turn, the role of the leader: the «chef de
bande» among children, editor of a journal (*Méridiens,* 1929),
captain of a Resistance detachment (1942-44), and solitary ruler
of his home in Provence (1952—). Independent, reserved,
clear-sighted, aware of society's imperfections but chary of
easy, ready-made solutions «dans le labyrinthe du politique et
du social»: such is the Captain of Céreste and the author of
Feuillets d'Hypnos, the poet of *Les Matinaux*: «Je n'ai ni chaud

ni froid: je gouverne. Cependant, n'allongez pas trop la main vers le sceptre de mon pouvoir» («Centon,» *Les Matinaux*).

René-Emile Char, we remember, had grown up in simulated aristocratic conditions. He knew that his grandfather had borne the proud name of Charlemagne. (It was not until much later that he learned of his true origins, «fils de rien et promis à rien,» as he tells in *La Nuit talismanique*) (4). The childish imagination quickly transposed the *fin-de-siècle* home of *haute bourgeoisie* dimensions into a mediaeval setting of castles and kings, and the grown man held fast to the illusion, constantly feeling the «Obligation, sans reprendre souffle, de raréfier, de hiérarchiser êtres et choses empiétant sur nous.» («Baudelaire mécontente Nietzsche,» *ibid.*). The royal *nous* is Char's most characteristic pronoun, the imperative, his dominant mode and the apostrophe his favorite rhetorical device. Vocabulary taken from feudal society and religious imagery abound in his work: *blason, cavalier, château, chevalerie, couronne, se couronner, courtois, Créateur, dynastie, empereur, félon, gouverner, gouverneur, les grands, maître, maîtriser, Majesté, martyr, mécène, ma monarchie solitaire, noble, noblesse, Octroi, octroyer, pouvoir, Prince, prophète, règne, roi, royal, royaume, sceptre, Seigneur, seigneurie, (noble) semence, siège pur, souverain, souveraineté, sublime, Suzerain, trésor.* These are Char's words, many of them from *Fureur et Mystère* and often capitalized or used as titles. The poems of *Fureur et Mystère* have, besides, headings like «Afin qu'il n'y soit rien changé,» «Vivre avec de tels hommes,» «L'Ordre légitime est quelquefois inhumain,» «Ne s'entend pas,» «Redonnez-leur,» «A la Santé du serpent,» and «Assez creusé,» all imperatives, actual or implied. Char's poetry is depersonalized by the frequent «on» and «l'homme»-constructions and by the use of infinitives or past participles in preference to conjugated verb forms.

The title «Assez creusé» is taken from a footnote to the

---

(4) Char's paternal grandfather, we remember, was a foundling who received the name of Charlemagne, which he abbreviated to Char-Magne, further abridged to Char by the poet's father.

ballet *La Conjuration,* where Char mentions the people he has known: Irène and Claude, the revolutionaries; Gilles, Michel and Henri, the hunters; Marie, Jérôme, beings beauteous; Yvonne and Blanche. The enumeration ends with the cry: «Assez creusé! Assez creusé!» This exclamation is explained by the prose poem of the same title from *La Fontaine narrative,* 1947. It is the next to the last text of *Fureur et Mystère* and reads as follows:

> Assez creusé, assez miné sa part prochaine. Le pire est dans chacun, en chasseur, dans son flanc. Vous qui n'êtes ici qu'une pelle que le temps soulève, retournez-vous sur ce que j'aime, qui sanglote à côté de moi, et fracassez-nous, je vous prie, que je meure une bonne fois.

The pessimistic note, sign of his «héritage intellectuel,» as Char called it, will be muted in later works. But the imperative mode and the syntactical setting of the poem recur throughout the volumes of the 50's and 60's.

We have in «Assez creusé» a structure characteristic of Char, i.e., the implied dialogue between an unnamed *vous* and the poet's *je* (or *nous*). The *vous* is all-inclusive (the second sentence mentions *chacun*) and designates mankind as a whole. It is nameless, faceless, and obviously inferior to *je*: «Vous qui n'êtes ici qu'une pelle que le temps soulève...» (The passage reminds us of the «Exploit du cylindre à vapeur» to be examined later, and of a text from *Recherche de la Base et du Sommet,* «Trois respirations,» which defines the power of the poet thus: «La parole soulève plus de terre que le fossoyeur ne le peut.») Char again sets himself apart from ordinary mortals and assumes even greater stature by shifting, once again, from an initial *je* to the royal *nous*: «Fracassez-nous, je vous prie...» It is evident that the plural *nous* does not include a second person, but stands for the poet and his *alter ego,* «sa part du prochain» (5). Gilles, Michel, Henri and the rest are interest-

---

(5) The quotation is taken from «Prouver par la vie,» a poem

ing only insofar as they enrich the personality of the speaker and fulfill his wishes. From the royal *nous,* we quickly switch back to the original first person singular, and the poem ends: «Fracassez-*nous, je* vous prie, que *je* meure une bonne fois.»

The *vous-nous* confrontation of «Assez creusé» is a product of Char's surrealist experience and a sign of his social awakening. It is first used significantly in *Dehors la nuit est gouvernée,* published in 1938. Prior to this time, Char's poems are constructed predominantly around the first person singular of lyric poetry (6). In the 1938 collection, one poem in particular, entitled «Tous compagnons de lit,» has been read as Char's new socialist manifesto. A recent critic writes:

> As expressed by «Tous compagnons de lit,» this particular act of living provides a basis for unifying all men...
>
> The assimilation of «je» into «nous» offers a more general and yet more familiar frame of reference. The plural «nous» reflects the unity of man and poet against the common menace (7).

The author goes on to speak of Char's «exaltation of communal action» in *Feuillets d'Hypnos* and of the «current of fraternal feeling» in *Dehors la nuit est gouvernée.*

The poet's *je* is not mentioned anywhere in «Tous compagnons de lit,» and is not assimilated into, but replaced by the first person plural. The poem is built, in the main, around a dialectic of *nous vs. vous.* The text is obviously related to «Assez creusé.» Again the *vous* is a plural and represents a group of inferiors who may be seen, but not heard. The «compagnons de lit» of the title are defined as:

---

of *Dehors la nuit est gouvernée:* «Je lègue ma part du prochain / A l'aiguilleur du convoi de mythes / Qui s'élabore au quai désert.» The scene is similar to that outlined in «Assez creusé.»

(6) Or else the term «le poète» is used, especially in the aphorisms of *Moulin premier* (1936).

(7) Virginia A. La Charité, *op. cit.,* p. 83.

Pourvoyeurs d'or mais à peine moins chétifs
   qu'une motte de chiendent dans un hectare
   en friche
Ils étreignent enfin ce présent digne d'eux
Qu'un devenir de maîtres leur brisait... (8).

Though the social status of these «purveyors of gold» is not indicated, they remind one of the «équipe d'ouvriers» who in «Les Rapports entre parasites,» a poem of *Abondance viendra,* were said to quarter mud, «cette autre pierre précieuse.» The earlier abstraction comes alive in the clod of grass. In both poems, those who equate mud and gold (an elemental equation noted by Jung) are set in contrast to the upper class, the masters, the poets, *nous.* Char speaks of the «sommeil fraternel» already celebrated by one of his early mentors, Heraclitus, who wrote: «Les hommes, dans leur sommeil, travaillent fraternellement au devenir du monde» (9). Char points to the «outils infranchissables conquis sur la paresse et l'exploit de travail» and to the «beauté populaire aux horloges innocentes.» He seemingly sings the new reign of the proletariat.

In «Tous compagnons de lit,» the silent, antiphonal *vous* are called upon to torture and, finally, to kill (like their companions of «Assez creusé») the superior nous:

Chers allongés qui avez amené le sang prestigieux
   sur des hauteurs où ne se montre guère
   l'amertume
Vous réparerez vite dans l'écrin de vos lois la
   place chaude que nous y aurons un instant
   occupée

---

(8) All quotations are taken, unless otherwise indicated, from the 1949 edition of *Dehors la nuit est gouvernée précédé de Placard pour un chemin des écoliers* (Paris: G. L. M.).

(9) Yves Battistini, *Héraclite d'Ephèse.* Traduction nouvelle et intégrale avec introduction et notes par Yves Battistini. Avant-propos de René Char (Paris: Aux Editions «Cahiers d'Arts,» 1948), no. 87.

Mieux

Vous nous frapperez d'interdiction vous maltraiterez
　　nos figures amovibles (10)
Est-ce exact l'oasis commence à briller par delà
　　la décollation de la mer végétante guenille
　　théâtrale
Notre langue commune dans l'éternité sous le
　　toit gardien de nos luttes c'est le sommeil
　　cet espéranto de raison
Nous ne tolérons pas d'être interrompus par la
　　laideur comédienne d'une voix
Nous ne nous avouons pas vaincu quand dans
　　l'homme debout le mal surnage et le bien
　　coule à pic.

In this fourth and final stanza of the poem, who is the *nous*,
the «sang prestigieux» lifted to the heights «où ne se montre
guère l'amertume»? The word *amertume* is a 1949 variant
of the poem which again sends us back to «Les Rapports
entre parasites.» Here, in 1933, the poet was summoned
to «bâtir une postérité sans amertume.» And in this same
text which called upon the slaves to strangle their master,
the poet himself was identified with that master and, perhaps,
even with Christ: «Entre les cuisses du crucifié se balance la
tête créole de poète. La lave adorable dissout la roche florissante.» Clearly, the two poems have an identical theme.

I think we witness in «Tous compagnons de lit» a struggle
between the poet's conscious intentions and his subconscious
feelings (and the assumption will be verified by a grammatical
or typographical slip). On the one hand, and in keeping with
the spirit of the times, Char would use the collective *nous* to
speak of all ordinary mortals (11). He would sing the «exal-

---

(10) The word *amobiles* given in the collection is a misprint.
The 1937 manuscript shows *amovibles* which I substitute here.
(Catalogue Exposition Maeght, 1971). The 1971 edition corrects
the 1949 misprint.

(11) In June 1936, Eluard had said: «Le temps est venu où tous
les poètes ont le droit et le devoir de soutenir qu'ils sont profondé-

tation of communal action,» the «utilité collective,» by fusing *nous* and *vous* into one group of equals, «tous compagnons de lit... chers allongés.» All members of this group would share one common language, «cet espéranto de raison,» the confused and artless language of dream that Breton thought proper for the new poetry by, of, and for all people.

Subconsciously, however, the poet sets himself apart from the sleepers, begs them to be excluded from their group: «Vous réparerez vite... la place chaude que nous y aurons un instant occupée...» These are imperatives of the kind the poet had given in «Les Rapports entre parasites» and «Assez creusé.» And again, he sees in himself the master, the Christlike figure offering himself up to be stoned, to die the martyr's death: «Vous nous frapperez d'interdiction vous maltraiterez nos figures amovibles...» For as he leaves the surrealist chapel, Char knows that there is one thing better than simulated dream.

The last stanza of «Tous compagnons de lit» reminds one of Sandburg's «Flash Crimson» from *Smoke and Steel,* 1920, containing lines like

> I shall cry to God to give me a broken foot.
> I shall ask for a scar and a slashed nose.
> I shall take the last and the worst...
> And yet—of all «and yets» this is the bronze
>   strongest—
> I shall keep one thing better than all else;
>   there is the blue steel of a great star of early
>   evening in it; it lives longer than a broken foot
>   or any scar.
> The broken foot goes to a hole dug with a shovel
>   or the bone of a nose may whiten on a
>   hilltop—and yet—«and yet»—
> There is one crimson pinch of ashes left
>   after all; and none of the shifting winds

ment enfoncés dans la vie des autres hommes, dans la vie commune.» For a good overview of the period, see Jacques Gaucheron, «Un grand moment dans la poésie française,» *Europe,* juillet-août 1974, numéro spécial: *La Poésie et la Résistance.*

that whip the grass and none of the pounding
rains that beat the dust know how to touch
or find the flash of this crimson...

The main difference between the two poems lies in the fact
that Sandburg, the socialist, has room for God. Char does
not, but the attitude of the two poets towards their own
creation—and the definition of poetry it implies—are similar
in the lines quoted. The poet must offer himself up as a martyr
so that from his blood may spring the flash of crimson that
is poetry. The poet is the superior being who, not unlike
Christ, must take upon himself the sins of the world. His
blood must flow like lava to break up inert matter, to bring
flowers from dead rock: «La lave adorable dissout la roche
florissante.» An aphorism of *La Bibliothèque est en feu,*
written nearly twenty years after «Tous compagnons de lit,»
sums up the early poem in one sentence: «La beauté fait son
lit sublime toute seule, étrangement bâtit sa renommée parmi
les hommes, à côté d'eux mais à l'écart» (12).

The question has never been raised why in two parallel
passé composé constructions near the end of «Tous compagnons
de lit,» there is participial agreement in one case and not in
the other. The last two lines of stanza four began, we
remember:

Nous ne tolérons pas d'être interrompus...
Nous ne nous avouons pas vain*cu* (*sic*)...

The two half lines rhyme, but only for the ear. A mere
misprint? Nothing but a typographical slip? Then why does
it occur, one might ask, not only in the 1949 publication
of *Dehors la nuit est gouvernée,* but also in the subsequent
edition of 1971? In a letter to the author (28 February,
1974), Char states: «'Nous ne nous avouons pas vain*cu*,' faute
non intentionnelle, faute d'inattention. Il faut lire vain*cus*.»

---

(12) For Char, the words *beauté* and *poésie* are synonymous.

However, the October 1936 manuscript shows two singular past participles (13), as does the 1938 edition. There are other instances of non-agreement in Char's poems. In «Cruauté,» for example, the poet writes: «Nous nous galvanisons dans les cendres qui nous ont vomi,» a line not unrelated to the verses quoted from Sandburg and from «Tous compagnons de lit.» «Versant,» another poem of *Le Marteau sans maître,* opens with these lines:

> Donnons les prodiges à l'oubli secourable
> Impavide

The last adjective does not make much sense in the framework of the poem if read as a modifier of *oubli.* In a recent text, Char asks: «Sommes-nous... plus végétal que la fleur du mirabilis?» (*La Nuit talismanique,* 1972). It is interesting to note that Char is often deliberately ambiguous. He chooses invariable adjectives as modifiers of the ambivalent *nous* or references to parts of the body, which would remain singular in any case. Another text of *La Nuit talismanique* begins: «Verbe d'orages raisonneurs qui ne se cassent pas, qui demeurent suspendus au-dessus de notre tête comme un banquier à court d'argent.» Often, the second partner in the *nous* alliance is not a human being, but an inanimate object, as in these lines: «O ma petite fumée s'élevant sur tout vrai feu, nous sommes les contemporains et le nuage de ceux qui nous aiment!» (*ibid.*).

There is another instance of non-agreement in *Fureur et Mystère.* The poem «La Sorgue, chanson pour Yvonne» is an interesting example of the frequent pronoun shifts so typical of Char (14). Stanzas 1 and 2 establish a liaison between the poet and the river, the poet speaking first on his own behalf:

> Rivière...
> Donne aux enfants de *mon* pays...

---

(13) Published in the Catalogue Exposition Maeght, 1971.
(14) Indeed, it is perhaps due to these frequent pronoun shifts that Char's poetry sometimes seems ambiguous or difficult. Especially in the early poems, where the poet still believes in the

Rivière où l'éclair finit et où commence *ma* maison,
Qui roule aux marches d'oubli la rocaille de *ma*
raison.

The nine lines that follow evoke those who (beside the poet)
depend on the river's benevolence. The river assumes social
significance. Then follows the stanza:

Rivière des meilleurs que *soi,* rivière des
brouillards éclos,
De la lampe qui désaltère l'angoisse autour de
son chapeau.

And the poem ends with the first mention of a *nous* which
is, however, an obvious singular:

Rivière au cœur jamais détruit dans ce monde
fou de prison,
Garde-nous violent et ami des abeilles de l'horizon.
(*La Fontaine narrative,* 1947).

It is as though the poet had tried—in vain—to get outside
himself by going from an implied *je* to the indefinite *soi* and,
at last, to the plural *nous*... only to put it to singular use!

There is more than a typographical slip in «Tous compagnons de lit.» The poem that the critics would read as the
«exaltation of communal action» really ends in the celebration
of a singular *nous,* the royal *we* incarnated by the man at the
top, the *homme debout.* Mentioned here for the first time,
this *upright* man (in the physical and moral sense) will become
Char's symbol for the superior being, the master, the poet. In
a radio address of 15 August, 1946, he defined the concept of
truth (and beauty, and poetry) as follows: «Des mots échangés
tout bas au lendemain de 1940 s'enfouissaient dans la terre
patiente et fertile de la révolte contre l'oppresseur et deve-

---

Rimbaldian dictum of «Le Je est haïssable,» the speaker often refers
to himself indiscriminately as *je, tu, il, nous,* and *vous.*

naient progressivement des hommes debout... Miracle de la conscience, de cette sensation de l'évidence qui, selon Claude Bernard, a nom vérité.» Char will accept his equals, men like Louis Curel de la Sorgue, «un homme à présent debout, un homme dans un champ de seigle, un champ pareil à un chœur mitraillé, un champ sauvé» («Fenaison,» *Seuls demeurent*). But while he apparently hails «Tous compagnons de lit,» he finally admits that there is no room at the top for the parasites, the fatalists, the idle pessimists, for them that sleep the hollow sleep of straw:

> Le grand bûcher des alliances
> Sous le spiral ciel d'échec
> C'est l'hiver en barque pourrie
> Des compagnons solides aux compagnons liquides
> Des lits de mort sous les écorces
> ...
> Sur la paille des fatalistes
> L'écume d'astre coule tout allumée
> Il n'y a pas d'absence irremplaçable.
>
> («Chaîne,» *Poèmes militants,* 1932).

«La menace s'est polie. La plage qui chaque hiver s'encombrait de régressives légendes... se prépare aux êtres à secourir» («Calendrier,» *Seuls demeurent*). There *is* a development in Char's poetry that goes from the early surrealist anarchy (15) of *Ralentir Travaux* and «la Justice éteinte» to the realist's engagement in the Resistance. However, *La Conjuration,* once a part of *Fureur et Mystère,* is still closer in spirit to *Dehors la nuit est gouvernée* than to *Seuls demeurent*. Though dated 1946, it was probably written—at least in part— before Char's participation in the Resistance. The hero or *premier danseur* of *La Conjuration* is a certain «homme- miroir,

---

(15) In his letter quoted earlier, Char objects to the word *anarchy,* commenting: «'Anarchy' n'est pas le mot qui convient. Pas du tout. *Ralentir Travaux,* c'est la révolte et le refus, non l'anarchie.»

prince des nœuds.» His very name is reminiscent of the young Char's fable-like creations that had very little in common with creatures of flesh and blood. Perhaps this «homme-miroir» is the masculine counterpart to Char's early heroine Artine, 1930, whom he had defined as «la transparence absolue.» The later hero attracts to himself all those who would seek in his mirror their own image. Yet, even while reflecting the world, the prince (in workers' clothes!) renounces it, keeps aloof from the crowd, «divorcé d'avec l'humain.» His motions are characterized by egoism, nonchalance, and a defiant absolutism. He is incapable of compromise, incapable of contact and unwilling to risk the pollution that would cause the flower to yield the fruit. And so the «homme-miroir» dies as the flower dies, the diurnal diamond «pur de compromis.» In a sense, he is the least «fraternal» of Char's heroes, and that may explain why the ballet was not included in the second (1962) edition of *Fureur et Mystère*.

Char's wartime poetry and prose ring a different note. A text dating from 1953 (in *Le Rempart de brindilles*) which I read as a reflection on the years 1940-45, perhaps explains why the poet chose to exchange roles with the partisan. In a string of infinitives which are really self-given imperatives (a device typical of Char), man's role is defined as follows:

> Echapper à la honteuse contrainte du choix entre l'obéissance et la démence, esquiver l'abat de la hache sans cesse revenante du despote contre laquelle nous sommes sans moyens de protection, quoique étant aux prises sans trêve, voilà notre rôle, notre destination, et notre dandinement justifiés. Il nous faut franchir la clôture du pire, faire la course périlleuse, encore chasser au delà, tailler en pièces l'inique, enfin disparaître sans trop de pacotilles sur soi. Un faible remerciement donné ou entendu, rien d'autre.

These, the realistic calculations of the intelligent man aware of the evils and the dangers of his age, these and a healthy

Selbsterhaltungstrieb—coupled with the poet's deeply rooted love for his homeland—this is what drove Char to the *maquis*. It was to keep his sanity that the poet, in his own words, escaped (*échapper, esquiver, franchir*) and exchanged the security and warmth of his «island»-home for the cold and vulnerable mountaintops of the Basses-Alpes. Char the strong, the sane man, the fundamental optimist could not find employment—literally or figuratively—in the weak and stagnant society of his day. *Oisif, désœuvré,* these are key-words in *Le Marteau sans maître,* and they describe not only Char's own state, but the general tenor of the society in which he lived: «Pessimistes aux abois, un mot-percuteur: désœuvré. Nombre d'autres touchent, esclaves, leur ration de fouet» (*Moulin premier*).

> Hypothétique lecteur
> Mon confident désœuvré...
> («Confronts,» *Poèmes militants*).

Here Char's parody of Baudelaire ends. He does not find «son semblable, son frère» and cannot share in the materialistic pessimism that was his intellectual heritage, nor live in the state of cowardly inertia it fostered. «L'univers de la matière est plus mensonger que le monde des dieux. Il est loisible de le modifier et de le retourner,» Char declares in «Outrages,» a series of aphorisms dated 1944-67. He the healthy man cannot breathe the poisonous vapors of corruption, despotism, injustice breathed by the «confidents désœuvrés,» the «compagnons de lit.» In a sense, Char acts out in *Fureur et Mystère* and in the *maquis* of Céreste the role he had assigned to himself ten years earlier. Only now that he has come face to face with death, he no longer wants to be appointed the sacrificial lamb. Now that oppression on the one hand and anarchy on the other («l'obéissance et la démence») are threatening to bring about the actual extinction of justice, the «agneau mystique» makes way for the «renard». Now that the war is on and death never more than a second away, Char has no time for the intellectual luxury of meditations on suicide or the slaying of martyrs: «Enfin disparaître sans trop de pacotilles sur soi. Un faible remerciement donné ou entendu, rien d'autre.» Char's new attitude, which is, in fact, more fraternal than his early aspirations to martyrdom, is a by-product of the changed times and circumstances.

«Fantôme sans asile, aux actions sans mérite … Vous sentez-vous ainsi?» (*Moulin premier*). This is the question Char faced in 1935, at the end of his surrealist venture. And perhaps ironically, the *maquis* provided both the *asile* and the *actions*. Though the experience of Céreste did not, of course, change Char's basic make-up, it did lend a new dimension to his poetry. By 1940, it was no longer possible for the poet to withdraw from the crowd. He could not remain the solitary romantic figure, the «grande brouette des marécages» of *Le Marteau sans maître*. Char now was forced into direct contact with other, ordinary people and these, creatures of flesh and blood, seem to replace the earlier «hommes emblématiques» of his poetry, the symbolic heroes with their awesome capitals: *le Balancier, le Borgne, l'Ecumeur de mémoire, l'Elagueur, l'Equarrisseur, le Justicier des courants humains* and the *Novateur de la lézarde* (all from *Le Marteau sans maître*).

The nameles, faceless, motionless second and third persons (*vous, il, elle, ils, elles, ceux qui, celles qui*, etc.) of the early poems now begin to live. There is, in *Seuls demeurent,* the haunting tale of the young girl who goes about the hills of Provence gathering the fragile branches of the mimosa tree («Congé au vent»). There is Louis Curel de la Sorgue, the upright man formed by the river. We meet the eel-fishers («Violences») and the blacksmith who spends his days bent over the forge («Fréquence»). To a friend killed in action, Char dedicates «Eléments,» the story of a woman and her child on the point of death.

But note how Char goes about describing these people. The mimosa gathering girl resembles a painting. Like Botticelli's Primavera, she is the incarnation of Spring. Char recalls how he searched very long for the one word which, to his mind, captures the essence of the poem, the word *chimère* in the last line of «Congé au vent»: (16) «Peut-être aurez-vous la chance de distinguer sur ses lèvres la chimère de l'humidité de la Nuit?»   Louis Curel de la Sorgue, the poet's friend, is described through the *biais* of the river.   The poem that bears his name sketches a landscape rather than the portrait of a man.   And what of the titles of these poems? «Congé au vent,» «Violences,» «Fréquence,» «Eléments.» Focusing on the larger cosmic phenomena, they exclude man. Char's *dramatis personae,* though they now have names and, sometimes, even particularized functions in time and space, still keep about them the aura of symbols.   When the poet writes, in «Allégement»: «Du torrent épars de la vie arrêtée j'avais extrait la signification loyale d'Irène,» we know that the girl has been reduced (or, rather, elevated) to the etymology of her name.   Like the *chimère* of «Congé au vent,» Irène is the symbol of peace.

«Il n'y a pas de chimère.   Pourtant des hommes, jamais bien établis, en incarnent les traits furtifs et dégrisants,» Char writes in 1964 («Violette blanche pour Jean-Paul Samson,» *Recherche de la Base et du Sommet,* 1965).   The poet's heroes still remain the exceptional beings endowed with supernatural powers, like the «donneur de liberté» who—though he has lost the capital—keeps company with earlier figures of *Le Marteau sans maître.*   The poet reserves to him an «exemplaire destin» and invests him with the power of charming the wild beasts of the forest («L'Epi de cristal...»).   These heroes have about them something of the *Märchengestalt* with which they share the elusiveness of their appearance (the «personne à peine indiquée» in «L'Eclairage du pénitencier») and the permanence of the symbol they embody.

The words *frère, sœur, compagne, compagnon, compère, semblable* (n.), are used with increasing frequency in *Seuls demeurent,* along with the group *secours, secourir, secourable*: «La plage qui chaque hiver s'encombrait de régressives *légen-*

---

(16) Reported from a private interview with the poet, April 1970.

6

des, de *sibylles* aux bras lourds d'orties, se prépare aux *êtres à secourir*» («Calendrier»). Char would like to be the «frère secourable» of those that serve with him the common cause of the *maquis*. But he still looks upon himself as «l'exclu et le comblé» («L'Eclairage du pénitencier»), different from and superior to the ordinary *maquisards*. He even reverts to the old manner of his first aphorisms by referring to himself with the reverential «le poète»: «Le poète est retourné pour de longues années dans le néant du père. Ne l'appelez pas, vous tous qui l'aimez.» This is the «Début du partisan.» The poem in which Char tries to describe his own place in the *maquis* bears the title: «L'Absent,» the absent one, who is qualified as «ce frère brutal mais dont la parole était sûre, patient au sacrifice, diamant et sanglier, ingénieux et secourable,» and who could be found «au centre de tous les malentendus tel un arbre de résine dans le froid inalliable.»

«Le poète passe par tous les degrés solitaires d'une gloire collective dont il est, de bonne guerre, exclu...» Char does not feel at ease among «ses semblables, ses frères,» his newly discovered brethren. He cannot identify with the many people whose close company is suddenly forced upon him, and he feels again the *gêne* that he knew during his schooldays in Avignon. The poet is repulsed by the drudgery of everyday existence in which life would involve him as witness or victim. To the company of men, he prefers the flowers. The story of the eel-fishers («Violences») ends as follows:

> ... Et chaque nuit le même manège se répétait dont j'étais le témoin sans nom et la victime. J'optai pour l'obscurité et la réclusion.
>
> Etoile du destiné. J'entr'ouvre la porte du jardin des morts. Des fleurs serviles se recueillent. Compagnes de l'homme. Oreilles du Créateur.

But a voice recalls «L'Absent» from the paradise of dream: «Vecteur infaillible de l'homme au rat quand cette voix jamais refoulée, basse comme l'absence, répète: 'Tu n'échapperas pas. Tu *es* parmi nous'» («Ecrasez-leur la tête avec un gourdin, je veux dire avec un secret,» *La Nuit talismanique*). The poet has turned partisan, has been linked at last to the «difformité des chaînes de chaque être» («Ne s'entend pas»). To André Breton, Char writes at the end of the war: «J'ai de la difficulté à me reconnaître sur le fil des évidences dont je suis l'interné et le témoin, l'écuyer et le cheval» (17). The former *fidèle* of the surrealist chapel has entered a new arena. Already in 1930, in the letter addressed to «Chère Artine,» the poet had written: «J'ai l'impression que vos rêves majeurs ne m'atteignent plus comme par le passé, dans toute ma chair vive. Notre rencontre remonte à Octobre 1929. Depuis cette date les hippodromes ont cessé de m'être favorables» (*Le Surréalisme au Service de la Révolution*, no. 3) (17a). The diary of Hypnos continues the leavetaking. The peasant partisans of the *maquis* have no use for the «souris de l'enclume» (*Feuillets d'Hypnos*, no. 52) and the «marteau sans maître.» The threatened men of Céreste find no comfort in the old Pythian oracles. Reality has replaced dream, and action, prophecy.

The earlier note of joyous sacrifice has gone out of Char's Resistance poems. Nausea and fear, anguish and solitude, these are components of *Fureur et Mystère* that critics have overlooked. In a very real sense, the *maquis* was for Char a prison in which he was caught like an animal in the closed circle of the arena («Et chaque nuit le même manège se répétait dont j'étais le témoin sans nom et la victime»). Tacked to the wall of this prison, the poet kept an *image* that was never to leave him again, the *Prisonnier* of Georges de la Tour:

> La reproduction en couleurs du *Prisonnier* de Georges de la Tour, que j'ai piquée sur le mur de chaux de la pièce où je travaille, semble, avec le

---

(17) «La Lettre hors commerce,» in *Recherche de la Base et du Sommet.*

(17a) In his *René Char: Dichtung und Poetik,* Franz Mayer recounts how, in conversation, Char identified Artine as Lamartine. A poet's joke on the critic? Antonin Artaud would seem a more likely *destinataire* of the «Farewell.»

temps, réfléchir son sens dans notre condition. Elle serre le cœur mais combien désaltère!... La femme explique, l'emmuré écoute. Les mots qui tombent de cette terrestre silhouette d'ange rouge sont des mots essentiels, des mots qui portent immédiatement secours. Au fond du cachot, les minutes de suif de la clarté tirent et diluent les traits de l'homme assis... Le Verbe de la femme donne naissance à l'inespéré mieux que n'importe quelle aurore.

Reconnaissance à Georges de la Tour qui maîtrisa les ténèbres hitlériennes avec un dialogue d'êtres humains.

(*Feuillets d'Hypnos*, no. 178).

To the poem «Gravité» from *Dehors la nuit est gouvernée,* 1938, Char adds at this time (1945) the subtitle: «L'emmuré.» Like the passage above, «Gravité» describes the «homme abrupt dans sa prison» who awaits the healing and redemptive powers of woman, the liberation through love. One day, Char will come to know «le Verbe de la femme [qui] donne naissance à l'inespéré.» One day he, too, will be able to join with Georges de La Tour in the celebration of the red terrestrial angel. For the present, however, he must learn to live in the company of men («Vivre avec de tels hommes»), peasants, workers, whose physical strength and beauty he may admire, but whose spirit he cannot penetrate. One of these, a *garagiste* from the Vaucluse, remembers:

Je considère que Char était extrêmement handicapé par rapport à un homme comme moi. Je veux dire que je suis un homme normal, normal en tout. Physiquement, moralement, intellectuellement. Lui, au contraire, était exceptionnel et, si j'ose dire, anormal en tout; avec la double conséquence que cela dut le rendre particulièrement repérable à ses ennemis, et dut lui rendre particulièrement difficile de se plier aux exigences de l'action en commun (18).

_____

(18) *L'Herne*, March 1971, p. 203. The testimony is by M. Jean

Better than the learned commentators of *Fureur et Mystère,* the companions of the *maquis* knew that Char by his very nature was not made for communal action. From the beginning the poet's place was never really among, but always above the partisans of Céreste, where the reign of Alexander was established:

> Ecartez-vous de moi qui patiente sans bouche;
> A vos pieds je suis né, mais vous m'avez perdu;
> Mes feux ont trop précisé leur royaume;
> Mon trésor a coulé contre votre billot.
>
> Le désert comme asile au seul tison suave
> Jamais ne m'a nommé, jamais ne m'a rendu.
>
> Ecartez-vous de moi qui patiente sans bouche:
> Le trèfle de la passion est de fer dans ma main.
>
> Dans la stupeur de l'air où s'ouvrent mes allées,
> Le temps émondera peu à peu mon visage,
> Comme un cheval sans fin dans un labour aigri.

This is Char's 1945 «Post-scriptum» to *Le Visage nuptial* (*Seuls demeurent*). The poet has been momentarily silenced; he is waiting «sans bouche,» like his fellow partisans, «acteurs à la langue coupée («La Liberté passe en trombe,» 1946). His fire has been put out, his treasure (i.e., his poetry) upon collision with the butcher's block (the *maquis*) has sunk to the bottom of the sea. But the poet will not die. He will simply exchange the «tison suave» for the «trèfle de fer,» and a new leader, the partisan, is born, whose name will not be writ on water.

«Successives enveloppes! Du corps levant au jour désinté-gré, des blanches ténèbres au mortier hasardeux, nous restons constamment encerclés, avec l'énergie de rompre» (*La Nuit*

Fernand, «chef de la Section Atterrissage Parachutage (S. A. P.), département de Vaucluse.»

talismanique). The post-scriptum quoted above is a sequel to
«Fenaison.» Only now one horse has left the arena, has
broken out of his prison and, like the winged Pegasus, taken
to the sky. The lamb has risen from the sand that was to
have been the altar of its sacrifice. The desert has been left
behind and man, once «enclavé dans la chevalerie pythienne»
or crouched on the prison floor, man has risen to his feet:

> Voici le sable mort, voici le corps sauvé:
> La Femme respire, l'Homme se tient debout.
> («Le Visage nuptial»).

Char at last has found a place within—and yet outside—
his society. He has taken his place among those who belong
neither to society, nor to the world of dream: «Quelques
êtres ne sont ni dans la société ni dans une rêverie,» Char says
in «Cotes,» a series of aphorisms of *Dans la pluie giboyeuse*,
1968. «Ils appartiennent à un destin isolé, à une espérance
inconnue. Leurs actes apparents semblent antérieurs à la première inculpation du temps et à l'insouciance des cieux. Nul
ne s'offre à les appointer. L'avenir fond devant leur regard.
Ce sont les plus nobles et les plus inquiétants.»

The reign of Alexander will be stern: «Le trèfle de la
passion est de fer dans ma main.» The partisan has come to
bring the sword. He will be as exacting, as uncompromising
as the poet. His companions remember:

> ... Il savait être très dur avec les hommes quand
> il le fallait... Il leur serrait la vis. Il fallait être
> dur pour commander des fauves comme certains
> l'étaient à l'époque, et ce n'est pas pour rien que
> nous avions droit de vie et de mort sur nos hommes.
> Ainsi, au début, les hommes qui entraient dans ses
> maquis étaient-ils un peu désorientés et réticents...
> Puis, très vite, s'instaurait une confiance absolue.
> Ce n'est pas facile et c'était exceptionnel de main-
> tenir pendant des mois et des années une dureté et
> des précautions pourtant indispensables, et plus

difficile encore de les teinter de cette humanité sans lesquelles elles sont insupportables (19).

To this, the testimony of Jean Fernand, Char's closest friend and adjoint, Pierre Zyngerman (alias Léon Saingermain) adds: «... Char sut obtenir de chacun des actes extraordinaires, des renoncements incroyables; il nous amenait presque à un état de sublimation de nous-mêmes» (20).

Immediately after the «Post-scriptum» quoted above, there follows the third section of *Seuls demeurent, Partage formel,* a collection of aphorisms dealing, in the main, with the nature of poetry and the functioning of the poetic imagination. Structurally, *Partage formel* resembles the earlier *Moulin premier,* first published in 1936 and appended to *Le Marteau sans maître* in 1945. Char again speaks in short passages of poetic prose and refers to himself in the third person of *le poète.* However, as the title implies, *Partage formel* marks a clear division between Char's surrealist apprenticeship and his new position, defined as follows:

> Après la remise de ses trésors... et l'abandon de ses sueurs, le poète, la moitié du corps, le sommet du souffle dans l'inconnu, le poète n'est plus le reflet d'un fait accompli. Plus rien ne le mesure, ne le lie... (LIII).

This aphorism and «Post-scriptum» tell the same tale. The poet has handed over his treasure and has left the sacrificial ground. Char speaks again of «la remise de ses trésors» in *Partage formel* (XXII): «Compagnons pathétiques qui murmurez à peine, allez la lampe éteinte et rendez les bijoux. Un mystère nouveau chante dans vos os. Développez votre étrangeté légitime.» I read in this text a juxtaposition of the surrealists' cult of the marvelous and of the new and legitimate

---

(19) *Ibid.,* p. 204.
(20) *Ibid.,* p. 206.

étrangeté of the partisans. A note from *Feuillets d'Hypnos* (no. 61) further explains:

> Un officier venu d'Afrique du Nord, s'étonne que mes «bougres de maquisards» comme ils les appelle, s'expriment dans une langue dont le sens lui échappe, son oreille étant rebelle «au parler des images.» Je lui fais remarquer que l'argot n'est que pittoresque alors que la langue qui est ici en usage est due à l'émerveillement communiqué par les êtres et les choses dans l'intimité desquels nous vivons continuellement.

Char the idolater has turned iconoclast; he has broken down the false idols of precious stone: «Fureur et mystère tour à tour le séduisirent et le consumèrent. Puis vint l'année qui acheva son agonie de saxifrage» (*Partage formel,* XIII) (21). Now man is made the measure of all things, man and the seemingly barren rocks of his earth: «Devant les précaires perspectives d'alchimie du dieu détruit—inaccompli dans l'expérience—je vous regarde formes douées de vie, choses inouïes, choses quelconques, et j'interroge: 'Commandement interne? Sommation du dehors?'» («Mission et révocation,» the last text of *Partage formel,* and the only one to have a title).

For Char, the inner and the outer commands («commandement interne, sommation du dehors») are not always in accord. The outer world, the *maquis,* would make of him a tool of history, a recorder of reality, a *chroniqueur* of events. The poetic imagination resists:

> Le poète transforme indifféremment la défaite en victoire, la victoire en défaite, empereur prénatal seulement soucieux du recueil de l'azur.
> Quelquefois sa réalité n'aurait aucun sens pour

---

(21) The word *saxifrage* is an important one for Char who in *La Parole en archipel* will write an «Hommage» to Höderlin with the title: «Pour un Prométhée saxifrage.»

lui, si le poète n'influençait pas en secret le récit
des exploits de celle des autres (*ibid.*, III + IV).

The outside world would summon Char to renounce the
chimeras and fables of his early years, keeping his mind strictly
on the *hic et nunc* reality of the *maquis*. But here the opening
lines of *Partage formel*:

> L'imagination consiste à expulser de la réalité
> plusieurs personnes incomplètes pour, mettant à
> contribution les puissances magiques et subversives
> du désir, obtenir leur retour sous la forme d'une
> présence entièrement satisfaisante. C'est alors l'inex-
> tinguible réel incréé.

In this passage, the poet defines the role of every artist
whose task it is to give to the seemingly shapeless contours of
reality an aesthetically satisfying form. He thanks men like
Heraclitus and Georges de La Tour for having shown the way:
«je vous sais gré d'avoir de longs moments poussé dehors de
chaque pli de mon corps singulier ce leurre: la condition humaine incohérente...» (*ibid.*, IX). At the same time, however,
the poet is also aware of the snares of an artistic creed inspired
by the «magic and subversive powers of desire.» A moral
judgment is implied. Hypnos-Alexander must reconcile the
roles of poet and partisan. He writes:

> Sans doute appartient-il à cet homme, de fond
> en comble aux prises avec le Mal dont il connaît le
> visage vorace et médullaire, de transformer le fait
> fabuleux en fait historique. Notre conviction in-
> quiète ne doit pas le dénigrer mais l'interroger, nous,
> fervents tueurs d'êtres réels dans la personne succes-
> sive de notre chimère. Magie médiate, imposture,
> il fait encore nuit, j'ai mal, mais tout fonctionne à
> nouveau.
> L'évasion dans son semblable, avec d'immenses
> perspectives de poésie, sera peut-être un jour pos-
> sible (*ibid.*, LV).

Again, the pronoun shifts (*il, nous, je*) are typical of Char and reflect the ambiguity of his situation. By referring to himself successively as *cet homme, nous,* and finally *je,* he is able to enter into dialogue with himself, exposing his own doubts about the validity of his art, questioning his own convictions as artist and man, poet and partisan. Will he be able to substitute history for fable, *êtres réels* for *chimères?* It is the last sentence of the text above that opens up—though hypothetically only—new vistas of Char's poetry: «L'évasion dans son semblable, avec d'immenses perspectives de poésie, sera peut-être un jour possible.» True identification with another human-being does not come for Char until the completion of *Lettera amorosa,* 1964, but the «évasion dans son semblable» is begun in Céreste.

Feuillets d'Hypnos, 1943-1944, dedicated to Albert Camus, forms the center section of *Fureur et Mystère.* First published in 1946, it elicited enthusiastic commentary from people like Etiemble (22). The title refers to the pages of a diary kept by Captain Alexander and his alter ego, Hypnos, during Char's service in the *maquis.* Though the poet would have us believe that he wrote these diary notations «comme une ménagère consigne ses comptes sur un calepin,» (23) many of the 237 separately numbered entries are aphorisms or prose poems of a high literary order, and there is even one true poem in free verse (no. 221). Given the care with which Char generally revises his texts, it is unlikely that these leaves were, as he says, «plus souvent survolées que relues» (24). But the poet was aware of the objections that could have been raised, in some quarters, to the artistic activity of the partisan who

---

(22) Even when, due to an unfortunate quarrel over Rimbaud texts, Etiemble and Char write each other rather uncomplimentary letters, Etiemble still finds a privileged place apart for *Feuillets d'Hypnos.* (v. *Le Dernier Couac,* Paris: G. L. M., 1958).

(23) Reported by Pierre Berger, «Conversation avec René Char,» *La Gazette des Lettres,* 15 juin 1952.

(24) I have seen a typescript of *Feuillets d'Hypnos* with many manuscript corrections in the poet's hand.

claimed to have left poetry behind. The times had changed. The days when an Apollinaire could send home from the front the glorious hymns to war found among his *Calligrammes,* were gone. Char published nothing during the years of his military engagement, and when the *Feuillets d'Hypnos* do appear in print, they are prefaced by a sort of *in apologia*:

> Ces notes n'empruntent rien à l'amour de soi, à la nouvelle, à la maxime ou au roman. Un feu d'herbes sèches eût tout aussi bien été leur éditeur. La vue du sang supplicié en a fait une fois perdre le fil, a réduit à néant leur importance...
> Ce carnet pourrait n'avoir appartenu à personne...
> Ces notes marquent la résistance d'un humanisme conscient de ses devoirs, discret sur ses vertus, désirant réserver *l'inaccessible* champ libre à la fantaisie de ses soleils, et décidé à payer le *prix* pour cela.

Surrealism has left its imprint on Char who, in a way, tries to answer in his war journal the contradictory demands of Breton's manifestoes. First of all, the poet disclaims any artistic merit. Anyone, he says, could have written these notes; anyone and no one. The very choice of his *nom de plume* (Hypnos) recalls Char's «sommeil fraternel» of «Tous compagnons de lit.» The purpose of *Feuillets d'Hypnos* was not to enrich French literature, nor to bring glory to their author. (Paradoxically, that is, of course, precisely what the journal did!) And secondly, Char's notebook, while it was to be a document of social and political protest, was yet to remain a book free from dogma, «discret sur ses vertus» and following no party-line. This, however, does not place *Feuillets d'Hypnos* outside of or above all aesthetic and moral preoccupations, as predicated by Breton. Instead, Char pleads, quite simply, for a new humanism conscious of its duties. To the poet's mind, these duties include not only the Resistance organized on the mountaintops of the Basses-Alpes, but also the «résistance d'un humanisme... désirant réserver *l'inaccessible* champ libre à la fantaisie de ses soleils, et décidé à payer le *prix* pour cela.»

In a «Postface» to *Dehors la nuit est gouvernée,* Char writes: «L'inaction ce devoir nous quitte. Les tâches du réveil s'allument distinctes des berges de leur trajectoire... Le printemps gronde. Quel goût ont les outils?» (25). In Céreste, the *marteau* has accepted its *maître,* and the tasks of the waking man are spelled out in the notebook of Hypnos: «Autant que se peut, enseigne à devenir efficace, pour le but à atteindre mais pas au delà. Au delà est fumée. Où il y a fumée il y a changement» (no. 1). Again, Char directs his imperatives towards himself, reminding himself to stay within the role he has assumed. I know of no better description of Captain Alexander than that given, once again, by his adjoint Pierre Zyngerman, who writes: «Je ne sais quelle qualité faisait de lui l'homme de l'efficacité de chaque jour» (26). This is Char's humble but extremely difficult task: to rule, to command, to lead his men without the reassuring support of an established set of political values or formal truths of any kind, of which he says:

> ... Le génie de l'homme, qui pense avoir découvert les vérités formelles, accommode les vérités qui tuent en vérités qui *autorisent* à tuer. Parade des grands inspirés à rebours sur le front de l'univers cuirassé et pantelant! Cependant que les névroses collectives s'accusent dans l'œil des mythes et des symboles, l'homme psychique met la vie au supplice sans qu'il paraisse lui en coûter le moindre remords...
>
> (*Feuillets d'Hypnos,* no. 37).

Nothing but the «efficacité de chaque jour» has any value or meaning for the men of Céreste who will be judged accord-

---

(25) In the 1938 edition, this «Postface» was called «Validité,» a significant title, restored in the 1971 edition.

(26) *L'Herne, no. cit.,* p. 206.

ing to how well they serve that *efficacité*. Char's men remember:

> ... Et de fait, sitôt mis en présence d'Alexandre, je compris que je ne connaîtrais pas le découragement avec ce camarade... Il me jaugea, tandis que de mon côté également je le jaugeais. En trois jours, j'avais pris une leçon mais lui étais devenu dévoué... J'étais désormais prêt à exécuter strictement les missions qu'il m'ordonnerait, quels que soient les risques pourvu qu'elles soient franches et précises... C'est ainsi que nous passâmes lui et moi un pacte à la vie à la mort qui dure encore... (27).

This is the testimony of Bruno Charmasson, one of Char's *agents de liaison,* who appears under his pseudonym, Arthur le Fol, in *Feuillets d'Hypnos,* where the poet says of him: «Sa fringale d'action doit se satisfaire de la tâche précise que je lui assigne. Il obéit et se limite, par crainte d'être tancé!... Fidèle Arthur, comme un soldat de l'ancien temps!» (no. 9). Another entry in *Feuillets d'Hypnos* (no. 196) further illustrates Char's concept of «fraternal action»: «Cet homme autour duquel tourbillonnera un moment ma sympathie *compte* parce que son empressement à servir coïncide avec tout un halo favorable et mes projets à son égard.»

Char's idea of the efficient ruler—and, therefore, a definition of his own newly assumed task—can best be deduced from a letter that Hypnos wrote to his adjoint, laying down the principles of conduct for the ruler and the ruled:

> ... Stoppez vantardise. Vérifiez à deux sources corps renseignements. Tenez compte cinquante pour cent romanesque dans la plupart des cas. Apprenez à vos hommes à prêter attention, à rendre compte exactement, à savoir poser l'arithmétique des situations... Avec les hommes de l'équipe soyez rigoureux

---

(27) *Ibid.,* p. 204.

> et attentionné. Amitié ouate discipline. Dans le
> travail, faites toujours quelques kilos de plus que
> chacun, sans en tirer orgueil... Suggérez les précau-
> tions; laissez-leur le mérite de les découvrir... Con-
> trariez les habitudes monotones. Inspirez celles que
> vous ne voulez pas trop tôt voir mourir. Enfin,
> aimez au même moment qu'eux les êtres qu'ils
> aiment. Additionnez, ne divisez pas... (no. 87).

Be not effusive, but correct. Teach not by doctrine, but by
example. Do not dictate, but inspire, and leave the «inaccessible champ libre à la fantaisie de ses soleils.» These are
the commandments of Char's new moral code. These are the
ingredients of a new humanism conscious of its duties, the
anguished existential humanism «précédé d'aucun testament»
(no. 62), not securely anchored in any book of laws, but daily
exposed to the merciless tides of reality.

To the *maquisards,* that reality was a matter of life and
death, and this is the only truth that «le Capitaine Alexandre»
tried to teach his men, many of whom undoubtedly joined the
Resistance inspired by a narrowly defined idealism. Char says
of them:

> Ils se laissent choir de toute la masse de leurs
> préjugés ou ivres de l'ardeur de leurs faux princi-
> pes. Les associer, les exorciser, les alléger, les
> muscler, les assouplir, puis les convaincre qu'à partir
> d'un certain point l'importance des idées reçues est
> extrêmement relative et qu'en fin de compte «l'affai-
> re» est une affaire de vie et de mort et non de
> nuances à faire prévaloir au sein d'une civilisation
> dont le naufrage risque de ne pas laisser de trace
> sur l'océan de la destinée, c'est ce que je m'efforce
> de faire approuver autour de moi (no. 38).

This lesson postulates that the complexity of life cannot be
reduced to ideas, and that, therefore, we cannot hope to for-
mulate—and much less, to know—any absolute truths. We
should, thus, be careful not to turn temporary convictions into

ideologies that kill: «Le génie de l'homme, qui pense avoir découvert les vérités formelles, accommode les vérités qui tuent en vérités qui *autorisent* à tuer,» noted Hypnos. «Parade des grands inspirés à rebours sur le front de l'univers cuirassé et pantelant!»

Man's salvation, however, is not in knowing, but in asking questions, in keeping alive his conscience and his consciousness: «Fidèles et démesurément vulnérables, nous opposons la conscience de l'événement au gratuit...» (*ibid.*, no. 164). The *gratuit* ceases to exist in man's awareness thereof, and even death acquires meaning, as in view of it, man defines his life: «Juxtapose à la fatalité la résistance à la fatalité. Tu connaîtras d'étranges hauteurs» (*Le Bulletin des Baux*).

> J'aime ces êtres tellement épris de ce que leur cœur imagine la liberté qu'ils s'immolent pour éviter au peu de liberté de mourir. Merveilleux mérite du peuple. (Le libre arbitre n'existerait pas. L'être se définirait par rapport à ses cellules, à son hérédité, à la course brève ou prolongée de son destin... Cependant il existe entre *tout cela* et l'Homme une enclave d'inattendus et de métamorphoses dont il faut défendre l'accès et assurer le maintien.)
> (*Feuillets d'Hypnos,* no. 155).

Char believes in the value of man's freedom and in the possibility of meaningful existence. Though, in his terms, man's action can have an absolute value only for the dead, it is not devoid of meaning, as it lays the foundation for «les consciences qui en héritent et la questionnent» (*ibid.*, no. 187). Outwardly, man must define his parameters by serving particularized functions in time and space: as poet or partisan, he must engage himself on different roads, in accordance with the necessities of the day. But at the center, the questioning conscience remains free, free to doubt, to change, to grow. In the *Lettre hors commerce* (to André Breton, 1947), Char writes: «La permission de disposer, accordée à l'homme, ne peut être qu'infinie, bien que notre liberté se passe à l'intérieur de quelque chose dont la surface n'est pas libre, de quelque chose qui est conditionné.» In *Feuillets d'Hypnos,* the poet draws upon one of his favorite symbols, the almond, to paint his picture of man:

> N'étant jamais définitivement modelé, l'homme est receleur de son contraire. Ses cycles dessinent des orbes différents selon qu'il est en butte à telle sollicitation ou non. Et les dépressions mystérieuses, les inspirations absurdes, surgies du grand externat crématoire, comment se contraindre à les ignorer? Ah! circuler généreusement sur les saisons de l'écorce, tandis que l'amande palpite, libre... (no. 55) (28).

Near the end of *Feuillets d'Hypnos* (as again near the end of *Le Poème pulvérisé*), Char offers up a prayer—a prayer not to God, but to life—that man may come to know the value of his freedom without killing that within himself which makes freedom possible, «l'amande [qui] palpite,» the questioning conscience:

> O vie, donne, s'il est temps encore, aux vivants un peu de ton bon sens subtil sans la vanité qui abuse, et par-dessus tout, peut-être, donne-leur la certitude que tu n'es pas aussi accidentelle et privée de remords qu'on le dit. Ce n'est pas la flèche qui est hideuse, c'est le croc (no. 220).

I think that Char's role in the *maquis* was both more complex and more subtle than either factual accounts of missions accomplished or fraternal eulogies inspired by a narrow idealism can tell. Eluard understood the full meaning of that role when, in 1945, he dedicated a copy of «Au rendez-vous allemand» to René Char «qui reconstitue un univers défait en

---

(28) Mauricette Raymond has studied the symbol of the almond in the poetry of Char. (v. «Le symbole de l'amande,» *L'Herne, no. cit.,* pp. 121-123).

lui imposant sa règle et sa loi, règle de lys et loi d'ébène.» In Céreste, Captain Alexander was forced to elaborate for himself and for his fellowmen rules of conduct aimed at satisfying the «efficacité de chaque jour,» an efficacy constantly questioned and redefined. The revolutionary platform assigned to the partisan-poet becomes a questionable abstraction. «Destruction révolutionnaire de l'ordre établi: il n'y avait pas solution de continuité des batailles surréalistes livrées par Char à sa mobilisation les armes à la main. Simplement, une logique assumée avec rigueur jusqu'à ses extrêmes conséquences» (28a).

Doubt, continual self-examination, humility and faith in the basic values of man, faith in life: these were the things needful to the *maquisards*. It was the unwritten task of their leader to kindle in them hope and faith: «Ensoleiller l'imagination de ceux qui bégaient au lieu de parler, qui rougissent à l'instant d'affirmer. Ce sont de fermes partisans» (no. 60). In a «Note sur le maquis,» dated 1944, Char defined his mission thus: «Faire longuement rêver ceux qui ordinairement n'ont pas de songes, et plonger dans l'actualité ceux dans l'esprit desquels prévalent les jeux perdus du sommeil» (*Recherche de la Base du Sommet*).

One will look in vain in all of Char's works for a true «Resistance poem,» or even for a patriotic piece, of the kind that a Péguy or an Aragon could turn out with such ease. Georges Louis Roux, the poet's host of Céreste, explains:

> Quand il [Char] était à Céreste, il venait chez nous écouter la radio anglaise et nous parlions des événements et des hommes. Un écrivain qui, quelque temps après la défaite, s'était répandu en poèmes exaltés sur la France déchirée, excitait particulièrement son ironie et ses sarcasmes... Dieu sait si Char vomissait l'ignominie dans laquelle nous étions plon-

---

(28a) Raymond Jean, «René Char ou le refus,» *Europe,* juillet-août 1974, p. 87.

7

gés, mais, pour lui, la dignité commandait de se taire
et d'agir, ce qu'il fit jusqu'à la Libération; d'autre
part, ce n'était pas seulement la France qui comptait,
mais quelque chose d'universel et de fondamental:
le sens même de la vie et le destin des hommes, sur
qui pesait un effroyable danger d'asservissement et
de dégradation (29).

Char has nothing but disdain for those who, after the
Liberation, quickly claimed for themselves medals, decorations
and victory celebrations. In a letter to Francis Curel, he writes
in 1946: «Ne songeons pas aux couards d'hier, auxquels se
joindront les nôtres ambitieux, qui s'accoutrent pour la tournée
des commémorations et des anniversaires. Rentrons. Les
clairons insupportables sonnent la diane revenue» (*Recherche
de la Base et du Sommet*). Though he admits the inevitable
nature of his acts, «le Capitaine Alexandre» never glories in the
massacres he commands and writes, again to Francis Curel,
1943: «Je veux n'oublier jamais que l'on m'a contraint à
devenir—pour combien de temps?—un monstre de justice et
d'intolérance, un simplificateur claquemuré, un personnage
arctique qui se désintéresse du sort de quiconque ne se ligue
pas avec lui pour abattre les chiens de l'enfer» (*ibid.*).

After the Liberation, Char refuses to testify in the war
trials: «Refus de siéger à la Cour de Justice, refus d'acca-
bler autrui dans le dialogue quotidien retrouvé, décision tenue
enfin d'opposer la lucidité au bien-être, l'état naturel aux hon-
neurs, ces mauvais champignons qui prolifèrent dans les cre-
vasses de la sécheresse et dans les lieux avariés, après le premier
grain de pluie. Qui a connu et échangé la mort violente hait
l'agonie du prisonnier ... Les enragés de la veille, ces auteurs
du type nouveau de 'meurtrier continuel,' continuaient, eux, à
m'écœurer au-delà de tout châtiment» (Letter to Francis Curel,
1948). The poet proclaims instead a new era of tolerance
and forgiveness: «Nous sommes partisans, après l'incendie,

---

(29) *L'Herne, no. cit.*, p. 198.

d'effacer les traces et de murer le labyrinthe. On ne prolonge pas un climat exceptionnel. Nous sommes partisans, après l'incendie, d'effacer les traces, de murer le labyrinthe et de relever le civisme» (*ibid.*). Unlike the patriots who could produce, on command, their «poèmes exaltés sur la France déchirée,» Char found no cause for exultation, no abstract certainty or truth in the real world where poetry had been replaced by victory celebrations on the one hand, and criminal proceedings on the other.

René Char will not be seen at the meetings of the Anciens Résistants, some of whom he considers as corrupt and morally reprehensible as the enemy they fought. In his war journal he noted: «La qualité des résistants n'est pas, hélas, partout la même! A côté d'un Joseph Fontaine, d'une rectitude et d'une teneur de sillon…, combien d'insaisissables saltimbanques plus soucieux de jouir que de produire! A prévoir que ces coqs du néant nous timbreront aux oreilles, la Libération venue…» (*Feuillets d'Hypnos*, no. 65). And again: «Je vois l'homme perdu de perversions politiques, confondant action et expiation, nommant conquête son anéantissement» (*ibid.*, no. 69). Typically, Char gives credit for the success of the Resistance to the leaders, the «hommes intelligents et clair-voyants» that commanded the spoiled children, the poor workers, the fanatics, the «paysans au patriotisme fort obscur, d'imaginatifs instables, d'aventuriers précoces voisinant avec les vieux chevaux de retour de la Légion étrangère…» («Note sur le maquis»).

True to the friends he made among the partisans of Céreste and among the *loyaux adversaires* on the other side of an arbitrary line, the poet yet proclaims no loyalty towards any socially or politically defined group or ideology. No party has been successful in inscribing René Char in its lists. The poet is interested in individual man, not in the credoes published by more or less enlightened governments. He fights for indi-vidual justice, testifies in favor of Louis Fernandez and Albert Camus, but has little patience with summary verities proclaimed from rostrum or pulpit.

For Char, the war had settled nothing. The basic questions of life and death, right and wrong, good and evil had not been answered by political expediency, and the victor's truth was, for him, as uncertain as that of the vanquished. The poet had succeeded in transforming «vieux ennemis en loyaux adversaires,» but the problems facing both remained the same. No self-satisfied hymns of praise, no apostrophes to a glorious national future follow upon the *Feuillets d'Hypnos.* The simple songs and tales of *Les Loyaux Adversaires,* the third section of *Fureur et Mystère,* go back to the years before World War II. Many of these poems tell of Char's childhood («Le Thor,» «Cur secessisti») not nostalgically, but searchingly: «Que disais-tu? Tu me parlais d'un amour si lointain / Qu'il rejoignait ton enfance» («L'Ordre légitime est quelquefois inhumain»). In the *Lettre hors commerce* to Breton, Char writes: «Ce n'est pas moi qui ai simplifié les choses, mais les choses horribles m'ont rendu simple, plus apte à faire confiance à certains au fond desquels subsistent, tenaces, les feux mourants de la recherche et de la dignité humaine (cette dignité si mal réalisable dans l'action et dans cet état hybride qui lui succède) ailleurs déjà anéantis et balayés, méprisés et niés... La transvaluation est accomplie. L'agneau 'mystique' est un renard, le renard un sanglier et le sanglier cet enfant à sa marelle.»

In accordance with the hopes expressed by the partisan of Céreste, the poet of the Sorgue returns to his beginnings «dans une insatisfaction nue, une connaissance à peine entrevue et une humilité questionneuse.» In a beautiful prose poem that has about it the aura of a fairy-tale or of a *récit de rêve,* Char tells the story of a primaeval forest «où le soleil n'a pas accès mais où, la nuit, les étoiles pénètrent.» In this virgin forest, the poet would live the existentialist's life of eternal beginnings, a life perpetually redefined according to the necessities of every day. Here he would forget the doctrines and experiences of the *maquis* that threatened to weigh down and bind those who could not—or would not—break with the past:

... Je me gouvernais sans doctrine, avec une véhémence sereine. J'étais l'égal de choses dont le secret tenait sous le rayon d'une aile. Pour la plupart, l'essentiel n'est jamais né et ceux qui le possèdent ne peuvent l'échanger sans se nuire. Nul ne consent à perdre ce qu'il a conquis à la pointe de sa peine! Autrement ce serait la jeunesse et la grâce, source et delta auraient la même pureté. («Pénombre»).

The «Argument» of *Le Poème pulvérisé,* the next section of *Fureur et Mystère,* transposes the mesage of the fairy-tale into more explicit prose:

Comment vivre sans inconnu devant soi?
Les hommes d'aujourd'hui veulent que le poème soit à l'image de leur vie, faite de si peu d'égards, de si peu d'espace et brûlée d'intolérance...

Here Char breaks free of the *maquis.* Most of the texts contained in *Le Poème pulvérisé* were written after the poet's return to L'Isle-sur-la-Sorgue. Against the background of his childhood home are set the new fables, fairy-tales and songs that go back not only to Char's own youth, but yet farther back to the beginnings of man.

In «L'Extravagant,» a fable-like prose poem, «le Capitaine Alexandre» lays down his post and René Char takes leave of his «compagnons de lit»:

... Par la nuit d'hiver fantastiquement propre parce qu'elle était commune à la généralité des habitants de l'univers qui ne la pénétraient pas, le dernier comédien n'allait plus exister. Il avait perdu tout lien avec le volume ancien des sources propices aux interrogations, avec le corps heureux qu'il s'était plu à animer auprès du sien... Aujourd'hui il rompait avec la tristesse devenue un objet aguerri, avec la frayeur du convenu. La terre avait faussé sa persuasion, la terre, de sa vitesse un peu courte, avec son imagination safranée, son usure crevassée par les actes des monstres. Personne n'aurait à l'oublier car l'utile ne l'avait pas assisté, ne l'avait pas dessiné en entier au regard des autres. Sur le plafond de chaux blanche de sa chambre, quelques oiseaux étaient passés mais leur éclair avait fondu dans son sommeil.

The last comedian, he who tried to rouse from sleep the companions of the *maquis,* the partisan has died. The old and fallow earth—trampled down by the feet of monsters—will cover up the past with its false persuasions and stale emotions. The actor has played out his role, and the games are up. Char returns to his old manner of confronting a superior being (in this case, «L'Extravagant» or «il») with «la généralité des habitants de l'univers.» And note that the superiority of «L'Extravagant» is not based on any merit acquired in the service of Céreste. On the contrary, it is that part of himself which he kept hidden from the «regard des autres,» the profile alone, which gives meaning to his life and justifies his superiority. «Comment vivre sans inconnu devant soi?» The birds of lightning that crossed his sleep, the poems softly whispered into the night but never published in the *maquis,* will guide the poet into the light of day.

Char has broken loose from his prison physically and mentally. He has escaped death. Nothing now interests him but life itself:

> Illusoirement, je suis à la fois dans mon âme et hors d'elle, loin devant la vitre et contre la vitre, saxifrage éclaté. Ma convoitise est infinie. Rien ne m'obsède que la vie («Le Météore du 13 août») (30).

For Char, poetry and life are one, and so the poems of *Le Poème pulvérisé* testify to the new light, the freedom that he has found: «Pourquoi *poème pulvérisé?* Parce qu'au terme

---

(30) Again the poet refers to himself with the word *saxifrage,* the breaker of stone, for which cp. note 21, *supra.*

de son voyage vers le Pays, après l'obscurité pré-natale et la dureté terrestre, la finitude du poème est lumière, apport de l'être à la vie» (*La Bibliothèque est en feu,* 1956).

In his search for a new meaning to life, Char goes back to the beginnings of western civilization, to classical Greece («Hymne à voix basse») and even farther back to the pre-Socratic world of Heraclitus, the world of cosmic harmony where fire, earth, air, water, snake and bird, seagull and shark, could live together as *loyaux adversaires:* (31)

> Il y aura toujours une goutte d'eau pour durer plus que le soleil sans que l'ascendant du soleil soit ébranlé (*A la Santé du serpent,* V).

Yes and *no,* past and future had no meaning in that world: «*Ceci n'est plus,* avais-je coutume de dire. *Ceci n'est pas,* corrigeait-il» («Suzerain»). Man lived in the eternal presence of the *éclair,* in the *nunc stans* of lyric poetry:

> Lyre sans bornes des poussières,
> Surcroît de notre cœur.

The poem called «Lyre» is the last text of *Le Poème pulvérisé,* and it sums up very well the message of this section. If man (and his poetry) are to live, they must shake the fetters imposed upon them by national and ideological frontiers, and rise above «la morne démarche du quotidien» («L'Extravagant»):

> Né de l'appel du devenir et de l'angoisse de la rétention, le poème, s'élevant de son puits de boue et d'étoiles, témoignera presque silencieusement, qu'il n'était rien en lui qui n'existât vraiment ailleurs, dans ce rebelle et solitaire monde des contradictions.
> («Argument,» *Le Poème pulvérisé*).

---

(31) For a fuller discussion of Heraclitus and Char, v. Philip E. Cranston, «René Char, poète outil: A l'instant du poème,» *French Review,* special issue no. 1, Winter 1970, pp. 17-24.

From Lautréamont, Rimbaud, and the *maquis,* Char learned that destruction must be an integral part of creation. Words, elements, forms, ideas, laws, must be perpetually decomposed and reconstituted if life is to continue (32). Like Heraclitus, Char knows that «Nos orages nous sont essentiels» (*Contre une maison sèche,* 1972). And while destruction is inevitable, man-made constructions are not without value: «Dans l'ordre des douleurs la société n'est pas fatalement fautive,» concludes the poet, «malgré ses étroites places, ses murs, leur écroulement et leur restauration alternés» (*ibid.*). With Heraclitus and Breton, Char affirms that, in the end, destruction and creation, life and death are all part of the same cycle, and that in man's oneness with that cycle lies his strength, his health, and his humanity:

> Le chasseur de soi fuit sa maison fragile:
> Son gibier le suit n'ayant plus peur.
> Leur clarté est si haute, leur santé si nouvelle,
> Que ces deux qui s'en vont sans rien signifier
> Ne sentent pas les sœurs les ramener à elles
> D'un long bâillon de cendre aux forêts blanches.
> («Les trois sœurs,» *Le Poème pulvérisé*).

It is but a small step from the obscure forests of primaeval existence to the white forests of eternal light, from the hunter of the earth to Orion. In the allegory of «Les trois sœurs,» Char reaches a Dantesque serenity; his poem has become pure light (33). I do not know whether his late friend Martin Heidegger was thinking of lines like these in one of the poems recently dedicated by the philosopher to the poet. But

---

(32) It is according to the principles of destruction and recomposition that Char organizes his own poems and anthologies. V., for example, his 1956 collection called *En trente-trois morceaux,* in which he reprints only bits and pieces of earlier poems. (Paris: G. L. M.).

(33) Indeed, Char's definition of poetry—«la finitude du poème est lumière»—might well be applied to the *canti* of the *Paradiso.*

Heidegger's «Dank» seems to capture the same serenity, the same landscape, and the same light:

> Sichverdanken: Sichsagenlassen das Gehören in
> das vereignend-brauchende Ereignis.
> Wie weit der Weg vor diese Ortschaft, von der uns
> das Denken in fügsamer Weise gegen sich selber
> denken kann, um so das Verhaltene seiner
> Armseligkeit zu retten.
>
> Was aber arm ist, selig wahrt es sein Geringes.
> Dessen ungesprochenes Vermächtnis
> gross behaltet's im Gedächtnis:
>   Sagen die Alêtheia als: die Lichtung:
>   die Entbergung der sich entziehenden Befugnis (34).

Le Poème pulvérisé spoke of the destruction necessary to creation; *La Fontaine narrative,* the last section of *Fureur et Mystère,* celebrates the freedom resulting from that destruction. *Le Poème pulvérisé* contained the poems of earth; *La Fontaine narrative* is made up of water, fire and air. Already in 1945, in his «Post-scriptum» to *Le Visage nuptial,* Char had attempted the synthesis of earth and sky, water and air:

> Le temps émondera peu à peu mon visage,
> Comme un cheval sans fin dans un labour aigri.

Even in the apparent bleakness of his *maquis* prison, Char had kept alive the hope that one day he, too, would rise like the winged Pegasus to strike the Helicon mountain from which *La Fontaine narrative,* the Hippocrene fountain, would flow.

When the war is over, Char sings the celebration of that fountain and of the sea, the river, the torrent which in the very wake of destruction prepare the bed from which new life will spring. In a text fittingly called «Les premiers instants,» he describes his new awakening to life: «La modicité quotidienne avait fui, le sang jeté était rendu à sa chaleur. Adoptés

---

(34) Martin Heidegger, «Gedachtes,» *L'Herne, no. cit.,* p. 186.

par l'ouvert, poncés jusqu'à l'invisible, nous étions une victoire qui ne prendrait jamais fin.» Once again, I think the *nous* here is a royal plural. Char is celebrating his own victory, not the one-time conquest of the enemy, but the continual victory over his «héritage intellectuel,» the idle pessimism of the «compagnons de lit»:

> J'aime qui respecte son chien, affectionne ses outils, n'écorce pas l'arbre pour en punir la sève, ne mouille pas le vin hérité, se moque de l'existence d'un monde exemplaire.
>
> («Peu à peu, puis un vin siliceux,» *La Nuit talismanique*).

Like his early mentor Rimbaud, Char has abandoned «le boulevard des paresseux, les estaminets des pisse-lyres, pour l'enfer des bêtes, pour le commerce des rusés et le bonjour des simples» («Tu as bien fait de partir, Arthur Rimbaud!»). As always, Char's poetry is a reflection of his life. It is from the solitude of his home in Provence that he bids farewell to the *compagnons de Paris* and to the partisans of Céreste. Solitude is the price man must pay for his freedom. If he is to be completely free, he alone must choose to doubt or to believe («A une ferveur belliqueuse»), to love or to hate («Fastes»), to create or to destroy («Le Martinet,» «Madeleine à la veilleuse»), to live or to die («Assez creusé»). The man that would be truly free must break his human bondage. Like the hunter of the earth that finally takes his place in the sky, the poet must find his way out of the *selva oscura* of the earth into the white forests of air.

Fureur et Mystère ends with one of the most unusual love-poems I know, a poem written from the heights «où ne se montre guère l'amertume» and, like the *Paradiso,* a poem of pure light:

Allégeance

> Dans les rues de la ville il y a mon amour. Peu importe où il va dans le temps divisé. Il n'est plus

mon amour, chacun peut lui parler. Il ne se souvient plus; qui au juste l'aima?

Il cherche son pareil dans le vœu des regards. L'espace qu'il parcourt est ma fidélité. Il dessine l'espoir et léger l'éconduit. Il est prépondérant sans qu'il y prenne part.

Je vis au fond de lui comme une épave heureuse. A son insu, ma solitude est son trésor. Dans le grand méridien où s'inscrit son essor, ma liberté le creuse.

Dans les rues de la ville il y a mon amour. Peu importe où il va dans le temps divisé. Il n'est plus mon amour, chacun peut lui parler. Il ne se souvient plus; qui au juste l'aima et l'éclaire de loin pour qu'il ne tombe pas?

Love and poetry (which, for Char, are synonymous) must be as free as the sun that defines for all men the hour and the season, but remains itself without time and space: «Peu importe où il va dans le temps divisé.» Like the sun, love and poetry must circulate freely «sur les saisons de l'écorce,» always serving, yet everywhere above the needs of the day.

The sun is not bound by the laws of man, yet everyone partakes of its light: «Il n'est plus mon amour, chacun peut lui parler.» The sun does not function according to man-made principles of ethics or aesthetics, yet everyone delights in its radiance: «Il ne se souvient plus; qui au juste l'aima et l'éclaire de loin pour qu'il ne tombe pas?» The poet, likewise, cannot be made prisoner of any literary or political engagement, of surrealism or the *maquis*.

In an essay called «La Responsabilité des poètes modernes,» dedicated to Albert Camus, Char's friend René Ménard writes:

> Beaucoup de jeunes poètes s'interrogent sur leur droit de consacrer le meilleur d'eux-mêmes à la poésie, tandis que tant d'autres hommes souffrent dans

la misère et le délaissement. Certains croient conci-
lier leur vocation avec les exigences de leur conscience, en dévouant leurs poèmes à quelque idéal politique ou social. Ceux qui ne trouvent pas dans leurs
convictions assez d'élan pour ainsi «s'engager,»
comme l'on dit, ou bien surmontent leurs scrupules,
ou bien se taisent. Ces troubles sont fréquemment
exploités avec des intentions étrangères à la Poésie.
Aussi, convient-il d'écarter ce faux problème.

La poésie moderne, dans ses expressions que l'on
peut dire meilleures parce qu'elles emportent l'as-
sentiment d'hommes qui témoignent sur bien d'autres sujets de leur vigueur et de leur sensibilité
d'esprit, n'a pas pour fin première une recherche
esthétique...

Une telle poésie est nécessairement «engagée,» non
envers une idéologie quelconque, mais dans la vie,
au sens le plus strict. Conscience elle-même, elle
n'a nul besoin de se réclamer d'autres vérités que
de la sienne...

... La vocation de la Poésie est de sensibiliser les
rapports de l'esprit avec le monde et avec lui-même,
lorsque la raison est impuissante à en rendre compte.
Là est la responsabilité du poète, là est son engagement... (35).

Claude Vigée has commented, in a similar vein, on the «instrument suspect par excellence, qui fausse la condition véritable
de l'homme et exprime le contraire de sa situation,» the language of the «engagement» (36).

Fureur et Mystère should not be read as a documentary on

(35) René Ménard, «La Responsabilité des poètes modernes,»
(Rome, *Botteghe Oscure*, no. 14, 1954). In the same issue, Jackson
Matthews published his translations of *Feuillets d'Hypnos* and
Lettera amorosa.
(36) Claude Vigée, *Révolte et Louanges, essais sur la poésie
moderne* (Paris: José Corti, 1962), p. 104.

the Underground, for the songs of Hypnos—dedicated to cloud and bird, river and sun—are engaged in the totality of life, in the «prodige qu'est la vie humaine dans sa relativité» (37).

---

(37) A first version of this chapter appeared in *The Modern Language Review,* July 1976, as «René Char's *Fureur et Mystère: Poésie engagée?*»

Les Busclats

II

INTIMATE SPACE: IMAGINATION'S WAY

1

THE DREAM: «EAUX-MÈRES»

> Le présent-passé, le présent-futur. Rien qui précède
> et rien qui succède, seulement les offrandes de
> l'imagination.
> («Aromates chasseurs,» *Aromates chasseurs*, 1975).

In *Le Surréalisme au Service de la Révolution* (no. 6), Char
published a prose text called «A quoi je me destine,» dated
11 February, 1932 and dedicated to Paul Eluard. Of this piece
which, as «Eaux-mères,» becomes part of *Abondance viendra*
in 1934, the poet says:

> This text, taken as a whole, is the account of a
> dream. Only the parts in italics are waking im-
> pressions which came to me in the process of tran-
> scribing the dream. I thought I should not discard
> them, since they insisted so strongly on being
> recorded. They will be found precisely in the order
> in which they occurred (1).

In the 1945 publication of *Abondance viendra*, Char—having moved away from surrealism and more interested now in
literary form than in automatic writing or dream transcrip-
tions—does make minor changes in both the account of the

---

(1) I am translating from Char's footnote, given in *SSR* and
Abondance viendra.

dream and in the waking impressions, interspersed in italics. These changes consist, in the main, of deletions and clarifications. We must, nevertheless, believe the poet when he says that the text is, in fact, the faithful recounting of an actual dream. As such, «A quoi je me destine» is a piece unique in Char's repertory and one which must be consulted in an exploration of the poet's «intimate space,» to which I should like to turn here. It is difficult to make cuts in a dream narration, which I therefore quote, in the original 1932 version, without deletions, despite the extraordinary length:

La propriété de ma famille à l'Isle-sur-Sorgue. A l'ouest, une vaste étendue de prairies. Le foin a été enlevé. Pour bien marquer les divisions, outre les rideaux d'arbres dépouillés de leurs feuilles, quelques sombres carrés de betteraves d'une espèce bâtarde, très basse. Tout cela rapidement aperçu. Je constate avec satisfaction que la vue est libre. A l'horizon et comme point final du panorama, une chaîne de montagnes me fait facilement songer à un renard bleu. Mon attention est attirée par un large fleuve, sans sinuosité, qui s'avance vers moi, creusant son lit sur son passage. Son allure très lente est celle d'un promeneur un peu las. Je n'éprouve pas d'inquiétude. Quelques centaines de mètres me séparent de lui. En son milieu, marchant dans le sens du courant, de l'eau à la ceinture, je distingue, côte-à-côte, ma mère et mon neveu âgé de sept ans. Je remarque que le niveau de l'eau est le même pour tous les deux, bien qu'ils soient l'un et l'autre de taille visiblement différente. Ils me racontent la promenade agréable qu'ils viennent de faire; promenade complètement dénuée d'intérêt à mon avis. J'écoute très distraitement un récit où il est question d'un enfant que je ne connais pas, du nom de Louis Paul, disparu depuis peu de jours et dont on n'a pu réussir, malgré les efforts répétés et l'assurance qu'il s'est noyé dans le fleuve, à retrouver le corps. Ma mère se montre réservée dans le choix de ses termes. Systématiquement le mot «mort» n'est pas prononcé. Elle dit: «La perte du fil.» Ce qui me laisse rêveur.

Dans les sous-sols de la maison d'habitation. Je suis dans une pièce infiniment peu attirante, probablement une ancienne cuisine désaffectée. Un alambic est accroché à un clou de la plinthe. Une corde à linge fortement nouée à ses deux extrémités traverse la pièce dans le sens de la largeur. Un placard dont on a ôté les battants qui est aussi une forge et une mare laisse voir à peu de distance un foyer de coke de gaz allumé et une pancarte, de la destination de celles des hommes-sandwich sur laquelle est écrit en caractères Braille «Electricien de Vénus.» *J'ai l'impression que, mettant à profit la confusion qui règne, les vers de farine ont dévoré le sel à l'Equateur.* Entre ma mère. Elle porte sans effort un cercueil de taille ordinaire qu'elle dépose, sans un mot, à mes pieds. Sa force seule m'est un profond sujet d'étonnement. En vain je m'essaie à soulever le cercueil. Cet objet *creux destiné à être longuement fécondé* me surprend d'ailleurs par sa forme invariable et son aspect extérieur d'une grande propreté. On l'a passé à l'encaustique. Je suis flatté. Je questionne ma mère. Sur le ton de la conversation elle m'apprend la présence du cadavre de Louis Paul, à l'intérieur. Mais aussitôt elle détourne les yeux, très gênée et murmure à court de souffle: «C'est la logique,» phrase que j'interprète par «C'est la guerre,» et qui provoque ma colère. *Nous ne sommes donc pas sortis des frontières du Premier Empire.* Je désire m'assurer du contenu exact du cercueil. Je dévisse les écrous. Le cercueil est rempli d'eau. L'eau est extrêmement claire et transparente. Contrairement à celle du fleuve c'est une eau potable, probablement filtrée. Je me penche assez intrigué: sous l'eau, à quelques centimètres, dans une attitude de souffrance indescriptible j'aperçois le corps d'un enfant d'une huitaine d'années. La position des membres, par ce qu'elle représente de désarticulation horrible, m'émeut vivement. Les chairs sont bleues et noires, déchirées, *parce qu'il y a eu lutte*, mais curieusement disposées en particulier sur le front où elles empruntent le dessin d'une dentelle vénitienne. L'un des bras passe derrière la tête. La main appliquée sur la bouche est retournée. La paume est un cul de singe. C'est le premier noyé qu'il m'est donné de voir. Un monstre. Un chapeau de paille du genre canotier de première communion me surprend par son parfait état de conservation. Sur le ruban de couleur blanche, un mince filet de sang flotte sans parvenir à se détacher ni à troubler l'eau. C'est la sangsue *métisse*. Ma mère me prie de sortir. Je refuse. Elle attire mon attention sur ce qu'elle appelle tristement «Le retour des Boers fratricides.» A l'aide d'un gant de boxe elle tranche la corde *qui s'effondre avec un grand cri*. C'est un attentat. Quel poids. J'ai très peur. Je tire hâtivement le corps hors du cercueil. Durant cette opération je pense, non sans mélancolie, à certaine mort vraiment trop inhumaine. L'essentiel est de ne pas échouer. Je comprends mal. Maintenant je frictionne rudement le corps de l'enfant. J'exécute à plusieurs reprises les tractions de langue prévues. Mais je suis manifestement gêné, dominé par un sentiment de pudeur indicible. Ma mère se plaint de coliques. La raideur du corps de l'enfant s'est accrue. J'ai brusquement la conviction que cet enfant vit. *C'est l'évidence.* Tout à l'heure au fond de l'eau il louchait. *C'était l'octroi.* Je multiplie de plus en plus énergiquement mes frictions. Mais il faudrait qu'il rendît au moins une partie de l'eau absorbée. Sans cela il va couler de nouveau à pic. Sa bouche m'apparaît légèrement entr'ouverte. Où ai-je déjà vu ces lèvres? Au parc des Buttes-Chaumont: c'était l'arc du tunnel. Je guettais à l'entrée, la sourde et la muette. Je me rappelle avoir rêvé d'une exquise petite fille, *grande comme une bille* se baignant dans la conque d'une source, toute nue. Malgré des séjours prolongés dans l'eau, coupés de fréquents plongeons, elle n'était jamais parvenue qu'à mouiller les lèvres extérieures de son sexe et cela à son grand désespoir. C'était

Sangüe. Quelle aventure. *Autour de moi il pleut de la suie et du talc. Signes d'une conjonction d'astres dans le ciel favorable et défavorable à moins que le jour et la nuit écœurés du conformisme de l'actuelle création n'aient enfin conclu le grand pacte d'abondance.* Il n'y a rien de miraculeux dans le retour à la vie de cet enfant. Je méprise les esprits religieux et leurs interprétations mystiques. Je prends l'enfant entre mes bras et un immense amour m'envahit. J'aime cet enfant d'un amour maternel, d'une grandeur impossible à concevoir. Il va falloir changer ma règle d'existence. Ma tâche est désormais de le protéger. Il est menacé. On verra. Il est petit et je suis grand. Assis sur une chaise et le serrant contre moi, je le berce doucement, tendrement. Ma sœur, mère de mon neveu, se trouve là. Je la prie de m'apporter des vêtements secs. Il me tarde qu'elle me donne satisfaction pour la mettre dehors ensuite. Elle ne se montre pas très empressée. A cette minute je mesure toute l'étendue de son avarice. Je la menace de la tuer. Elle s'en va et revient bientôt avec un gracieux vêtement taillé dans un fibrôme *d'été.* Elle fait preuve dans ses explications d'une platitude et d'une bassesse dégoûtantes. Il semble que l'enfant sur mes genoux s'est transformé. Son visage vivant, expressif, ses cheveux châtains, en particulier, m'enchantent. Ils sont partagés par une raie impeccable. L'enfant m'aime profondément. Il me dit sa confiance et se blottit contre moi. Je suis ému aux larmes. Nous ne nous embrassons pas. Ma mère et ma sœur ont disparu. A la place qu'elles occupaient il y a une loupe noire *oubliée par le libérateur repoussant.*

«He is an abundant man,» Jackson Matthews said of Char, «in size, in vitality, in speech, in silences, in ideas and affections, in seriousness, gaiety, gentleness, violence» (2). But if

_____

(2) *René Char: Hypnos Waking. Poems and Prose selected and*

we listen closely, Char—in the very abundance of his work—
really always sings, like every authentic poet, one and the
same song (3). For him, that song is about love and death,
about love conveived as a deathbound struggle, and reborn.
This theme, for Char, is an intimate reality, a living reality
leading back to childhood memories translated in many of his
finest works. For the purposes of this essay, I have chosen
to examine from among these—as the poetic translation of the
dream—the second poem in the series called «Quatre âges,»
published in the *Placard pour un chemin des écoliers,* 1937,
and dedicated to the children of Spain, caught up in the Spanish
Civil War:

> J'ai étranglé
> Mon frère
> Parce qu'il n'aimait pas dormir
> La fenêtre ouverte.

> Ma sœur
> A-t-il dit avant de mourir
> J'ai passé des nuits pleines
> A te regarder dormir
> Penché sur ton éclat dans la vitre.

---

translated by Jackson Matthews (New York: Random House, 1956),
p. 280.

(3) «Chaque poète passe sa vie sur un seul poème dont les
quinze ou vingt versions les plus proches lui seront seules comptées,»
writes René Ménard in *La Condition poétique* (Paris: Gallimard,
1959), p. 16. In a similar vein, Heidegger wrote, the same year:
«Jeder grosse Dichter dichtet nur aus einem einzigen Gedicht. Die
Grösse bemisst sich daraus, inwieweit er diesem Einzigen so anver-
traut wird, dass er es vermag, sein dichtendes Sagen rein darin zu
halten» (*Unterwegs zur Sprache,* Pfullingen: Verlag Günther Neske),
p. 37. These are answers Georges Mounin («Situation présente de
René Char,» *op. cit.*) could have made to Alain Bosquet who accused
Char, in the 1950's, of «une certaine stagnation, ... une éthique
qui n'évolue guère, ... une esthétique où la virtuosité et même
l'inertie ont pris la place de l'invention.» By this time, Mounin
himself had voiced some doubts about «la grandeur de Char.»
Trapped in his politically predicated ethics and aesthetics, Mounin
parted ways with the poet around 1947, after the publication of
Le Poème pulvérisé. On poetry as invention, see *La Bibliothèque*

The poem that shows the children on the point of death is in the form of a dialogue, of which Char said: «La beauté naît du dialogue, de la rupture du silence et du regain de ce silence» (*Le Bulletin des Baux*). It was the dialogue which, quite naturally, led the poet to the writing of plays (*Le Soleil des eaux*, 1946, *Sur les hauteurs*, 1947, *Claire*, 1948, *L'Homme qui marchait dans un rayon de soleil*, 1949), and to the ballet, the dialogue of movement (*La Conjuration*, 1946, *L'Abominable homme des neiges*, 1952) (4). In these dialogues, all of which end in silence and death, some critics would hear only the voice of the poet's social conscience. Pierre Berger, for example, writes of the *Placard pour un chemin des écoliers*:

> Ce placard, nous avons été quelques-uns, en 1937, à nous l'accrocher au cœur. Nous n'avons jamais pu l'en arracher, tant il est vrai qu'on n'arrache pas les proclamations écrites avec le sang... Une fois de plus, il se confirme que l'homme ne peut rien bâtir sans la présence des démons. C'est ainsi qu'ils ne cessent de s'intégrer à l'inspiration de Char. La chaleur apporte ensuite son offrande. Déjà, en 1936, quand il commença d'écrire *Placard pour un chemin des écoliers*, l'incendie léchait sa porte. Le sourire des enfants au seuil du martyre ne se devinait qu'à travers les flammes (5).

But the birth of a poem is of a more intimate and less circumstancial nature than that outlined above.

Nor do I believe, as discussed at some length in the next chapter, that the dialogue engaged in by Char is one of poetry vs. reason. Poetic dialogue is related to, but not dependent on, the philosopher's dialectics. The deadly confrontation of

---

est en feu: «Celui qui invente, au contraire de celui qui découvre, n'ajoute aux choses, n'apporte aux êtres que des masques, des entre-deux, une bouillie de fer.»

(4) Char's collected theater was published under the title *Trois coups sous les arbres* (Paris: Gallimard, 1967).

(5) Pierre Berger, *René Char* (Paris: Seghers, 1951), p. 12.

two children recorded in «Quatre âges» predates any social upheaval such as the Spanish Civil War. This confrontation already came in the dream narrative of 1932. It recurs in «Eléments» (*Fureur et Mystère*), the story of a mother and her child, stillborn or about do die; it was announced by «Artine,» Char's first long prose poem of love which ended with the proclamation: «Le poète a tué son modèle.»

The text of the «Quatre âges» series is among those seemingly simple but deeply moving and haunting poems which, like the «Berceuse pour chaque jour,» 1956, have about them something of the archetypal mystery of the folksong. The death and sadness of which they sing (to such a deceptively simple tune) come to us like echoes from a far distant land. The love of which they speak is the *amor de lonh* of the troubadour tradition. The fear of dawn and discovery are heard in the Provençal *albas* as in the Breton *lais*.

In *Fête des arbres et du chasseur,* 1948, his longest «dialogue,» Char wrote:

> Nous avons en nous une suite de chansons qui nous flanquent, ailes de communication entre notre souffle reposé et nos fièvres les plus fortes. Pièces presque banales, d'un coloris clément, d'un contour arriéré, dont le tissu cependant porte une minuscule plaie. Il est loisible à chacun de fixer une origine et un terme à cette rougeur contestable. («Prologue.»)

The red wound, the fever of night and the light of dawn are caught in the reflections of the window closed upon the sleepers of «Quatre âges.»

The impressions, however fluid, recorded in the text ultimately called «Eaux-mères,» are anchored in several word clusters and complexes which could be divided as follows: 1.) The Family (*bâtard, ma mère, mon neveu, un enfant*); 2.) Water (*un large fleuve vs. les vêtements secs, l'eau claire et transparente, potable, filtrée, vs. celle du fleuve*); 3.) The Cord, with its connotations of the labyrinth (*creuser, les soussols, une corde à linge fortement nouée vs. un fleuve sans sinuosité, la confusion, les vers de farine, gêné, une dentelle vénitienne, un ruban, un mince filet de sang*); 4.) *L'attentat,* a word which really lacks a precise English translation in its complex meaning of outrage and crime (*disparu, noyer, la mort, la perte, une forge vs. une mare, un cercueil, le cadavre, la guerre, la colère, la lutte, déchiré, le noyé, un monstre, troubler, fratricide, un gant de boxe, un grand cri, inhumain, échouer, évidence, octroi, désespoir, menacer, tuer, platitude...bassesse... dégoûtantes, vs. vivre, création, abondance, grandeur*; 5.) Physical dexterity and strength (*la force, les efforts vs. sans efforts; soulever, poids, vs. las, lent, peur, mélancolie, rêveur*).

The negative side of the fourth list seems to be, at first glance, the most important, judged by the number of entries. And so it does not surprise us that the critics and the general reader have, by and large, approached Char as the poet of violence and revolt (6). Those who have known him personally have helped to propagate the poet's image as the *Übermensch,* «un géant, aux épaules larges, aux gestes lents,» naturally upright, «haut, grand, immense,» (8) fearless in the face of adversity and death: «Et de mettre aussitôt en parallèle cette attitude naturelle avec l'apparence extérieure d'un homme que sa haute stature et sa large carrure installent confortablement à la surface de la terre, où ses membres jouent avec aisance dans l'air» (9). André Gascht categorizes Char as one of those «robustes gars du Midi parmi lesquels il vécut les années du maquis» (10). And Gabriel Bounoure adds: «De la mansuétude des enfances rêveuses—mais emplies de grandes attentes—sortent, d'aventure, par décrets assez diaboliques, les

---

(6) I shall discuss the theme of violence in Char's work in Chapter 3. A recent American dissertation, entitled: *Eclairs: A Study of Invisibility and Violence in the Poetry of René Char* (Nancy Kline Piore, Tufts Univ.) investigates the same subject.

(7) Georges Mounin, *Avez-vous lu Char?* (Paris: Corti, 1957), p. 23.

(8) Pierre Berger, *op. cit.,* p. 25.

(9) André Gascht, *Charme de René Char* (Bruxelles: Le Thyrse, 1957), p. 12.

(10) *Ibid.,* p. 15.

hommes d'audace, dont le poignet est fort, les réfractaires, les partisans, ceux qu'offensera toujours la seule idée du profit... Sortent aussi les poètes, qui appartiennent, en droit ou en fait, à la même équipe» (11).

In an earlier chapter, I tried to portray a different Char, the poet as I have known him, and as he describes himself in «Biens égaux»: «De si loin que je me souvienne, je me distingue penché sur les végétaux du jardin désordonné de mon père, attentif aux sèves, baisant des yeux formes et couleurs que le vent semi-nocturne irriguait mieux que la main infirme des hommes.» I wonder whether the painters of the fearless warrior-hero ever listened to *Les Cloches sur le cœur,* and whether anyone ever took seriously the cry ending the second stanza of «Tenailles,» a poem of that collection:

> Joie ingénue plaisir morbide
> Effluve diaphane et fétide
> Qui se concrétise puis se meurt
> Amour jouir peur peur peur peur

If we are to define the object of the poet's fear, we must return to the dream narration of the young man. «Eaux-mères» is the account of a child mysteriously drowned and ressuscitated. It is the story of birth and death by water. Curiously —and conveniently—those critics who have spoken of Char as the poet of violence and war have also insisted on the element of fire in his poetry. They have overlooked all references to water, so prevalent in Char's work (11a). The poet of the Isle-sur-Sorgue naturally speaks of the river, of the old village fountains of Provence, and of the Fontaine de Vaucluse which, in the summer, lies peacefully and mysteriously still at the foot of the rocks, an almost motionless lake. «Un lac!» cries the poet of «La Frontière en pointillé.» «Qu'on nous l'accorde!

---

(11) «Céreste et la Sorgue,» *L'Arc,* no. 22, été 1963, p. 25.
(11a) For a good discussion of the elements in Char's poetry, see Mary Ann Caws, *René Char* (Boston: Twayne, 1977), chapter 4: «The Elements of the Poem.»

Un lac, non une source au milieu de ses ajoncs, mais un pur lac, non pour y boire, un lac pour s'offrir au juron glacé de ses eaux estivales. Qui sollicites-tu? Nul n'est prêteur, nul n'est donnant» (*Aromates chasseurs*).

It is here that we must look for a fuller understanding of the dream. «L'être voué à l'eau,» said Bachelard, «est un être en vertige. Il meurt à chaque minute, sans cesse quelque chose de sa substance s'écroule. La mort quotidienne n'est pas la mort exubérante du feu qui perce le ciel de ses flèches; la mort quotidienne est la mort de l'eau. L'eau coule toujours, l'eau tombe toujours, elle finit toujours en sa mort horizontale... La mort de l'eau est plus songeuse que la mort de la terre: la peine de l'eau est infinie» (*L'Eau et les rêves,* p. 9). And Heraclitus, whom the young poet knew so well, wrote: «C'est la mort pour les âmes de devenir eau, c'est la mort pour l'eau de devenir terre. De la terre vient l'eau, et de l'eau provient l'âme» (*Fragments,* no. 42). Those who see in Char only the giant pitched against thunder and lightning cannot know the object of his fear. He who confronted destiny on the mountaintops of Céreste is without arms against the *mare tenebrarum* of night and dream.

Is it accurate to say that the poet *confronts* his destiny? Like Utrillo, Char has a predilection for people and objects seen from behind. Is it a predilection, or the fear of meeting them face to face? In the *pointe-sèche* of Valentine Hugo accompanying the first edition of *Placard pour un chemin des écoliers,* the sister of the «Quatre âges» dialogue is shown with her back turned to her brother. Her face is seen only as a reflection in the window, as the text dictates. Both children are lying down, and again this is an attitude overlooked by the critics. (It may be interesting to remember that the *Placard* poems were conceived during Char's convalescence, following the blood poisoning that brought him so near to death and kept him confined to his bed for many months.)

For René Char, the upright position is not, as the critics would have it, «l'attitude naturelle avec l'apparence extérieure d'un homme que sa haute stature et sa large carrure installent confortablement à la surface de la terre.» The word *debout* is, in Char's poetics, a superlative, attained only by means of struggle and pain: «Comment agressé de toutes parts, croqué, haï, roué, arrivons-nous cependant à jouir, debout, debout, debout, avec notre exécration, avec nos reins?» (*A une sérénité crispée*). The man who, in 1944, while fighting in the Resistance, broke an arm and injured his spinal column, rejoices in the victory over the fall.

«L'essentiel est de ne pas échouer,» said the dreamer of «Eaux-mères.» And the verb (*échouer*) has all the impact of its etymological derivation. In 1936, in *Moulin premier,* the poet noted: «Il advient au poète d'échouer au cours de ses recherches sur un rivage où il n'était attendu que beaucoup plus tard, après son anéantissement.» Again, *échouer* is used with the meaning of *to fall*. To fall is to die, to assume the horizontal position of the enemy (water, *un rivage*). «Je n'ai pas peur,» said Hypnos. «J'ai seulement le vertige. Il me faut réduire la distance entre l'ennemi et moi. L'affronter *horizontalement*.» Bachelard, an early friend of the poet, defined the horizontal enemy: «L'être voué à l'eau,» he wrote, «est un être en vertige... L'eau coule toujours, elle tombe toujours, elle finit toujours en sa mort horizontale. ...»

The brother strangled in the «Quatre âges» poem will die by the death of water. The passage through the glass (window or mirror) is for Char's figures the passage to death. «Je glisse en liberté au travers des blés murs / Nulle haleine ne teint le miroir de mon vol,» he wrote of «L'Oiseau spirituel» (*La Parole en archipel*). Even his flight is, from the start, pure horizontal movement. It is a gliding across the mirror into freedom, and death.

This horizontal death was already confronted by the shifting faces of «Eaux-mères»: by the mother-sister and the child-nephew pairs. Note that the female figures have rather uncomplimentary roles in the dream. The narrator fears his mother and detests his sister. The mother is strong, but distant. Her very strength is an outrage, and a menace to the dreamer. She cuts the cord which strangled—and returned to life—the child drowned in the «objet *creux destiné à être longuement fécondé*.» The waking impression underlines the symbolism of birth sketched by the dream. It is the mother, the *magna mater* of the «Eaux-mères» that detains the power of life and death. The act of birth is a traumatic experience. The dreamer is afraid of the «sous-sols de la maison» and of the «corde... fortement nouée» that symbolize prenatal life.

Mixed with the fear of his mother is the narrator's jealousy. He would like to claim for himself—against all natural and legal evidence and logic—the natural resurrection («il n'y a rien de miraculeux») of the child. He would like to substitute himself for both mother and sister and reserve to himself the unspoken love of the reborn child. It is, in fact, the narrator (not the dream-sister) who shows himself to be avaricious and hostile, hostile not only to the figures of the dream, but also to the waking world symbolized by «le libérateur repoussant» that destroys the illusions of sleep.

While it is rightly thought, by most critics, that biography has no place in literary interpretations, we must nevertheless call on one of Char's rare autobiographical notes to explain the confused images of «Eaux-mères.» Three children, all about the same age, are variously represented in the dream as the unknown child, the narrator's nephew, and the narrator himself, seen as a small boy at the family estate. Obviously, all three children evoked here are but different dream configurations of the poet himself who expresses in «Eaux-mères» a sense of non-belonging and non-identity, calling himself, in the later version of the text, *le bâtard de l'eau*. The female characters, his mother and his sister, mother of the drowned child, likewise fuse into the single figure of a mother who is strong, logical, efficient, but lacking in warmth, affection and understanding for the child. A waking impression situates the events of the dream at the «*frontières du Premier Empire*,» an interesting detail, because the poet's maternal great-grand-father, Auguste Chevalier, was imprisoned by Napoleon III for his Republican leanings!

The note supplied by the *Arrière-Histoire* to the prose

poem «Jacquemard et Julia» of *Le Poème pulvérisé* gives us several insights into Char's family situation. The poem, we remember, speaks of the great «Jadis» of primordial harmony, beauty and love, of a world at peace with itself where «les sources ne compliquent pas à plaisir leurs parcours» (recalling the «fleuve sans sinuosité» of the dream). Reminiscent of a Provençal *canso,* this lyrical evocation depicts «les cavaliers du jour» patiently waiting, in quest of their love, beneath the closed castle windows. This is how the story ends:

> L'inextinguible sécheresse s'écoule. L'homme est un étranger pour l'aurore. Cependant à la poursuite de la vie qui ne peut être encore imaginée, il y a des volontés qui frémissent, des murmures qui vont s'affronter et des enfants sains et saufs qui *découvrent.*

The poet gives the following explanation of this text:

> Jacquemard, c'est mon père, qui mourut quand j'avais onze ans. Julia, c'est la sœur de ma mère qu'il avait épousée en premières noces, à vingt ans, si ce que me contait ma grand-mère est exact. (Il n'y a pas lieu d'en douter.) Julia décéda après une année de mariage. Mon père qui l'aimait d'un amour d'amant adolescent eut un très grand chagrin. A la gloire de leur flamme éphémère ce poème est dédié. Il n'entre, ce faisant, dans mon esprit aucune intention désobligeante envers ma mère qui se montra toujours bonne pour moi, bien que maladroite parfois.

I have already discussed René-Emile's particular situation within the Char household, on which the text above, not published until after Mme Char's death in 1953, sheds some new light. The story of Emile Char's first marriage, told to the young boy by his maternal grandmother, must have left a deep impression on the sensitive child, in whom it seems to have inspired a sense of guilt. For, if his mother's sister had lived, he, René-Emile, would never have been born. Julia, to whom—although he did not know her—the poet lovingly dedicates the poem of primordial beauty and harmony, Julia had to die so that he might live. When his father joins her, the young boy is left alone, an orphan:

> Nous avons répété tout seuls la leçon de vol de nos parents. Leur hâte à se détacher de nous n'avait d'égal que leur fièvre à se retrouver deux, à redevenir le couple impérieux qu'ils semblaient former à l'écart; et rien que lui. Abandon à nos chances, à leur contraire? Eux partis, nous nous rendîmes compte qu'au lieu de nous lancer vers l'avant, leur leçon enflammait nos faiblesses, portait sur des points dont la teneur, d'un temps à un autre, avait changé. L'art qui naît du besoin, à la seconde où le besoin en est distrait, est un vivre concordant entre la montagne et l'oiseau.
>
> («Bons voisins,» *L'Effroi la joie,* 1969).

Has anyone pointed out the apparent need for justification that permeates so much of Char's poetry? «Eaux-mères» speaks of *logique, évidence,* and *octroi.* The dreamer interprets the phrase «C'est la logique» as «C'est la guerre.» The waking hand rejects the logic and the changing evidence of day:

> Contradictions persuasives
> Qui dévitalisent l'éveil
> Courte vie au salaire enchevêtré de la cascade
> Evidence mutable

There is a struggle in Char's poetry between apparent evidence and hidden truth. And whatever the later philosophical ramifications of the question, this struggle must have its origin in the poet's private and secret «plaie chimérique.» In *Rougeur des Matinaux* he writes: «L'évidence et ses à-peu-près sont collectifs. La vérité est personnelle.» It is to this personal truth that Char would dedicate his poetry and his life. The truth that would keep alive—as does the dream—the

multiple faces of the dead; a truth that would kill the living
child, pierce the poet with the arrow of Orion, which will,
however, flower and bear fruit in the green wound, the fertile
field of the sky:

> Le dard d'Orion. Le trèfle étoilé. Dans la garri-
> gue, miroir du ciel diurne.
> Le trèfle obscurci... La cicatrice verte.
> La trombe de la souffrance, le balluchon de l'es-
> poir.
> («La Frontière en pointillé,» *Aromates chasseurs*).

The hammer, the scythe, the knife and the arrow nurture the
truth, the life-bearing wound of the poem, «le champ de la
blessure... de tous le plus prospère» (*Fureur et Mystère*).

«Tu es dans ton essence constamment poète,... constamment avide de vérité et de justice,» wrote Char. «C'est sans
doute un mal nécessaire que tu ne puisses l'être assidûment dans
ta conscience» (*A la Santé du serpent*). The logic, evidence
and justice of day do not coincide with the truth sought by
Char in poetry and dream. For that truth lies in the substitutions of the nephew—drowned or stillborn—for the young
narrator, in the confusion of mother and sister, in the peaceful
coexistence of Julia, René-Emile's sister, and his father's first
wife (and sister of his mother), after whom Julia Char was
named.

Against these assertions of the subconscious are pitted the
fears of the waking man, who, aware of the legitimacy
supported by legal evidence, yet feels as uncertain of his place
as his foundling grandfather (who received the proud name of
Charlemagne!) must have felt. Embarrassment and torment
result from the confrontation of external evidence and personal
truth, a truth expressed in the dream and having its origin,
at least in part, in the stories told to the young boy by his
maternal grandmother.

> Nous nous sommes soudain trop approchés de
> quelque chose dont on nous tenait à une distance

mystérieusement favorable et mesurée. Depuis lors
c'est le rongement. Notre appuie-tête a disparu.
                              («Pour renouer,» 1954).

The brother and sister of «Quatre âges,» in the waking night,
will try to bridge the mysterious distance from evidence to
truth.

                         *   *   *

«J'ai étranglé mon frère...» Who is this sister of the
dream? Is it Char's mother, or her sister, or the sister of the
poet? Whose face is reflected in the window, and who turns
her back to the poet? Char's poetry goes in quest of the
mysterious being, only half perceived, elusive and unknown,
discussed by Maurice Blanchot in an article called «René Char
et la Pensée du Neutre» (12). «L'Inconnu,» writes Blanchot,
«est un neutre; l'inconnu n'est ni objet ni sujet; cela veut dire
que penser l'inconnu, ce n'est nullement se proposer le 'pas
encore connu', objet de tout savoir encore à venir, mais ce n'est
pas davantage le dépasser en l'absolument inconnaissable, sujet
de pure transcendance, se refusant à toute manière de connaître
et de s'exprimer.» According to the philosopher, this «neuter»
object or subject does not belong to the realm of light, but to
a region «étrangère à celle découverte dans et par la lumière.»
In Blanchot's (and Heidegger's) terms, the unknown is that
which does not fall immediately within our vision, without,
however, being hidden from sight, «ni visible ni invisible, ou
plus justement se détournant de tout visible et de tout invisible» (13). It is in the chiaroscuro half-light of early dawn
that we must try to read the dialogue of the «Quatre âges.»
    Despite its abrupt opening, this dialogue is a lyrical song
of love, softly whispered into the night. «J'ai étranglé mon
frère...» What a curious opening for a love-song! Who is
the strange female figure that opens the dialogue? Is it Caesia,

———
(12) *Ibid.,* pp. 9 ss.
(13) *Ibid.*

the *virgo caesia* that appeared as the title heroine in a poem of *Les Cloches sur le cœur,* and again in «Profession de foi»? The sister watched over by the amorous brother always returns as the «Inconnue connue» of *Le Poème pulvérisé,* the woman caught in the mirror or window, admired—but not touched—by her lover. Neither visible nor invisible, she is the young woman that turns her back, like the mimosa-gathering girl of «Congé au vent.» She is the nameless unknown of *Partage formel,* she is Iris, «nom propre de femme, dont les poètes se servent pour désigner une femme aimée et même quelque dame dont on veut taire le nom» (*Lettera amorosa*). She is the *domna* of the troubadours: young, beautiful, mysterious, inaccessible, loved in secret, «la libre et rare fille» («Neuve,» from *Deux poèmes, 1937*).

Illusory and evasive, she is the «grande Passante sans gage» of *L'Homme qui marchait dans un rayon de soleil* and «L'Amie qui ne restait pas» of the *Poèmes des deux années, 1955.* She is the «Passante de Sceaux» and the woman waiting in the «Passe de Lyon» of *La Parole en archipel.* She is the creature who—in her very presence—eludes us. She is Claire, defining love as «une capacité d'absence» and the *destinataire* of *Lettera amorosa,* «cet être que l'absence s'efforce de placer à mi-longueur du factice et du surnaturel.»

This being, like Artémis-Aurélia, easily assumes different shapes and forms, even splits into separate entities, appearing and disappearing at will, like Char's early heroine, Artine, defined as «la transparence absolue»; like «Anoukis l'Etreigneuse» of *Les Matinaux* who is also Jeanne and «L'Etrangère»; like the «Minutieuse» of *La Paroi et la prairie, 1952,* and «L'Une et l'Autre» of *La Parole en archipel.*

Added to this «femme dédoublée» is the «Revenante,» the girl or woman believed to be dead and returning to life, like Lola Abba of *Le Marteau sans maître* and the mother of the «attaché d'ambassade» who, already in the coffin, miraculously comes to life again when a bone stuck in her throat is coughed up («Réserve romancée,» *Moulin premier*). Even if these creatures dead and ressuscitated seem to bear the unmistakable stamp of surrealism, the recurrent theme of the woman dying and reborn is accompanied in Char's poetry by too much personal concern and anguish to be the simple exercise of an apprentice in the school of Breton. «Le poème va vers l'absence, mais c'est pour récompenser avec elle la réalité totale; il est tension vers l'imaginaire, mais c'est qu'il vise à 'la connaissance productive du Réel',» writes Blanchot (14). By the death—or absence—of the girl or woman loved by the poet, comes his realization of the truth which surpasses the evidence and justice of day.

When she is allowed to die a natural death, the woman loved by Char perishes by the death of water, «la mort songeuse, la mort quotidienne de l'eau.» This is the fate of the mother and child about to be drowned («Eléments»), of the mother, sister and child of «Eaux-mères,» of «ces femmes, vagues de la mer, qui se brisent» (*Feuillets d'Hypnos*) and of the «vagues grandes femmes blanches qui fendent la mer» (*Abondance viendra*).

More frequently, however, the woman evoked by the poet dies a violent, unnatural death. She is strangled or slain by her lover. She dies at the most beautiful time of the year, and at the height of her love, in the very act of nuptial union, in the warm summer night closing in on the lovers. «Enfin, si tu détruis, que ce soit avec des outils nuptiaux,» dictated the poet of *Rougeur des matinaux*.

It does not seem to be the same women who, in Char's poetry, is drowned or slain. The latter, a creature of summer, perishes as if by fire when her image, held prisoner by the walls of a closed room, bursts upon the window. «L'été chantait sur son roc préféré quand tu m'es apparue,» «l'été et notre vie étions d'un seul tenant,» the poet wrote of her in *Fureur et Mystère*. The pleasures enjoyed by this woman and her lover are felt to be an outrage («Eaux-mères» spoke of an

---

(14) Maurice Blanchot, *La Part du feu* (Paris: Gallimard, 1949), p. 110.

attentat), for to the creature of fire, the other, unknown woman, drowned in the December waters, has been sacrificed. Psychologically speaking, this woman did not die a natural death. She was killed by the lovers of summer who drove her from the house and from the nuptial bed.

«Parallèle du cœur,» a poem of *Les Cloches sur le cœur,* made first mention of the crime:

> Pour que le même amour revienne
> Me labourer le cœur
> A cette cheminée qui fume
> A cette maison qui saigne
>
> Et que le vide soit meilleur
> Qu'ils soient heureux ceux qui tuèrent
> Par haine de ce qui dure

The text, retitled «Le Sol de la nuit,» appears in *Art bref suivi de Premières alluvions,* 1950, in the following revised version:

> Pour que le même amour revienne
> A cette cheminée qui fume
> A cette maison qui saigne
> Et le vide serait meilleur
> Qu'ils soient heureux ceux qui tuèrent
> Dans la mansarde du serpent.

The serpent, although here lodged in the attic, sends us back to the «sous-sols de la maison» mentioned in the dream. There the poet found himself, we remember, in a room described as «infiniment peu attirante,» traversed by a «corde à linge fortement nouée» and furnished with a cupboard that was at once a forge and a pond. Combining the properties of fire and water, earth and air, the serpent is the «marginal being» who, according to the poet, «unit la lumière à la peur» («Le Serpent,» *La Paroi et la prairie*). Emissary of the underworld, he glides through the open window of the nuptial chamber to draw from their self-appointed paradise the dreamer and his love.

«Ta nuit je l'ai voulue si courte que ta marâtre taciturne fut vieille avant d'en avoir conçu les pouvoirs,» says a mysterious voice in «L'Eclairage du pénitencier,» a text of *Seuls demeurent*. The prisoner who listens must be the narrator himself who accepted, on external evidence, the «marâtre taciturne» that usurped the place of the lawful wife and mother.

The drowned woman, breaking the ice of the wintry lake (and the glass of the window) returns at night to the room from which she was banished:

> Qu'elle vienne, maîtresse, à ta marche inclinée,
> Ou qu'elle appelle de la brume du bois;
> Qu'en sa chambre elle soit prévenue et suivie,
> Epouse à son carreau, fusée inaperçue.
> Sa main, fendant la mer et caressant tes doigts
> Déplace de l'été la borne invariable.
>
> («Vermillon,» *Poèmes des deux années*).

She beckons the dreamer to leave the room, to follow her, to look upon the shore where she awaits lover and child:

> «Scrute tes paupières,» me disait ma mère, penchée sur mon avant-sommeil d'écolier. J'apercevais flottant un petit caillou, tantôt paresseux, tantôt strident, un galet pour verdir dans l'herbe. Je pleurais. Je l'eusse voulu dans mon âme, et seulement là.
>
> («Dédicace,» *Lettera amorosa*).

A much later text («Lombes,» *Aromates chasseurs*) names the flower: «Quelle barbarie experte voudra bien de nous demain? Savoir que ce qui existait avant nous se trouve à présent devant, comme au jardin d'hiver une orchidée saignante, par césarienne.» The Song of *Lettera amorosa* linked orchid and iris in the

> Cadeau le plus ancien des prairies au plaisir
> Que la cascade instille, que la bouche délivre.

And a prose poem of *Retour amont,* «Tracé sur le gouffre,» associates the «plaie chimérique» and the flower:

Dans la plaie chimérique de Vaucluse je vous ai regardé souffrir. Là, bien qu'abaissé, vous étiez une eau verte, et encore une route. Vous traversiez la mort en son désordre. Fleur vallonnée d'un secret continu.

Though he knows that he must return to the shore from which he came, the schoolboy is, nevertheless, fascinated by the reflection of the sister's face and susceptible to the snares and false brilliance of night. It is then that the unknown, mysterious woman intervenes:

Ce qui m'a mis au monde et qui m'en chassera n'intervient qu'aux heures où je suis trop faible pour lui résister. Vieille personne quand je suis né. Jeune quand je mourrai. La seule et même passante.

(*Feuillets d'Hypnos*).

The passing female figure returns as the young and jealous mother (sister), trying to reclaim her child: «Iris. Nom spécifique d'un papillon, le nymphale iris, dit le grand mars changeant. Prévient du visiteur funèbre» (*Lettera amorosa*). Secretly, the dreamer knows that he must die to join the woman of water, to whom he rightfully belongs:

Du bleibst, du bleibst
einer Toten Kind,
geweiht dem Nein meiner Sehnsucht,
vermählt einer Schrunde der Zeit,
vor die mich das Mutterwort führte,
auf dass ein einziges Mal
erzittre die Hand,
die je und je mir ans Herz greift.
(«Vor einer Kerze,» *Von Schwelle zu Schwelle*, 1955).

Paul Celan, Char's friend and translator, knew the anguishing personal truth discovered by the dreamer of «Quatre âges.»

The woman of night is a figure of punishment and atonement, «Femme de punition / Femme de résurrection»:

> Femelle redoutable, elle porte la rage dans sa morsure et un froid mortel dans ses flancs, cette connaissance qui, partie d'une noble ambition, finit par trouver sa mesure dans nos larmes et dans notre jugulation. Ne vous méprenez pas, ô vous entre les meilleurs dont elle convoite le bras et guette la défaillance.
>
> («Rougeur des Matinaux»).

She is the avenging angel who rises in the night, slaughters the sacrificial animal and falls back into sleep, reconciled:

> O tué sans entrailles!
> Tué par celle qui fut tout et, réconciliée, se meurt;
> Lui, danseur d'abîme, esprit toujours à naître,
> Oiseau et fruit pervers des magies cruellement sauvé.
> («Homme-oiseau mort et bison mourant,»
> La Paroi et la prairie, 1952.)

By forcing the dreamer out into the open, she puts out the fire reflected in the window, delivering the poet, «homme-oiseau mort,» to the merciless hands of water and wind.

* * *

> J'ai étranglé
> Mon frère
> Parce qu'il n'aimait pas dormir
> La fenêtre ouverte...

Why was the brother punished? Because he turned his back on life. Because in the red window of night («vitre inextinguible») he held captive a sterile image and, bent over that image, killed his love by stifling it. The dreamer was strangled because he would not sleep by the window opened to light, and space, and air. René Char, child of the *mistral,* why should he fear the wind? Because it cools the fires of night, shattering the glass and the *amorosa visione.* «Et ai paor que'l gilos vos assatge / Et ades sera l'alba!» (Giraut de Bornelh).

But was the face reflected in the window not that of a false idol? «Comment, faible écolier, convertir l'avenir et détiser ce feu tant questionné, tant remué, tombé sur ton regard fautif?» («Mirage des aiguilles,» *Retour amont*). The 1963 text restates the question answered, in 1936, by the poem of «Quatre âges.» It was the sister's hand that corrected the faulty vision of the schoolboy. As he died, the brother passed through the opened window, and the «verre voué aux tourments» became «la vitre de l'heureux.»

Giacometti killed Caroline, the poet killed Artine, and the sister of the dream strangled her brother. The artist killed his model, repudiated «tout ce par quoi le rêve et l'inconscient et l'irréel pouvaient devenir un monde qui prétendît se suffire et dispenser du vrai» (15). The poet killed art, for the sake of life, from which art must spring.

«J'ai tué mon frère...» With this curious and moving love-song René Char leaves the *chemin des écoliers* of symbolism and surrealism. Henceforth, he will not remain fixed on his own image, he will not seek to drown himself «à la surface d'un étang» (*Le Marteau sans maître*). He will dream, instead, of houses without windows («J'habite une douleur,» *Le Poème pulvérisé*), or of windows neglected by man («Qu'il vive!» *Les Matinaux*). «'Supprimer la fenêtre ou non?' Ce n'est pas le mur qui questionne, ni le maçon, mais l'absurde habitant» (*A une sérénité crispée*).

* * *

Va mon baiser, quitte le frêle gîte,
Ton amour est trouvé, un bouleau te le tend.

---

(15) Georges Mounin, *op. cit.,* p. 7.

La résine d'été et la neige d'hiver
Ont pris garde.
> («Sur la paume de Dabo,» 1953).

Char has followed the call of the «Inconnue,» and has moved from the «chambre close» to «La Chambre dans l'espace» (*La Parole en archipel*).   He has sent his love out into the streets of the city («Allégeance,» *Fureur et Mystère*), has set his sister free to leave the house: «Je ne retiendrai pas votre bouche pour l'empêcher de s'entrouvrir sur le bleu de l'air et la soif de partir» («Marthe,» *Le Poème pulvérisé*).

Notre arrivée avant le givre
Et les feux chantants de l'hiver
A l'auberge où il fait bon vivre
Augure le départ amer

Il faut courir à la forêt
Se mesurer avec le vent
Dire aux pluies à leur volonté
Assez de ce jeu ruisselant

Etre épris du très seul adieu
Celui qui rompt la main brutale
Qui engrange sans fin les lieues
Celui qui luit sur les joues sales

Oiseau jamais intercepté
Ton étoile m'est douce au cœur
Ma route tire sur sa raie
L'air s'en détourne et l'homme y meurt
...
> («Sur le livre d'une auberge,» *Premières
> alluvions*).

Having passed the test of fire and water («feux chantants» and «jeu ruisselant»), the poet who has come to know the personal truth hidden behind the closed shutters of night, gives himself up to the wind, confident that through the sacrifice of his love he will come to know a pleasure far greater than that enjoyed by those who killed for love «dans la mansarde du serpent,» or in the «sous-sols de la maison.» For by death of the illusion comes the birth of the poem.

> Il faut que craque ce qui enserre cette ville où tu te trouves retenue. Vent, vent, vent autour des troncs et sur les chaumes.
> J'ai levé les yeux sur la fenêtre de ta chambre. As-tu tout emporté? Ce n'est qu'un flocon qui fond sur ma paupière.
>
> (*Lettera amorosa*).

The triple repetition of the word *vent* is the answer to the cry «Peur peur peur peur» heard many years earlier in *Les Cloches sur le cœur*. The mature poet celebrates his newly found freedom in «Devancier,» a poem of *Retour amont*:

> J'ai reconnu dans un rocher la mort fuguée et mensurable, le lit ouvert de ses petits comparses sous la retraite d'un figuier. Nul signe de tailleur: chaque matin de la terre ouvrait ses ailes au bas des marches de la nuit.
> Sans redite, allégé de la peur des hommes, je creuse dans l'air ma tombe et mon retour.

As the illusion of night is shattered, fear is conquered, and the poem emerges: «Au commencement était la peur, puis la résistance à l'objet de la peur, ensuite le verbe...» (*A une sérénité crispée*). As he leaves the closed chamber, «l'objet *creux destiné à être longuement fécondé*» and the «auberge où il fait bon vivre,» the poet casts one last glance at the now naked window of the empty house. Has the sister, then, taken everything from him on her flight to freedom? On the contrary, by forcing open the shutters, she has set free the vistas of infinity that are the domain of the poem. «En disparaissant,» writes Char in *Aromates chasseurs*, «nous retrouvons ce qui était *avant* que la terre et les astres ne fussent constitués, c'est-à-dire l'espace. Nous sommes cet espace dans toute sa dépense. Nous retournons au jour aérien et à son allégresse noire.» As she dies, Julia—like Caroline—becomes «ce beau visage sans antan qui allait tuer le sommeil, dans le miroir de notre regard, provisoire receveur universel pour tous les yeux futurs» («Célébrer Giacometti,» *Retour amont*).

In his *Lettera amorosa,* quoted earlier, the poet spoke of the snowflake left by the fleeing woman, a flake that melts on the poet's eyelid. A text from *La Bibliothèque est en feu,* 1957, equated the event of the poem with the down-feather falling, in winter, onto the poet's window. «Le Nu perdu,» a poem of *Retour amont,* elaborates on the image: «Porteront rameaux ceux dont l'endurance sait user la nuit noueuse qui précède et suit l'éclair... La rage des vents les maintient encore dévêtus. Contre eux vole un duvet de nuit noire.» Surely, snowflake and feather are but two representations of one symbol which stands for poetic creation. When asked: «Comment me vint l'écriture?», Char answered: «Comme un duvet d'oiseau sur ma vitre, en hiver. Aussitôt s'éleva dans l'âtre une bataille de tisons qui n'a pas, encore à présent, pris fin.»

«Rien n'est produit, créé ni même montré pour jamais, que par l'accumulation des distances et le déchirement, césarien, des suites,» wrote Georges Blin in his preface to *Commune Présence.* The poet who has qualified poetry as «un chant de départ,» as a «course perpétuelle vie-mort-vie, tendue vers l'Idéal du mieux» («En compagnie,» *N. R. F.,* Dec. 1966), bids farewell to his sister, and to the woman that waited for him in the «Passe de Lyon,» to whom he says:

> ... Vous me conduirez à la fenêtre où vos yeux voyagent, d'où vos faveurs plongent quand votre liberté échange sa lumière avec celle des météores, la vôtre demeurant et la leur se perdant. Avec mes songes, avec ma guerre, avec mon baiser, sous le mûrier ressuscité, dans le répit des filatures, je m'efforcerai d'isoler votre conquête d'un savoir antérieur, autre que le mien. Que l'avenir vous

entraîne avec des convoiteurs différents, j'y céderai, mais pour le seul chef-d'œuvre!

Flamme à l'excès de son destin, qui tantôt m'amoindrit et tantôt me complète, vous émergez à l'instant près de moi, dauphine, salamandre, et je ne vous suis rien.

The masterpiece of which the poet speaks belongs to all men. The serpent or salamander, the flame or fountain are not for him to crush. The flower, «iris jaune des rivières» is not his to pluck. In the closed chamber of the house, it would soon fade and die. Sown into the wind, however, this flower —combining the properties of fire and water, earth and sky, man and woman—turns into the rainbow whose beauty is enjoyed by all: «Iris. Nom d'une divinité de la mythologie grecque, qui était la messagère des dieux, et qui, déployant son écharpe, produisait l'arc-en-ciel» (*Lettera amorosa*). The flower and the woman—though slain by man—live on in the promise of the rainbow, scintillating in space, untouched and undefiled by human hand:

> ... Te voici nue et entre toutes la meilleure seulement aujourd'hui où tu franchis la sortie d'un hymne raboteux. L'espace pour toujours est-il cet absolu et scintillant congé, chétive volte-face? Mais prédisant cela j'affirme que tu vis; le sillon s'éclaire entre ton bien et mon mal. La chaleur reviendra avec le silence comme je te soulèverai. Inanimée.
>
> («Biens égaux,» *Le Poème pulvérisé*).

The rough, uneven hymn of «Eaux-mères» has been hewn into the pure prism of water and sun. The poet has defined —and purified—the object of his fear. He has reconciled the multiple and seemingly incompatible faces of life and love, the woman of water and the woman of fire, mother and sister, nephew and child: «Iris. Les yeux bleus, les yeux noirs, les yeux verts, sont ceux dont l'iris est bleu, est noir, est vert.» He no longer sees their existence as mutually exclusive, nor does he remain fixed in his own confused and anguishing world of dream. He leads us back, instead, to the land of the fairy-tale, and to Greek mythology, to the intimations of immortality that speak of peace, and joy.

Zephyros killed Ὑάκινθος and the flower was born. The wind destroyed the reflection in the window, and life entered the closed chamber of dream. The bleeding orchid of the earth is made whole in the cool radiance of the rainbow. The nights of false brilliance are turned into «Les Nuits justes»:

> Avec un vent plus fort,
> Une lampe moins obscure,
> Nous devons trouver la halte
> Où la nuit dira «Passez»;
> Et nous saurons que c'est vrai
> Quand le verre s'éteindra.
>
> O terre devenue tendre!
> O branche où mûrit ma joie!
> La gueule du ciel est blanche.
> Ce qui miroite, là, c'est toi,
> Ma chute, mon amour, mon saccage.
> (*Les Matinaux*).

There is, in *Lettera amorosa*—Char's longest love poem, begun in 1952, but revised and republished many times—(16) one section, set off from the rest in quotation marks, which is a true poem in free verse, entitled:

Chant d'Insomnie:

> «Amour hélant, l'Amoureuse viendra,
> Gloria de l'été, ô fruits!

---

(16) The first fragment of *Lettera amorosa*, entitled «Pourquoi le ciel se voûte-t-il?», was published by P.-A. Benoit in 1952. The first complete version of the poem appeared in 1953 (Gallimard). The second edition is given in *La Parole en archipel*, 1962, followed by a third revision in 1963. The «version définitive» of *Lettera amorosa* is given in *Commune Présence*, 1964.

La flèche du soleil traversera ses lèvres,
Le trèfle nu sur sa chair bouclera,
Miniature semblable à l'iris, l'orchidée,
Cadeau le plus ancien des prairies au plaisir
Que la cascade instille, que la bouche délivre.»

The ancient gift of water and sun remains, distilled in the light of the rainbow—lips traversed by the arrow of the sun—and in the yellow flower of the Sorgue: «Iris plural, iris d'Eros, iris de *Lettera amorosa.*» The letter closes with a dedication to the flower:

> Merci d'être, sans jamais te casser, iris, ma fleur de gravité. Tu élèves au bord des eaux des affections miraculeuses, tu ne pèses pas sur les mourants que tu veilles, tu éteins des plaies sur lesquelles le temps n'a pas d'action, tu ne conduis pas à une maison consternante, tu permets que toutes les fenêtres reflétées ne fassent qu'un seul visage de passion, tu accompagnes le retour du jour sur les vertes avenues libres.

The faulty vision of the schoolboy, caught in the illusory fire of night, has been corrected by the sister who accompanied the poet on the *Chemin des écoliers.* As he left that road, the poet's vision sharpened, bringing into focus—via the iris of the eye—outer and inner reality, individual perception and the light of the sun itself, the light and the world:

> En cette fin des Temps aux travestis enfantins, c'est à une lumière du crépuscule, *non fautive,* que nous vouâmes notre franchise. Lumière qui ne se contractait pas en se retirant, mais demeurait là, nue, agrandie, péremptoire, se brisant de toutes ses artères contre nous (17).

---

(17) It is Char who underlines the adjective, *non-fautive.*

This is the epilogue of *Le Chien de cœur,* texts composed by Char during and following the night of 3-4 May, 1968, which brought him, once again, so near to death:

> Je crus que la mort venait, mais une mort où, comblé par une compréhension sans exemple, j'aurais encore un pas à faire avant de m'endormir, d'être rendu éparpillé à l'univers pour toujours.

When in *La Bibliothèque est en feu* Char writes: «La poésie me volera ma mort,» I think we must take his statement quite literally. It was the act of writing that saved the poet from death, in the anguish of night and the agony of Céreste. It was the poem which made possible the simultaneous existence of mother and sister, nephew and child, evidence and truth.

«Hypnos saisit l'hiver et le vêtit de granit. L'hiver se fit sommeil et Hypnos devint feu,» wrote Hypnos, the poet-brother of Alexander, captain of the *maquis.* The rest, as he put it, being up to man, René Char made of winter, night, and death the poem of summer, dawn, and love (18).

> Oreiller rouge, oreiller noir,
> Sommeil, un sein sur le côté,
> Entre l'étoile et le carré,
> Que de bannières en débris!
>
> Trancher, en finir avec vous,
> Comme le moût est à la cuve,
> Dans l'espoir de lèvres dorées.
>
> Moyeu de l'air fondamental
> Durcissant l'eau des blancs marais,
> Sans souffrir, enfin sans souffrance,
> Admis dans le verbe frileux,
> Je dirai: «Monte» au cercle chaud.
> («Dernière marche,» *Retour amont,* 1966).

---

(18) The first version of this chapter was published as: «Sous le signe d'Iris: René Char, poète d'amour,» in *French Review,* Special Issue, no. 1, Winter 1970.

10

2

THE WAKE: «SILLAGE» AND OTHER SIGNALS

> Quelquefois mon refuge est le mutisme de Saint-Just à la séance de la Convention du 9 Thermidor. Je comprends, oh combien, la *procédure* de ce silence, les volets de cristal à jamais tirés sur la *communication*.
>
> («Feuillets d'Hypnos,» no. 185, 1943-1944).

> Je vais parler et je sais dire, mais quel est l'écho hostile qui m'interrompt?
>
> («Outrages,» *Le Chien de cœur*, 1944-1967.)

«Il n'y a pas d'humanisme poétique de la modernité,» wrote Roland Barthes some twenty-five years ago. He qualified modern poetry as «un discours plein de terreur, c'est-à-dire qu'il met l'homme en liaison non pas avec les autres hommes, mais avec les images les plus inhumaines de la Nature» (1). In the critic's view, poets since Mallarmé—and René Char foremost among them—have done away with the dialogue of classical literature for which they substitute the terror of individual words, words unconnected to each other and unrelated to the world around them.

And yet, one of the most insistent themes recurring throughout the poetry of Char is the problem of communica-

---

(1) Roland Barthes, *Le Degré zéro de l'écriture* (Paris: Editions du Seuil, 1953), p. 72.

tion. The urgency of this problem may explain his popularity with a certain group of young French intellectuals who have long since written off other contemporary poets—and poetry in general—as irrelevant. Perhaps it is this theme also which has led Char critics—Berger, Mounin, Gascht, and Hubert Juin, to mention just a few (2)—to insist on the «fraternal» aspect of his poems.

For René Char, the struggle to get outside the soliloquy, the effort to break down a wall within himself, is a very personal, almost physiological necessity apparent even in his earliest verse. I shall not study here in detail the poet's first published volume, *Les Cloches sur le cœur*. Char himself destroyed the greater part of this work, which he dismisses as inconsequential juvenilia (3). I shall respect his judgment by limiting myself to two pieces from *Les Cloches*, «Prêt au dépouillement» and «Sillage,» both of which have been republished in later collections. I also include in this discussion Char's earliest published poem, «Ce soir,» even though it only appeared once (in a literary journal) and never became part of a larger work. The text is well known to Char's readers, and even if it is, as its author remarks, a mere prank, a pastiche of the inferior verse published by a small regional magazine (4), «Ce soir» still makes a significant contribution to our understanding of the poet's evolution.

---

(2) Pierre Berger, *René Char* (Paris: Seghers, 1951); Georges Mounin, *La Communication poétique, précédé de Avez-vous lu Char?* (Paris: Gallimard, 1969); André Gascht, *Charme de René Char* (Bruxelles: Le Thyrse, 1957); Hubert Juin, «La Poésie et la fraternité,» *Critique*, 96 (mai 1955), pp. 409-14.

(3) In a letter to the author (3 November, 1972), Char refers to his early work as the «récréations» of an adolescent, and he comments: «Il n'y a que de bons et de mauvais poèmes, hélas! les premiers n'aidant pas les seconds et vice versa.» The letter was sent in response to the original version of this chapter, published in *PMLA* 87, 1972, pp. 1016-22.

(4) In the same letter, Char says of «Ce soir»: «Ce chèvrefeuille... est un canular dont le seul mérite consista à 'tromper' une revue régionaliste qui avait usurpé ce splendide mot: *Le Feu*. D'où cette tentative de pastiche des poèmes habituels qu'elle publiait...» *Le*

In addition to these texts, I examine here two poems, «Jouvence» and «Sur le volet d'une fenêtre» from *Premières alluvions,* an anthology of Char's early work (some of it rescued from *Les Cloches*). I also touch upon «Possible,» part of the first edition of *Arsenal,* 1929, written, the poet insists, «dans l'ignorance du surréalisme» (5). All the texts discussed here —and that was the primary consideration in choosing them— are known to predate Char's personal contact with Eluard and the Paris surrealists in the fall of 1929.

«Ce soir,» dating back, perhaps, to 1923, was published in April 1929 in the review *Le Feu* (Aix-en-Provence). It seems, at first glance, nothing more than a schoolboy's embroidery on a troubadour *motif*:

Feu, which advertised itself as «la plus vivante, la meilleur marché» of literary reviews, was first published in Paris before becoming, in 1918, «l'Organe du Régionalisme méditerranéen,» published in Aix-en-Provence. The journal's editor, Emile Sicard, wrote verse of the «dolorisme de salon»—type given below:

Le Jardin du Silence et la ville du roy

Pourquoi mon cœur est-il cette coupe fragile
   Qui ne peut contenir
Toute la terre rouge et tous les champs fertiles,
   Et tout leur avenir?

Pourquoi ne suis-je pas aussi grand que moi-même
   Quand je vois mon pays?
Pourquoi ne puis-je pas serrer tout ce que j'aime
   Dans mes bras éblouis?
...
Les cyprès, ces soldats des champs, montent la garde.
Le pas d'un chemineau résonne. L'ombre garde
Je ne sais quelle extase et quel ravissement
Qui semble un bras de mère autour d'un cou d'enfant.
Cybèle est endormie au seuil de chaque asile.
C'est un soir de faiblesse humaine et d'évangile.

Here is the cypress, and the child. Perhaps also the cemetery, the absent loved one, and the «faiblesse humaine» of Char's narrator (*Le Feu,* no. 91, novembre 1912).

(5) In a private interview, August 1973.

Le chèvrefeuille en fleurs frissonne, languissant,
Au vieux mur décrépi, tout boursouflé de pierre;
Tes volets se sont clos ce soir à ma prière,
Le chèvrefeuille en fleurs se dresse éperdument
L'âme de tes parfums erre en ce doux moment, ...
Je devine ta voix en ce soir de misère,
Mon cœur est cet enfant tout délirant de fièvre,
Et qui clame sa peur de mourir, grimaçant.
Quelque chose a glissé sur ma joue, lentement,
Un cyprès quelque part apaise un cimetière;
Ton souvenir est là qui rôde et qui espère,
Je suis lâche ce soir! Je t'aimais tant!
Et sur mon désespoir la nuit grave s'étend.

In the poem, the lover stands, at night, before the beloved's
closed window, singing his languishing strains to the unseen
lady. The poem has Baudelairean echoes—*âme, parfums,
fleurs*—although the general atmosphere also takes us back to
mediaeval love lyrics. The slightly precious note: «quelque
chose a glissé sur ma joue» for «j'ai pleuré,» would not have
been out of place in troubadour verse (6).

There is a certain vagueness about the poem (*quelque chose,
quelque part*) whose structure—if we take from it the mediaeval trappings of the *chèvrefeuille*—hinges upon the implied
dialogue of a *je* and a *tu,* the latter seen only in the form of its
possessive adjective correlatives: *ton, tes.* The third line,
«Tes volets se sont clos ce soir à ma prière,» is modulated by
line 11: «Ton souvenir est là qui rôde et qui espère.» The
two lines rhyme with each other, as well as with line six:
«Je devine ta voix en ce soir de misère,» echoed, in turn, by
line 12: «Je suis lâche ce soir! Je t'aimais tant!»

The verbs of the poem, nearly all in the present tense,
describe three opposing motions: *se clore, rôder,* and *errer*

---

(6) Georges Mounin also raises the question of possible *précieux*
elements in Char's poetry (*op. cit.*, pp. 197-222). Claude Vigée links
Char's «penchant au maniérisme» and his taste for the *précieux* to
what he calls the «orfèvrerie parnassienne» (*Révolte et Louanges,*
Paris: José Corti, 1962, p. 114).

seem to suggest the circle; *se dresser* and *glisser* indicate vertical movement, and the poem ends on the horizontal *s'étend,* which serves not only to personify *la nuit grave,* but also to underscore the general inadequacy of the poet («je suis lâche») who lets himself be covered by night and *désespoir.* The final idea suggested by the poem is one of cowardice and weakness. Note, by the way, that *rôder* is the only word to bring a purely animal notion into the predominantly vegetal setting of the poem. Despite his «admirable bestiaire,» to quote Jean Starobinski, (7) Char will always remain first and foremost a poet of the vegetal world. As he looks back, nearly sixty years old, to his literary beginnings, Char remembers: «L'aubépine en fleurs fut mon premier alphabet» (*L'Age cassant,* 1966).

In «Ce soir» the desired dialogue between the narrator's *je* and the unseen lady is hinted at structurally, but is not, in fact, begun. The poet realizes that it is he who is at fault. If, instead of remaining at the bottom of the ladder and relegating his love to the imperfect, he had imitated the *chèvrefeuille,* (7a) if he had made the «Saut en hauteur» (*Les Cloches sur le cœur*), or Breton's «saut vital,» and opened the window, communication would have been established. The speaker would have heard quite clearly the *confuses paroles* which now he can only guess at («Je devine ta voix»), and the walls separating him from his beloved would have become «les murs de camaraderie» (*ibid.*).

In a later—and much more virile—poem, the dialogue seems to take place. I do not think, however, that the implied second person of «Ce soir» and the actual *tu* of «Sillage» suggest the same personae. The first poem implies an actual confrontation of two speakers; the second reads like a soliloquy. In «Sillage,» the poet enters into dialogue with himself, con-

---

(7) «René Char et la définition du poème,» *Liberté* 10, Montréal, juillet-août 1968, p. 25.
(7a) Vines, trees, and rivers, like nerves, establish relationships by linking inner and outer space, vertical and horizontal planes.

demning his own *plaintes* and *gémissements* of an earlier period:

> Ce col enroulé de tes plaintes
> Au recueil du couchant sonore
> N'est-il pas par son mutisme
> Le symbole froid de jadis
>
> Où à chaque étage de nue
> Tu retrouves mêlés aux brousses
> Les gémissements que tu proférais
> Pour rassurer ton orgueil
>
> Il n'est de similitude
> Entre tes doigts gaînés de peau
> Badinant avec le feuillage
> Amorphe de ce haut-fourneau
> Sur un tabouret de nuage
>
> Et les arrhes de sol qui patinent les champs

The poem is printed above in its original version, as it appeared in *Les Cloches sur le cœur.* When «Sillage» was reworked for inclusion in *Premières alluvions,* 1946, its title was changed to «Sillage noir,» and the last two stanzas of the poem were deleted. Char kept only the first line of stanza three and added to it two new verses, not previously published, so that the third stanza reads, in the 1946 version:

> Il n'est de similitude
> Il n'est que solitude
> Il n'est qu'aboiement et chien

He then substituted for the original last two lines of the poem the final stanza of «La Tête sous l'oreiller,» a poem of *Arsenal,* which I quote from the manuscript copy sent to Eluard: (8)

---

(8) Bibliothèque Littéraire Jacques Doucet, Paris. The ms. is dated 13 February, 1931.

L'amour qui s'était assoupi
Comme la mer sous une vague
Garde un visage de momie
Et parle une langue de sable.

There were two minor changes: stanzas one and two of the original version were consolidated into one, and line two of stanza two changed its verb to the imperfect:

Tu retrouvais mêlés aux brousses

«Sillage» is, like «Ce soir,» an evening poem. The regular alexandrines of the earlier poem have been replaced by not quite so regular octosyllables (which Char will favor down to his latest poems). Rhyme has given way to assonance. But «Sillage» shares, connotatively, much of the vocabulary of «Ce soir,» though it is quite different in tone.

The word *froid* above echoes the earlier *frissonne* (both, furthermore, attributed to vertical objects); *plaintes* and *gémissements* are variations on the theme of *languissant, prière,* and *désespoir*; *jadis* modifies *ton souvenir* of «Ce soir»; the *brousses* (and, in the original version, *le feuillage amorphe*) replace the earlier *chèvrefeuille*. «Chaque étage de nue» recalls the image of the flower climbing the wall. «Je t'aimais tant,» the poet's cry of «Ce soir,» is modulated in the more laconic «amour qui s'était assoupi,» which also recalls the final image of night spreading its wings over the poet's despair, like «les arrhes de sol qui patinent les champs.» «Je t'aimais tant» is further echoed by the two imperfects of «Sillage»: «tu retrouvais,» and «tu proférais.»

The sets have been changed between «Ce soir» and «Sillage.» From the closed courtyard of a Provençal *mas* the poet has gone out into the open plain, and it is not a wall he faces now, but a mountain (that most virile of Char's symbols, reappearing in much of his later verse) (9). However, this is

_____
(9) I realize, of course, that the word *col* here also suggests the neck, and a collar, meanings which help to explain the word

a mountain the poet will not climb: «Et comme fut longue à venir à nos épaules la montagne silencieuse» («La Frontière en pointillé,» *Aromates chasseurs*). At the foot of the rock lies the body of water in which the face of the beloved finally appears: «Seule des autres pierres, la pierre du torrent a le contour rêveur du visage enfin rendu» («La Scie rêveuse,» *Dans la pluie giboyeuse,* 1969).

At first, however, this is a dead face: «L'amour qui s'était assoupi... / Garde un visage de momie.» It speaks in the distant, shifting, fleeting voice of sand, making communication impossible. Of Char's contributions to *Ralentir Travaux,* we remember these lines from «Isolée à ravir»:

> Elle a jeté un pont de soupirs
> Sur la mer inhabitable
> Elle a quitté ses habits de terre
> Mis ses habits de sable
> Elle parle une langue de liège...

This is more than a variation on the legend of the Loreley. While a dialogue has not been established between the poet and his love, a bridge has been thrown from earth to water.

The 1934 edition of *Le Marteau sans maître* contained the poem «Drames» (dedicated to Char's former wife, Georgette Goldstein), reading, in part:

> Quand je partirai longuement
> Ce sera dis-tu la marche à peau de tigre
> Tu sais casser les mots que j'aime
> Comme glisse l'écume de la géométrie
> Sur le cénotaphe du géomètre
> Sur la piste du cratère je tournerai
> Pour conclure les réactionnaires seront consumés
>   dans les retraites végétales
> La réalité niée dans le dernier meurtre

---

mutisme associated with *col.* The mountaintop in its cold and quiet solitude is not an infrequent image in Char's mature poetry.

> Le pont macabre sera enfin jeté
> Entre la terre blanche et le ciel jaune
> La présence et l'absence réconciliées
> Dans un monde sans aspect
> Tous les loisirs de la vapeur

The theme of reconciliation through communication runs through all of Char's poetry.

In «Sillage,» and the lines from *Ralentir Travaux,* nature has begun to communicate with the poet. The sea has been humanized, has been made habitable. Though at this particular moment it is quiet and seemingly dead, we know that the water has been stirred. A wake appears on its surface, marking the passing contact with another object. Nature speaks, but, as yet, its language is artless and diffuse.

«Bel édifice et les pressentiments,» a poem of *Le Tombeau des secrets,* 1930, expresses the same anxiety in the face of the amorphous body of water to which the poet seeks to give human form:

> J'écoute marcher dans mes jambes
> La mer morte vagues par-dessus tête
>
> Des yeux purs dans les bois
> Cherchent la tête habitable (10)

Man and the world have not become one. The poet who tries to listen but does not understand («écoute mais n'entend pas,» *Lettera amorosa*) remains fixed in his solitude. Only indistinct sounds are heard, like the murmuring of the dead sea, and the barking of distant dogs. The last line of the final version of «Sillage,» retitled «Sillage noir,» seems to go back—perhaps unconsciously—to «ton souvenir est là qui rôde» of «Ce soir.» While the earlier poem spoke only of the impossibility of communication, «Sillage noir» hints at a reason for the poet's failure: «les gémissements que tu proférais / *Pour rassurer ton*

---

(10) My quotation is, again, taken from the copy sent to Paul and Gala Eluard.

orgueil.» Why did the schoolboy speak? Was it not to reassure his own vanity, to revel in the melodiousness of his own voice given over to sighs and lamentations? Was he, then, prepared to listen to someone else, or did he not speak to sustain the *amour-propre* banned by Breton from poetic dialogue? (11)

Perhaps it is his *lâcheté,* as Char himself calls it, and his lack of will that poems such as «Sillage» and «Prêt au dépouillé-ment» try to combat. The latter, besides being one of Char's earliest prose poems, is the first to bear one of those magnificent Char titles that are in themselves a poem, «Prêt au dépouillement»:

> Par ce temps de soleil veule, de douceur sans contrariété, il est inacceptable que la distance soit telle. Pourtant à mon corps sans limite tu ne saurais opposer cette faible terre ou cet azur trop réel. Ta voix est décharnée, intraduisible, et c'est tout juste en l'écoutant si cette verge dont je me cingle le mollet ne devient pas le plus vil instrument de supplice.

«Prêt au dépouillement» is a poem of day, and all of Char's readers know that day will be the privileged time of his most striking poems, from «Prêt au dépouillement» to *Les Matinaux* and beyond. While in «Ce soir» the poet spoke only of his *lâcheté,* he now asserts his pride. His «corps sans limite» assumes cosmic proportions far greater than «cette faible terre ou cet azur trop réel.» It is not with an idealized nature or an ideological *azur* that the poet hopes to establish communication. He does not seek the Mallarméan ideal, but the real world of shadows and shades, where contraries are abolished, where sky, earth and water commune. But before he can attune his ear to that Heraclitean harmony, the poet must wake up

---

(11) André Breton, *Manifestes du Surréalisme* (Paris: Gallimard, 1963), p. 49. Breton's discussion of poetic dialogue appeared in the first Surrealist Manifesto, published in 1924.

and stand up, whip himself into consciousness, cast away his pride and learn to listen and to understand: «Le contraire d'écouter est d'entendre. Et comme fut longue à venir à nos épaules la montagne silencieuse.»

«Et c'est tout juste en l'écoutant si cette verge dont je me cingle le mollet ne devient pas le plus vil instrument de supplice.» How different is the ending of this prose poem from that of the other texts examined! For the first time, we actually see the poet standing up (*debout* will become a key word in Char's vocabulary), fully awake and aware of his impotence. From «ce col enroulé de tes plaintes» he goes to «cette verge dont je me cingle le mollet.» From *désespoir* he passes to action, from *plaintes* to self-inflicted *supplice*. *Chèvrefeuille —feuillage amorphe—brousses—verge,* the (de-)gradation is evident. «Je suis lâche» becomes «je me cingle le mollet.» The erotic overtones are obvious. (Perhaps one could even see in the «col *enroulé*» and the «mollet *cinglé*» first hints at the serpent which will be the most important animal in Char's bestiary.)

I think we have in «Prêt au dépouillement» a double attempt at dialogue, that of the poet with the universe, and the poet's dialogue with himself, the cosmic body, as it were, in conversation with the limited mind, enslaved by its literary predecessors. Both attempts are unsuccessful, and the poet rebels against his own *faiblesse,* his inability to translate («ta voix est...intraduisible») the distance from the ground to the window, from earth to sky, even on a day like this («Par ce temps de soleil veule»), when the impressionistic half-light of early morning would seem to favor the abolition of contraries, when communication between sky and sea, earth and water should be as self-evident in his verse as in an Elstir painting. The poem ends in failure, but in the poet's awareness of and rebellion against that failure lies the first promise of ultimate success. Char's new hope is expressed in «Possible,» a poem from *Arsenal*:

Dès qu'il en eut la certitude
A coup de serrements de gorge
Il facilita la parole.

Elle jouait sur les illustrés à quatre sous
Il parla comme on tue le fauve
Ou la pitié.

Ses doigts touchèrent l'autre rive
Mais le ciel bascula si vite
Que l'aigle sur la montagne
Eut la tête tranchée.

The effort has been too great. Communication is not established through violence; the poem cannot be forced into existence: «l'aigle sur la montagne / Eut la tête tranchée.»

The cosmic communication sought by the poet is first hinted at in a text from Char's literary beginnings. «Jouvence,» dated 1923-25, is a contemporary of «Sillage,» though it is not published until 1946, as «Jouvence I,» in *Premières alluvions.*

Ceux qui partent pour les nuages
Se séparent de leur raison
La mer ouverte à l'œil unique
Est leur taciturne horizon

The first line of the poem reminds us of «A l'horizon,» a quatrain dedicated to André Breton and published in *Le Tombeau des secrets,* 1930:

Ceux qui partent pour les nuages
Croient solide comme un roc
A l'avenir de la mer
Ouverte à l'œil unique

I do not know whether «Jouvence I» is, in fact, Char's «praise of those poets who endeavor to infuse a new spirit in poetry, one which will give man a new understanding of his existence» (12). The poem does recall the figure of Orlando separated from his *raison* and the popular image of the poet lost «dans les nuages.» In an early prose text, Char also speaks—praisingly—of the traditional notion of poetic folly: «Toute poésie doit naître libre et un peu folle,» he writes in 1924 (13). The quatrain of 1923-25 does not, however, opt in favor of those who «partent pour les nuages.» It does represent a movement away from «cette faible terre» and «cet azur trop réel.» But the mere substitution of one horizon for another, the sky for the sea, does not in itself bring about any significant change. The sea will remain as taciturn as the mountain wrapped in its *mutisme*.

It is the symbol of the cloud (first introduced in «Sillage») which will eventually bring together earth and sky and thus establish a dialogue (13a). «Dans nos interminables songeries devant le ciel,» writes Gaston Bachelard, «dès que les nuages descendent sur la table de pierre, dans le creux de nos mains, il semble que tous les objets s'arrondissent un peu, qu'une pénombre blanche habille les cristaux. Le monde a notre dimension, le ciel est sur terre, notre main touche le ciel» (14). Symbol of the amorphous («le feuillage / Amorphe de ce haut-fourneau / Sur un tabouret de nuage,» wrote Char), the cloud is, nevertheless, a dynamic image as it suggests two opposing movements: the vertical motion of ascension, with its concomitants of insecurity and risk, and the movement (or stillness) of the circle, connoting security, stability, and warmth.

---

(12) Virginia A. La Charité, *op cit.*, p. 20.

(13) A prose text first published by Georges Mounin in *Les Temps Modernes*, nos. 137-38, juillet-août 1957, pp. 277-78.

(13a) In *A une sérénité crispée* (contained, in 1965, in *Recherche de la Base et du Sommet*), Char writes: «Le devoir d'un Prince est, durant la trêve des saisons et la sieste des heureux, de produire un Art à l'aide des nuages, un Art qui soit issu de la douleur et conduise à la douleur.» For a discussion of the cloud symbol in Hölderlin, see Martin Heidegger, *Erläuterungen zu Hölderlins Dichtung* (Frankfurt: Klostermann, 1963), pp. 15-17.

(14) Gaston Bachelard, *L'Air et les songes: Essai sur l'imagination du mouvement* (Paris: Corti, 1943), p. 217.

It is interesting to see how two later texts of René Char illustrate this double aspect of the cloud. In *Les Loyaux Adversaires* (*Fureur et Mystère,* 1948) figures «Cette fumée qui nous portait,» a prose poem that will lend its title to the opening section of Char's 1964 anthology, *Commune Présence*. In it, the poet combines the image of the cloud with that of the mountain to reinforce the theme of ascension, announced by the title:

> Cette fumée qui nous portait était sœur du bâton qui dérange la pierre et du nuage qui ouvre le ciel. Elle n'avait pas mépris de nous, nous prenait tels que nous étions, minces ruisseaux nourris de désarroi et d'espérance, avec un verrou aux mâchoires et une montagne dans le regard.

This text combines again the notions of *errer* (in *désarroi*) and *espérer* (*espérance*) as we found them in «Ce soir.» The mature poet repeats the itinerary traveled in his youth. From «cette faible terre» he seeks to rise like smoke to horizons beyond «cet azur trop réel,» horizons that stand out like «une montagne dans le regard.» If his journey is to be successful, the lock that holds his jaws (we are reminded again of the lines from «L'Egalité») must be broken, and the poet must find «la parole qui délivre,» the word that will lift him from his earthbound *désarroi* to *espérance*.

The poem suggests both horizontal and vertical movement (*verrou, montagne*), but the tension felt in «Ce soir» is resolved here by the dominant image of the circle, suggested by the words *pierre, nuage,* and *ciel.* Bachelard in his prose («dès que les *nuages* descendent sur la table de *pierre*...») has once again uncovered one of the intricate associative processes of the poetic imagination: «du bâton qui dérange la pierre et du nuage qui ouvre le ciel.» The last image takes us back to the «mer ouverte à l'œil unique» and perhaps to the title «Sillage,» if we think of the wake left by the cloud as it «opens» the sky.

In «Sur les hauteurs,» a poem from *Les Matinaux,* Char

likens his own destiny to that of the cloud and speaks of the precarious nature of their mutual existence:

> Attends encore que je vienne
> Fendre le froid qui nous retient.

> Nuage, en ta vie aussi menacée que la mienne.

Again there is the suggestion of a breaking down or opening up (*fendre*) of a hostile element, *le froid,* which reminds us of *le symbole froid,* the mountain of «Sillage» standing in proud and silent isolation. Instinctively the poet knows—even in his early verse—that the cloud will be his ally in the quest for meaningful communication with the world around him.

In the poem «Jouvence I,» the dual symbolism of the cloud is already suggested. The verbs of lines one and two—*se séparer, partir*—introduce the theme of risk, while the nouns of lines three and four—*mer, œil, horizon*—suggest roundness and security, a world at rest. *Partir* and *se séparer* also modify the theme of absence, introduced in «Ce soir» by words such as *deviner* and *souvenir.* But something has happened between «Ce soir» and «Jouvence.» The latter title stands by itself in contrast to «le vieux mur décrépi» of the earlier poem. In «Jouvence,» the *volets clos* of «Ce soir» have been opened; a way out of the «closed valley» is seen. Though no voice is heard and the horizon remains still, the sea—once likened to a *visage de momie*—has begun to live. It has opened its *œil unique.*

In the 1950 edition of *Premières alluvions,* a second stanza, undated, is added to «Jouvence I»:

> Ceux qui mentent aux nuages
> Sont ménagers de leur raison
> La mer ouverte à l'œil multiple
> Est leur famélique horizon.

In an early prose text, «Mesures pour rien,» published in the Paris review *Le Rouge et le Noir* (no. 8, mars 1929), Char

— 161 —

identified those who «mentent aux étoiles»: «Je m'insurge contre nos aînés dont la plupart sont nos pires ennemis, conscients ou non... Pour faire le point ils mentent aux étoiles. Quelle vilaine action!» While those who lie to the stars and «Ceux qui mentent aux nuages» are clearly related, the new second stanza of «Jouvence» implies no moral-aesthetic judgment. Those who keep their reason but lie to the clouds (by denying them, like Mallarmé?) are no better and no worse than «ceux qui partent pour les nuages,» the romantics, the dreamers. The poet does not choose between «Jouvence I» and «II.» The structure of the quatrains supports his neutral position. «Ce soir» spoke in the naïve and touching tone of a confession, by use of the romantic *je*. The «Jouvence» texts achieve distancing by introduction of an invisible narrator and, more particularly, by means of the demonstrative pronoun constructions (*ceux qui*) so typical of Char. «Ceux qui, aux premières heures de la nuit, ratent leur lit,» writes the poet in 1947 («L'Extravagant»). In «La Patience» he speaks of «ceux qu'il faut attacher sur terre»; in «Les Transparents,» 1950, appears «celui qui part.» The poem «Centon,» 1950, mentions «ceux qui regardent souffrir le lion dans sa cage,» and one of the more recent Char texts, «Les Apparitions dédaignées» (*Le Chien de cœur,* 1969) points to «ceux qui ont installé l'éternel compensateur.»

The speaker of the «Jouvence» quatrains does not engage himself or his own responsibility. Again, the cloud symbol fits in well with the linguistic structure of the poem. «La rêverie des nuages reçoit un caractère psychologique particulier,» writes Gaston Bachelard. «Elle est une *rêverie sans responsabilité*» (15). And yet I do not think that the image of the cloud is, for Char, sufficient unto itself. It does not replace human contact, as it seems to do for Baudelaire, who writes: «Chose curieuse, il ne m'arriva pas une seule fois, devant ces magies liquides et aériennes, de me plaindre de l'absence de l'homme» (*Curiosités esthétiques*).

---

(15) Bachelard, *op. cit.,* p. 212. The italics are Bachelard's.

Quite to the contrary, the cloud represents, in Char's poetic universe, the mediator between man and the world. It establishes communication not only between the various elements, but also between these elements and man, and, finally, between the poet and another human being: «L'infini attaque mais un nuage sauve,» wrote Char in *La Bibliothèque est en feu.* Those who have experienced the mercilessly cloudless sky of Provence will know the true meaning of that aphorism.

A near contemporary of «Jouvence I» is the quatrain called «Sur le volet d'une fenêtre,» one of Char's most serenely beautiful poems:

> Visage chaleur blanche
> Sœur passante sœur disant
> Suave persévérance
> Visage chaleur blanche.

The shutters of «Ce soir» have been opened, and reflected in the window is seen a face with the reassuring warmth of a sister's face, a sister qualified by the rather uncommon attribute: *disant.* The wall has, at last, been broken down (or climbed), communication has been established with someone other than the poet's *alter ego.* Like the child to whom he compared himself in «Ce soir,» the poet first learned to see, then, to listen, and, finally, to understand. The listless murmurs of sand and sea, the unintelligible barkings of dogs have given way to the voice of the «sœur disant.»

In the «Visage chaleur blanche» I cannot help but see again the image of the cloud. The quatrain has, moreover, all the lightness, the swiftness of air, the whiteness and the warmth of a cloud. «Le nuage, mouvement blanc... Tous les objets s'arrondissent un peu, ... une pénombre blanche habille les cristaux,» wrote Bachelard. Char himself associates face and cloud in a 1964 addition to his longest and most unusual love poem, *Lettera amorosa,* which reads: «Je ne confonds pas la solitude avec la lyre du désert. Le nuage cette nuit qui cerne ton oreille n'est pas de neige endormante, mais d'embruns enlevés au printemps.» At the death of Adrienne Monnier, Char recalls «sa personne... comme un doux nuage gris teinté de rose» («Au revoir, Mademoiselle,» dated «20 août, 1955»). And again, in a much later text, «Destination de nos lointains» (*La Nuit talismanique*), Char writes: «O ma petite fumée s'élevant sur tout vrai feu, nous sommes les contemporains et le nuage de ceux qui nous aiment!» In «Traversée,» from «Sept parcelles de Luberon» (*Retour amont*), the poet asks:

> Que faut-il,
> La barre du printemps au front,
> Pour que le nuage s'endorme
> Sans rouler au bord de nos yeux?

It is the cloud which, taking on the shape of the beloved's face, translates the distance from sky to earth, speaking the words sought by the poet:

> Qui appelle encore pour un gaspillage sans frein?
> Le trésor entrouvert des nuages qui escortèrent notre vie.
> («Baudelaire mécontente Nietzsche,» *La Nuit talismanique*).

«Ce soir» seemed to lack direction: vertical, horizontal, and circular motions were indicated. «Sur le volet d'une fenêtre,» on the other hand, seems to glide in the air, a perfect circle. There is no visible movement; there is no tension of tenses. There are no verbs, only a present participle, but this one all-important: *disant*. At last the hidden partner of «Ce soir» is not only seen, but heard. The poet has established contact with the world. From the «feuillage amorphe» of «Ce soir» he has brought forth the rose that is poetry.

«Jouvence des Névons,» a poem of *Les Matinaux* quoted earlier, retraces Char's poetic itinerary from soliloquy to dialogue, from solitude to communication:

> Dans l'enceinte du parc, le grillon
> ne se tait que pour s'établir davantage.

Dans le parc des Névons
Ceinturé de prairies,
Un ruisseau sans talus,
Un enfant sans ami
Nuancent leur tristesse
Et vivent mieux ainsi.

Dans le parc des Névons
Un rebelle s'est joint
Au ruisseau, à l'enfant,
A leur mirage enfin.

Dans le parc des Névons
Mortel serait l'été
Sans la voix d'un grillon
Qui, par instant, se tait.

In the beginning, the child and the river are alone, each locked, like the speaker of «Ce soir,» in his own *tristesse* and despair. Against this solitude, this distance («il est inacceptable que la distance soit telle...») the child rebels, and he learns to see: «leur mirage enfin.» Child and river become one, reflecting and defining each other (16). As they grow together, they assume cosmic proportions, communicating, in the end, with the whole world, via the cricket's voice. In the park of the Névons are heard at last «les paroles amoureuses» of the earth that the poet will rediscover in «Le Bois de l'Epte.» In the loving communion of man and nature, man and man, death and despair are overcome: «Mortel serait l'été /Sans la voix d'un grillon...»

I do not think—as several critics do—that the dialogue engaged in by Char is one of reason vs. poetry. Rather, the poet engages all of himself, his reason and his poetry—«ceux

---

(16) In the first edition, this union was made explicit in the note: «L,enfant, le ruisseau, le rebelle ne sont qu'un seul et même être qui se modifie suivant les années. Il brille et s'éteint tour à tour, au gré de l'événement, sur les marches de l'horizon.» This is later compressed into the epigraph of the poem's definitive version.

qui mentent aux nuages» and «ceux qui partent pour les nuages»—in a quest for meaningful communication with an *Umwelt* which, if uninterrogated, would remain hostile or absurd: «L'infini attaque mais un nuage sauve.» The dialogue is, for Char, a necessary prerequisite for life and the guarantee for poetic survival.

In a commentary on his play *Le Soleil des eaux,* the poet writes:

> Je crois que la poésie, avant d'acquérir pour toujours, et grâce à un seul, sa dimension et ses pouvoirs, existe préliminairement en traits, en spectre et en vapeur dans le dialogue des êtres qui vivent en intelligence patente avec les ébauches autant qu'avec les grands ouvrages vraiment accomplis de la Création. La menace quasi constante d'anéantissement qui pèse sur eux est leur plus sûre sauvegarde. L'apprentissage du poète qui a lieu en pareille compagnie est un apprentissage privilégié.
> («Pourquoi du *Soleil des eaux*,» 1951).

A recent prose poem, «Lenteur de l'avenir,» shows the poet fully aware of the road traveled since «Ce soir,» and of the journey yet ahead:

> Il faut escalader beaucoup de dogmes et de glace pour jouer de bonheur et s'éveiller rougeur sur la pierre du lit.
> Entre eux et moi il y eut longtemps comme une haie sauvage dont il nous était loisible de recueillir les aubépines en fleurs, et de nous les offrir. Jamais plus loin que la main et le bras. Ils m'aimaient et je les aimais. Cet obstacle *pour le vent* où échouait ma pleine force, quel était-il? Un rossignol me le révéla, et puis une charogne.
> La mort dans la vie, c'est inalliable, c'est répugnant; la mort avec la mort, c'est approchable, ce n'est rien, un ventre peureux y rampe sans trembler.

J'ai renversé le dernier mur, celui qui ceinture les nomades des neiges, et je vois—ô mes premiers parents—l'été du chandelier.

Notre figure terrestre n'est que le second tiers d'une poursuite continue, un point, amont.

(Retour amont).

Many of Char's mature poems, from «Le Visage nuptial,» 1938, to *Aromates chasseurs,* 1975, will contain dialogues, actual or implied. What, then, makes the poet publish, in 1969 (*Le Chien de cœur*), the anguished question with which I began: «Je vais parler et je sais dire, mais quel est l'écho hostile qui m'interrompt?» To this question, which he follows with the dates 1944-67, Char himself knows the answer. It was the *maquis* which silenced and still threatens to interrupt the poet. It was the Captain of Céreste who killed what the poet of the Sorgue fought so long to revive. «Depuis là,» says René Char, referring to the massacres of the *maquis* and his part in them, «j'ai perdu le chant» (17).

---

(17) In a private interview, April 1970.

3

FROM WATER TO VAPOR, VIOLENCE TO MAGIC:

«EXPLOIT DU CYLINDRE À VAPEUR»

> La formule magique dévore la gerbe d'épis
> Le grand météore de l'insomnie
> Enflamme l'incurable vertèbre tournante du médium
>
> Poésie riche de conséquences
> («Les Liaisons sentimentales de l'image,» *Poèmes militants*, 1934).
>
> La violence était magique,
> L'homme quelquefois mourait,
> Mais à l'instant de l'agonie,
> Un trait d'ambre scellait ses yeux.
> («Cet amour à tous retiré,» *Les Matinaux*, 1950).

In his *Histoire du Surréalisme*, (1) Maurice Nadeau pays only passing attention to René Char whom he mentions pêle-mêle with other newcomers to the «second wave» of surrealism, men like Dali and Buñuel who joined Breton's camp in 1929. Marcel Raymond sets aside Char and Gisèle Prassinos as notable exceptions to the blind followers of Breton who «montrent jusqu'où peuvent aller les possibilités ornementales de la rhétorique de l'absurde» (2). Jean-Louis Bédouin in *La Poésie Surréaliste* prints only two texts from *Ralentir*

---

(1) Maurice Nadeau, *Histoire du Surréalisme* (Paris: Editions du Seuil, 1964), p. 131.
(2) Marcel Raymond, *De Baudelaire au Surréalisme* (Paris: José Corti, nouvelle édition revue et remaniée, 1966), p. 350.

Travaux, «Page blanche,» and «Décors,» neither one of which contains verses by Char (3). A recent critic, Georges Mounin, underlines «l'effort par où Char échappe au surréalisme figé pour demeurer poète vivant» (4). John H. Matthews writes: «Like Eluard's, Char's originality came in the years subsequent to his association with surrealism. As with Eluard, those who respect and like Char's poetry generally ignore its ties with surrealism (4a).

The poet's own attitude towards his surrealist apprenticeship is expressed in two letters preserved in *Recherche de la Base et du Sommet,* 1965. The first of these, the «Lettre hors commerce» already quoted, was sent to André Breton on 18 February, 1947 and contains the following reflections:

> Où en suis-je aujourd'hui? Je ne sais au juste. J'ai de la difficulté à me reconnaître sur le fil des évidences dont je suis l'interné et le témoin, l'écuyer et le cheval. Ce n'est pas moi qui ai simplifié les choses, mais les choses horribles m'ont rendu simple, plus apte à faire confiance à certains, au fond desquels subsistent, tenaces, les feux mourants de la recherche et de la dignité humaine (cette dignité si mal réalisable dans l'action, et dans cet état hybride qui lui succède) ailleurs déjà anéantis et balayés, méprisés et niés... C'est te dire que si certains prodiges ont cessé de compter pour moi, je n'en défends pas moins, de toute mon énergie, le droit de s'affirmer prodigieux. Je ne serai jamais assez loin, assez perdu dans mon indépendance ou son illusion, pour avoir le cœur de ne plus aimer les fortes têtes désobéissantes qui descendent au fond du cratère, sans se soucier des appels du bord...

---

(3) Jean-Louis Bédouin, *La Poésie Surréaliste* (Paris: Seghers, 1964), pp. 355-356.

(4) Georges Mounin, *La Communication poétique précédé de Avec-vous lu Char?* (Paris: Gallimard, 1969), p. 89.

(4a) John H. Matthews, *Surrealist Poetry in France* (New York: Syracuse Univ. Press, 1969), p. 114.

Tu peux faire figurer à cette Exposition «qui je fus» en 1930-1934. Je puis dire en quelques lignes, si tu le désires, mon affection durable pour ce grand moment de ma vie qui ne connut jamais d'adieu, seulement les mutations conformes à notre nature et au temps. Rien de banal entre nous. Nous avons su et saurons toujours nous retrouver côte à côte, à la seconde excessive de l'essentiel. Notre particularité consiste à n'être indésirables qu'en fonction de notre refus de signer le dernier feuillet, celui de l'apaisement. Celui-ci s'arrache—ou nous est enlevé.

Char juxtaposes with these lines, which seem to mark him as one of the «derniers fidèles» of surrealism, a letter addressed to Henri Peyre in 1963, in which he explains:

Le mariage d'un esprit de vingt ans avec un violent fantôme, décevant comme nous sommes, nousmêmes, décevants, ne peut être que le fait d'une révolte naturelle qui se transporte sur un miroir collectif, ou plutôt sur un feu compagnon qu'un rapide divorce des parties bientôt éteindra. Parce que ce que nous cherchions n'était pas découvrable à plusieurs, parce que la vie de l'esprit, la vie unifilaire, contrairement à celle du cœur, n'est fascinée, dans la tentation de la poésie, que par un objet souverain inapprochable qui vole en éclats lorsque, distance franchie, nous sommes sur le point de la toucher...
Le surréalisme a accompli son voyage; l'Histoire lui a aménagé des gares et des aéroports, en attendant d'en trier dans une bibliothèque routinière les beautés et les poussières, ce qui demeurera son enfantillage, mais aussi son faste et ses justes imprécations. Que notre jeunesse n'ait pas pensé à cela, elle a eu bien raison. Ce n'est pas à moi qu'il appartient d'examiner contradictoirement le surréalisme dans ses effets, les détestables et les autres. Une source devenant ruisseau, inondant des terres, salissant les murs, n'est point *fautive*. L'homme, n'est-ce

pas, n'est qu'un excès de matière solaire, avec une ombre de libre arbitre comme dard. Sur un cratère d'horreurs et sous la nuit imbécile s'épanouit soudain, au niveau de ses narines et de ses yeux, la fleur réfractaire, la nova écumante, dont le pollen va se mêler, un pur moment, à son esprit auquel ne suffisaient pas l'intelligence terrestre argutieuse et les usages du ciel (5).

In recent years, Char has refused to be classified in anthologies of surrealist poetry, as he has always refused all labels and categorizations. Yet whatever the poet's public statements or private motives, Char's participation in the surrealist movement—if never a whole-hearted commitment—is, nevertheless, a fact of literary history, a fact which, furthermore, played a decisive role in the development of the poet and the man.

Between 1929-1934, Char signed a number of surrealist tracts, including the questionnaire in defense of Buñuel's film *L'Age d'or,* 1931, and *La Planète sans visa,* 1934, which protested Trotsky's expulsion from France and French territory. Char participated in *L'Affaire Aragon,* 1932, and in the creation of Breton's second version of *La Révolution Surréaliste,* the movement's official organ, rebaptized, in 1930, *Le Surréalisme au Service de la Révolution,* to mark, as Aragon recalls, its anti-individualist and materialist evolution:

> L'entrée dans le groupe surréaliste de certains éléments (Char, Dali, Buñuel) qui possèdent des moyens d'expression extrêmement précieux pour la vie de ce groupe et l'extension de son action a compensé au-delà de ce qu'on pouvait espérer le départ de tant de velléitaires confus et de littérateurs décidés. Le groupe ainsi renforcé a fondu une revue: *le S. A. S. D. L. R.* manifestant, par cette modification

---

(5) This last text appears first in the 1965 edition of *Recherche de la Base et du Sommet.*

de l'ancien titre (*la R. S.*), le sens général anti-indivi-
dualiste et matérialiste de son évolution... (6).

Under the auspices of the *Editions surréalistes,* Char published,
we remember, *L'Action de la Justice est éteinte* in 1931 and
Le Marteau sans maître in 1934.

The latter, which is the poet's first *florilège* of his early
verse, contained, in 1934, five sections: *Arsenal,* 1927-29;
Artine, 1930; *L'Action de la Justice est éteinte,* 1931; *Poèmes
militants,* 1931-33, and *Abondance viendra,* 1932-33.   While
Char was not an official member of the Paris group after 1934,
works like *Moulin premier,* 1935-36; *Placard pour un chemin
des écoliers,* 1937, and *Dehors la nuit est gouvernée,* first
published in 1938, still show surrealist traits.

During his brief surrealist apprenticeship, Char gained, I
believe, two important insights: 1.) the realization that the
existing socio-political order was in need of re-examination,
and 2.) the certainty that violence and destruction would not
solve the problems faced by his—or any—generation.   A third
step remained to be taken, but the last and decisive mile men
like Char and Eluard had to walk alone, after the dissolution
of their formal association (7).   The *fureur* and revolt against
society had to lead back to the *mystère* of the individual.
Alone, and within himself, René Char sought the answer to
the apparent contradictions of a world shared by partisan and
poet, violence and magic.   I would attempt to show here some
aspects of Char's development through and beyond surrealism,
an evolution from the anarchy of *Le Marteau sans maître,* to
the harmony of *Les Matinaux.*

«Jusqu'à nouvel ordre, à la poésie courtisane, brut opposer
le poème *offensant,* tige de maçonnerie, résidence et parc
d'attractions, de sécurité, d'agression et de reconnaissance du
lecteur» (*Moulin premier,* XXXIV) (8).   The keynotes of

---

(6) Nadeau, *op. cit.,* p. 141.
(7) Others, like Aragon—perhaps afraid of self-confrontation—
opted in favor of a new alliance, a new platform.
(8) All quotations that follow are taken from the 1963 edition

Char's poetry between 1930-34 are given by words such as *attentat, barbare, blasphème, bourreaux, brutal, cadavre, carcan, cataclysme, catastrophe, coup, couteau, crasse, créneau, crever, crime, cruel, égorger, fer, gratter, matraque, meurtre, offensant, pourriture, rage, résistance, révolution, rude, saigner, sang, sauvage, scandale, sévère, suicide, supplice, tomber, trancher, tuer, viol, violence, violent*—almost all unknown to *Les Cloches sur le cœur.*

The new titles, too, are significant. *Arsenal* adds the poem «Masque de fer.» *L'Action de la Justice est éteinte,* dedicated to André Breton, announces the new reign of anarchy. The third section of *Le Marteau sans maître, Poèmes militants,* has titles like «Métaux refroidis,» «Chaîne,» «Minerai» (later called «Les Asciens»), «Le Supplice improvisé,» «Fanatisme» (a poem originally dedicated to Tristan Tzara and retitled «Cruauté» in the 1945 edition), and «Bourreaux de solitude.» The collection itself seems to borrow its title from «Balles animales,» a poem of *Les Cloches sur le cœur,* which ended:

> Le fil se dévide
> Aux soies des drapeaux
> Dont les franges vibrent
> Au choc des marteaux

The once harmless tool has become—as in Rimbaud's poem «Le Forgeron»—the revolutionary's weapon. However, the last two sections of *Le Marteau sans maître* strike a gentler note, and long passages of *Abondance viendra,* dedicated to Eluard, are made up of meditative prose.

Char's theoretical writings of this period underline his new concept of poetry. In *Le Surréalisme au Service de la Révolution,* no. 4, 1932, he published «Propositions-Rappel,» a prose text from which some of the aphorisms of *Moulin premier* are borrowed. The article begins:

---

of *Le Marteau sans maître, suivi de Moulin premier* (Paris: José Corti). Variants between this and previous editions are pointed out when significant.

Ce qui fait la qualité d'un esprit poétique, c'est la proie de plus en plus dangereuse qu'il assigne au pouvoir illimité de son action.

And the statement ends:

La pensée poétique vivante de ce que vous désirez semblera pouvoir être énoncée dans sa meilleure forme quand les images symboliques *quitteront* leur signification pacifique, exactement comme le locataire a pris congé dans le temps du propriétaire —c'est ainsi qu'on doit voir le mouvement *sortir* de l'immobilité—ne résisteront plus au néant qui les aspire et, se détruisant réciproquement, viendront s'identifier à leurs cendres primitives. Descendance révolutionnaire.

«Devant les responsabilités du poème, sans hilarité, j'aime à croire le poète capable de proclamer la loi martiale pour alimenter son inspiration. L'étincelle dépose» (*Moulin premier,* VII). Char's new poetics is illustrated in a poem of *L'Action de la Justice est éteinte,* entitled «Les Soleils chanteurs,» which I quote below in its definitive (1963) version. This text mentions the kinds of violence—natural catastrophies, accidents, suicide, sickness, crime—which the young surrealist poet would call upon to revitalize poetry:

Les disparitions inexplicables
Les accidents imprévisibles
Les malheurs un peu gros
Les catastrophes de tout ordre
Les cataclysmes qui noient et qui carbonisent
Le suicide considéré comme un crime
Les dégénérés intraitables
Ceux qui s'entourent la tête d'un tablier de forgeron
Les naïfs de première grandeur
Ceux qui descendent le cercueil de leur mère au fond
    d'un puits
Les cerveaux incultes
Les cervelles de cuir

Ceux qui hivernent à l'hôpital et que leur linge éclaté
   enivre encore
La mauve des prisons
L'ortie des prisons
La pariétaire de prisons
Le figuier allaiteur de ruines
Les silencieux incurables
Ceux qui canalisent l'écume du monde souterrain
Les amoureux dans l'extase
Les poètes terrassiers
Les magiciens à l'épi
Règnent température clémente autour des fauves
   embaumeurs du travail.

The 1934 version also made reference to

Ceux qui assassinent les orphelins jouant du clairon
...
Les artisans incendiaires
La traite des vampires
Le blasphème exterminateur

and ended with the «embaumeurs»

Travaillant sur les cadavres des sifflets

These lines are deleted in the definitive version of the poem,
which adds lines 13, 15, 16, and 17 quoted above.

   Another text of *L'Action de la Justice est éteinte,* entitled
simply «Poème,» adds to the previous list «le crime passionnel,
le viol, l'attentat à la pudeur, sources authentiques de la poésie.» «Le Cheval de corrida,» part of the original *Poèmes
militants,* 1931-1933, but deleted from later editions, similarly
stated:

Le nœud du suicide dénonce le soin méticuleux des
   intraitables
...
Que la ventouse d'immortelle brise les sortilèges de
   glu dans les silos des asiles d'aliénés

...
L'hyène et la fourmi vautours de l'amour
Dénudant le cadavre refroidi de la batteuse suprême

It is believed, at this time, that poetry, the «rose violente,» is best cultivated in a violent «climat de chasse.» Crime is not only honorable, but essential to the emergence of new art forms.

Breton's *beauté convulsive* is sought by Char in every destructive act that would break down the established order of things. In *Le Surréalisme au Service de la Révolution,* no. 3, 1931, he published the poem «Arts et Métiers,» which becomes «Métaux refroidis» in *Poèmes militants.* The original text read, in part, as follows:

Touriste des crépuscules
Dans tes parcs
Le filon de foudre
Se perd sous terre
Or nocturne

Habitant de l'espace de la femme que j'aime
Le vert-de-gris des bêches va fleurir
...
Sa forme est révolutionnaire dans le sang
Entre ses mains
Ma tête
Avec ses bancs et ses promenades
Ma tête
Ne vaut pas
Une pierre pour la fracasser
Un marécage pour l'enliser
Un lac pour la noyer
Une hache pour la trancher
Une cartouche de dynamite pour la pulvériser
Un tombeau pour la souiller
Un charbon pour la dessiner
Un pont pour la traverser
Un scandale pour la retirer
Un crime pour l'honorer

— 177 —

Introuvable sommeil
Arbre couché sur ma poitrine
Pour détourner les sources rouges
Faudra-t-il te suivre longtemps
Dans ta croissance éternelle

As it passes into the *Poèmes militants,* this text is de-personalized: «Ma tête» is replaced by «La tête lointaine nébuleuse,» and the crimes perpetrated upon it pass from the virtual to the actual state. «Une pierre pour la fracasser» is turned into «La pierre qui la fracasse;» «Un crime pour l'honorer» becomes «Le crime qui l'honore,» etc. Personal revolt turns into generalized revolution. Char now advocates a poetry of action that will *pulverize* the statuesque verse of the Parnassians and the Mallarméan ideal of «la tête lointaine nébuleuse.» In 1947, he will publish *Le Poème pulvérisé.*

This new poetry requires a new language. Gone is the melancholy tone of *Les Cloches sur le cœur,* gone the late-romantic *plaintes* of «Ce soir.» «Les mondes éloquents ont été perdus» is Char's paraphrase of Verlaine (*«La Main de Lacenaire,» L'Action de la Justice...*). He no longer aims for the polished quatrains of his beginnings, but looks instead for «les mots à forte carrure,» Breton's «phrases qui cognent à la vitre,» words couched in the staccato rhythms of everyday speech.

In the best surrealist tradition (and following Lautréamont, whom he read at this time), Char speaks of revolt against the order of nature, against the established socio-political order, and against the ethic and aesthetic codes imposed by man upon both. Hence references to sickness, suicide, fratricide, matricide, regicide, and to the generally unaccepted forms of love. To Sade, rediscovered by Apollinaire and celebrated by the surrealists, Char writes an «Hommage» which ends: «Sade, l'amour enfin sauvé de la boue du ciel, l'hypocrisie passée par les armes et par les yeux, cet héritage suffira aux hommes contre la famine, leurs belles mains d'étrangleur sorties des poches» (*Le Surréalisme au Service de la Révolution,* no. 2, 1931). This text, originally a contribution to Breton's inquiry into the «Actualité de Sade,» reappears, with variants, in the *Poèmes militants.* In *Moulin premier* (XLIV), Char celebrates Onan in these terms: «Onan consommé—suave sécheresse—le trajet de son sperme pose un problème de magie formelle...» In *Placard pour un chemin des écoliers,* Char will tell of a young girl's love for a puma. In the passage just quoted from *Moulin premier,* magic and violence—here, violence to nature—are associated explicitly for the first time. Such an association was already implied, however, in the enumerations of «Les Soleils chanteurs» that linked the «disparitions inexplicables» and the «accidents imprévisibles» to the «magiciens à l'épi.»

Char finds his most suitable metaphors for the alliance of violence and magic in the world of the mineral. He describes the poet as a wheelbarrow living «dans les nacelles de l'enclume» («Poètes,» *L'Action de la Justice...*), writing his poem «la tête sur la pointe de [son] couteau» («L'Artisanat furieux,» *ibid.*). In the same vein, he speaks of the «conflits mortels d'origine minérale mystérieuse, constituant dans le règne une nouveauté dont le déni d'amour radicalement insoluble semble l'expression naturelle» («Poème,» *ibid.*), and he writes of the «pierre catastrophique» which is poetry («L'Instituteur révoqué,» *ibid.*). The original version of «Les Asciens,» «Minerai,» contained these lines:

> Le cheval conducteur n'appartient pas à la platitude
> historique
> Mais à la poésie criminelle

The text also mentions the «nœud du métal / Qui donne la mort / Sans laisser de trace,» lines which end the original and the revised versions of the poem. In «Le Cheval de corrida,» Char spoke of the «gaz carboniques,» and expressed the hope

> Que les métaux voient leur lit déserté par la mollesse
> des époux
> Que la culture pompe sans relâche l'eau du tombeau

«L'Accident dans la plaine,» later retitled simply «Plaine,» originally ended with the line: «Et le roulement de la tôle qui voile la vue des monuments.» The 1934 version of «Domaine» (*Abondance viendra*) introduced the reader to

> ... les mines du Salut la Rêverie Féodale, le mythe du Pied Calciné au sommet de la Tour Pariétale, l'obscur tourniquet pulmonaire, l'hectare phosphorescent, fébrile bourgeon noir...

A text entitled «Intégration» (*ibid.*) contains this apostrophe to chalk:

> Craie, qui parla sur les tableaux noirs une langue plastique dérivée du naphte—auditoire civil, de santé moyenne,—j'évoque les charmes de tes épaisseurs voilées, siège de la cabale.

The poem «Voyageur sans tunnel,» which became «L'Oracle du grand oranger» (*L'Action de la Justice est éteinte*) shows, in 1934, the following lines:

> Tête écorchée
> Une pincée de soufre dans une assiette à cet usage
>
> Et remue le tonneau amer
> Un jet de vitriol voici les courtes baleines
> Mobiles du grand oranger

In the *Poèmes militants,* Char celebrates the «Métaux refroidis,» the «herbe de plomb... herbe de mâchefer» («Vivante demain») and «l'oiseau rouge des métaux» («L'Historienne»). In *Abondance viendra,* he mentions the «radium sauvage» («Les Rapports entre parasites»), the «chaînes magnétiques» (*ibid.*), the «cœur chloroformé» («Devant soi,» *ibid.*), and, finally, «les multiples propriétés occultes dérivées du phosphore poétique autonome meurtrier» (*Moulin premier,* XII).

«Je ne sais pas d'où viennent à René Char ses images empruntées au vocabulaire de la chimie,» writes Georges Mounin (*op. cit.,* p. 45). John H. Matthews sees in chemicals and metals militant elements that underline the theme of revolt. He writes:

> The image of rot and decay is resisted in Char's poetry by the introduction of the image of transformation, involving chemical change. The figure of the rotting corpse is replaced by that of metals resistant to rust and, in the context of alchemical thought, susceptible to modification and elevation, rather than deterioration and decay. More than representatives of resistance and purification, these bright metals attract Char because they take on the lustre of revolt. In his view, they are worthy of mention among the active, militant elements which should hold our attention in the universe about us (*op. cit.,* p. 118).

Chemicals, metals, and machinery are, of course, «natural» ingredients in early twentieth century verse. In the poetry of René Char, they represent that which is permanent. *Imputrescible* is one of the poet's earliest *mots-thèmes,* already found in the poem «Drames» included in the original *Poèmes militants,* 1931-33. The poetry of alchemy and metal also rings in a farewell to romantic verse and its endless hymns to nature. By his celebration of the «unnatural,» Char aims to «charger d'explosif» the «épais guano des migrations romantiques» (*Moulin premier*) (9). His metal hammer beats the rhythm of *Les Matinaux* and dictates even the final eloquence of Orion: «Il te fut prêté de dire une fois à la belle, à la sourcilleuse distance les chants matinaux de la rébellion. Métal rallumé sans cesse de ton chagrin, ils me parvenaient humides d'inclémence et d'amour» («Eloquence d'Orion,» *Aromates chasseurs*).

Chemicals and metal must be an integral part of Char's

---

(9) References to excrements are frequent in Char's early poetry, which is full of Rimbaldian echoes.

«intimate space.» In the *récit de rêve,* «A quoi je me destine,» examined earlier, the poet records his vision of «une pièce infiniment peu attirante, probablement une ancienne cuisine désaffectée. Un alambic est accroché à un clou de la plinthe... Un placard dont on a ôté les battants qui est aussi une forge...» The furnace and the hearth, the smithy's and the baker's are the favorite resting-places on «imagination's way.» But quite aside from literary fad and private fancy, are chemicals not the most secret, most elusive, most «magical» of man's weapons? And to those born, like Char, into World War I, was not gas the atomic bomb of the day?

In Char's post-surrealist poetry, references to metals and chemicals are rare. There are the notable exceptions of the «coq de fer» in «Déclarer son nom,» a poem of 1959 that recalls the year 1917, and the «abeille de fer» of «Apparition d'Aerea,» a prose poem first published in 1962 (10). Both are symbols of war. The call to arms is, however, in the end, muted into the whisper of stars, as Orion, «pigmenté d'infini et de soif terrestre» no longer sharpens his arrow on the ancient scythe, but

> Les traits noircis par le fer calciné,
> Le pied toujours prompt à éviter la faille,
> Se plut avec nous
> Et resta.

> Chuchotement parmi les étoiles.
> («Evadé d'archipel,» *Aromates chasseurs*).

Evocations, or rather, provocations of violence of any type diminish in Char's poetry after 1938. At least, violence and aggression are no longer seen in the same light. It is no longer the poem or the poet that is «offensant d'agression,» but the world around them.

---

(10) The poem is republished as «Aux portes d'Aerea» in *L'Arc,* no. 22, été 1963, p. 49, before becoming part of *Retour amont* (Paris: G.L.M., 1965, and Gallimard, 1966).

At the time of the Spanish Civil War, René Char dedicates his *Placard pour un chemin des écoliers* to the children of Spain:

> Enfants d'Espagne, j'ai formé ce **PLACARD** alors que les yeux matinals de certains d'entre vous n'avaient encore rien appris des usages de la mort qui se coulait en eux. Pardon de vous le dédier. Avec ma dernière réserve d'espoir.
>
> Mars 1937 (11)

Throughout the dedication, Char contrasts his own pastoral childhood with that prepared in 1937 for the children born to violence and war. He juxtaposes the natural green world of fruits, flowers and prairies to the unnatural red and murderous world of steel. The dedication begins:

> Enfants d'Espagne, —ROUGES, oh combien, à embuer pour toujours l'éclat de l'acier qui vous déchiquète; — A Vous.

The songs and fables of this collection (finally republished in 1971), are among the most haunting poetry Char ever wrote, and one would have to go back all the way to the anonymous Spanish *romances* of the fifteenth and sixteenth centuries to find a poem that would equal the mysterious beauty of such poems as, for example, «Compagnie de l'écolière.»

A reverse process of the one noted in *Le Marteau sans maître* takes place in these poems of 1934-36. Whereas the natural world was once condemned to death through calcification, we now see even the mineral world come alive. Though already in «Arts et Métiers,» 1931, Char had expressed the hope that «le vert-de-gris des bêches va fleurir,» his early poetic universe was more aptly described by these lines from «Les

---

(11) All quotations that follow are taken, unless otherwise indicated, from the 1949 edition of *Dehors la nuit est gouvernée précédé de Placard pour un chemin des écoliers* (Paris: G.L.M.).

Rapports entre parasites» (*Abondance viendra*): «Témoin, dans les relais de ton esprit réaliste, le règne végétal est figuré par la plante carnivore, le règne minéral par le radium sauvage, le règne animal par l'ascendant du tigre.» The 1931 poem «Drames» speaks with similar condescension of «le règne végétal»:

> Pour conclure les réactionnaires seront consumés
> dans les retraites végétales
> La réalité niée dans le dernier meurtre

This is a world dehumanized by the word, a world in which man's part is death.

This *Weltanschauung,* reminiscent of Lautréamont's, gives way, in later poems, to a complete reversal of values. In the poems of 1935-46, the mineral assumes the properties of the animal—or, even more frequently—vegetal world, now seen in a more favorable light. For this world—though it is of a vital and ever changing nature—yet does not grow out of hand like *Le Marteau sans maître.* It is a world friendly to man, in which the poet—and the children—move with ease. Everything lives in the mind of a child. Everything seemingly inert changes place and shape:

> Tu marches comme un incendie de forêt
> Puma mon bien-aimé
> ...
>
> Aussitôt les pierres se gonflèrent à éclater
> Les crottins s'enfuirent...
> («Allée du confident, II,» *Placard pour un
> chemin des écoliers*)

Among the most beautiful of Char's opening lines are the following from «Compagnie de l'écolière» (*ibid.*):

> Je sais bien que les chemins marchent
> Plus vite que les écoliers
> Attelés à leur cartable

> Roulant dans la glu des fumées
> Où l'automne perd le souffle

In a much later poem, «Griffe,» from *La Nuit talismanique,*
1972, he comes back to the same theme:

> Marcheur voûté, le ciel s'essouffle vite;
> Médiateur, il n'est pas entendu;
> Moi je le peins bleu sur bleu, or sur noir.
> Ce ciel est un cartable d'écolier
> Taché de mûres.

The poet achieves an extraordinary swiftness in these poems
which show all matter in perpetual motion. The roads run
along more quickly than the children on their way from school.
Autumn and the sky are out of breath, «l'horizon devient rose
il bouge» («Les Oursins de Pégomas»).

Preference is now given to vegetal matter:

> Nous écrasons les derniers squelettes vibrants du
>   parc idéal
> D'un bout à l'autre de la distance hors mémoire
> Nous apparaissons comme les végétaux complets
> Envahisseurs du nouvel âge primitif...

In the new primitive age announced above by «Les Asciens»
(*Poèmes militants*), the stars have a «tige émoussée;» even
metal grows like a flower: «Ce wagonnet détaché de son train
s'établit tige» («Validité,» later retitled «Postface,» *Dehors la
nuit...*). The original poem of *Arsenal* called «La Guerre sous
roche» becomes «Transfuges» in the 1934 edition, and begins:

> Sang enfin libérable
> L'aérolithe dans la véranda
> Respire comme une plante

The human body itself is made to partake of the vegetal
world. All heaviness is taken from it. The poet now speaks
of the «ajoncs de son sang» («Compagnie de l'écolière,»

Placard...), and of «le lierre de [son] corps» («Les Vivres du retour,» *ibid.*). In *Dehors la nuit est gouvernée,* this type of imagery also abounds. The title poem begins: «Peuples de roseaux bruns...» and speaks of «l'île de son ventre,» of the «printemps de sa ville.» The next poem opens with an address to «Tous compagnons de lit florissants... .» In the same text, the first line of stanza four originally read:

> Chers allongés qui avez amené le sang prestigieux
> sur des hauteurs où ne se montre guère de
> *légumes*

a reading restored in the 1971 edition of *Placard...* . As late as 1972, Char asks, in a hymn to night: «... sommes-nous, au déclin de ce jour, plus végétal que la fleur du mirabilis?» (*La Nuit talismanique*).

In the poems of 1934-38, the poet—«apprenti de la combustion»—bursts in upon himself. The revitalization of poetry is no longer achieved through explosive violence and arbitrary aggression upon nature (practiced by the sorcerer's apprentice of *Le Marteau sans maître*), but by renewal from within. The poet looks at himself, at his own creation, at his own past:

> A ton tour d'entrer en éruption
> Tablier du forgeron ciel charnel de ma sombre
> enfance
>> («Dépendance de l'adieu,» *Dehors la nuit
>> est gouvernée*).

Man cannot relate to the world by destroying it. Rather, he must adjust his vision so as to bring the apparent chaos of the universe into proper focus. He must seek to discover veiled and secret relationships visible only to the inner eye:

> Je retiens de ce fluide qui se desserre me tourmente
> par un foulage de buées sans entrailles comme
> dans cette conjecture de la dégradation du Chas-

seur répétée par le papier à fleurs d'une minime
chambre
...

Que la chambre des machines se couche à tes pieds
...
O moule moisi de beauté en retrait sombre de la
forge des reins
Tu étais sortie tu allais passer
Vérité répétition neuve
Entre semelle et talon à l'air à l'arraché.

(«Confins,» ibid.).

Stars become flowers painted on a child's bedroom wall. The
machine, like a dog, lies down at the feet of man. Nature is
no longer the enemy, above and beyond us. It has come
down to our level and accepted the rule of man. In the diary
kept during his years in the *maquis,* the mature Char wrote
the following observation: «Résistance n'est qu'espérance.
Telle la lune d'Hypnos, pleine cette nuit de tous ses quartiers,
demain vision sur le passage des poèmes» (*Feuillets d'Hypnos,*
no. 168). And this full moon of hope which watches over
the poet and his art takes on the color of sage: «La lune est
d'étain vif et de sauge» (*ibid.,* no. 148). Though once a hostile
element, the celestial body now partakes of the healing power
of the plant (*salvus*) and comes to the rescue of poet and partisan. Orion, returning to the earth, offers the aromatic herb
that heals and joins, as in marriage, winter and summer, earth
and sky: (12)

Un bouquet de thym en décembre, une griffe de
sauge après neige, de la centaurée dès qu'elle aimera,
un échelon de basilic, la renouée des chemins devant
sa chambre nuptiale...

---

(12) In *La Nuit talismanique,* the herb also mediates between
expression and description, poetry and painting. The caption under
a wax bas-relief entitled «La Sauge des villages,» reads: «Entre
l'exprimé et le décrit, j'offre la fleur de sauge.»

Que le ciel, lorsqu'elle sortira, lui donne son vent
rapide.
(«La Dot de Maubergeonne,» *Aromates chasseurs*).

In *Feuillets d'Hypnos* all of nature participates in the quest
for harmony. The red metal birds of *Poèmes militants* turn
into the white birds of peace, «les météores hirondelles»
(no. 175) that speak with a voice of gold (no. 230). In *La
Nuit talismanique,* the poet again remembers the meteor-bird
metaphor:

Les arbres ne se questionnent pas entre eux, mais
trop rapprochés, ils font le geste de s'éviter. De
la chênaie s'élance trois fois l'appel du coucou,
l'oiseau qui ne commerce pas. Pareil au chant votif
du météore.

(«Volets tirés fendus»).

The meteor suggests the arrow and the sting, made harmless in
Orion's land:

Qui cherchez-vous brunes abeilles
Dans la lavande qui s'éveille?
Passe votre roi serviteur.
Il est aveugle et s'éparpille.
Chasseur il fuit
Les fleurs qui le poursuivent.
Il tend son arc et chaque bête brille.
Haute est sa nuit; flèches risquez vos chances.

Un météore humain a la terre pour miel.
(«Réception d'Orion,» *Aromates chasseurs*).

In Char's post-surrealist poetry, everything once heavy and
destructive suddenly becomes light and life-bearing. His world
undergoes the vegetal transformations of Maldoror. In the
Poèmes militants, even the grass was made of lead and stone.
Now lead is melted; it flows like oil and is, in the end, transformed into the alchemist's gold:

> Fils cette nuit nos travaux de poussière
> Seront visibles dans le ciel
> Déjà l'huile du plomb ressuscite
> («Courbet: Les casseurs de cailloux,»
> *Dehors la nuit est gouvernée*).

Rocks are pulverized into sand. Stones are no longer instruments of torture and death, «pierres catastrophiques,» but agents of nature's healing power: «Limon secouru nuit guérie» («Dépendance de l'adieu»). The rock is made fertile:

> Sable paille ont la vie douce le vin ne s'y brise pas
> Du colombier ils récoltent les plumes
> De la goulotte ils ont la langue avide
> Ils retardent l'orteil des filles
> Dont ils percent les chrysalides
> Le sang bien souffert tombe dans l'anecdote de
>   leur légèreté.
>   («Courbet: Les casseurs de cailloux»).

As the body takes on the properties of vegetal matter, so the mineral assumes human form. Char now sees in the rock the protective form of an eyelid («l'écueil en forme de paupière,» «Le Tireur d'oublies»). The forge becomes «la forge des reins» («Confins») . Everything is taken down one step (judged by Char's original scale of values), so that the mineral world completely disappears or else is subjugated to the animal will: «Que la chambre des machines se couche à tes pieds»!

«Haine nous te fendrons le roc avant de tomber à genoux,» proclaims the speaker of «Tous compagnons de lit.» The poet's admiration is no longer reserved for the harsh or the unnatural. Only one poem of *Dehors la nuit est gouvernée, «Octroi,»* keeps the cold and dehumanized imagery of Char's surrealist verse. I would presume that it is an early piece, and it is not among the best in the collection:

> Au sommet du glacier de l'Assiette
> Voulez-vous me passer votre main
> ...

Entre le cylindre et la route
Rien ne retient les cantonniers
De partager notre horreur
Des chemises véreuses comme des églises

Voix amies le plomb des fourchettes
Navre l'ivoire de la langue
...

The slightly pretentious and precious note («l'ivoire de la langue»), the sophisticated humor («passer *la main,*» not, for example, *le pain*), the fashionable anti-religious metaphor (all this in the best Breton tradition of «le merveilleux est toujours beau, n'importe quel merveilleux est beau,» a credo to which the young Char may have subscribed) would lead me to believe that «Octroi» was written in the early 1930's.

For already in *Placard pour un chemin des écoliers,* Char has surpassed this early manner and exchanged what I would call «le merveilleux de manufacture» (the poet himself speaks of «la Sainte de manufacture» in *Le Marteau sans maître*) for the marvelous of a fairy-tale entitled «Exploit du cylindre à vapeur.» Of this poem, which reads like the transposition of a true childhood recollection, Georges Mounin writes:

> Mais c'est le «Cylindre à vapeur» qui est à lui tout seul un roman de l'enfance. Un conte plus beau que tous ceux de Grimm ou de Perrault, dans lequel au lieu d'un fantastique à base de folklore, le poète restitue l'une de ces nombreuses aventures de notre véritable enfance où le fantastique est issu, sans artifice, de la vision même de l'enfant que nous nous souvenons d'avoir été (*op. cit.,* p. 121).

We may not agree with the critic's rhyming comparisons, but the «Cylindre à vapeur» is certainly the most fabulous—in the fairly-tale sense of the word—story told by the young poet. Here Char succeeds in creating a world he had only hoped for in *Poèmes militants,* as he transforms an ordinary steamroller into the symbol of:

Tout ce qui se détache convulsivement de l'unité
    du monde
De la masse débloquée par la simple poussée d'un
    enfant
Et fond sur nous à toute vitesse
Nous qui ne confondons pas les actes à vivre et les
    actes vécus
Qui ne savons pas désirer en priant
Obtenir en simulant
...

                    («L'Historienne,» *Poèmes militants*).

Better than all the aggressive verse of *Le Marteau sans maître,*
«Exploit du cylindre à vapeur» captures «tout ce qui se détache
convulsivement de l'unité du monde,» the *beauté convulsive*
sought by Breton.

The poem's story line seems simple enough. It opens by
contrasting the adult world, «laid comme un gendarme,» with
the marvelous world of childhood «which believeth all things»:

Nous autres sommes disposés
A tout espérer à tout croire
Nous faisons tourner nos toupies
Dans le rayon de vos battoirs
Par vent de neige et canicule
Grandes personnes étrangères
Pour un royaume de lézards
Nous ne vous tolérerions pas enrolé volontaire
Notre univers s'élance
Du point d'obsèques de votre raison

Une merveille la ficelle
D'elle qu'avez-vous obtenu
Un colis laid comme un gendarme
Car les filets sont l'invention
Du fantastique des poissons

Vous qui prétendez démêler les rides de nos sources
—Lequel est architecte et lequel est maçon?—

> Vos conceptions ne s'harmonisent guère
> Mais vous signez ensemble
> Tu es le soldat du traité
> Lourdaud qui pends la crémaillère
> Et endosses l'éboulement

After having set the stage for his «grand Guignol» («Une merveille la ficelle...»), the poet begins the actual story of the steamroller as it makes its way through the wintry ground:

> Dans la prairie où nous allions fumer
> Entre deux orages les gelées blanches y étendaient
>   leur peau
> Vint se garer un cylindre à vapeur
> Flexible comme une courtilière avec une énorme
>   tête de génie

«Dans la prairie où nous allions *fumer*,» writes the poet, not, as one might have expected, *jouer*. This is a fairy-tale «pour grandes personnes,» the kind that Breton had called for. Something of a circus atmosphere is generated by the poem. The steamroller has a «tête de génie.» It is driven by two gaily dressed men. In the trailer behind it, a pregnant and fickle woman awaits delivery:

> Des deux hommes qui le montaient
> Nous connûmes leurs foulards
> ...
>
> La roulotte contenait une femme enceinte
> Les Ponts et Chaussées fermaient les yeux
> Le trio ajournait à plaisir le temps de la délivrance

The show is accompanied by the sound of the rains, beating down like drums and interrupted by shouts of joy every time the sun reappears:

> Une interminable semaine
> Les tambours de la pluie tapèrent à se crever

Par la lucarne du grenier
Un ban de hourras fut poussé
En l'honneur du soleil réapparu
Charge au galop des galoches
Vers le pré tout saisi d'ajoncs

The «cylindre à vapeur» *is* the sun, melting away the hoarfrost, laying bare the flowers of the meadow. The machine, once a destructive force and the enemy of man, is now working for his benefit and pleasure, without upsetting the socio-political order—the Highway Department winks both eyes!—and without harming the order and beauty of man's natural environment. The steamroller turns into a kind of giant cricket that lives in perfect harmony with nature:

Le cylindre à l'écart plaqué sur l'horizon tel un
  mythe millénaire
Se cernait d'exotisme
Que nous étions heureux dans la prairie
Sous la protection de l'Ami
…
Quelque couleuvre aux anneaux gourds
A-t-elle expiré en cylindre
Qu'une dune se traîne
Maintenant là où il avait empire
…
L'Ami s'était creusé un grand trou dans la terre
  et avait tiré la boue sur lui
Cet exploit ne troubla rien
Aucune bêche ne fut dérangée
La fatalité se donna raison
En secret nous la commuâmes
Puis la roulotte un matin s'en fut derrière un
  Autre

The steamroller combines the properties of the snake with those of the moal-cricket. It can dig under the earth and jump up into the air. For the grown man who has kept alive the child's sense of wonder, the machine assumes exotic properties.

Transformed first into an ordinary insect, it is finally likened to a mythical being «plaqué sur l'horizon.» Then the actual machine, having accomplished its «exploit,» disappears, the trailer buries itself underground, leaving only the *bête innommable* (*La Paroi et la prairie*, 1952), sketched upon the horizon. Like the poet's later «Cerfs noirs» (*ibid.*), the steamroller has turned into pure vapors, leaving behind all the heavy machinery of earth:

Cerfs, vous avez franchi l'espace millénaire,
Des ténèbres du roc aux caresses de l'air

The tool has been freed from the parentheses of reason, from science and technocracy, to assert the miracle of its own being: (12a)

«Une science autoritaire se détache du groupe de ses sœurs modestes et brocarde le prodige de la vie dont elle tire une monnaie de peur. Toujours l'idée avilissant l'objet. La bête est devenue fabuleuse et spumeuse...

(«Lombes,» *Aromates chasseurs*).

«Et tant de conscience finit par tapisser l'éphémère. Chère roulotte!» («Aromates chausseurs,» *ibid.*). Char's youthful steamroller-cricket has all the ligthness and swiftness of air... and of Apollinaire's hymn to aviation. Char, who was an early admirer of Apollinaire, may well have remembered in the «Cylindre à vapeur» certain verses of «Zone.» The last stanza of the poem presents, furthermore, a typically Apollinairian

---

(12a) It is interesting to see Char come back, almost forty years after the «Cylindre à vapeur,» to the notion of the destructive tool made harmless by art. In his 1976 text accompanying the water-colors of Wifredo Lam, he writes: «La réplique à l'imagination chez un tel peintre est confondante puisque la faulx parvient à donner la vie au lieu de la prendre. Il est vrai, l'outil-roi n'existe qu'en vol...» (*De La sainte famille au Droit à la paresse*, Paris: Le Point cardinal, 1976).

device. The poet turns to his imaginary audience in the form of direct address: «Vous qui...» And the poem ends on the octosyllable, a favorite meter of both Apollinaire and Char:

> Vous qui ne croyez pas aux prodiges
> Aux crimes des feux follets
> A la ponte d'étoiles noires
> Sur les routes empierrées
> C'est vrai vous n'êtes que des hommes
> La vapeur que vous respirez
> Est de la vapeur de fantôme.

This last stanza underlines again the contrast between *nous autres*: artists, children, poets who can transform reality, and *vous autres*: ordinary mortals content to live in the ugly world of the gendarme. There is an immense pride in these lines: «Vous n'êtes que des hommes!» You are but men; you breathe but the ordinary (poisonous) vapors of the machine. But I the poet, I who believe in *prodiges* (a favorite word of Apollinaire and Char), I have seen in those vapors a *tête de génie*. I have named the *bête innommable* that is not found in your dictionaries of reason:

> Notre univers s'élance
> Du point d'obsèques de votre raison

I have transformed the *phosphore meurtrier* into the *ignis fatuus*. I have reduced the terror of gas war to the magic beauty of the will-o'-the-wisp. I have turned the crimes of war into the «crimes des feux follets,» into the «magiques assassinats d'insectes» (*Lettera amorosa*). My world is lifted up and reborn as yours is buried by the steamroller and destroyed.

* * *

> Le loriot entra dans la capitale de l'aube.
> L'épée de son chant ferma le lit triste.
> Tout à jamais prit fin.

3 septembre 1939 (*Fureur et Mystère*, 1948).

Then came World War II. Violence and aggression, once the intellectual prerogatives of an artistic elite, now became the ugly reality of everyday and every common life. Char, sent off to fight in Alsace, writes notes in a very different key:

> Saison d'animaux pacifiques, de filles sans méchanceté, vous détenez des pouvoirs que mon pouvoir contredit; vous avez les yeux de mon nom, ce nom qu'on me demande d'oublier.
>
> Glas d'un monde trop aimé, j'entends les monstres qui piétinent sur une terre sans sourire. Ma sœur vermeille est en sueur. Ma sœur furieuse appelle aux armes.
>
> La lune du lac prend pied sur la plage où le doux feu végétal de l'été descend à la vague qui l'entraîne vers un lit de profondes cendres...

This is the world of «Donnerbach Mühle,» a text that the poet dates «Hiver 1939.» In 1940, René Char, having joined the Resistance, seemingly bids farewell to the poet: «Le poète est retourné pour de longues années dans le néant du père. Ne l'appelez pas, vous tous qui l'aimez...» («Chant du refus,» *Neuf poèmes pour vaincre,* 1940-44).

Though Char continues to write, he publishes nothing during the difficult years of the Resistance. In a letter sent from the front (1941) to his good friend Francis Curel, he explains:

> ... Je ne désire pas publier dans une revue les poèmes que je t'envoie. Le recueil d'où ils sont extraits, et auquel en dépit de l'adversité je travaille, pourrait avoir pour titre *Seuls demeurent*. Mais je te répète qu'ils resteront longtemps inédits, aussi longtemps qu'il ne se sera pas produit quelque chose qui retournera entièrement l'innommable situation dans laquelle nous sommes plongés. Mes raisons me sont dictées en partie par l'assez incroyable et détestable exhibitionnisme dont font preuve depuis le mois de juin 1940 trop d'intellectuels parmi ceux dont le nom jadis était précédé ou suivi d'un prestige bienfaisant,

d'une assurance de solidité quand viendrait l'épreuve
qu'il n'était pas difficile de prévoir...

(*Recherche de la Base et du Sommet*, 1965).

Seuls demeurent finally appeared in February 1945. When
the larger war-time anthology *Fureur et Mystère* is published
in 1948, it contains no hymns to victory. There is not in all
of Char's poetry or prose of this period any of the playfulness
and exuberance of Apollinaire's *Calligrammes*. To this day,
one of the aspects Char most admires in the work of «Guy au
galop» is precisely this seemingly carefree verse written by
Apollinaire during his service at the front, where his sense of
wonder and joy was not troubled by the fear of annihilation
(13). Char's is a fundamentally different nature, and he is
fighting a different kind of war. In his letter of 28 February,
1974, quoted earlier, he writes: «La guerre de 1914 avait
libéré les enfants... Avec celle de 1940 ce fut tout le contraire: Les guerres sont totalitaires aujourd'hui et à géométrie
variable.» Char's war journal, *Feuillets d'Hypnos,* written
«dans la tension, la colère, la peur» (Preface), consists of cold
tactical calculations, philosophic meditations, short lyrical in-
termezzi and angry outcries against the senseless violence of
war. On a *carte inter-zones* the poet writes, on 8 November,
1942: «Je suis aujourd'hui pareil à un chien enragé enchaîné
à un arbre plein de rires et de feuilles» (*Fureur et Mystère*) (14).

In the midst of death and destruction, caught up in the
absurdity of war, Char forgets the lessons of surrealism and

---

(13) Char's reflections on Apollinaire are reported from a private
interview, April 1970.

(14) The quotations that follow are taken from the 1962 edition
of *Fureur et Mystère* (Paris: Gallimard), consisting of *Seuls demeurent* (1938-1944), *Feuillets d'Hypnos* (1943-1944), *Les Loyaux Adversaires* (1946), *Le Poème pulvérisé* (1945-1947) and *La Fontaine
narrative* (1947). The entries in Char's war diary are numbered.
These numbers follow my quotations from *Feuillets d'Hypnos*, in
the 1962 arrangement.

the songs of Maldoror. He denounces the murderous world
of the machine. In his diary he asks:

> Le cerveau, plein à craquer de machines, pourra-t-il
> encore garantir l'existence du mince ruisselet de rêve
> et d'évasion? L'homme, d'un pas de somnambule,
> marche vers les mines meurtrières, conduit par le
> chant des inventeurs...
>
> (*Feuillets d'Hypnos*, no. 127).

The poet now rebels against his intellectual heritage, against
the easy and comfortable superiority of the pessimist whom
he had once imitated, and he notes:

> Nous sommes des malades sidéraux incurables
> auxquels la vie sataniquement donne l'illusion de la
> santé. Pourquoi? Pour dépenser la vie et railler
> la santé?
> (Je dois combattre mon penchant pour ce genre
> de pessimisme atonique, héritage intellectuel...)
> (*ibid.*, no. 80).

He who had once called on the «dégénérés intraitables» and
on the «silencieux incurables» to revitalize poetry, he would
now prefer to leave the «routes de la mémoire...couvertes de
la lèpre infaillible des monstres» and seek refuge «dans une
innocence où l'homme qui rêve ne peut vieillir» («Envoûtement
à la Renardière,» *Seuls demeurent*, 1938-1944).

Violence and aggression are no longer gratuitous, sickness
and death no longer the subject matter of revolutionary poetry.
Face to face with the reality of war, Char seeks to return to
childhood innocence and peace, to the world of health to which
his first postwar aphorisms, gathered under the title of *A la
Santé du serpent*, 1945-1947, are dedicated. The collection
opens with the cry: «Je chante la chaleur à visage de nouveau-
né, la chaleur désespérée (*Fureur et Mystère*).

During his service in the *maquis*, Char makes to himself
the following promise:

> Si j'en réchappe, je sais que je devrai rompre avec
> l'arôme de ces années essentielles, rejeter (non re-
> fouler) silencieusement loin de moi mon trésor, me
> reconduire jusqu'au principe du comportement le
> plus indigent comme au temps où je me cherchais
> sans jamais accéder à la prouesse, dans une insatis-
> faction nue, une connaissance à peine entrevue et
> une humilité questionneuse.
>
> (*Feuillets d'Hypnos*, no. 195).

Humility is not only a new word, but a new concept in Char's poetry. The aggressiveness, the revolt, the violence of *Le Marteau sans maître* do not recur in his postwar verse. Though Char will never again recreate the carefree atmosphere of the «Cylindre à vapeur» and never again write with that lightness of touch, some of the texts he publishes in *Les Matinaux*, 1950, recapture—if in a more subdued key—themes of the *Placard pour un chemin des écoliers*. One of the better known poems of the 1950 collection is a piece called «Cet amour à tous retiré»:

> Sur la terre de la veille
> La foudre était pure au ruisseau,
> La vigne sustentait l'abeille,
> L'épaule levait le fardeau.
>
> Les routes flânaient, leur poussière
> Avec les oiseaux s'envolait,
> Les pierres s'ajoutaient aux pierres,
> Des mains utiles les aimaient.
>
> Du moins à chaque heure souffrante
> Un écho devait répéter
> Pour la solitude ignorante
> Un grêle devoir d'amitié.
>
> La violence était magique,
> L'homme quelquefois mourait,
> Mais à l'instant de l'agonie,
> Un trait d'ambre scellait ses yeux.

Les regrets, les basses portes
Ne sont que des inductions
Pour incliner nos illusions
Et rafraîchir nos peaux mortes.

Ah! crions au vent qui nous porte
Que c'est nous qui le soulevons.
Sur la terre de tant d'efforts,
L'avantage au vaillant mensonge
Est la franche consolation!

The differences and similarities between this piece and those quoted from *Placard pour un chemin des écoliers* are evident. Again, the poem is an effort at levitation, and Char returns to the favorite form of his beginnings: the octosyllabic quatrain. But the pace has changed. The roads above idle along in their heavy imperfect rhythms. They no longer fly away, faster than children on their way from school. They need exclamation points to lift them from their pedestrian ground. The stones remain attached to the earth or rise, at best, only as high as man, the builder, can reach. They are no longer murderous or magic stones, but the real stones of the earth that serve utilitarian functions. Man's reach, it seems, no longer will exceed his grasp.

These lines do not succeed in recreating the aeriness of the «Cylindre à vapeur.» They are heavier. Yet, like the earlier poem, «Cet amour à tous retiré» also ends on the affirmation of the marvelous, of the supra-terrestrial world of phantom and fable. Only now the poet openly admits that this fable is a lie: «L'avantage au vaillant mensonge...» But what of it? Is it not the *vaillant mensonge* or «Le Glorieux Mensonge,» as Mallarmé would have it, that will lead us out of the houses of low doors, houses built of utilitarian stone? «Ah! crions au vent qui nous porte / Que c'est nous qui le soulevons»!

«Cet amour à tous retiré» contains the verses which opened this chapter:

La violence était magique,
L'homme quelquefois mourait,

Mais à l'instant de l'agonie,
Un trait d'ambre scellait ses yeux.

By means of the «Glorieux Mensonge» which is poetry, René Char has come to terms with the inner and outer chaos of his world, with the contradictory existences of partisan and poet. Magic has taken from violence the terror of destruction and death. The eyes of the dying man are sealed by amber, the solidified transcendental light, «ayant l'expansion des choses infinies.» As he dies, man—like the steamroller—is magically transformed. All earthly heaviness is taken from him. He is made light as a ray of sunshine; he is lifted from the earth and rejoins the ἠλέκτωρ Ὑπερίων , the *mythe millénaire* (15).

«Présence d'esprit,» a poem of *Arsenal* retitled, in 1945, «Robustes météores,» is, I think, a perfect *raccourci* of the road traveled by the poet:

Dans le bois on écoute bouillir le ver
La chrysalide tournant au clair visage
Sa délivrance naturelle

Les hommes ont faim
De viandes secrètes d'outils cruels
Levez-vous bêtes à égorger
A gagner le soleil.

The poem brings together elements from every period of Char's literary development. The personification of the title, «Robustes météores,» recurs in the «météores hirondelles» and the «voix d'or du météore» of *Feuillets d'Hypnos*. Already in *Abondance viendra*, 1933, the chrysalis is Char's favorite emblem of things to be. Line three of «Robustes météores» recalls a poem from the first edition of *Arsenal*, 1929, «La Délivrance naturelle,» which ends:

---

(15) The French word *ambre* has, of course, kept some of the original connotations of the Greek ἤλεκτρον, in expressions such as «un homme fin comme l'ambre.»

Dans quelle forêt bout le ver?
Enfin délivrés les grands chemins
Montent au clair visage
Là où les hommes ont faim
De viandes secrètes d'outils cruels
Je tiens bêtes à égorger
A gagner le soleil.

The image of the «viande secrète» also appeared in the original first line of «Masque de fer» (*ibid.*): «Ne tient pas qui veut sa viande secrète,» before *viande* was changed to *rage* in 1934. The theme of the earthbound creature that is lifted—by magic—to the sky, is part of «La Délivrance naturelle» and of another early *Arsenal* poem, «Bonne aventure» (omitted from the 1934 and all subsequent editions), which ends with these lines, all in capitals:

CETTE POIGNEE ENFIN FABULEUSE
D'AVENTURIERS QUI SE PROPOSENT DE
GAGNER LE SOLEIL

It is also found in «Sur parole,» a poem of *Ralentir Travaux,* which Char starts out with these lines:

Il y a des flammes
Plus voyantes que les mains qui roulent les
        cauchemars
Sur la mémoire

On gagne le soleil par enchantement

There are obvious similarities between «Robustes météores» and «Cet amour à tous retiré.» Violence and magic are once again associated. Man and all animals must pass through death, must be strangled or slain with «outils cruels,» must offer up their «viande secrète» to reach, like the chrysalis, their «délivrance naturelle.» Only after death will they be lifted, as by enchantment, to the realm of the sun, where man and the «bêtes égorgées» will live on forever, transformed into the eternal animals of the sky: «Pour seul soleil: le bœuf écorché de Rembrandt» (16).

«Moi, si cela avait pu dépendre de ma volonté, j'aurais voulu être plutôt le fils de la femelle du requin, dont la faim est amie des tempêtes, et du tigre, à la cruauté reconnue: je ne serais pas si méchant» (*Les Chants de Maldoror,* I).   Char counters the wish of Lautréamont with one of his most serene poems, «Le Requin et la Mouette,» the fable of peace (17). Here, the tiger has lain down with the lamb, the shark, with the seagull.   Cruelty has been taken from the animal world:

> Je vois enfin la mer dans sa triple harmonie, la mer qui tranche de son croissant la dynastie des douleurs absurdes, la grande voilière sauvage, la mer crédule comme un liseron.
>
> Quand je dis: *j'ai levé la loi, j'ai franchi la morale, j'ai maillé le cœur,* ce n'est pas pour me donner raison devant ce pèse-néant dont la rumeur étend sa palme au-delà de ma persuasion. Mais rien de ce qui m'a vu vivre et agir jusqu'ici n'est témoin alentour. Mon épaule peut bien sommeiller, ma jeunesse accourir. C'est de cela seul qu'il faut tirer richesse immédiate et opérante. Ainsi, il y a un jour de pur dans l'année, un jour qui creuse sa galerie merveilleuse dans l'écume de la mer, un jour qui monte aux yeux pour couronner midi.   Hier la noblesse était déserte, le rameau était distant de ses bourgeons.   Le requin et la mouette ne communiquaient pas.
>
> O Vous, arc-en-ciel de ce rivage polisseur, approchez le navire de son espérance.   Faites que toute

---

(16)   A quote taken from *Contre une maison sèche,* a text dated «Juillet 1969, juillet 1970,» and first published in the special Char issue of *L'Herne,* 1971.

(17)   In his *Arrière-Histoire du Poème pulvérisé* (Paris: Jean Hugues, 1953, second edition, 1972), Char explains how «Le Requin et la Mouette» came into being: «C'est au Trayas au bord de la Méditerranée durant l'hiver de 1946 que le thème du *Requin et la Mouette* s'est imposé à moi.   J'allais voir Henri Matisse à Vence et

fin supposée soit une neuve innocence, un fiévreux
en avant pour ceux qui trébuchent dans la matinale
lourdeur.

(*Le Poème pulvérisé*, 1945-1947).

The poet has lifted the laws of man and burst the narrow
confines of a man-made reality, for which he has substituted
the «glorieux mensonge.» Not through violence («rien...n'est
témoin alentour»), but through the magic of poetry he has
changed the established order of things, solved the apparent
contradictions of nature. He has recaptured the original
harmony of the Heraclitean universe, has recreated «Les premiers instants» where shark and seagull could live together as
loyaux adversaires, where earth and sky were united and man
still believed in the promise of the rainbow:

> Nous regardions couler devant nous l'eau grandis-
> sante. Elle effaçait d'un coup la montagne, se
> chassant de ses flancs maternels. Ce n'était pas un
> torrent qui s'offrait à son destin mais une bête
> ineffable dont nous devenions la parole et la sub-
> stance. Elle nous tenait amoureux sur l'arc tout-
> puissant de son imagination. Quelle intervention
> eût pu nous contraindre? La modicité quotidienne
> avait fui, le sang jeté était rendu à sa chaleur. Adop-
> tés par l'ouvert, poncés jusqu'à l'invisible, nous
> étions une victoire qui ne prendrait jamais fin.
> («Les premiers instants,» *La Fontaine narra-
> tive,* 1947).

The destructive forces of nature have been put to creative
use. They have torn man away from his houses of low doors,
lifted him beyond the *modicité quotidienne,* forced him into

---

nous en parlions. Ces parfaites noces le hantaient. Poème qui
s'est acquitté par le charme écumant qu'il m'a procuré, encore
après sa fugue, tel le chant d'un coq brutal dans l'âme, maître du
silence qui le suit.»

the open, where he will join the *bête ineffable* whose victory shall have no end.

«Ainsi, il y a un jour de pur dans l'année, un jour qui creuse sa galerie merveilleuse dans l'écume de la mer, un jour qui monte aux yeux pour couronner midi.» As Char leaves the surrealist chapel, blasphemy gives way to prayer: a prayer that everything violent may be made calm, everything corrupt, made pure. A prayer that man, though he may stumble and fall, will ultimately rise—«luire et s'élancer—prompt couteau, lente étoile»—(18) to take his place among the stars: «Peu d'un astre: mi-homme, mi-lune, mi-soleil» (19).

In his new humility, René Char has found the poem for which Lautréamont—and the surrealists—had looked in vain (20).

> Avec mes dents
> J'ai pris la vie
> Sur le couteau de ma jeunesse.
> Avec mes lèvres aujourd'hui,
> Avec mes lèvres seulement...
>
> Courte parvenue,
> La fleur des talus,
> Le dard d'Orion,
> Est réapparu.
> («Jeu muet,» *Dans la pluie giboyeuse,* 1968).

---

(18) *La Nuit talismanique,* p. 13.
(19) *Ibid.,* p. 26.
(20) The original version of this chapter appeared in the *Forum for Modern Language Studies* (The Univ. of St. Andrews, Scotland), vol. X, No. 1, January 1974, with the title: «Violence and Magic: Aspects of René Char's Surrealist Apprenticeship.»

Le Bois de l'Epte

III

SPACE IN MOTION: THE REBEL'S ROAD

1

WINTERREISE: LE POÈME PULVÉRISÉ

> Mais quelles sont les lois qui corrigent et redressent
> ce que les lois qui infestent et ruinent ont laissé
> inachevé? Et sont-ce des lois? Y a-t-il des déroga-
> tions? Comment s'opère le signal? Est-il un troi-
> sième espace en chemin, hors du trajet des deux
> connus? Révolution d'Orion resurgi parmi nous.
>
> (*Aromates chasseurs*).

In 1972, Jean Hugues brought out the second edition of the *Arrière-Histoire du Poème pulvérisé*, (1) René Char's commentary on the nineteen texts (plus an introduction, «Argument») that comprise the postwar collection of poems, prose poems and aphorisms gathered under the title of *Le Poème pulvérisé*. These texts—most of which had appeared separately or in small groups in various journals and reviews—were first published as a volume in 1947 (Paris: Fontaine) (2). The poem which gave its title to the collection had appeared in the October-November 1945 issue of *Poésie 45* (Paris), and was renamed «J'habite une douleur» in *Le Poème pulvérisé*. The texts of the 1947 collection, with minor variants and additions, later became a part of *Fureur et Mystère*.

---

(1) *Arrière-Histoire du Poème pulvérisé* (Paris: Jean Hugues, 1972). Unless otherwise stated, all quotations that follow are taken from this edition.

(2) The first English translations of *Le Poème pulvérisé* appeared in January 1948, in the Paris review *Transition Forty-Eight*, no. 1.

Until now, the *Arrière-Histoire du Poème pulvérisé* (which began as a manuscript commentary written by the poet into one copy of the *Poème*) (3) was less readily available to the general reader than the texts commented upon. Limited in its original edition to 120 copies (Jean Hugues, April 1953), the *Arrière-Histoire* reached a larger public when it appeared in the *N. N. R. F.* of June 1953. The present edition (expanded to 1000 copies) maintains the original arrangement, i.e., each text of *Le Poème pulvérisé* is printed with the author's commentary, in italics, following it. The volume contains all the original texts, plus an «Avant-Propos» written by Char for the *N. N. R. F.* publication of the *Arrière-Histoire*. The new edition also reproduces the original frontispiece, a color lithograph—a silhouette portrait of the poet—by Nicolas de Stäel.

In his commentary on the «Argument» of *Le Poème pulvérisé* Char writes: «Lorsque furent achevés et réunis les dix-neuf textes qui composent *Le Poème pulvérisé,* il me sembla qu'un argument était nécessaire pour marquer l'autonomie et la dépendance à la fois de chaque poème à l'égard des autres...» (*Arrière-Histoire*). It is from this angle, i.e., from the viewpoint of the collection's structural unity, that I have chosen to examine here both *Le Poème pulvérisé* and Char's explanatory notes—some of them poems in their own right—supplied by the *Arrière-Histoire*.

The texts of *Le Poème pulvérisé* follow, first of all, a chronological order. Putting aside for a moment the «Argument,» and the tripartite poem «Les trois sœurs,» which is at once the exposition and the summing up of the work as a whole, we see that the real beginning of *Le Poème pulvérisé* is to be found in «Biens égaux,» which is, in fact, the earliest text of the collection, begun in 1937, and first printed in 1938

---

(3) The copy is dedicated to Yvonne Zervos and preserved in the Bibliothèque Littéraire Jacques Doucet, Paris. A variant study of the original MS notes and the printed version of the *Arrière-Histoire* might prove interesting.

in *Dehors la nuit est gouvernée*. There follows «Donnerbach Mühle,» a prose poem recalling Char's military service in the Vosges and dated «Hiver 1939.» The fifth text, «Hymne à voix basse,» was composed for a Paris exhibition organized by Yvonne Zervos in 1946 in support of the Greek Resistance. Most of the poems that follow first appeared in print that same year. The last three texts of *Le Poème pulvérisé*, «L'Age de roseau,» «Chanson du velours à côtes,» and «Lyre» also seem to be the last by date of composition. The manuscript of «Chanson du velours à côtes» is dated April 1947; «L'Age de roseau» and «Lyre» appeared together, that same year, in the Paris review *84*, no. 1.

But chronology is not the only—or the most important—element in the structure of *Le Poème pulvérisé*. I have borrowed the title of this chapter, *Winterreise,* from the Schubert song cycle not because I think that the tone of Char's poetry in any way resembles the romantic strains of a Wilhelm Müller. Such an analogy would, indeed, be absurd. A comparison between *Die Winterreise* and *Le Poème pulvérisé* will, in fact, show how Char breaks away from the romantic tradition and is much closer in spirit to Hölderlin than to any of the later German or French poets. But there are thematic and structural similarities between the two works: both of them form a cycle, both describe a journey in space and time, a journey into winter... and death.

Char's journey begins with a cry to arms and the sound of a lyre:

> La seconde crie et s'évade
> De l'abeille ambiante et du tilleul vermeil.
> Elle est un jeu de vent perpétuel,
> Le dé bleu du combat, le guetteur qui sourit
> Quand sa lyre profère: «Ce que je veux, sera.»

These lines from «Les trois sœurs,» the liminary text of *Le Poème pulvérisé,* are not fully understood by the reader until he has reached the last poem of the collection, «Lyre»:

> Lyre sans bornes des poussières,
> Surcroît de notre cœur.

In a note supplied by the *Arrière-Histoire,* Char further defines his lyre:

> Lyre nuptiale. Lyre sans merci.
> Du ciel tombe une plume d'aigle.
> (Rarement trouvée.)

This association of the nuptial lyre with the fallen eagle-feather is, in turn, not really grasped until the reader has accompanied the poet on his journey through *Le Poème pulvérisé.*

Schubert's romantic hero is the dejected lover who has made the classic journey from May to December (both months chosen, of course, for their symbolic value). In May he came to the strange city in quest of the fair maiden that was to be his bride. In December he leaves her village, hoping to forget her and himself, in death. Char's wanderer likewise set out on a sunny day, «sur une route de lavande et de vin,» in quest of his first love: «Nous avons marché côte à côte dans un cadre enfantin de poussière à gosier de ronces, l'un se sachant aimé de l'autre...» («Biens égaux»). But like his distant German cousin, he, too, is quick to realize that youth and love are subject to the laws of time and space. The child of «Les trois sœurs» (the Parcae), introduced in the exposition of *Le Poème pulvérisé,* is a stillborn illusion:

> Trois Parques soufflent sur les doigts de l'homme
> qu'elles ont désiré enfant. Vainement.
> > *(Arrière-Histoire).*

Like the singer Orpheus, the poet of «Biens égaux» will travel to the underworld in search of his lost love. On his lyre he will play an epithalamium and an elegy: «Lyre nuptiale. Lyre sans merci.» The early poem already ends on the affirmation of a reunion after death:

L'espace pour toujours est-il cet absolu et scintillant
congé, chétive volte-face? Mais prédisant cela,
j'affirme que tu vis; le sillon s'éclaire entre ton bien
et mon mal. La chaleur reviendra avec le silence
comme je te soulèverai, Inanimée.

Schubert's *Winterreise* begins at night. Darkness and cold
characterize the season and the hour of the lover's departure:

> Ich kann zu meiner Reisen
> Nicht wählen mir die Zeit,
> Muss selbst den Weg mir weisen
> In dieser Dunkelheit.

Yet there is a certain voluptuousness for the romantic wanderer
as for the soldier of World War II in the presence of the moon
whose rays—caught in the ice of the lake or scintillating («cet
absolu et scintillant congé») on the snowy paths of the forest—
simulate the warmth of summer on a cold winter night:

> Es zieht ein Mondenschatten
> Als mein Gefährte mit,
> Und auf den weissen Matten
> Such' ich des Wildes Tritt.

«Donnerbach Mühle» sums up Müller's lines in one sentence:
«La lune du lac prend pied sur la place où le doux feu végétal
de l'été descend à la vague qui l'entraîne vers un lit de profondes cendres.»
  The illusion is shattered—as the house is burnt down, the
poem pulverized—and the waves come to rest in «un lit de
profondes cendres.»

> Der Wind spielt drinnen mit den Herzen
> Wie auf dem Dach, nur nicht so laut.
> Was fragen sie nach meinen Schmerzen?
> Ihr Kind ist eine reiche Braut.

The primary destructive agent in *Le Poème pulvérisé*—as in
the Schubert song cycle—is the wind. I have already exam-

ined the significance of this element in Char's poetry, but no discussion of the 1947 collection would be complete without reference to one of the poet's most constant symbols which is, furthermore, the prime mover of *Le Poème pulvérisé*. René Char concluded his *N. N. R. F.* introduction to the *Arrière-Histoire* with these remarks: «La vraie lumière, celle qui a raison par la particularité et la toute-puissance de ce qu'elle nomme... c'est-à-dire, la lumière mentale... relève doucement le vent qui tombe durant sa course, quand il s'efforce de venir en aide aux hommes dans le désespoir.»

On the one hand, the wind is, then, a friend to man, lifting him from his earthbound existence and despair to the Olympian heights of pure light and joy. On the other hand, however, each uprooting—no matter how poor the original soil—implies suffering, struggle and pain. The wind destroys that which is whole, stirs up that which is silent and symbolizes, like the second of «Les trois sœurs,» the deathbound strife of every human existence. Thus the *creator spiritus,* the life-giving breath of the wind, is at the same time the symbol of death, «le guetteur qui sourit / Quand sa lyre profère: 'Ce que je veux, sera.'» Man—and whole civilizations with him—flees the vermilion tree of death, (4) and is uplifted by the winds... only to go down again (like the house in the forest and the waves of the sea) to a bed of deep ashes.

«Hymne à voix basse,» the text that follows «Donnerbach Mühle,» puts the experience of the individual into the larger context of the history of Western civilization:

> L'Hellade, c'est le rivage déployé d'une mer géniale d'où s'élancèrent à l'aurore le souffle de la connaissance et le magnétisme de l'intelligence, gonflant d'égale fertilité des pouvoirs qui semblèrent perpé-

---

(4) While both the *olivier* and the *tilleul* of «Les trois sœurs» are native to Char's Provençal settings, I rather suspect that the *tilleul vermeil*—with its symbolic color of mourning—is of German import. In Schubert's *Winterreise* it is also the *Lindenbaum* that invites the weary wanderer to suicide and eternal rest.

tuels; c'est plus loin une mappemonde d'étranges montagnes: une chaîne de volcans sourit à la magie des héros, à la tendresse serpentine des déesses, guide le vol nuptial de l'homme libre enfin de se savoir et de périr oiseau; c'est la réponse à tout, même aux détours du labyrinthe...

Every authentic poem—whether it take for its apparent subject matter the Vietnam War, the *maquis* or the Greek Resistance movement—is going to make an essential statement about the inner universe of its author and his relationship to the world. And so in «Hymne à voix basse,» Char would celebrate not only the eventual liberation of Greece, but his own freedon from the laws of human existence. Perhaps, after all, man need not return to the labyrinth that is, at once, the cradle and the tomb. Perhaps he can escape the sting of the serpent, assume the properties of the bird and, by magic, fly to the Olympian heights where he will join the immortal gods and heroes of old. Perhaps he can rise, like the phoenix, from this bed of ashes and sand to deny time and space in a world not bound by the laws of nature known to man.

The old and shopworn metaphor does not convince the poet. «J'habite une douleur,» the prose poem after whose original title the collection is named, marks a turning point in *Le Poème pulvérisé*. It is here that the poet bids farewell not only to his private sufferings and sorrows, but to the whole tradition of melodious and self-indulging poetry:

Ne laisse pas le soin de gouverner ton cœur à ces tendresses parentes de l'automne auquel elles empruntent sa placide allure et son affable agonie... D'autres chanteront l'incorporation mélodieuse, les chairs qui ne personnifient plus que la sorcellerie du sablier...
Tu n'as fait qu'augmenter le poids de ta nuit. Tu es retourné à la pêche aux murailles, à la canicule sans été. Tu es furieux contre ton amour au centre d'une entente qui s'affole. Songe à la maison parfaite que tu ne verras jamais monter...

Qu'est-ce qui t'a hissé, une fois encore, un peu plus haut, sans te convaincre?
Il n'y a pas de siège pur.

There are no easy, ready-made, magical solutions to the problems of everyday existence, and individual man cannot escape the sting of the serpent, the sting of death. «J'habite une douleur» expresses the realization that we are locked in the sphere of our sorrow which no wind can dispel. The note of the *Arrière-Histoire* further explains:

> C'est là, je crois, l'un de mes poèmes les plus «achevés;» l'aliment qui le compose ne se détériora pas, ne toucha la moelle de l'air que complètement «enveloppé.» J'étais à cet instant lourd de mille ans de poésie et de détresse antérieure. Il fallait que je l'exprime. J'ai pris ma tête comme on saisit une motte de sel et je l'ai littéralement pulvérisée... De cette illusion atroce est né *J'habite une douleur,* plus quelque calme.

The passage above, while it describes an act of violence and destruction, yet introduces a first note of optimism into *Le Poème pulvérisé.* The act of pulverization takes place here. Thematically, «J'habite une douleur» is the central text of the collection. In it, Char prepares the sacrifice of his own life, a sacrifice that will guarantee the authenticity and thereby the survival of his art. A thousand years of poetry («l'incorporation mélodieuse») and many summers of personal happiness are put on the chopping-block of reality (the winters of Céreste) and offered up to the winds. Yet something of the poem remains after the sacrifice: «L'aliment qui le compose ne se détériora pas, ne toucha la moelle de l'air que complètement enveloppé...» The essence of the poem is enveloped in its own protective coating, just as the delicate white flower of «Le Muguet,» the messenger of summer, is sheathed in its leaves for protection against the cold winter winds. However, the *Arrière-Histoire* adds a word of caution to the jubilant notes of «Le Muguet»: «Comment ne pas conserver derrière son oreille, pour assurer la continuité du muguet, le brin de thym écarlate de la superstition!»

«Seuil,» the text which follows, again puts personal experience into the larger context of the history of the world. It is a retelling of the Biblical story of the flood, applied to *poetic* creation:

> Quand s'ébranla le barrage de l'homme, aspiré par la faille géante de l'abandon du divin, des mots dans le lointain, des mots qui ne voulaient pas se perdre, tentèrent de résister à l'exorbitante poussée. Là se décida la dynastie de leur sens.
>
> J'ai couru jusqu'à l'issue de cette nuit diluvienne...

The poet has escaped the wrath of men and the vengeance of God; he has come out of the diluvian night. The romantic singer (Wilhelm Müller) celebrated his victory with the proud assertion:

> Lustig in die Welt hinein
> Gegen Wind und Wetter!
> Will kein Gott auf Erden sein,
> Sind wir selber Götter!

«Seuil» is, like «Le Muguet,» a hymn to survival. But again the *Arrière-Histoire* adds a note of caution:

> Soustraits au naufrage!
> Pourquoi s'interdire d'espérer? Et que l'effort, le courage et l'amour viendront à bout du destin chaque jour plus menaçant pour les rescapés en si petit nombre, il ne faut pas en douter...

The poet would substitute himself for God, who has abandoned man. Having survived the deluge (and World War II), he has rescued from shipwreck the essential words, those that guarantee his existence on earth: *effort, courage, amour.* Will they suffice to safeguard against death?

«L'Extravagant,» a sort of twentieth century fable, follows the Biblical flashback. The hero of that fable is the man (poet, soldier, wanderer) endowed to the utmost with one of the essential words: courage. The story begins: «Il ne déplaçait pas d'ombre en avançant, traduisant une audace tôt consumée, bien que son pas fût assez vulgaire... Le gel furieux effleurait la surface de son front sans paraître *personnel*...» Wind and ice are no obstacles to the course of «L'Extravagant.»

Char is, of course, using that word in its etymological sense of *extra vagans*. The Extravagant is the wanderer who has left behind the sure terrain of the earth and ventured into the great unknown. He is no ordinary traveler in quest of ordinary adventure: «Tel n'était pas ce marcheur que le voile du paysage lunaire, très bas, semblait ne pas gêner dans son mouvement.» He glides, birdlike, through the air. There is no effort in his movement, and... no love. These, we remember, were the other two words rescued by the poet, and they are words discarded by the «fabulous» wanderer who seems to have broken with the past and with the human condition. For he would deny the warmth of summer, and of love:

...Il avait perdu tout lien avec le volume ancien des sources propice aux interrogations, avec les corps heureux qu'il s'était plu à animer auprès du sien lorsqu'il pouvait encore assigner une cime à son plaisir, une neige à son talent. Aujourd'hui il rompait avec la tristesse devenue un objet aguerri, avec la frayeur du convenu. La terre avait faussé sa persuasion, la terre, de sa vitesse un peu courte, avec son imagination safranée, son usure crevassée par les actes de monstres. Personne n'aurait à l'oublier car l'utile ne l'avait pas assisté, ne l'avait pas dessiné en entier au regard des autres. Sur le plafond de chaux blanche de sa chambre, quelques oiseaux étaient passés mais leur éclair avait fondu dans son sommeil.

Le voile du paysage lunaire maintenant très haut déploie ses couleurs aromatiques au-dessus du per-

sonnage que je dis. Il sort éclairé du froid et tourne
à jamais le dos au printemps qui n'existe pas.

The poem which began like a dream-recital ends in a night-mare. Char prefers not to speak of the circumstances which produced this particular text. In his commentary, he writes: «Le sujet de ce poème est une affreuse circonstance que je ne veux pas décrire, une marche au supplice. Hypnos rompit le rêve et découvrit le cauchemar.» Quite apart from actual circumstances, however, the text describes the death (the murder?) of one of the key terms strong enough to survive the deluge: courage. Courage alone kills and is killed in turn. When Hypnos wakens to the call of Alexander, the poet dies with the enemy. The wanderer of the air, «le céleste, le tué» (5) is thrown back unto the earth: «Le voile du paysage lunaire maintenant très haut déploie ses couleurs aromatiques au-dessus du personnage que je dis.» Man, however coura-geous, cannot survive for very long in isolation, in the cold, pure and rarefied atmosphere of a lunar landscape: «Il n'y a pas de siège pur.» If he is to live, he will have to re-establish contact with the earth, with the sun, and with his fellow-men (5a).

«Rire de soi, se reclasser momentanément dans l'ambiance conventionnelle où se complaisent la plupart, est excellent,» comments the *Arrière-Histoire* on «Pulvérin,» the text that follows «L'Extravagant.» In the Schubert song cycle, a bitter, ironic laughter breaks up the dream-recital:

Wie hat der Sturm zerrissen
Des Himmels graues Kleid!
Die Wolkenfetzen flattern
Umher in mattem Streit.

---

(5) «Le céleste, le tué» is a title given by Char to one of his drawings included in *La Nuit talismanique,* 1972. It represents a bird with one white and one black wing, symbolizing day and night, life and death.

(5a) For a different interpretation of «L'Extravagant,» see Mary Ann Caws, *The Presence of René Char,* pp. 205-206.

Und rote Feuerflammen
Zieh'n zwischen ihnen hin:
Das nenn' ich einen Morgen
So recht nach meinem Sinn!

Char also follows his *Mondgesang* with a hymn to the sun.
«Pulvérin» is the description of a new dawn, a sunlit morning
full of promise and hope:

> La nouvelle sincérité se débat dans la pourpre de
> la naissance. Diane est transfigurée. Partout où
> l'arche du soleil développe sa course, partout essai-
> me le nouveau mal tolérant. Le bonheur est modifié.
> En aval sont les sources. Tout au-dessus chante la
> bouche des amants.

The wanderer of outer space has returned to the earth with its
imperfections and sorrows, but with its promises, also, of a
new, modified form of happiness heard in the lovers' song.

«Affres détonation silence» is a summing-up of the two
texts that precede it and a logical conclusion to both. It is
also a retelling, on a realistic plane, of the fable of «L'Extravagant»: the prediction of that hero's imaginary death comes
true in the execution of Roger Bernard, Char's poet-friend
killed in action. The explosion (*détonation*) of the myth and
of the nightmare occurs in «Pulvérin.» Silence follows upon
the death of the poet:

> Aujourd'hui, le vieux réfractaire faiblit au milieu de
> ses pierres, la plupart mortes de gel, de solitude et
> de chaleur. A leur tour les présages se sont assoupis
> dans le silence des fleurs.

«Affres détonation silence» is set in the Moulin du Calavon
that once gave shelter to animals and men: «Le Moulin du
Calavon. Deux années durant, une ferme de cigales, un château
de martinets. Ici tout parlait torrent, tantôt par le rire, tantôt
par les poings de la jeunesse.» The poem is a recasting, in a

Provençal setting, of the earlier «Donnerbach Mühle,» which ended: «Tonnerre, ruisseau, moulin.» «Affres détonation silence» (punctuated in the *Fureur et Mystère* renditions) picks up where «Donnerbach Mühle» left off. When both mills (farms, castles) are destroyed, the poet seeks a new *lieu de sûreté* for the survival of poetry. «Affres détonation silence» ends in the suggestion of a re-established dialogue:

> Ne cherchez pas dans la montagne; mais si, à quelques kilomètres de là, dans les gorges d'Oppedette, vous rencontrez la foudre au visage d'écolier, allez à elle, oh, allez à elle et souriez-lui car elle doit avoir faim, faim d'amitié.

The message of these lines is clear: the true poem cannot set itself comfortably apart in the shelter of mountain and stone. It must be subjected to the test of life, to the thrust of the air from which, like the flower, it must return intact (6). The background note to «Affres détonation silence» is a farewell letter to Roger Bernard, to whom Char writes:

> Cher Roger,
> On n'écrit pas aux morts... A peine aux disparus. Mais tu étais poète. C'est leur privilège à ces souffrants, à ces mal connus, aux poètes, d'être pliés dans des enveloppes à face heureuse, jetés au voyage et non brisés comme du bois de fagot...
> Je t'embrasse, mon compagnon des forêts extra-ordinaires... Le temps d'une vie, c'est à peine la distance d'un sentier à une route... Une route?...

The road traveled by the poet of *Le Poème pulvérisé* leads not only into the future and outer space, but, more frequently, inward to the poet's own past. The distance

---

(6) The original title of «Affres détonation silence» names the spirit of the air in the «Territoire d'Ariel.» (The original version of the poem was published in the Paris journal *Action*, 2 novembre 1945.)

covered by the individual is measured against the progress of the collective conscience and consciousness of man. By a process of chronologically arranged *télescopages,* Char first sets his own experience against the backdrop of ancient Greece, then moves forward to Biblical times and finally, in «Jacquemard et Julia,» creates a mediaeval fairy-tale setting to correspond to scenes from his own childhood:

> Jadis l'herbe, à l'heure où les routes de la terre s'accordaient dans leur déclin, élevait tendrement ses tiges et allumait ses clartés. Les cavaliers du jour naissaient au regard de leur amour et les châteaux de leurs bien-aimées comptaient autant de fenêtres que l'abîme porte d'orages légers.
>
> Jadis l'herbe connaissait mille devises qui ne se contrariaient pas. Elle était la providence des visages baignés de larmes. Elle incantait les animaux, donnait asile à l'erreur. Son étendue était comparable au ciel qui a vaincu la peur du temps et allégi la douleur.
>
> Jadis l'herbe était bonne aux fous et hostile au bourreau. Elle convolait avec le seuil de toujours. Les jeux qu'elle inventait avaient des ailes à leur sourire (jeux absous et également fugitifs). Elle n'était dure pour aucun de ceux qui perdant leur chemin souhaitent le perdre à jamais.
>
> Jadis l'herbe avait établi que la nuit vaut moins que son pouvoir, que les sources ne compliquent pas à plaisir leur parcours, que la graine qui s'agenouille est déjà à demi dans le bec de l'oiseau. Jadis, terre et ciel se haïssaient mais terre et ciel vivaient.
>
> L'inextinguible sécheresse s'écoule. L'homme est un étranger pour l'aurore. Cependant à la poursuite de la vie qui ne peut être encore imaginée, il y a des volontés qui frémissent, des murmures qui vont s'affronter et des enfants sains et saufs qui *découvrent.*

«Jacquemard et Julia,» dedicated to Char's father and his first wife, Julia, is the first of three texts in *Le Poème pulvérisé* that attempt the reconciliation of earth and sky, history and myth, individual death and collective survival.

A visit to the ancient and deserted ruins of Les Baux, where —whipped by the winds and burnt by the sun—nothing but the stone survives, inspired in the poet the following reflections:

> Juxtapose à la fatalité la résistance à la fatalité. Tu connaîtras d'étranges hauteurs.
>
> La beauté naît du dialogue, de la rupture du silence et du regain de ce silence...
>
> La durée que ton cœur réclame existe ici en dehors de toi.
>
> Oui et non, heure après heure, se réconcilient dans la superstition de l'histoire. La nuit et la chaleur, le ciel et la verdure se rendent invisibles pour être mieux sentis.
>
> Les ruines douées d'avenir, les ruines incohérentes avant que tu n'arrives, homme comblé, vont de leurs parcelles à ton amour. Ainsi se voit promise et retirée à ton irritable maladresse la rose qui ferme le royaume.

In *Le Bulletin des Baux,* the path of the poet-wanderer in quest of the unknown is clearly mapped out. Unlike the «Extravagant,» who would leave the earth and sever all human ties in search of superhuman powers, the poet must walk patiently and lovingly among the ruins of civilizations past, to deliver from the great unknown *Jadis,* caught in the silent stone, the indestructible elements that may withstand the test of time. Not in the realm of angels, but among his fellowmen, the poet must try to discover the relationships of word and world. As Antonin Artaud once put it: «Mais il faut aller à pas lents sur la route des pierres mortes, surtout pour qui a perdu la *connaissance des mots.* C'est une science indestructible et qui explose par poussées lentes. Et qui la possède ne la connaît pas. Mais les Anges aussi ne la connaissent pas, car toute vraie connaissance est *obscure*. L'Esprit clair appartient à la matière» («Position de la chair»).

It is for the poet to break the silence of the ages, to save from oblivion the essential words: effort, courage, love, words that will give new life to the deserted cities, castles, temples. The poet must make the incoherent ruins of ages past communicate with his own time: he must seek to understand their language and to translate for his fellowmen the harmonic oneness of the world. He must recompose a world that is whole with the fragments of that which has been uprooted, eroded, or otherwise destroyed by the inimicable *tempus edax rerum*.

«Le Requin et la Mouette,» the parable discovered simultaneously by Char and Matisse in the winter of 1946, on the shores of the Mediterranean, closes the cycle of restoration and reconciliation. In this prose poem, Char celebrates the return to the *Jadis* sung in «Jacquemard et Julia,» a return to the perfect harmony of the primordial universe to which the artist can, momentarily, restore the world of man. Here shark and seagull live in perfect communion, each respecting the other's integrity and freedom. Char has arrived at a new definition of love, a love akin to the Christian concept of *caritas*. «Marthe» and «Suzerain,» the texts that follow, are the consecration of that love. In his commentary on «Marthe,» Char writes: «Résolution en jubilation du temps vécu dans l'être aimé. L'arc des eaux jaillissantes, quelle beauté! Quelle victoire! Marthe, en songeant à Lazare.» The beloved is compared to a fountain whose waters—always offered up to the wind, yet forever returning to the original source—will never run dry. Man—all men—may freely drink from that fountain without becoming prisoner of the well, without impeding the free flow of the «chiare, fresche e dolci acque» sung by Petrarch. The prose poem ends as follows:

> Je n'entrerai pas dans votre cœur pour limiter sa mémoire. Je ne retiendrai pas votre bouche pour l'empêcher de s'entrouvrir sur le bleu de l'air et la

soif de partir. Je veux être pour vous la liberté
et le vent de la vie qui passe le seuil de toujours
avant que la nuit ne devienne introuvable...

In *La Parole en archipel,* the 1961 anthology, René Char
weaves into «La double tresse» the poem «Chaume des
Vosges,» expressing a traditional view of love, and «Sur la
paume de Dabo,» a text showing the transformation accomplished by *Le Poème pulvérisé.* «Chaume des Vosges,» a contemporary of «Donnerbach Mühle,» is a poem of winter, and
a hymn to night:

> Beauté, ma toute-droite, par des routes si ladres,
> A l'étape des lampes et du courage clos,
> Que je me glace et que tu sois ma femme de
>   décembre.
> Ma vie future, c'est ton visage quand tu dors.

«Sur la paume de Dabo,» which follows, is dated «Eté 1953»:

> Va mon baiser, quitte le frêle gîte,
> Ton amour est trouvé, un bouleau te le tend.
> La résine d'été et la neige d'hiver
> Ont pris garde.

Char's narrator has come a long way from his early songs
of *Weltschmerz* and his egocentric preoccupation with personal
gratification. By viewing his own experience in the light of
the life-cycles of mankind (as recorded by mythology, history,
or the Bible), the poet has at once lost his own identity (preserved, however, by the poem) and reached a higher and more
meaningful level of consciousness unknown to Schubert's
wanderer and to the poets locked in the romantic tradition. In
the opening text of *Le Rempart de brindilles* (*Poèmes des
deux années,* 1955), Char defines the mission of poetry, as
he has come to see it:

> Le dessein de la poésie étant de nous rendre souve-

rains en nous impersonnalisant, nous touchons, grâce
au poème, à la plénitude de ce qui n'était qu'esquissé
ou déformé par les vantardises de l'individu.

Les poèmes sont des bouts d'existence incorruptibles
que nous lançons à la gueule répugnante de la mort,
mais assez haut pour que, ricochant sur elle, ils
tombent dans le monde nominateur de l'unité.

In *Le Poème pulvérisé,* Char found the «poèmes de la totalité
illuminée, de la résurrection insensée.»

As «Marthe» sang the love of woman, so «Suzerain»
celebrates the communion of men: free and noble spirits, men
of the open forests and fields, artisans, hunters, and fishermen
of the Vaucluse.   In his commentary on «Suzerain,» the poet
asks:

Où sont-ils ces êtres libres et détirés? Morts,
morts, morts... Mais ils continuent de vivre en moi,
oh combien! Je vous les transmettrai, amis, ennemis. Qu'ils inspirent les uns et avisent les autres!

Just as the fountain, from which all men drink, continues to
flow, so the words of free men, recorded by the poet, are
transmitted to all.

«A la Santé du serpent,» the group of twenty-seven aphorisms that follows, is a recapitulation of *Le Poème pulvérisé,*
retracing —*en raccourci*—the journey from summer to winter
to spring, from birth to death, to resurrection.   The first three
aphorisms are a rephrasing of the words that guarantee life
on earth:

I

Je chante la chaleur à visage de nouveau-né, la
chaleur désespérée.

In the face of the hopeless aftermath of the war, the poet finds
the courage to sing anew the hymn to life.

II

Au tour du pain de rompre l'homme, d'être la
beauté du point du jour.

All of nature must participate in an effort to restore the purity
and the beauty of early morning and the beginnings of mankind.

III

Celui qui se fie au tournesol ne méditera pas dans
la maison. Toutes les pensées de l'amour devien-
dront ses pensées.

The man that communicates with nature will again communicate with his fellowmen and speak the redeeming words of
love.

In the aphorisms that follow, the speaker contemplates his
departure, his journey beyond the earth:

XVII

Mon amour, peu importe que je sois né: tu deviens
visible à la place où je disparais.

XX

Ne te courbe que pour aimer. Si tu meurs, tu
aimes encore.

«A la Santé du serpent,» the toast offered to the health of
the serpent, seems, paradoxically, a toast also to the death
of man. In the context of Western culture, the serpent is, of
course—quite apart from its Biblical connotations—the enemy
of man. The snake seems the antithesis of the bird, which
Le Poème pulvérisé hailed as the symbol of man's highest
aspirations. The serpent is the ruler of the labyrinth from
which man attempted to escape, just as the bird is the king
of the air in which «L'Extravagant» tried, in vain, to survive.
Does the health of the serpent not imply the death of the bird
—ergo, of the poet—as foretold by «Les trois sœurs»?

Meurent les yeux singuliers
Et la parole qui découvre.
La plaie qui rampe au miroir
Est maîtresse des deux bouges.

Violente l'épaule s'entrouvre; ·
Muet apparaît le volcan.
Terre sur quoi l'olivier brille,
Tout s'évanouit en passage.

But by the death of the poet comes the resurrection of the poem which, separated from its creator, is at last free to live its own life in a world not bound by the laws of time and space. The poem is a world unto itself, in which the wind —the ruler of the antithetical world—comes to rest, where shark and seagull, serpent and bird are joined.

Mais tout coïncidera à nouveau
Serpent passe soleil mouche franchit lune...
(«L'Essentiel intelligible,» *Dehors la nuit est gouvernée*).

When Char draws his serpent, it resembles a bird, the bird which he calls «L'Oiseau exorciseur,» and of which he writes:

Au-dessus des contradictions partielles sont apparues les identités antagonistes qui, elles, mettent fin (7).

In his commentary on «A la Santé du serpent,» the poet explicitly links snake and bird:

Je répète «A la santé du Serpent!»
Et mon toast est tourné vers vous, en cercle au sol et sur les branches, empressés ou hostiles, oiseaux!

_____
(7) «Le Serpent» and «L'Oiseau exorciseur,» both in *La Nuit talismanique*.

The toast to the serpent is also a toast to the bird, and to man. Char gives us the final element of the equation only in a much later text entitled «Tables de longévité,» which ends on the exhortation:

Souvenez-vous de cet homme comme d'un bel oiseau sans tête, aux ailes tendues dans le vent. Il n'est qu'un serpent à genoux.
(*Dans la pluie giboyeuse*, 1968).

«A la Santé du serpent» concludes with a definition of the new poetry advocated by Char:

XXVI

La poésie est de toutes les eaux claires celle qui s'attarde le moins aux reflets de ses ponts.
Poésie, la vie future à l'intérieur de l'homme requalifié.

This new poetry will not seek its own echo, its reflection in the pond. It lives in anticipation of things yet to be, not in nostalgia for bridges already crossed. It believes in the power of the living word substituting for a dying world. For «Out of the living word / come flower, serpent, and bird» (Howard Nemerov, «The Book of Kells»).

The poem is the flower found in the incoherent ruins of Les Baux, «la rose qui ferme le royaume.» It is the flower of peace: «Il maintint la rose au sommet jusqu'à la fin des protestations» («Maurice Blanchot,...» *Dans la pluie giboyeuse*). It is the rose of the winds and the *rosace* of cathedrals, the flower which, like the poem, is composed of many fragments gathered from the past, united and brought into presence by the word: «La rose! Le champ de ses allées éventerait même la hardiesse de la mort» («Front de la rose,» *Poèmes des deux années*). It is the flame emitted by the serpent: «La fleur est dans la flamme, la flamme est dans la tempête.» And perhaps it is the serpent itself. It is earth, fire, air and water, all elements in one. As the serpent is offered up by

the peasants of Luchon, in their midsummer bonfires, the
people pray that the rains may fall and bring fertility to their
fields: «Une rose pour qu'il pleuve. Au terme d'innombrables
années, c'est ton souhait» («A la Santé du serpent,» XXVII).

> La beauté déferlait de sa gaine fantasque, donnait
> des roses aux fontaines... Il se pencha sur le visage
> anéanti...

Fire, air, earth, and water, all elements are one in the kingdom
of poetry, in the fragments of Heraclitus and in *Le Poème
pulvérisé.*

* * *

> Yeux qui, croyant inventer le jour, avez éveillé le
> vent, que puis-je pour vous, je suis l'oubli.
>> («A la Santé du serpent,» XXV).

In the three texts which close the cycle of *Le Poème pulvérisé,* the poet comes to terms with death, accepting night as
an integral part of life. In «L'Age de roseau» he asks the
question: «Monde las de mes mystères, dans la chambre d'un
visage, ma nuit est-elle prévue?» The commentary on the
poem bears the subtitle:

> Dialogue en forme de salut:

> —Long insouci devant vous, poignard de rosée.
> —Long embellie, passant gracieux.

> Ainsi se rafraîchissait mon enfance meurtrie.

The salvation and the health of the poet are in his passing on,
in the journey beyond his own past. In «Chanson du velours
à côtes,» the text that follows, the dialogue is enlarged to
include all creation and destruction, day and night:

> Le jour disait: «Tout ce qui m'accompagne, s'atta-
> che à moi, se veut heureux. Témoins de ma comé-
> die, retenez mon pied joyeux. J'appréhende midi

et sa flèche méritée. Il n'est de grâce à quérir pour prévaloir à ses yeux. Si ma disparition sonne votre élargissement, les eaux froides de l'été ne me recevront que mieux.»

Day is, of course, the symbol of life, the stage where war and death are prepared. Night, its logical conclusion, is the hour of the dejected lover's departure, his *Winterreise* into death. It is the hour when «le dernier comédien,» the extravagant wanderer, is brought to fall.

La nuit disait: «Ceux qui m'offensent meurent jeunes. Comment ne pas les aimer? Prairie de tous mes instants, ils ne peuvent me fouler. Leur voyage est mon voyage et je reste obscurité.»
Il était entre les deux un mal qui les déchirait. Le vent allait de l'un à l'autre; le vent ou rien, les pans de la rude étoffe et l'avalanche des montagnes, ou rien.

The mediator between day and night, life and death, is the wind, symbol of courage, effort, strife, of man's struggle to reach the summits from which he is always thrown back again onto the ground. The somewhat strange title of the dialogue, «Chanson du velours à côtes,» is explained by the *Arrière-Histoire*:

Le poète n'est-il pas ce montagnard qui récidive sans cesse et que l'assaut répété des sommets remet sur ses pieds?... Cependant il meurt. Va poète, et que le velours te tienne, t'empêche de glisser...

His task having been accomplished, the poet can continue his journey through the dark winternight, confident that «l'homme n'accomplit rien de franchement infructueux. Il ne perd que ce qu'il se plaira ensuite à rechercher. L'intrigue, le désespoir sont sa lanterne, la poésie est son bâton» (*ibid.*). The staff of poetry is Char's answer to the staff of the Parcae. It is the poem that helps man—collective man—to survive, physically and mentally, in a world threatened by man-made wars and God-ordained catastrophies. It is the magic wand of poetry that leads man through the dark journey of winter into the light of spring.

> On ne tue point la rose
> Dans les guerres du ciel.
> On exile une lyre.
> («Déshérence,» *Retour amont*) (7a).

The texts of *Le Poème pulvérisé* culminate in the joyful notes of the «Lyre,» the last poem of the collection. Char's lyre of dust is the symbol of the pulverized poem, blasted free of the human hand that held it prisoner. It is the fountain freely flowing from the rock, the *éclair* emerging from the cloud, the flames emitted by the serpent, the flower blooming in the wind. It is the instrument set free of the artisan and the artist, «le marteau sans maître» and the «lyre sans merci.» Limitless lyre of dust, greater by far than any single human heart (or love), spanning all time and space, played not only in the underworld, by the singer Orpheus, but set against the expanse of the sky, plucked by the constellation of stars (8).

> Et moi qui avance en chantant
> Clown musical aux braises des sun-lights
> Sur instrument à cordes.

Those were the last lines of «Flexibilité de l'oubli,» a poem of *Les Cloches sur le cœur*. The stringed instrument is not yet named, but the adolescent's poem already traces the outline

---

(7a) The original version of this stanza (dated «13 janvier 1965») has a fourth line: «Et qui le peut, la suive.» (Bibliothèque Littéraire Jacques Doucet). Two previous titles, «Chant des frontières» and «Profil sous une rose» are shown crossed out at the head of the poem.
(8) The original title of the poem was «Le Titre silencieux» (MS Doucet), referring, perhaps, to the poet's departure.

of the mature poet's lyre. During the war, when the French were deliberately kept from contact with everything German, Char was determined to discover for himself the rich cultural heritage of the enemy that even he, the enemy, could not destroy. It was during these years that he read Rilke and Trakl and Hölderlin. In September 1940, Char arranges and corrects a collection of fourteen Hölderlin fragments translated by Alzir Hella and Olivier Bournac. Among these, there is this passage:

> Accordez-moi un seul été, ô tout puissants,
> Accordez-moi encore un automne pour mûrir mon chant,
> Afin que mon cœur, rassasié de ce doux feu,
> Puisse ensuite mourir.
>
> L'âme qui dans la vie n'a pas eu sa divine satisfaction
> Ne trouve pas non plus de repos dans l'Orcus souterrain;
> Si, au contraire, je réussis le saint labeur
> Que j'ai dans le cœur, la poésie,
>
> Alors bienvenu sera le silence du royaume des ombres
> Même si ma lyre ne m'accompagne pas,
> Je serai satisfait, car, pour un temps
> J'aurai vécu comme les dieux et cela m'aura suffi. (9)

Char has succeeded in his «saint labeur;» he has been granted the summer and the autumn «pour mûrir [son] chant;» he has traveled one step further than his German cousin on his winter's journey. His suicide has not misfired, and his voluntary death is not an act of despair, but a joyful sacrifice of the creator to his creation. «Ce qui me console,» writes

_____

(9) The little book of Höderlin fragments in French translation is preserved in the Bibliothèque Littéraire Jacques Doucet.

Char, «lorsque je serai mort, c'est que je serai là—disloqué, hideux—pour me voir poème.» The poet has offered up his own love (and life), has pulverized his poem, so that the particles liberated from it (fire, earth or water) might be carried by the winds to all the corners of the earth.

> Lyre nuptiale. Lyre sans merci.
> Du ciel tombe une plume d'aigle.
> (Rarement trouvée.)

In *Le Poème pulvérisé,* the poet has accomplished «le vol nuptial de l'homme libre enfin de se savoir et de périr oiseau» («Hymne à voix basse»). Müller's bird was the crow. Char, like Browning, has found the eagle-feather:

> I crossed a moor, with a name of its own
> And a certain use in the world no doubt,
> Yet a hand's-breadth of it shines alone
> 'Mid the blank miles round about:
>
> For there I picked up on the heather,
> And there I put inside my breast
> A moulted feather, an eagle-feather!
> Well, I forget the rest.

An early text of *Les Cloches sur le cœur,* called «Arrière vertige des tremplins,» first spoke of the feather trophy reserved to the artist. The poem ended:

> Un trophée une plume d'ange
> En chaque main un sort nouveau
> Et leurs cheveux couvrent leurs âmes
> Gloire vous soit rendue
> Vous que n'a pu retenir au sol
> Factice l'épanchement vénéneux
> De mille seins de jeunes vierges

Char's early heroes were—in the Mallarmé-Verlaine tradition—

the circus artists, musical clowns and acrobats, but their ambitions (and their fate) foreshadow those of the poet.

Lyre sans bornes des poussières,
Surcroît de notre cœur.

How different is the ending of *Le Poème pulvérisé* from that of Müller's *Winterreise!* As the Schubert cycle ends, his singer, to be sure, also plays the *Leier*. His, however, is not the Greek λύρα, the noble lyre of Orpheus or the *lyra* of the sky, but the humble *Leierkasten,* the barrel-organ of the poor itinerant player who, like the dejected lover, has not found hope or joy in this life and who, having no faith in his art, cannot believe in the poem that has taken flight.

«Que notre lit d'amour se prolonge après nous et dresse sa pénombre dans un regard qui rêve, oui, cela a de quoi rendre heureux («Verbe d'orages raisonneurs»). This text of *La Nuit talismanique,* 1972, reaffirms the position taken in 1947. Effort, courage, and love, all three are necessary to man on his *Winterreise* through life. But only love, the greatest among them, will lead beyond winter, night, and death to «la résurrection insensée.»

«Pourquoi *poème pulvérisé?* Parce qu'au terme de son voyage vers le Pays, après l'obscurité pré-natale et la dureté terrestre, la finitude du poème est lumière, apport de l'être à la vie» (*La Bibliothèque est en feu,* 1956) (10).

---

(10) The original version of this chapter appeared in *French Review,* Special Issue No. 5, Spring 1973.

2

OUT OF THE LABYRINTH: CHAR AND RIMBAUD

> ... Mais si je savais ce qu'est Rimbaud pour moi,
> je saurais ce qu'est la poésie devant moi, et je
> n'aurais plus à l'écrire.
>
> (René Char, «Arthur Rimbaud,» 1956).

Rimbaud's name figures in a prose poem, in interviews, and in several critical essays by Char aimed at assessing the poet's role in literary history (1). In a conversation with Edith Mora, Char is reported to have said: «S'il faut parler d'influence, je dirai: Rimbaud» (*Les Nouvelles Littéraires,* 16 septembre 1965). But only one Char text—the reply to a survey conducted and published in 1938 by the Cahiers G. L. M.—specifically acknowledges the poet's indebtedness to Rimbaud. Cautioning first against all influence studies, Char then names, nevertheless, three of his mentors: Heraclitus, Lautréamont, and Rimbaud: «J'ai tiré produit d'Héraclite, l'homme magnétiquement le mieux établi, du Lautréamont des poésies, de Rimbaud aux avant-bras de cervelle. Ces trois-là commandent au personnel de la voûte» («La Poésie indispensable,» *Recherche de la Base et du Sommet,* 1965).

---

(1) The following works by Char, to be discussed later, mention Rimbaud by name: «Tu as bien fait de partir, Arthur Rimbaud!,» a prose poem of *Fureur et Mystère* (Paris: Gallimard, 1948); «La Poésie indispensable,» an essay first published by the Cahiers G. L. M., 1938; «En 1871,» dated 1951; «La Conversation souveraine,» 1953; «Arthur Rimbaud,» 1956, published as an Introduction to Char's

Rimbaud was, of course, one of the literary ancestors claimed by the surrealists, and many of the contributors to the G. L. M. survey mention his name. However, I tend to believe that for Char, «l'enfant de Charleville» (2) was a personal discovery. He who in 1928 (before direct contact with the Paris group had been established) prefaced his first volume of verse with the unfinished *ars poetica* given below must have known the «Délires» of Rimbaud. *Les Cloches sur le cœur* opens, we remember, with these lines, in italics:

> *parquer son espoir illimiter sa faiblesse un*
> *suicide moral ne pouvait me suffire*
> *bribe par bribe détruire sa personnalité j'ai*
> *engendré une folie régulière*
>
> *la nuit est mesquine quand les adieux*
> *quadrangulaires* (3).

The revolutionary tone does not, we recall, prevent Char from writing in *Les Cloches sur le cœur* plaintive confessional poetry reminiscent of Baudelaire and Apollinaire, or medita-

---

edition of Rimbaud's *Œuvres* (Paris: Le Club français du livre, 1957); *Le Dernier Couac*, a controversy with Etiemble arising over the reading of a Rimbaud text, and «Page d'ascendants pour l'an 1964.» All my quotations from Char's critical essays are contained in the second edition of *Recherche de la Base et du Sommet* (Paris: Gallimard, 1965). Another text, «Arthur Rimbaud boulevard d'enfer», written in collaboration with Jacques Dupin (Paris: s.n., 1951), and reprinted as «Sous un portrait d'Arthur Rimbaud» in *Soleil*, no. 6, juin 1951, is not included in *Recherche...* There is another text, called «Réponse à une enquête à propos de Rimbaud,» dated «8 octobre '54» and addressed to the *Figaro Littéraire*, reading, in part: «La parole de Rimbaud qui m'enserre peut-être le plus étroitement est celle de l'année 1873, son 'expérience,' sa vraie vie plutôt—s'achevait. Tout ce qu'il avait conquis et qu'il allait perdre s'étalait miraculeusement devant ses yeux. La citadelle idéale des lampes qu'il se préparait à abandonner s'allumait pour longtemps sans lui, pour nous.» (Bibliothèque Littéraire Jacques Doucet).

(2) Dismissing all labels, Char will admit only the factual identifications of Rimbaud: «l'enfant de Charleville,» and «Rimbaud le Poète» («Arthur Rimbaud»).

(3) Bibliothèque Littéraire Jacques Doucet, Paris.

tions along the lines of «Mallarmé lycéen.» Which could lead one to assume that he did not discover Rimbaud until about 1926, when most of the poems of *Les Cloches* had been written (4). That would make the volume's preface—as is so often the case—an afterthought.

Critics have commented on various Rimbaldian echoes in *Le Marteau sans maître,* 1934, Char's first major collection. Here, the verbal cascades, expressions of revolt, scatological references, preoccupation with violence and destruction, but also Char's interest in alchemy and vision, his experiments with dream narration and oracular verse could, I presume, be profitably explored. But even when so delimited, Rimbaud's legacies may become confused with the bequests of Lautréamont («Rimbaud règne, Lautréamont lègue») (5), or, indeed, with lists of creditors drawn up by Breton (which included, among many, the Marquis de Sade).

I am inclined to think that Char did not come to grips with Rimbaud until his own poetry had matured. During the early years, I see the influence as largely cerebral and, therefore, superficial («Rimbaud aux avant-bras de cervelle»), without any of the poetic magnetism attributed to Heraclitus. In the 1930's, Rimbaud provided the surrealists with a workable platform duly memorized, exploited (and, we might add, disfigured, much as a philosopher and a composer were maimed, *outre-Rhin,* to serve political objectives).

From the outset, the differences between Rimbaud and Char are many and profound. The latter, a «Méridional» and fundamental rationalist, never indulges in artificially induced

---

(4) It is doubtful whether Char in 1928 had come across Rimbaud's early *huitain* beginning:

Oh! si les cloches sont de bronze,
Nos cœurs sont pleins de désespoir!

It is tempting to see here the suggestion of Char's title, *Les Cloches sur le cœur.*

(5) The juxtaposition should invite re-examination of Lautréamont's *Poésies.*

visions (6). Char does not believe in the *sorcellerie du sablier* (his words) or in the supernatural powers of the poet. He never descends to the depths of *Une Saison en enfer,* nor does he reach the *Illuminations* of Rimbaud. Char lacks the latter's spontaneity, and his breathless enthusiasm. His poetry never assumes the frenetic movement of «Le Bateau ivre»; he knows neither the «extase» nor the «cauchemar» of Rimbaud («Nuit de l'enfer»), nor his «luxure... magnifique» («Mauvais sang»), the frank eroticism and baroque sensuality, the profusion of forms and colors (in particular, gold). His canvases rarely have the sweep or the *ampleur* of Rimbaud's.

In search of models, Char looks to ancient Greece; Rimbaud, to the Middle Ages. Rimbaud writes in the impressionistic half-light of the Ardennes, or under the «ciels mouillés» of Paris. Char's poem is refined in the intense light of Provence. Rimbaud's *Illuminations* are all expansion; Char's aphorisms, the ultimate contraction. Char's outlines are as sharp as Rimbaud's are fluid. Nature, in Char's poetry, is frequently described with the exactness of scientific observation. Rimbaud's fauna and flora belong to the world of dream. Rimbaud's «Alchimie du Verbe» is a rapid succession of verbal substitutions. Char, working along Bachelardian lines, seeks the gradual transformation of a single *matière.* His poems are, for the most part, visual compositions reflecting a material reality. Most of Rimbaud's visions have the structure of an «opéra fabuleux» («Délires: II»). After *Le Marteau sans maître,* Char writes little narrative poetry, and he almost never indulges in autobiography.

The two poets differ by both temperament and training. While Rimbaud repeatedly reminds us: «Je suis de race inférieure de toute éternité» («Mauvais sang»), Char, an aristocrat by nature, would never have felt at home in «Ma Bohême» or among the «Chercheuses de poux.» His poetry does not have the popular ring of Rimbaud (or even Eluard). His vision

---

(6) This may explain, in part, Char's summary dismissal of Michaux.

does not focus on «Les Pauvres à l'église» or «Les Etrennes des orphelins.» Char's poetry is almost completely devoid of humor (7). Rimbaud rebelled against the Parnasse. Char struggles with Romanticism and the symbol forests of Baudelaire: «Sans vous défigurer, nous saurons vous charger d'explosif, épais guano des migrations romantiques» (*Moulin premier,* 1934-1935).

Char also accomplished, as it were, a second revolution when, around 1940, his break with surrealism became final. While Breton was waiting to take the ship to America, Char served the cause of the *maquis,* and the two never re-established a working relationship (8). The war changed the direction and the impact of *Le Marteau sans maître.*

As the takes leave of the surrealists (who, by this time, had themselves renounced «le culte des hommes»), Char writes the first text which I read as a conscious reassessment of Rimbaud. The long prose poem «Suzerain» of *Le Poème pulvérisé,* 1947, is one of the poet's rare autobiographic narratives (9). Reviewing his childhood and the simple men that made it, for him, «un crépuscule admirable,» Char concludes: «Ce monde net est mort sans laisser de charnier. Il n'est plus resté que couches calcinées, surfaces errantes, informe pugilat et l'eau bleue d'un puits minuscule veillée par cet Ami silencieux.» Of this unidentified and nameless friend, he says:

> ... Il m'offrait, à la gueule d'un serpent qui souriait, mon impossible que je pénétrais sans souffrir. D'où venait cet Ami? Sans doute, du moins sombre, du moins ouvrier des soleils. Son énergie que je jugeais

---

(7) As far as I can recall, only James Lawler has touched upon the question of humor in Char's poetry. V. «René Char's *Quatre Fascinants,*» in *About French Poetry from Dada to «Tel Quel»; Text and Theory* (Detroit: Wayne State Univ. Press, 1974).

(8) Char's rather diplomatically worded «Lettre hors commerce» to André Breton, 1947, should be consulted in this connection.

(9) It is interesting that in his explanatory note to the poem given in *Arrière-Histoire du Poème pulvérisé,* Char does not mention Rimbaud.

grande éclatait en fougères patientes, humidité pour
mon espoir. Ce dernier, en vérité, n'était qu'une
neige de l'existence, l'affinité du renouveau. Un
butin s'amoncelait, dessinant le littoral cruel que
j'aurais un jour à parcourir. Le cœur de mon Ami
m'entrait dans le cœur comme un trident, cœur
souverain, égaillé dans des conquêtes bientôt ré-
duites en cendres, pour marquer combien la tentation se déprime chez qui s'établit, se rend. Nos
confidences ne construiraient pas d'église; le mutisme reconduisait tous nous pouvoirs.

Il m'apprit à voler au-dessus de la nuit des mots,
loin de l'hébétude des navires à l'ancre. Ce n'est
pas le glacier qui nous importe mais ce qui le fait
possible indéfiniment, sa solitaire vraisemblance.
Je nouai avec des haines enthousiastes que j'aidai
à vaincre puis quittai. (Il suffit de fermer les yeux
pour ne plus être reconnu.) Je retirai aux choses
l'illusion qu'elles produisent pour se préserver de
nous et leur laissai la part qu'elles nous concèdent.
Je vis qu'il n'y aurait jamais de femme pour moi
dans MA ville. La frénésie des cascades, symboli-
quement, acquitterait mon bon vouloir.

J'ai remonté ainsi l'âge de la solitude jusqu'à la
demeure suivante de L'HOMME VIOLET. Mais il
ne disposait là que du morose état civil de ses
prisons, de son expérience muette de persécuté, et
nous n'avions, nous, que son signalement d'évadé.

Evocations of «Le Bateau ivre» and biographical references
point to Rimbaud, as does Char's attitude towards the nameless *Ami, L'HOMME VIOLET*:

O, suprême Clairon plein des strideurs étranges,
Silences traversés des Mondes et des Anges:
—O l'Oméga, rayon violet de Ses Yeux!

In the beginning, Rimbaud the violet and violent man, (10)

---

(10) Rimbaud sees himself as «un gros ours aux gencives violet-
tes» in the prose poem «Bottom» (*Les Illuminations*).

is the sovereign («cœur souverain»), exercising, by his word, the power of life and death over his vassal. However, in the end, Rimbaud himself is reduced to nothingness, to the «morose état civil» and «son signalement d'évadé.»

As early as 1944, in the prose poem called «Calendrier» (*Seuls demeurent*), Char the vassal relinquishes the fief held for his suzerain:

> J'ai lié les unes aux autres mes convictions et agrandi ta Présence. J'ai octroyé un cours nouveau à mes jours en les adossant à cette force spacieuse. J'ai congédié la violence qui limitait mon ascendant. J'ai pris sans éclat le poignet de l'équinoxe. L'oracle ne me vassalise plus. J'entre: j'éprouve ou non la grâce.

While one might be inclined to interpret this text as Char's farewell to surrealism (the preface to the first *Manifeste du Surréalisme* ended on a new definition of *grâce* used to denote the effects of surrealist activity), it should be remembered that Breton explicitly denied the *oracular* power of poetry. But Char may be thinking, in «Calendrier,» of Rimbaud's search for a new religion, defined in «Mauvais sang» as follows: «C'est la vision des nombres. Nous allons à l'*Esprit*. C'est très-certain, c'est oracle, ce que je dis. Je comprends, et ne sachant m'expliquer sans paroles païennes, je voudrais me taire» (*Une Saison en enfer*).

Char's struggle with Rimbaud seems to be described in «Le mortel partenaire,» a prose poem of *Poèmes des deux années 1953-1954* (10a). The text is the narration of a boxing match and a suggestion of amorous combat. The partner, identified by the title as male, quickly changes sex and roles, and remains undefined until the end of the poem, which suggests that the assailant (*il*) was combating life itself (*la vie*), which has the power to kill. However, the poem

---

(10a) For a discussion of «Le mortel partenaire,» see Mary Ann Caws, *The Presence of René Char*, pp. 55-56.

also hints at a literary struggle. The definition of the arena: «Sur la blanche surface où se tenait le combat» suggests the boxing ring, the bed, and the white pages of a book. The ambiguities of love and war, the sports arena and the realm of poetic creation, are maintained throughout.

The combat takes place on the first day of summer: «Dans l'air de juin voltigeait le prénom des fleurs du premier jour de l'été.» We hear the echo of Rimbaud's «Aube» (*Les Illuminations*): «J'ai embrassé l'aube d'été... La première entreprise fut... une fleur qui me dit son nom.» The description of the assailant who would defy life—and is killed by it—also fits Rimbaud:

> ... A cet instant le premier dut à dessein prononcer à l'oreille du second des paroles si parfaitement offensantes, ou appropriées, ou énigmatiques, que de celui-ci fila, prompte, totale, précise, une foudre qui coucha net l'incompréhensible combattant.
> Certains êtres ont une signification qui nous manque. Qui sont-ils? Leur secret tient au plus profond du secret même de la vie. Ils s'en approchent. Elle les tue. Mais l'avenir qu'ils ont ainsi éveillé d'un murmure, les devinant, les crée. O dédale de l'extrême amour!

In «Tu as bien fait de partir, Arthur Rimbaut!,» a prose poem of *La Fontaine narrative,* the young poet is seen as a cannon-ball, propelled by the «absurd» *élan* of body and soul towards a goal it reaches only to destroy. But, says Char, «on ne peut pas, au sortir de l'enfance, indéfiniment étrangler son prochain.» In the dark silence of Africa, Rimbaud takes his place among the volcanoes «qui changent peu de place.» While these resemble—by the *éclat* accompanying their eruption—the earlier cannon-ball, a purely destructive force, they also spread, in the wake of the eruption, the lava that flows through the great void of the earth, bringing to it «des vertus qui chantent dans ses plaies.» When the volcano has been silenced, the lava-covered earth is transformed into the fertile vineyards and fields upon which we feed. It is in this sense that Char can conclude: «Tu as bien fait de partir, Arthur Rimbaud! Nous sommes quelques-uns à croire le bonheur possible avec toi!» Char will labor in the fields made fertile by the *Verbe* of Rimbaud. He will heal the wounds of the earth struck by lightning to bring forth from «Les Déserts de l'amour» the flower and the fruit of his poem.

During the 1950's, Char writes the major critical essays that mention Rimbaud. «En 1871,» a text dated 1951, discusses Rimbaud's place in literary history, and concludes: «Il n'a rien manqué à Rimbaud, probablement rien. Jusqu'à la dernière goutte de sang hurlé, et jusqu'au sel de la splendeur.» The ambiguous nature of *jusqu'à* (prepositional or adverbial?) and the adverb *probablement* give us pause. In «La Conversation souveraine,» 1953, mention of Rimbaud is reduced to two simple—but important—words: «Rimbaud règne.» The author, however, says nothing of Rimbaud's lordship over him, Char. Only Apollinaire and Reverdy are discussed as personal preferences and, perhaps, influences.

«Arthur Rimbaud,» 1956, the text originally published as an Introduction to a new edition of Rimbaud's *Œuvres* (Club français du livre), examines, in greater detail, the poet's originality. It also sheds some light on the nameless partner of the earlier prose poem. Thus, Char's «Suzerain» spoke of the lessons learned from the mysterious childhood friend: «La connaissance eut tôt fait de grandir entre nous. *Ceci n'est plus,* avais-je coutume de dire. *Ceci n'est pas,* corrigeait-il» (Char's italics). A lesson on which the critical essay elaborates: «La vraie vie, le colosse irrécusable, ne se forme que dans les flancs de la poésie. Cependant *l'homme n'a pas la souveraineté (ou n'a plus, ou n'a pas encore)* de disposer à discrétion de cette vraie vie, de s'y fertiliser, sauf en de brefs éclairs qui ressemblent à des orgasmes» (my italics). The passage names the combat engaged in by the poet and his «mortel partenaire.» It again defines Rimbaud's influence as the flash of lightning by which, in the end, the poet himself is killed. In the same essay, Char also describes Rimbaud's legacy as «les épines victorieuses, piquants qui furent annoncés par l'entêtant parfum des fleurs,» reminding us of the «prénom des fleurs» and «une fleur qui me dit son nom.»

Other passages in Char's Introduction recall «Suzerain.» The prose poem contained the aphorism: «La tentation se déprime chez qui s'établit, se rend.» It spoke of prisons and referred to the «expérience muette de persécuté... son signalement d'évadé.» These references are made explicit in the essay: «Rimbaud s'évadant situe indifféremment son âge d'or dans le passé et dans le futur. Il ne s'établit pas... Mais tout ce qu'on obtient par rupture, détachement et négation, on ne l'obtient que pour autrui. La prison se referme aussitôt sur l'évadé. Le donneur de liberté n'est libre que dans les autres...» (11).

The dual nature of Char's relationship to Rimbaud is delineated near the beginning of the essay: «Nous obéissons librement au pouvoir des poèmes et nous les aimons par force. Cette dualité nous procure anxiété, orgueil et joie.» Char admits that Rimbaud «nous entraîne, il nous soumet, consentants» by the power of his poem. But in love («nous les aimons par force») there is projection, servitude, influence. Rupture, detachment, and negation—characteristic of the life and work of Rimbaud—must, in the end, define Char's own position vis-à-vis him and all other literary influences (12). If he is to survive as poet, Char must overcome his «mortels partenaires,» while exploring, at the same time, «l'avenir qu'ils ont ainsi éveillé d'un murmure, ... O dédale de l'extrême amour!»

In at least one instance, Char seems to take up, consciously,

---

(11) We remember Rimbaud's cry in «L'Impossible» (*Une Saison en enfer*):

J'ai eu raison dans tous mes dédains: puisque je m'évade!

Je m'évade!

(12) The critical essays of the 1950's may achieve a catharsis along these lines. By naming and acknowledging his creditors, Char repays his literary debts, reaching, in the process, a greater awareness of his own quest.

where Rimbaud left off, entering the labyrinth of Daedalus and emerging the victor. He answers the «paroles si parfaitement offensantes» with «L'Inoffensif,» a prose poem of *Le Rempart de brindilles,* 1953, which illustrates, to my mind, both the abiding influence of Rimbaud and Char's progress beyond it (12a). «L'Inoffensif» reads like a sequel to «Les Déserts de l'amour,» Rimbaud's first experiment with the prose poem (following readings of Baudelaire in 1871). In an «Avertissement,» Rimbaud warns that these texts (only one has come down to us) were written by a «tout jeune homme,» a young man «si ennuyé et si troublé, qu'il ne fit que s'amener à la mort comme à une pudeur terrible et fatale. N'ayant pas aimé de femmes...» Thinly veiled confessions of his homosexual experiences end in expression of the hope that «cette Ame, égarée parmi nous tous, et qui veut la mort, ce semble, rencontre en cet instant-là des consolations sérieuses et soit digne.»

The narrative that follows is specifically introduced as a dream. In that dream, the narrator sees himself in the country-home of his parents. The «salle» and the «salon» are described, and the dinner-table, «très-grande.» Maid servants scurry about the house, and the dreamer remembers a priest in his «chambre de pourpre, à vitres de papier jaune: et ses livres, cachés, qui avaient trempé dans l'océan!» No other mention is made of him in the text. The narrator finds himself alone, in the kitchen, «ému jusqu'à la mort par le murmure» (one of Char's signal words!) «du lait du matin et de la nuit du siècle dernier.» From the kitchen, he passes into «une chambre très sombre,» where he is joined by one of the maids: «je puis dire que c'était un petit chien: quoiqu'elle fut belle, et d'une noblesse maternelle inexprimable pour moi: pure, connue, toute charmante! Elle me pinça le bras.» The dreamer does not recall her face: «ce n'est pas pour me rappeler son bras, dont je roulai la peau dans mes deux doigts;

(12a) For a discussion of «L'Inoffensif,» see Mary Ann Caws, *op. cit.,* pp. 121-126.

ni sa bouche, que la mienne saisit comme une petite vague désespérée, minant sans fin quelque chose. Je la renversai dans une corbeille de coussins et de toiles de navire, en un coin noir...» (13). Then night settles on the lovers:

> Puis, ô désespoir! la cloison devint vaguement l'ombre des arbres, et je me suis abîmé sous la tristesse amoureuse de la nuit.

The opening sentences of the last three paragraphs trace the growing sense of sadness and despair:

> 1. «J'étais dans une chambre sans lumière.»

> 2. «Je sortis dans la ville sans fin. O fatigue! Noyé dans la nuit sourde et dans la fuite du bonheur.»

> 3. «J'ai compris qu'elle était à sa vie de tous les jours; et que le tour de bonté serait plus long à se reproduire qu'une étoile.»

Each of the last three paragraphs speaks of the tears wept by the dreamer over the loss of his love:

> 1. «Alors, la femme disparut. Je versai plus de larmes que Dieu n'en a jamais pu demander.

> 2. «Enfin, je suis descendu dans un lieu plein de poussière, et, assis sur des charpentes, j'ai laissé finir toutes les larmes de mon corps avec cette nuit. —Et mon épuisement me revenait pourtant toujours.»

---

(13) In the essay «Arthur Rimbaud,» Char may be taking up Rimbaud's image of the «corbeilles de coussins et de toiles de navire» in the passage: «Et Rimbaud va du doux traversin d'herbe où la tête oublieuse des fatigues du corps devient une eau de source, à quelque chasse entre possédés au sommet d'une falaise qui crache le déluge et la tempête.» The passage could be applied to the later erotic evocations in «Les Déserts de l'amour.»

3. «Elle n'est pas revenue, et ne reviendra jamais, l'Adorable qui s'était rendue chez moi, —ce que je n'aurais jamais présumé. Vrai, cette fois j'ai pleuré plus que tous les enfants du monde.»

«L'Inoffensif,» a much shorter text, deletes from Rimbaud's narrative all purely descriptive and pseudo-realistic details. There are no references in Char's text to houses, rooms, servants or the dinner-table. The poem does away with all prosaic interpolations, such as «ce que je n'aurais jamais présumé,» and reads:

Je pleure quand le soleil se couche parce qu'il te dérobe à ma vue et parce que je ne sais pas m'accorder avec ses rivaux nocturnes. Bien qu'il soit au bas et maintenant sans fièvre, impossible d'aller contre son déclin, de suspendre son effeuillaison, d'arracher quelque envie encore à sa lueur moribonde. Son départ te fond dans son obscurité comme le limon du lit se délaye dans l'eau du torrent par-delà l'éboulis des berges détruites. Dureté et mollesse au ressort différent ont alors des effets semblables. Je cesse de recevoir l'hymne de ta parole; soudain tu n'apparais plus entière à mon côté; ce n'est pas le fuseau nerveux de ton poignet que tient ma main mais la branche creuse d'un quelconque arbre mort et déjà débité. On ne met plus un nom à rien, qu'au frisson. Il fait nuit. Les artifices qui s'allument me trouvent aveugle.

Je n'ai pleuré en vérité qu'une seule fois. Le soleil en disparaissant avait coupé ton visage. Ta tête avait roulé dans la fosse du ciel et je ne croyais plus au lendemain.

Lequel est l'homme du matin et lequel celui des ténèbres?

In the opening aphorism of *Le Rempart de brindilles,* Char writes: «Le dessein de la poésie étant de nous rendre souverains en nous impersonnalisant, nous touchons, grâce au poème, à la plénitude de ce qui n'était qu'esquissé ou déformé par les vantardises de l'individu.» «L'Inoffensif» begins where Rimbaud left off. The sunset—a mere pretext in Rimbaud's poem—becomes itself the subject of Char's text. Human presence and intervention are reduced to a minimum, and nature itself occupies, in «L'Inoffensif,» the center stage. Rimbaud mentions the family and the servants, the two women he has loved in dreams, «la servante» and «la Femme...dans la Ville,» plus a young priest (used, perhaps, to indicate the androgynous nature of the dreamer's love). Char restricts the human element to the narrator (*je*) and to an unidentified second person singular (*tu*), his *alter ego,* «l'homme des ténèbres» whose head is hurled, as the sun goes down, «dans la fosse du ciel.»

Rimbaud's numerous erotic evocations are as sensuous as they are desperate: «Elle me pinça le bras... Je ne me rappelle même plus bien sa figure: ce n'est pas pour me rappeler son bras, dont je roulai la peau dans mes deux doigts; ni sa bouche, que la mienne saisit comme une petite vague désespérée... je la pris, et la laissai tomber hors du lit, presque nue; et, dans ma faiblesse indicible, je tombai sur elle et me traînai avec elle parmi les tapis sans lumière!... Alors, la femme disparut.» In Char's poem, the sun is going down, without any erotic prelude. In fact, the feminine element in «L'Inoffensif» is reduced to one adjective, *entière.* Via the ancient symbol of man, the tree, the poet quickly focuses away from a presumed human figure to «la branche creuse»: «Ce n'est pas le fuseau nerveux de ton poignet que tient ma main mais la branche creuse d'un quelconque arbre mort et déjà débité.» The choice of the verb underlines the equation: man — tree. The word *débiter* calls to mind the branches cut from the dead tree as well as the now meaningless words spoken by an actor, and the debt owed (though presumably cancelled, through death) to a nameless creditor. The tree long dead no longer serves the narrator. The words it speaks no longer reach him. The vital energy, the *foudre* and the *éclair* have gone out of the *fuseau nerveux,* leaving, in their wake, nothing but dead branches. Several years later, in a 1964 addition to *Lettera amorosa,* Char will write: «La terre feule, les nuits de pariade. Un complot de branches mortes n'y pourrait tenir.»

In «L'Inoffensif,» Char names only the part of the body most nearly resembling the earth, and the sun: *ton visage, ta tête,* the very things Rimbaud would forget, recalling only the embrace, and the kiss. Char does not, in fact, establish human contact: «Je n'ai pleuré en vérité qu'une seule fois. *Le soleil...avait coupé* ton visage. *Ta tête avait roulé...*» He acknowledges, by means of a personification, the autonomous action of natural phenomena. For Char, the partners of the poem *are* the earth and the sun, darkness and light (not reduced to romantic metaphors). The verbs *rouler* and *tomber* are combined in the directional use of the preposition *dans,* which had a positional function in Rimbaud: «je roulai...dans mes deux doigts» becomes «ta tête avait roulé dans la fosse du ciel.» By his personification, Char actually dehumanizes the metaphor.

Rimbaud personifies nature in the traditional manner, making of it the reflection of the narrator's *état d'âme.* Like the early Char of «Ce soir,» he succumbs to the «tristesse amoureuse de la nuit» and drowns himself in «la nuit sourde.» Rimbaud's cry: «ô désespoir!» is countered by Char's logical conclusion: «impossible d'aller contre son déclin.» While Rimbaud sees himself «noyé dans la nuit *sourde,*» Char rejects the personification. «Il fait nuit,» he says. «Les artifices qui s'allument *me trouvent aveugle.*» Given the context, this is a realistic observation. Night is neither deaf nor attentive to man's despair. But the poet, blinded by the brilliance of the sun, may well be *aveugle* to the light of the stars. The choice of the adjective is consistent also with the structural differences between the two texts. Char's poem is a primarily visual composition; Rimbaud's, a lyrical confession.

Rimbaud seeks to possess—and thereby kills—the thing he loves. «Pleurant, je voyais de l'or - et ne pus boire,» he says in another poem («Alchimie du Verbe»). Char writes, in *Le Rempart de brindilles*: «La quête d'un grand Etre, n'est-ce qu'une pression de doigt du présent entravé sur l'avenir en liberté? Les lendemains non touchés sont vastes. Et là-bas est divin où ne retentit pas le choc de notre chaîne.» Rimbaud's poem has the finality of the *passé simple*: «je roulai...tombai...traînai.» The opening of Char's prose poem: «Je pleure quand le soleil se couche,» implying habitual action, is corrected, in the end, by evocation of a single act: «Je n'ai pleuré en vérité qu'une seule fois...» The imperfect which follows: «et je ne croyais plus au lendemain,» admits the possibility of change.

A rather lengthy parenthesis suggested by the repetition of the opening verb may shed additional light on the partner described in «L'Inoffensif.» The verb *pleurer,* not very frequent in Char's vocabulary, reappears in one other text of *Poèmes des deux années.* In the prose poem entitled «Marmonnement,» Char addresses himself to a wolf, an animal obviously chosen for all the erotic and religious overtones usually associated with it, and for the dual symbolism of life and death examined in the text:

> Pour ne pas me rendre et pour m'y retrouver, je t'offense, mais combien je suis épris de toi, loup, qu'on dit à tort funèbre, pétri des secrets de mon arrière-pays. C'est dans une masse d'amour légendaire que tu laisses la déchaussure vierge, pourchassée de ton ongle... Derrière ta course sans crinière, je saigne, je pleure, je m'enserre de terreur, j'oublie, je ris sous les arbres...

Char identifies his partner only by means of a question: «De plus, tu es inintelligible. Non-comparant, compensateur, que sais-je?» Reference to Rimbaud's oracles and «paroles... énigmatiques» was made in earlier texts. «Même, quelle langue parlais-je?» Rimbaud asks of himself in «Mauvais sang» (*Une Saison en enfer*). «Connais-je encore la nature? me connais-je?—*Plus de mots.* J'ensevelis les morts dans mon ventre,» an image that recalls the wolf's function in the fairy-tale, as well as the *homo homini lupus,* and, perhaps, the Minotaur. In the text dedicated to the «Epoux infernal» and the «Vierge folle» («Délires I,» *ibid.*), Rimbaud compares himself to the man of many names, in search of an identity: «il s'appelle Duval, Dufour, Armand, Maurice, que sais-je?» A passage that Char may remember in his description of the wolf: «Non-comparant, compensateur, que sais-je?»

In the essay «Arthur Rimbaud,» Char identifies the one who embodies the secrets of his «arrière-pays»:

> En voulant remonter aux sources et se régénérer, on ne fait qu'aggraver l'ankylose, que précipiter la chute et punir absurdement son sang. Rimbaud avait éprouvé et repoussé cette tentation: *«Il faut être absolument moderne: Tenir le pas gagné.»* La poésie moderne a un arrière-pays dont seule la clôture est sombre. Nul pavillon ne flotte longtemps sur cette banquise qui, au gré de son caprice, se donne à nous et se reprend...

The critical text shows a curious resemblance to the opening of Char's prose poem: «Pour ne pas me rendre et pour m'y retrouver...»

While Char's ambivalent attitude towards the animal and the struggle engaged in clearly recall «Le mortel partenaire,» the mere personification of the wolf would not permit identification with Rimbaud. «Le Loup criait sous les feuilles,» Rimbaud's early poem copied by Char into the Mercure edition of Rimbaud's *Vers et Prose,* 1924, is very different in tone and theme from Char's prose poem. The wolf is not a frequent animal in Rimbaud's extraordinary bestiary. It does appear in the «Bal des Pendus,» where it is specifically described as *funèbre*:

> Les loups vont répondant des forêts violettes:
> A l'horizon, le ciel est d'un rouge d'enfer...
>
> Holà, secouez-moi ces capitans funèbres
> Qui défilent, sournois, de leurs gros doigts cassés

Un chapelet d'amour sur leurs pâles vertèbres:
Ce n'est pas un moustier ici, les trépassés!

The wolf as a symbol of the (amorous and religious) warrior reappears in «Michel et Christine»:

Voilà mille loups, mille graines sauvages
Qu'emporte, non sans aimer les liserons,
Cette religieuse après-midi d'orage
Sur l'Europe ancienne où cent hordes iront!

As far as I recall, Rimbaud never refers to himself as a wolf, but does describe himself, in «Enfance I» (*Les Illuminations*) as «cette idole, yeux noirs et crin jaune, sans parents ni cour, plus noble que la fable.» In the opening text of *Une Saison en enfer,* comparing himself to a hyaena, Rimbaud writes: «Sur toute joie pour l'étrangler j'ai fait le bond sourd de la bête féroce,» a description worthy of «Le mortel partenaire» and no doubt remembered by Char in «Tu as bien fait de partir, Arthur Rimbaud.» In «Mauvais sang,» a text which also makes reference to his religious struggles, Rimbaud identifies his lineage as follows: «Ma race ne se souleva jamais que pour piller: tels les loups à la bête qu'ils n'ont pas tuée.» In the same text, he refers to himself as an animal, asking not to be judged by the tribunal of men: «Prêtres... je suis une brute.» In «Délires I» he again points to the savage nature of his ancestors: «Je suis de race lointaine: mes pères étaient Scandinaves: ils se perçaient les côtes, buvaient leur sang.»

«Derrière ta course sans crinière, je saigne, je pleure, je m'enserre de terreur, j'oublie, je ris sous les arbres,» wrote Char. And it is really the breathless rhythm of this sentence and the seemingly incongruous mention of the poet laughing under the trees that sent me back to *Une Saison en enfer.* Here, in the opening text referred to above, Rimbaud continues: «Je me suis allongé dans la boue. Je me suis séché à l'air du crime. Et j'ai joué de bons tours à la folie. Et le printemps m'a apporté l'affreux rire de l'idiot.» In «Deli-

res I,» the «Epoux infernal» repeats that laughter: «Hélas!
il avait des jours où tous les hommes agissant lui paraissaient
les jouets de délires grotesques; il riait affreusement, longtemps.» Rimbaud's laughter (following upon his suffering:
«Je suis en deuil, je pleure, j'ai peur,» *ibid*.) is the ultimate
despair. Read in this context, Char's gradation («je m'enserre
de terreur, j'oublie, je ris sous les arbres») makes very good
sense.

Another interpretation—quite different, but still pointing
to Rimbaud—is suggested by the ending of Char's prose poem:

> Continue, va, nous durons ensemble; et ensemble,
> bien que séparés, nous bondissons par-dessus le
> frisson de la suprême déception pour briser la glace
> des eaux vives et se reconnaître là.

The verb *bondir* and the narrator's determination to break up
the ice that covers the *eaux vives* suggest the liberation of
Ysengrin from the frozen waters of the lake. Oblique references to the *Roman de Renart* (Char made of the *renarde* his
own emblem of the *maquisard*) may, perhaps, be found in the
passage quoted earlier from «Suzerain,» where Char, assessing
his childhood, spoke of the «informe pugilat et l'eau bleue d'un
puits minuscule veillée par cet Ami silencieux.»

But the *eaux vives* mentioned in «Marmonnement» also
remind us of Rimbaud's «Bateau ivre» coming to rest in the
«flache / Noire et froide,» the «suprême déception.» And once
again there are, in Char's murmurings, echoes of Rimbaud's
«Aube.» Here, the poet is described on a walk resembling a
«course sans crinière» across the fields and into the woods
where the «eau...morte» comes alive: «Je ris au wasserfall
blond qui s'échevela à travers les sapins: à la cime argentée je
reconnus la déesse.» Seen in this context, Char's enumeration:
«je saigne, je pleure, je m'enserre de terreur» must be read
as a juxtaposition to: «j'oublie, je ris sous les arbres.» Char
does not acknowledge the goddess that would subjugate man.
Rimbaud's ending: «L'aube et l'enfant tombèrent au bas du

bois,» is rejected by Char who dismisses the supernatural («à la cime argentée...la déesse») as the «suprême déception.» Recognizing only the power of the poet and his creation, Char's poem ends: «...nous bondissons par-dessus le frisson de la suprême déception pour briser la glace des eaux vives et *se reconnaître* là.»

There is, in the end, no anguish in Char's mature poem, no weeping and no *désespoir*. Only the «frisson nouveau,» the anxiety—but also the joy—of anticipation. In his Introduction to Rimbaud's *Œuvres*, Char writes a passage we might well apply to his transformation of «Les Déserts de l'amour.» He asks:

> Qu'est-ce qui scintille, parle plus qu'il ne chuchote, se transmet silencieusement, puis file derrière la nuit, ne laissant que le vide de l'amour, la promesse de l'immunité? Cette scintillation très personnelle, cette trépidation, cette hypnose, ces battements innombrables sont autant de versions, celles-là plausibles, d'un événement unique: le présent perpétuel, en forme de roue comme le soleil, et comme le visage humain, avant que la terre et le ciel en le tirant à eux ne l'allongeassent cruellement (14).

Even the notion of cruelty is absent from «L'Inoffensif» (as is mention of *la nuit mesquine* that prefaced *Les Cloches sur le cœur*). Since every sunrise and every sunset is a unique event, it can occur only in a perpetual present that is without memory and, therefore, without regret. The continual recurrence of individual events forms a circle («en forme de roue comme le soleil») that is itself without beginning or end. An event perceived as scintillation, trepidation, or «frisson» (a word lacking a single English equivalent) cannot be defined in space and time. In the void, all things lose their name. That is why Char can assert, quite literally: «On ne met plus un nom à rien qu'au frisson.»

---

(14) Note the images recurring from «Le mortel partenaire.»

Char accepts the fact that man cannot hope to arrest the course of the sun. Though in «L'Extravagant» he apparently tried to return Rimbaud's «Vagabonds» (*Les Illuminations*) to the «état primitif de fils de soleil,» neither Char nor Rimbaud found «le lieu et la formule.» Like the «mortel partenaire,» Phaeton was killed by a flash of lightning and hurled into the darkness of the sea. How, then, should man hope to rival the sun?

Unlike the Prince of *Les Illuminations* («Conte») and the dreamer of «Les Déserts de l'amour,» Char's narrator does not kill the thing he loves, does not humiliate «le Pays qu'il révèle,» (15) does not reduce his love and happiness—in an effort to posses it—to «un petit chien.» The Minotaur and «Le mortel partenaire» are slain by the sword of Theseus and by the «foudre qui coucha net l'incompréhensible combattant» (16). But in L'Inoffensif,» the man of darkness, having been rendered non-violent and non-destructive, returns. Char compares his partner to a tree. Without its leaves that reach for the light (Char refers to the sun's going down as «son effeuillaison»), the branch will die. The hollow stem, deprived of its branches, can no longer speak the «paroles amoureuses» that awaken the earth. Without the «fuseau nerveux,» without the hand—the hand that writes—the arm is a useless tool. Char has, at last, freed himself from the strangling embrace of the «avant-bras de cervelle.» He has, to use a term of Harold Bloom's, «wrestled his precursor to a truce» (*Kabbalah and Criticism*), realizing that as the tree cannot survive without the sun, so «l'homme des ténèbres,» the man of darkness, cannot exist independent of «l'homme du matin,»

(15) Char applies the description to Rimbaud in «Page d'ascendants pour l'an 1964,» *Recherche de la Base et du Sommet*, 1965.

(16) «L'Inoffensif» and «Le mortel partenaire» follow directly upon each other in *Le Rempart de brindilles* and first appeared together in the *Cahiers du Sud*, no. 317, 1953. (Incidentally, it is Char himself who in the essay called «En 1871» sees the poet as carried off by the Minotaur.)

the man of light. The two are, as the poem's original title indicated, «false rivals.»

Man, said Char, does not have the sovereign power to dispose at will of the life formed «dans les flancs de la poésie sauf en de brefs éclairs qui ressemblent à des orgasmes.» And he continues:

> Et dans les ténèbres qui leur succèdent, grâce à la connaissance que ces éclairs ont apportée, le Temps, entre le vide horrible qu'il sécrète et un espoir-pressentiment qui ne relève que de nous, et n'est que le prochain état d'extrême poésie et de voyance qui s'annonce, le Temps se partagera, s'écoulera, mais à notre profit, moitié verger, moitié désert.

Another text of *Poèmes des deux années* celebrates Char's newly gained independence and his victory over the powers of darkness:

Victoire éclair

L'oiseau bêche la terre,
Le serpent sème,
La mort améliorée
Applaudit la récolte.

Pluton dans le ciel!

L'explosion en nous.
Là seulement dans moi.
Fol et sourd, comment pourrais-je l'être davantage?

Plus de second soi-même, de visage changeant, plus de saison pour la flamme et de saison pour l'ombre!

Avec la lente neige descendent les lépreux.

Soudain l'amour, l'égal de la terreur,
D'une main jamais vue arrête l'incendie, redresse le soleil, reconstruit l'Amie.

Rien n'annonçait une existence si forte.

Char has reconciled *Une Saison en enfer* and *Les Illumina-tions,* the man of darkness and the man of light, the serpent and the bird. He who once saw Rimbaud's work as «conduite à la perfection par Apollon et par Pluton» («Arthur Rimbaud») has now placed Pluto himself in heaven and whitewashed the leper of *Une Saison en enfer.* The changing faces of «L'Inoffensif,» the sun and the earth, the flame and the shadow come together as Char cultivates the ground made fertile by the «éclairs» sown by the serpent. The harvest is translated by the poet into «L'explosion en nous.» And, to underline the point, Char repeats: «Là seulement *dans moi.*» The struggle between love and terror («Marmonnement,» «Le mortel partenaire»), light and darkness ends in the «Victoire éclair.»

> Tous les faux désirs m'ont quitté
> Pour devenir d'inoffensifs promeneurs
> Les promeneurs paralysés à tête maternelle

It is as though Char remembered in 1953 these lines contained, some twenty years earlier, in «Vivante demain» (*Poèmes militants*), then discarded, and resurrected in «L'Inoffensif,» which continues the journey out of «Les Déserts de l'amour» into the orchard.

This journey points directly to *Lettera amorosa,* Char's longest poem of love which, in its original version, is a con-temporary of «L'Inoffensif.» The Letter has two epigraphs, one a quotation from Monteverdi, the other, the passage in italics given below:

> *Le cœur soudain privé, l'hôte du désert devient presque lisiblement le cœur fortuné, le cœur agran-di, le diadème.*

And the Letter proper opens: «...Je n'ai plus de fièvre ce

matin. Ma tête est de nouveau claire et vacante, posée comme un rocher sur un verger à ton image.»

It is not the loss of physical contact Char weeps in the opening line of «L'Inoffensif,» but the loss of vision (and, consequently, hope). Having seen a single sun rise and set, he is willing, in the end, to believe in—and to accept—the orderly and predictable cycle of night and day, darkness and light, independent of the nature of man: «Dureté et mollesse au ressort différent ont alors des effets semblables.»

Char has struggled with the man of darkness and defined «ce qu'est Rimbaud pour moi.» In the process, he has come to see more clearly his own goal, «ce qu'est la poésie devant moi,» the «espoir-pressentiment qui ne relève que de lui,» René Char.

> Mais, vrai, j'ai trop pleuré! Les Aubes sont
> navrantes.
> Toute lune est atroce et tout soleil amer...

wrote Rimbaud («Le Bateau ivre»). Unlike him, Char does not fear the «murmure du lait du matin» nor the «dédale de l'extrême amour.»

As his Introduction to Rimbaud's *Œuvres* comes to an end, Char takes leave of his «mortel partenaire» and former «Suzerain»:

> Comme Nietzsche, comme Lautréamont, après avoir tout exigé de nous, il [Rimbaud] nous demande de le 'renvoyer'. Dernière et essentielle exigence. Lui qui ne s'est satisfait de rien, comment pourrions-nous nous satisfaire de lui? Sa marche ne connaît qu'un terme: la mort...

Having entered the labyrinth of Daedalus and emerged unharmed, Char proclaims the immunity of *Les Matinaux* and celebrates, in *Lettera amorosa,* the «retour du jour sur les vertes avenues libres.» Orion, his sight restored by the rays of the rising sun, continues his eastward journey into the light (17).

(17) The original version of this chapter appeared in the *Kentucky Romance Quarterly*, 1974, no. 2, with the title: «*L'homme du matin... et celui des ténèbres.* Char and Rimbaud. Parallels and Contrasts.» Char, quoting Georges Bataille, speaks of the labyrinth in the original version of «Au lecteur,» published by Mary Ann Caws in *Poems of René Char.* Char's manuscript ends as follows: «'Cette fuite se dirigeant vers le sommet (qu'est, dominant les empires eux-mêmes, la composition du savoir) n'est que l'un des parcours du *labyrinthe*, mais ce parcours qu'il nous faut suivre de leurre en leurre, à la recherche de l'*être*, nous ne pouvons l'éviter d'aucune façon.'»

3

INTO THE SUN: CHAR AND BRAQUE

Pour seul soleil: le bœuf écorché de Rembrandt.
(*Contre une maison sèche,* 1971).

Probably no twentieth century poet since Apollinaire has known a more intimate and productive relationship with the great visual artists of his day than René Char. The exhibit organized in honor of the poet by the Maeght Foundation in April 1971 drew to Saint-Paul de Vence more art dealers and collectors than poets. (The scales may have tipped in favor of the latter when the exhibit traveled to Paris in the winter of the same year.) On display here were paintings and sculptures that have inspired Char's poetry: a woman's head by Georges de La Tour recalling «Madeleine à la veilleuse,» a poem first published in the *Mercure de France,* July 1948; a copy of the «Prisonnier» that Char had kept tacked to the walls of his hideout in Céreste, during the dark days of the Resistance; a figure painting by Corot, remembered by Char in «Une Italienne de Corot,» a text that appeared in the *Cahiers d'Art,* along with «Courbet: Les casseurs de cailloux,» both of which are included in *Dehors la nuit est gouvernée,* 1938. There were paintings by Paul Klee, to whom Char dedicated the text «Secrets d'hirondelles,» 1946, and the bronze «Tête d'Iris» (1890-91) by Rodin that the poet had seen in the Paris museum. It inspired the poem called «La Lisière du trouble,» dated 1948, and published in *Les Matinaux,* 1950:

Toutes les mains sur une pierre,
Les mains de pourpre et les dociles,
Pour deux actives qui distillent.

Mains, par temps sublime, que l'air fonde
    au même instant que l'arc;
Données par le parfum de l'iris des marais
    à ma lourdeur,
Un soir brumeux, de leur côté.

                                    (*Paris, Musée Rodin.*)

The Rodin bronze may be the *matière brute* of the many configurations of Iris attempted in the poet's *Lettera amorosa*, 1953. Char returns to the sculptor in a recent text (*24 janvier 1973*) entitled:

Rodin

Ces marcheurs, je les ai accompagnés longtemps. Ils me précédaient ou louvoyaient, balbutiants et cahotants, à la faveur d'un tourbillon qui les maintenait toujours en vue. Ils étaient peu pressés d'arriver au port et à la mer, de se livrer au caprice exorbitant de l'ennemi. Aujourd'hui la lyre à six cordes du désespoir que ces hommes formaient, s'est mise à chanter dans le jardin empli de brouillard. Il n'est pas impossible qu'Eustache le dévoué, le chimérique, ait entrevu sa vraie destination qui ne se comptait pas en instants de terreur mais en souffle lointain dedans un corps constant (1).

Along with the works of art and the artists that inspired Char's poetry (and we should add to these the nameless

---

(1) In *Argile*, no. 1, hiver 1973. In this new magazine dedicated to poetry, philosophy, and the fine arts, Heidegger, Char, and Braque appear side by side. The journal is edited by Claude Esteban whose wife, Denise, exihibited her paintings in Carpentras, not far from the home of Char who wrote the catalogue preface for the exhibit («Un droit perpétuel de passage,» dated «17 mai 1974»).

painters of Lascaux, as well as Giotto, Van Eyck, Uccello, Fouquet, Mantegna, Cranach, Carpaccio, Poussin, and Rembrandt, all mentioned, along with Georges de La Tour, among the «laines de mon nid rocheux»), (2) Maeght exhibited Char's texts illustrated by so many of the great contemporary artists: Salvador Dali, Kandinski, Picasso, Jean Arp, Matisse, Fernand Léger, Braque, Miró, Max Ernst, Giacometti, and others.

Char has always enjoyed a more than geographic proximity to the artists of the Midi (most of whom he first met during a temporary exile from his native Vaucluse, in the Paris years, 1929-1934, as a member of the surrealist group that thought to break down the barriers between poetry and painting.) Vision, in a very concrete sense, plays an important role in Char's poetry. His admiration for the pre-Socratics—for Heraclitus and Empedocles in particular—is based, in large measure, on the early philosophers' ability (lost to the later, more dogmatic schools) to fuse ideas and images, ideas anchored in a concrete outer reality, and subject, therefore, to the changing nature of that reality while always in harmony with it, one and indivisible. The visual image is not an adornment, but an inalienable part of the poetry of Char, and though with one possible exception («Dansons aux Baronnies,» 1964) he does not write anything like Apollinaire's *Calligrammes* or Reverdy's verbal *tableaux,* much of Char's poetry seems to be built according to intricate geometric designs proper to painting, sculpture, or architecture.

The present rapid overview cannot exhaust the wealth of fascinating material pertaining to Char and the visual arts: the poet's art criticism and his poems dedicated to painters and sculptors; Char and his illustrators and Char the painter in his own right. All of these subjects are, obviously, intimately connected. It is hoped that, one by one, they will be taken up again and examined at length by other critics.

Let me begin with a word about Char and his own art

---

(2) *Contre une maison sèche,* first published in the special Char issue of *L'Herne,* 1971.

work which, though rich and varied and revealing in many ways, is not central to the issues raised here. Char turned to practice of the visual arts during three years of insomnia, 1955-1958, when the spoken word was af if withheld from the poet. The longtime private possessions of the poet turned painter were not shared with the public until many years later, at the insistance of artists and friends, some of whom had seen Char's contributions to the «Dessins de poètes» exhibit organized in the Bateau-Lavoir, Paris, 1966.

Gathered under the title *La Nuit talismanique* (Skira, 1972) are poems carved into birch bark, emblems burned into pebble and stone, drawings and paintings done with the most primitive materials: fire and water, sealing-wax and tallow; and with a wide variety of tools: «Encre de Chine de couleur, bâtons de cire, pointes rougies au feu, écorces de bouleau, plumes, couteaux, crayons, clous, poinçons, pinceaux, cartons, bois, buvards humides» (*op. cit.,* p. 11). The stone and the word are fused into one poem:

> Cher Char chercheur de
> pierres dures sous la terre
> Qui savez les mettre au soleil
> Pour en faire des mots
> de plus pure matière
> 1955 avec tout ce qu'il
> peut y avoir de meilleur
> dedans
> Pierre Reverdy (3).

The dominant colors of the painter's palette are those already known to the readers of Char's poetry: red and black,

---

(3) «Vous êtes vous aussi...,» a text published in 1962 by P.-A. Benoit with a drawing by Braque, and reproduced in *L'Herne, no. cit.,* p. 221. For a detailed discussion of *La Nuit talismanique,* see Virginia A. La Charité, «Beyond the Poem: René Char's *La Nuit talismanique*,» *Symposium,* vol xxx, no. 1, Spring 1976.

the alchemist's colors, «la lune rouge et le géranium noir,» (4)
with occassional splashes of yellow, green, and a kind of mid-
night purple. Almost all the colors are subdued. Only the
light of a candle is shed—as in the de La Tour paintings so
much admired by Char—on the subjects of the poet-painter.
«L'unique condition pour ne pas battre en interminable retrai-
te,» Char writes in 1966, «était d'entrer dans le cercle de la
bougie, de s'y tenir, en ne cédant pas à la tentation de rempla-
cer les ténèbres par le jour et leur éclair nourri par un terme
inconstant» («Sur un même axe: I: Justesse de Georges de La
Tour,» *Dans la pluie giboyeuse*). Char's dominant form *is* the
circle.

His subjects are, for the most part, familiar to us from
the themes of his poetry: the serpent and the bird, the flower
and the sun. They enjoy, in his paintings, the same precarious relationship as that illustrated by shark and seagull in
the poem of that title («Le Requin et la Mouette,») and in
the drawings by Matisse that accompany the text.

From April to December 1929, Char—having left the Ecole
de Commerce of Marseille—directs, back in his native Isle, a
prestigious, if short-lived, literary review, *Méridiens,* which
already seeks to bring together poets and painters. André
Salmon and Philippe Soupault, Dali and Picasso are among the
contributors. Early in his career as a writer—and, no doubt,
under the influence of surrealism—Char turned to art criticism.
In February 1933, Breton's journal, *Le Surréalisme au Service
de la Révolution,* no. 6, engaged its contributors in various
exercises of subjective description. Char, Eluard, Giacometti,
and others were asked to describe «un morceau de velours
rose» (which Char attributes to Manet), and «L'Enigme d'une
journée,» a painting by Giorgio de Chirico. Through a series
of questions which the writer must answer regarding the nature

---

(4) «La Lune Rouge et le Géranium Noir» is a text contributed
by Char to José Corti's *Rêves d'encre* (Corti, 1945), dream images
with commentary by Char, Eluard, Julien Gracq and Gaston
Bachelard.

of the piece of velvet and the painting, the poet or painter, forced to free himself of all preconceived logical or critical cognizance, is asked to arrive at «la connaissance irrationnelle de l'objet.» The purpose of this exercise was not, of course, to produce a piece of traditional art criticism, but to engage poet and painter in what Char later called «la conversation souveraine,» an exchange of subjective reactions that reveal more about the observer than the observed and may, in the end, have very little to do with the object described. «This is the key to the surrealist approach to all forms of art,» wrote John H. Matthews. «The artistic merit of a given work —literary or pictorial, it makes no difference—appeals far less than the relationship that work establishes between subject and object—between what is perceived and the person who perceives it. A surrealist's imaginative sensibility is responsive above all to confrontation with a relationship that shatters reliance upon the habitual, challenging its capacity to limit our power of creative conjecture» (5). Char's commentary on the de Chirico painting is very close to the spirit of Chagall, painter of *Die Zauberflöte,* and one of the few great contemporary artists who, to my knowledge, has not collaborated with Char in any published work. However, one poem by Char, «A Paris,» June 1946, bears the post-script subtitle: «Marc Chagall (mis en poème par R. Char)»:

Seul le pays qui se trouve dans mon espoir
    est mon pays
J'y rentre comme on rentre chez soi, sans passeport.
Il est témoin de ma tristesse et de ma solitude.
Il me couche et me couvre d'une pierre parfumée,
En moi fleurissent des jardins, nos fleurs
    sont inventées, les rues de mon espoir...
Mais il n'y a pas de maisons, elles sont
    détruites au bord de l'enfance...
Leurs habitants vagabondent dans les airs
    à ma recherche.

---

(5) John H. Matthews, *Surrealist Poetry in France,* p. 216.

C'est pourquoi je souris quand mon soleil brille
    un peu ou bien je pleure comme une menue
    pluie dans le noir.
Il fut un temps où j'avais deux têtes,
Il fut un temps où ces deux visages
    se couvraient d'une teinte amoureuse
Et fondaient à l'horizon d'une rose.

Même si je vais en arrière, il me semble
    que c'est en avant
Dans la direction d'un haut portail.

Là s'étendent des steppes. Y passent
    la nuit les tonnerres éteintes et
    les éclairs brisés.

Char's first essay that could properly be called art criticism
was published in November 1937 by the Cahiers G. L. M.
It is a discussion of «La Jeunesse illustrée,» a painting by
Magritte, in which Char sees reflected one of his own early
themes, the theme of solitude and isolation. The article begins:
«Les nuances ont fini de nuire... Partout s'installe un temps
de grève grandiose. Et pas une présence d'homme, même sous
des traits de vapeur pour assortir le dénûment, y prélever
l'immédiate solitude...» Char sums up Magritte's art as
follows: «Avec René Magritte la beauté implantée totalise.
Elle patrouille et porte ostensiblement sur elle son *bien,*
plus un au-delà de connaissance et de problèmes que propulse
un devenir sauve-qui-peut.» And who among Char's readers
seeing these lines today will not call to mind immediately
the words that close the war journal of Hypnos fighting
in the *maquis* of Céreste: «Dans nos ténèbres, il n'y a pas
une place pour la Beauté. Toute la place est pour la Beauté.»
Char's earliest recorded texts dedicated to contemporary
artist friends are «Visage de semence,» a poem written to
Victor Brauner in 1938, and «Mille planches de salut,» a prose
text of 1939, dealing with the work of Picasso, of whom
he says:

L'œuvre de Picasso, consciemment ou involontaire-
ment prévoyante, a su dresser pour l'esprit, bien
avant qu'existât cette terreur, une contre-terreur
dont nous devons nous saisir et dont nous devrons
user au mieux des situations infernales au sein des-
quelles nous serons bientôt plongés. Face au
pouvoir totalitaire, Picasso est le maître-charpentier
de mille planches de salut (6).

We note here Char's concern for the moral mission of art.

After Dali (the painter of *Les Chants de Maldoror*) who
had done the poet's ex-libris («Le Silence ou la Liberté») and
the frontispiece of *Artine*, 1930, and Kandinsky, who did an
etching for *Le Marteau sans maître* in 1934, Picasso was Char's
first well-known collaborator. In January 1936, he supplied
the frontispiece of *Dépendance de l'adieu*, published by Guy
Lévis Mano. Picasso and Char continued their very productive
«conversation souveraine» right up to the 1973 catalogue of
the last Picasso exhibit in the Palais des Papes, Avignon.
«Picasso sous les vents étésiens,» the catalogue preface, is
Char's tribute to the dead friend, «sorcier évanoui» (7).

The first «functional» art criticism was written by Char for
the 1938 exhibit of drawings and gouaches by J.-M. Prassinos,
followed a year later by commentary on the works of Jean
Villeri, to whom Char dedicates a second article in 1948, and
a third, ten years later, on the occasion of another Paris exhibit
(Galerie Greuze) of Villeri's works. The first of these texts
appeared in *Art bref suivi de Premières Alluvions*, 1950, and
was revised, along with «Jean Villeri II, III,» for inclusion
in the second edition of *Recherche de la Base et du Sommet*,
1965. «Jean Villeri I» sets the tone of much of Char's art

---

(6) This text and all subsequent quotations from Char's commentary on the fine arts are taken, unless otherwise specified,
from the second edition of *Recherche de la Base et du Sommet*,
1965.
(7) Besides *Dépendance de l'adieu*, Picasso illustrated a ms. of
Placard pour un chemin des écoliers, 4 March, 1939; the 1945 edition
of *Le Marteau sans maître suivi de Moulin Premier* (Corti); *L'Esca-*

criticism which, for the most part, is really not criticism at all, but subjective meditation very close to poetry. Passages like: «Les enfants traversent la vitre et nagent vers le naufrage, chantier d'un château fort en bois d'épaves» could be transferred, unobtrusively, to prose poems like «Jacquemard et Julia.»

The early text also makes an important statement about Char's notion of the nature of visual imagery, as it links the vital energies of the universe to the conscious thought processes of the artist. Of Villeri, Char says:

> Cet homme utile croit aux couleurs, à celles dont le contact avec les énergies de l'univers, à la longue, est devenu inapparent afin d'être plus sensible. Le fer, le liège, le filin, l'arbre du gouvernail, l'étoile africaine, autant de *pensées* qui vous attendent pour vous prendre par la conscience.

«Jean Villeri II» elaborates on one of Char's fundamental themes, the nostalgia for the Heraclitean world of universal harmony: «Comme le monde était beau lorsqu'il n'avait que la largeur d'un visage et, pour l'assister, l'escorte du chant d'un oiseau! Il y avait une fraternité de dessin et de distance entre les choses, une égalité de traitement entre les êtres, qui comblaient le jour en vue du lendemain.»

In the winter of 1943, Char made the acquaintance of Ciska Grillet, who gave shelter to the partisans of Céreste. On the occasion of a Paris exhibit of her works in 1949, he writes for her a note of thanks which ends on the question: «L'art ne peut-il avoir recours, pour s'infléchir, à la salive de l'arbre fruitier? L'art qui rêve dans les vergers où fleurs et

---

lier de Flore (P.-A. Benoit, 1958); *Pourquoi la journée vole* (P.-A. Benoit, 1960), «Rougeur des matinaux,» presented to Yvonne Zervos in 1965; *La Provence point oméga,* two posters protesting the installation of atomic missile sites in Provence, 1966; and *Les Transparents,* 1967 (P.-A. Benoit). In 1969, the Editions Cercle d'Art published Picasso's drawings dated «27.3.66 — 15.3.68» accompanied by Char's text «Mille planches de salut.»

fruits ont raison ensemble?» Again, the text illustrates a favorite subject of the poet: the simultaneous existence of flower and fruit, two seemingly contradictory and mutually exclusive entities. At the same time, the commentary of 1949 shows a progression beyond the poet's appreciation of Picasso's work, written ten years earlier.

«Balthus ou le dard dans la fleur,» published by the *Cahiers d'Art* in 1945-46, makes first mention, in its title, of an image developed by Char in the «Chant d'Insomnie» of *Lettera amorosa*:

> «Amour hélant, l'Amoureuse viendra,
> Gloria de l'été, ô fruits!
> La flèche du soleil traversera ses lèvres...

The tribute to Balthus ends with the suggestion of the mysterious being, only half perceived and ever changing, to whom *Lettera amorosa* is addressed: «L'œuvre de Balthus est verbe dans le trésor du silence. Nous désirons la caresse de cette guêpe matinale que les abeilles désignent du nom de jeune fille et qui cache dans son corsage la clé des astres de Balthus.» The sting of the bee and the arrow of Orion are once again united.

In the same issue of the *Cahiers d'Art* appeared «Le Requin et la Mouette,» the subject discovered simultaneously by Char and Matisse. For the painter, this theme takes shape in a series of sketches. Char writes the well-known poem of that title, which will be included in *Le Poème pulvérisé*, 1947, accompanied by a black and white lithograph, the head of a woman (Lucienne Bernard?) by Matisse. In January 1947, the Galerie Maeght published, in its «Pierre à Feu» series, *Les Miroirs profonds,* an homage to Matisse, to which Char contributed the text entitled «Lyre pour des mondes internés,» a series of aphorisms taken from his *Feuillets d'Hypnos*, 1946.

In the simple yet fluid outlines of his drawings, the «bouleversante simplicité de lignes» noted by Eluard («Donner à voir»), in the burning reds and flowing blues of his paintings,

Matisse comes very close to the spirit of the young Char. The painter's black «Icarus» of 1947 hovers in the sky like Char's «Extravagant» of the same year. The death of Matisse in 1954 put an end to what might have been, in my view, one of the most fruitful «conversations souveraines» ever engaged in by poet and painter. As far as I know, Matisse left no other Char illustrations except an unpublished series of sketches for *Artine,* dated 1947-48.

At the time of *Le Poème pulvérisé,* Char discovers Pierre Charbonnier, the painter who captured the spirit of his native Isle in «Les eaux basses,» 1950, and «Moulins,» 1951. Charbonnier's work is exhibited at the Galerie Claude, Paris, June 1948. For the occasion, the poet writes the text that becomes «Pierre Charbonnier I» in *Recherche de la Base et du Sommet,* 1965, followed by a second article taken from the catalogue of the January 1958 Charbonnier exhibit at the galery J. C. de Chaudun. Excerpts from these texts and parts of a conversation between Char and Charbonnier are recorded in the catalogue of the Swiss exhibit of the painter's work in 1965 (Geneva, Galerie D. Benador). These texts emphasize the element of choice that must distinguish the art of painting from «les volontés de la peinture.» While all objects, however humble, may occupy the artist's field of vision, he must divest such objects of their common, ordinary, human *attaches,* by moving them into a realm of light where none but the most authentic among them will survive. «L'œuvre de Pierre Charbonnier,» Char concludes, «nous offre leurs amples ouvrages, communs et pourtant enchantés, mais presque toujours vides de ces mêmes hommes, ouvrages dès lors translucides, initiants, au sommet desquels ne s'affronte plus que le petit nombre rescapé des contradictions immortelles.» Char's defense of artistic realism, therefore, must not be confused with the photographic art later incorporated into painting.

In 1950, Pierre Charbonnier does a series of aquarelles to accompany a manuscript copy of «Quatre fascinants» and «La Minutieuse» offered to Yvonne Zervos, the longtime friend and *mécène* of so many poets and painters: Arp, Chagall, Klee, Max Ernst, Picasso, Man Ray, Giacometti, Léger, Miró, Char, Eluard, and Jacques Dupin. In 1929, Yvonne Zervos had opened in Paris the Galerie des Cahiers d'Art with the aim of introducing to the public many of the younger painters and to promote the foreign artists who had but recently arrived on the Paris scene or not yet crossed the border. During the difficult years of the German occupation, her galery became, furthermore, the regular meeting (and hiding-) place of many of the foremost thinkers, painters, and poets of the Resistance. They collaborated in the publication of the *Cahiers d'Art,* directed by Christian Zervos to whom, in 1938, Char had sent for publication his earliest texts inspired by paintings: «Une Italienne de Corot,» and «Courbet: Les casseurs de cailloux.»

In 1947, during the Festival d'Avignon, Yvonne and Christian Zervos organized the extraordinary «Exposition de peintures et de sculptures contemporaines.» Here for the first time Picasso, Braque, Klee, Matisse, Giacometti and Hélion were seen in the Palais des Papes. Yvonne conceived, but did not live to see, the last Picasso exhibit that opened in the Papal Chapel in 1973.

Yvonne
Qui l'entendit jamais se plaindre?

Nulle autre qu'elle n'aurait pu boire sans mourir
    les quarante fatigues,
Attendre, loin devant, ceux qui viendront après;
De l'éveil au couchant sa manœuvre était mâle.

Qui a creusé le puits et hisse l'eau gisante
Risque son cœur dans l'écart de ses mains.
                6 octobre 1963

This text, which is subtitled «La soif hospitalière» in *Retour amont,* 1966, is the homage Char pays to her who shared with him so much of his creative life, who discovered with him the *chimères* of the Vaucluse, retraced with him the outlines of La Petite-Pierre, the mountain village of Alsace where the young soldier had spent his first years of exile from home. Yvonne, along with Char's sister Julia, must have been the first to read the poet's *Lettera amorosa*. To Yvonne Zervos are dedicated nearly all the postwar poems of Char, many of which she inspired. She passed away in 1970 (8). A photograph of her hands by Man Ray, painted by Picasso in 1937, is among the poet's prized possessions. Char's interest in the visual arts, kindled by the surrealists, was kept alive and constantly renewed by Yvonne, whose judgments respected, in whose love he confided, and in whose company his own artistic vision was continually sharpened and refined.

As a tribute to the great patron of the arts, many painters have illustrated manuscripts of Char poems, offered to Yvonne (9). Among these, there is a copy of «Les Transparents» with illustrations by Louis Fernandez, done in 1949. In 1950, an exhibit of Fernandez, «cet allié de Zurbaran et de Vermeer» opened in Paris (Galerie Pierre). Char, in his «texte de présentation,» likens the painter to Nerval, calling both men artists of one theme, one passion, that haunts their waking creations and their dreams.

La Treizième revient... C'est encore la première;
Et c'est toujours la Seule...

In 1951, Fernandez draws a series of vignettes for *A une sérénité crispée,* the poet's first postwar collection of aphorisms. Three years later, he supplies an etching for the

---

(8) On the occasion of Yvonne's death, Char published a collection of his poems entitled simply, *Poèmes à Yvonne,* illustrated by P.-A. Benoit.

(9) Among the earliest of these mss. is «L'Homme qui marchait dans un rayon de soleil,» illustrated in 1949 with 16 aquarelles by Fernand Léger. Char's love for the small, elegantly bound and beautifully illustrated book is well known to his friends. Eluard referred to him as «mon petit bibliomaniaque.»

poem *Le Deuil des Névons,* published in a limited edition (Brussels: Le Cormier) (10).

There is another Fernandez exhibit in November 1968 (Galerie Iolas, Paris) and this time, Char contributes to the catalogue a true prose poem, «Rémanence,» taken from *Dans la pluie giboyeuse.* The poem is an investigation of the poet's own «état d'âme,» asking the self-directed question: «De quoi souffres-tu?» To which Char replies:

> De l'irréel intact dans le réel dévasté. De leurs détours aventureux cerclés d'appels et de sang. De ce qui fut choisi et ne fut pas touché, de la rive du bond au rivage gagné, du présent irréfléchi qui disparaît. D'une étoile qui s'est, la folle, rapprochée et qui va mourir avant moi.

The text fits the dreamlike but often cruel irreality of the painter's works. There is a hauntingly beautiful small oil (12×18 cm) by Fernandez called «Pêcheurs le soir.» It shows the bent figures of three pastel-clad fishermen trying to bring their white boat out of a *fond* of greens and blues, edged by an island that touches the horizon. The men seem to pull the boat not onto any visible shore, but into a realm of dark purple framed, on one side, by a small lozenge of black. No comfortable shore, even if the white bark were to reach it. Though movement is clearly indicated in the painting by the push and pull exerted on the boat by the men, the three stand—leaning heavily into the water—as if caught forever, while evening settles, in the unreal, cruel stillness of the sea. «Voici un peintre solitaire qui va enfin recréer la solitude,» wrote Char in 1950 (11). Louis Fernandez, painter of the «rose qui ferme le royaume,» the painter of silence (12).

---

(10) The book also contains the poet's horoscope («Horoscope d'un Poète») by Yves de Bayser.

(11) A manuscript preserved at the Bibliothèque Littéraire Jacques Doucet, Paris.

(12) Fernandez is one of the painters discussed by Fernand

Among the many exhibitors of the 1950's that call upon Char to write catalogue prefaces, there is Francis Picabia, «pareil à un fougueux coutelier, avec son assortiment qui jetait des éclairs» (1952). There is Victor Brauner's show at the Galerie de France in October 1952. Char recalls that he was among the first to have recognized Brauner's genius:

> J'ai le privilège d'être de ceux qui ont vu s'annoncer, se former puis grandir, atteindre l'un après l'autre—sans les torturer—les objectifs capitaux de la peinture de notre temps, l'œuvre de Victor Brauner. Le théâtre mental contemporain, du fait qu'il tire son spectacle des chimères de paille d'un Réel dédaigneusement fui—réel tellement inouï pourtant au niveau de l'être même!—est contraint de capituler. Et à la vue de tous, un récent réalisme, qui se voulut à la fois humble et ambitieux, est rapidement entré dans une précoce et muette vieillesse.

Again, as in his texts on Fernandez and Charbonnier, Char is concerned with the question of reality, and now, in a more technical sense, with realism in art. It is the «realistic» aspect of the works of Courbet, Zurbaran and Fernandez that interests the poet. And yet this realism is not to be confused with photographic reproduction. The geometric blocks that make up the frontispiece of *Le Deuil des Névons,* the exaggerated, almost Egyptian stiffness of «Le doux défunt,» a Char manuscript illustrated by Brauner in 1950, the immobility of his bestiary, all suggest an inner reality hidden from the uninitiated. The «Portrait analogique» that Brauner paints of Char in 1950 is composed of the symbols of his poetry: the flower and the bird, and the toast drunk to the serpent. It

---

Verhesen in an article entitled «René Char et ses alliés substantiels» (*Liberté,* vol. 10, no. 4, juillet-août 1968). Verhesen is, to my knowledge, the only critic to have written at length on the subject dealt with here.

shows the poet as the «grande brouette des marécages,» and as the point of a scale standing perfectly still amidst its opposing symbols. The figure resembles not Char, but the prehistoric warrior who might hunt his prey in the caves of Lascaux. Only those who know his poetry will recognize Char in «Le doux défunt.»

Victor Brauner feels very close to the poet and to poetry in general. He did a Char portrait in 1945 and designed the poet's ex-libris. His paintings have titles like «Le Poème,» 1946, and «Origine de la poésie,» 1957. There is an aquarelle called «Le poète renaît Char éveille l'homme,» done in 1950. The manuscripts illustrated by Brauner include, besides «Le doux défunt,» the text «Oiseaux que nous lapidons,» and «Le Viatique ou non,» 1950. Brauner also did some collages and gouaches for the manuscript of «De moment en moment,» 1957. Though the published version of *Quatre fascinants—La Minutieuse* was illustrated by Pierre Charbonnier, Char's private manuscript of the poems shows original aquarelles by Brauner.

Among the articles written by Char in the 1950's, there is one devoted to Lelia Caetani, 1954, and one to N. Ghika who, according to the poet, combines the tragic vision of ancient Greece with the solidity of Nietzsche. Ghika's work will survive, Char says, because it refuses to yield to the chaos of modern art which, like all chaos, is self-destructive:

> Le chaos dans les arts s'éteindra comme tous les chaos. Seuls appareilleront ceux qui l'auront éprouvé, en restant en possession de leurs ressources propres. N. Ghika est de ceux-là.

Char's original text was a preface to the 1958 New York exhibit of the painter's work. It is reprinted, with notes taken from the poet's conversations with the painter, in the *Cahiers d'Art* volume on Ghika published in 1965, by Yvonne and Christian Zervos. In honor of Yvonne, Ghika illustrated the manuscripts of «La Faux relevée» and «Nous avons» in 1958.

Jean Hugo's works were presented by the Cahiers d'Art galery in 1957. Char compares the painter and the «Mauvais vitrier» of Baudelaire. Unlike the latter, he says, Hugo *does* have glass of many colors, glass to make the magical windows, the windows of Paradise. Jean Hugo excels, in fact, in graceful miniature etchings that remind one of the art of the *vitrail*. He illustrates many of Char's *minuscules*: *La Fauvette des roseaux* and *Chanson des étages,* 1955; *A une enfant,* 1956; *Le Poète au sortir des demeures* and *Sur une nuit sans ornement,* 1957, followed by *Lied du figuier,* 1964, *Le Ramier,* 1967, and *Paris sans issue,* 1968. To Jean Hugo's first wife, Valentine, Char had sent, in 1935, copy of *Le Tombeau des secrets.* Valentine did the first Char portrait known to his readers, and five haunting dry-point etchings that capture the Pirandellean world of *Placard pour un chemin des écoliers,* 1937.

Another newcomer to the group of Char's collaborators in the 1950's was Wifredo Lam, who did five watercolors for *Le Rempart de brindilles* (Paris: Louis Broder, 1953) and illustrated a manuscript version of *A la Santé du serpent* in honor of Yvonne Zervos, 1951. Char turned to Wifredo Lam for illustrations of *Contre une maison sèche,* 1971 (12a).

In the 1950's, Char broadens his interests and turns to two new art forms: wood engraving and sculpture. He had sent copy of *Les Matinaux,* 1950, to Françoise and Nicolas de Staël. Staël and Char met in 1951, and together they published, in November of that year, twelve poems from *Le Poème pulvérisé,* accompanied by fourteen wood engravings and an original color lithograph. In December, these are exhibited at the Galerie Jacques Dubourg, Paris. For the occasion, Char writes the text «Bois de Staël,» which is his first recorded appreciation of an art form other than canvas painting. In his commentary, Char also makes the first explicit reference

---

(12a) For the exhibition of *Contre une maison sèche* as illustrated by Lam, Char wrote the text, *De La sainte famille au Droit à la paresse* (Paris: Le Point cardinal, 1976).

to Yéti, the «Abominable homme des neiges,» a theme he will take up later in the form of a «Ballet.» He writes: «Staël et moi, nous ne sommes pas, hélas, des Yétis! Mais nous nous approchons plus près qu'il n'est permis de l'inconnu et de l'empire des étoiles.» And the artist writes to Char, 9 November, 1953: «Il y a cela de vraiment merveilleux entre nous c'est qu'on peut se donner tout ce qui est possible et impossible sans limite parce qu'on ne voit pas la fin de nos possibilités.» The «Bois de Staël» are probably among the most successful examples of the «concordance» of two art forms. Pierre Granville comments on the enterprise: «En fait voici apparu à la mi-siècle un rare météore où la fraternité a sa forte part, mais où, davantage, le concept texte-image est foncièrement anti-illustratif, plain-chant laïque qui lie une rive à l'autre» (13).

In 1952, Char writes for Nicolas de Staël a true free verse poem, exalting the painter who has clothed the stone:

> ...
> O toile de rocher, qui frémis, montrée nue sur la corde d'amour!
> En secret un grand peintre va te vêtir, pour tous les yeux, du désir le plus entier et le moins exigeant.

The text reminds one of «Le coup,» Char's comparison between Rodin and Picasso included in *25 Octobre 1961*, published by P.-A. Benoit in honor of the painter. Char writes:

> Le coup de génie de Rodin est d'avoir su vêtir Balzac.
> Picasso, c'est Balzac nu; mais avec les mains de Rodin, la cape impétueuse et le destin de Picasso.

Among the works of Staël there is a color litho portrait of Char, published as the frontispiece of *Arrière-Histoire du*

---

(13) Pierre Granville's text, called «De deux colonnes érigées,»

Poème pulvérisé in 1953. On the occasion, Staël writes to Char: «Il y a des moments où je te vois comme un monument très rude.» The stark outlines of the white head set into an uneven orange-red circle against a dark blue rectangle convey the artist's concept of the poet. The catalogue of the 1971 Maeght exhibit shows, on the cover, another figure by Staël, the blue shadow of a man, poised as if about to take flight.

Nicolas de Staël committed suicide, from his Antibes villa, in March 1955. In a commemorative text called «Il nous a dotés,» Char writes a commentary (on a painting by Staël), published in *Le Nouvel Observateur* (18/3/65) as «Le Printemps de Staël»:

> Les années 1950-1954 apparaîtront plus tard, grâce à cette œuvre, comme des années de «ressaisissement» et d'accomplissement par un seul à qui il échut d'exécuter sans respirer, en quatre mouvements, une recherche longtemps voulue. Staël a peint. Et s'il a gagné de son plein gré le dur repos, il nous a dotés, nous, de l'inespéré, qui ne doit rien à l'espoir.

Staël left an aquarelle for the unpublished manuscript of «Claude Palun» (1952-53) and a series of *études* for «L'Abominable homme des neiges.» Char pays a final tribute to the artist in *Aromates chasseurs,* where he asks:

> Y a-t-il vraiment une plus grande distance entre nous et notre poussière finale qu'entre l'étoile intraitable et le regard vivant qui l'a tenue un instant sans s'y blesser?
> ... Nicolas de Staël, nous laissant entrevoir son bateau imprécis et bleu, repartit pour les mers froides, celles dont il s'était approché, enfant de l'étoile polaire (14).

---

was published in the catalogue of the 1971 «Exposition René Char» organized by the Galerie Maeght.

(14) Mary Ann Caws in her *René Char* (Twayne, 1977, p. 43)

It may be of interest to open here a short parenthesis on Char's relationship to the composers of his time and to music in general. He published a single commentary on music, «Entre la prairie et le laurier,» which first appeared in the *Cahiers de la Compagnie M. Renaud-J. L. Barrault* (no. 3, 1954). The text is reprinted in the first edition of *Recherche de la Base et du Sommet*, 1955, but excluded from the second publication of that anthology in 1965.

In the article, Char discusses how, until recently, poetry set to music was really always subservient to the latter: «Elle la poésie devenait sa doublure, sa monture, si bien que ces deux grands, intarissables et différents mystères, poésie et musique, ne consentaient à apparaître côte à côte que pour faire courir un sourire de commisération sur les lèvres venues pour savourer.» Char makes exceptions for *Don Giovanni* and *Pelléas et Mélisande*: «La tumultueuse unité, la féconde camaraderie, était donc possible?» Berg, Webern, Schönberg, and Bartok are named as the forerunners of new generations of composers who could bring about the successful fusion of poetry and music. The essay ends on a tribute to Pierre Boulez: «Aujourd'hui, Pierre Boulez nous invite à valider la conquête, à la mener plus avant, à tresser nos sèves ensemble. Soyons attentifs. Entre la prairie et le laurier, là où se concasse la pierre d'âme, commence une nouvelle aventure terrestre. La poésie de notre temps doit l'entendre et participer.»

To this critical essay, we should perhaps add the prose poem «Débris mortels et Mozart,» published in *La Bibliothèque est en feu*, 1957. However, Char seems to take his cue for the poem not from «La flûte enchantée» and «Don Giovanni» drawn on the Doucet manuscript of the text, but from the well-known prose of Saint-Exupéry. The poet writes:

> Sur la longueur de ses deux lèvres, en terre commune, soudain l'allégro, défi de ce rebut sacré, perce

---

considers Nicolas de Staël (along with Braque) the painter closest to the spirit of Char.

et reflue vers les vivants, vers la totalité des hommes et des femmes en deuil de patrie intérieure qui,
errant pour n'être pas semblables, vont à travers
Mozart s'éprouver en secret.

Char is not a musical poet, like, for example, Apollinaire,
Eluard, or even Saint-John Perse, all of whom—though in
quite different modes—exhibit strong musical affinities. When
Char speaks of *hymne* or *chant,* harp or lyre, we feel that for
him these are literary, not musical conventions. Music serves
to reinforce a visual image in texts like «Verbe d'orages raisonneurs...»: «Après avoir porté à sa plus haute fièvre la nuit
musicienne, le rossignol diminue la longueur de sa flamme...»
(*La Nuit talismanique*). Char's lyre is a visual configuration,
not a musical instrument.

The history of «L'Abominable homme des neiges» is interesting in this context. Staël, who had done sketches for the
sets of the ballet, goes in search of a composer. He approaches
Dallapiccola in Florence in February 1953, but the plans for a
collaboration fall through. He then stops to see Stravinsky in
New York, with equal lack of success. Finally Staël thinks of
asking Messiaen, but abandons the idea, discouraged. «On
manqua de persévérance,» Char remarks. The ballet is never
presented. Staël's unpublished *études* for the stage remain
just that.

Pierre Boulez has set to music several Char texts, the best
of these being, no doubt, his interpretation of *Le Marteau sans
maître,* which premiered in Baden-Baden, Germany, in 1955.
Boulez wrote the score for *La Conjuration,* staged—with sets
by Braque—in 1947. He composed «La Sorgue, chanson pour
Yvonne» and «Complainte du lézard amoureux» for a presen-
tation of *Le Soleil des eaux* at the Théâtre des Champs-Elysées,
Paris, 1950. Five poems of *Le Visage nuptial* were performed
in Cologne in 1957.

Boulez conducted Gilbert Amy's *Strophe,* based on the
poem «Tu ouvres les yeux,» presented in Brussels in 1966. In
1951, Jean-Louis Martinet had worked on «Congé au vent,»

«Hymne à voix basse,» and «Le Thor.»   Hélène Martin has
sung the «Chanson d'Insomnie» and the «Chanson des étages.»
In 1969, *Lettera amorosa* was presented as a ballet with music
by Claudio Monteverdi.

This is a meager showing for such a wealth of poetic output.   But Char's dense, aphoristic style does not lend itself
easily to musical interpretation.   Only Webern's short pieces
for orchestra come to mind, perhaps some of the moods of Berg.
No popular singer could compose the aphorisms of Char.   The
poet has not found his musician.

After painting and the «Bois de Staël,» Char turned to
sculpture.   He had known Giacometti since the days of *La
Révolution Surréaliste*.   Both poet and sculptor joined the
Paris surrealist group at roughly the same time (1929).   But
Char did not approach Giacometti until 1946, when the artist
did a watercolor for a manuscript version of «Les trois sœurs,»
the liminary poem of *Le Poème pulvérisé*.   In the tall, slender,
free and weightless statues of Giacometti I see the perfect
counterpoint to the poet Char, the «robuste gars du Midi,» the
giant of Provence, who in so many of his texts seeks the
«Territoire d'Ariel» that seems to be the Swiss sculptor's
natural habitat.   Char's first article dealing with Giacometti
dates from 1954:

> Un couple de Giacometti, abandonnant le sentier
> proche, parut sur l'aire. Nus ou non.   Effilés et
> transparents, comme les vitraux des églises brûlées,
> gracieux, tels des décombres ayant beaucoup souffert
> en perdant leur poids et leur sang anciens.   Cepen-
> dant hautains de décision, à la manière de ceux qui
> se sont engagés sans trembler sous la lumière irré-
> ductible des sous-bois et des désastres.

In 1955, Giacometti did a watercolor for *Poèmes des deux
années*; ten years later, he contributed four illustrations to
Retour amont, a collection of poems containing an homage to
the sculptor entitled «Célébrer Giacometti.»   The text figures

in the Giacometti exhibit organized in 1967 by the Galerie Engelberts, Geneva:

> En cette fin d'après-midi d'avril 1964 le vieil aigle despote, le maréchal-ferrant agenouillé, sous le nuage de feu de ses invectives (son travail, c'est-à-dire lui-même, il ne cessa de le fouetter d'offenses), me découvrit, à même le dallage de son atelier, la figure de Caroline, son modèle, le visage peint sur toile de Caroline—après combien de coups de griffes, de blessures, d'hématomes?—, fruit de passion entre tous les objets d'amour, victorieux du faux gigantisme des déchets additionnés de la mort, et aussi des parcelles lumineuses à peine séparées, de nous autres, ses témoins temporels. Hors de son alvéole de désir et de cruauté. Il se réfléchissait, ce beau visage sans antan qui allait tuer le sommeil, dans le miroir de notre regard, provisoire receveur universel pour tous les yeux futurs.

Giacometti and Char capture the world at a moment of crisis, in which procreation and death are frequently joined. Destruction is perceived as a provocation of movement and, therefore, life. Both Char and Giacometti frequently represent only a part of the human body, conceived as a self-propelled entity. The poet writes: «Je n'étais ce jour-là que deux jambes qui marchent» («Le Bois de l'Epte,» *Poèmes des deux années,* 1955). Giacometti sculpts the «Main prise au doigt» and the «Jambe qui marche» (bronze, 1958-59). Instead of painting the life model, the young Giacometti sketched a giant foot!

The poet and the sculptor seek to come to terms with an invisible reality they call *le vide,* a void which is not nothingness, but the unknown *existant* hidden from view. All being is a being-in-space waiting to be dis-covered. «Enfonce-toi dans l'inconnu qui creuse,» the poet commands (*Feuillets d'Hypnos,* no. 212), and the sculptor comments: «La sculpture repose sur le vide. C'est l'espace qu'on creuse pour construire l'objet et à son tour l'objet crée un espace.»

Both Char and Giacometti view their subjects as what Carl Burckhardt has called *Fernformen,* forms seen from a distance which disintegrate upon approach. They do not allow for contact, and vanish at close view. In Giacometti's «City Square,» 1948-49, four men are seen walking around a woman they cannot reach. The artist seeks an immaterial presence without individual qualities or characteristics. In Baudelaire's poetry, Madame Sabatier and Jeanne Dorval can be identified. We feel, in Eluard's work, the palpable differences between Gala and Nusch. Not so in Char and Giacometti. All their women share the qualities of Mélusine, Mathilde, and Nadja; all are without a face. Poet and sculptor capture the mystery, cruelty, and elusiveness of Being, visible in Giacometti's creations that are part animal, part machine. The sculptor's «Femme égorgée» of 1932 is not unlike Char's early heroines.

Both Giacometti and Char excel in the art of the *minuscule,* «victorieux du faux gigantisme des déchets additionnés de la mort.» Three years of the sculptor's production, it is said, could be fitted into six matchboxes. Many of his figures were cut razor-thin and disintegrated on contact. Many of Char's poems have appeared as tiny books, beautifully bound and illustrated.

The art of the *minuscule* is linked to the art of fragmentation practised by Giacometti and Char. The poet gathers his fragments *En trente-trois morceaux*; Giacometti works in plaster, the most ductile and perishable of materials. He wipes out a portrait, just as it seems finished, leaving the bare traces of a figure. Every one of his works is an unfinished piece, he says, which must be seen in relation to every other piece to make a whole. For the totality of life can be caught only for the moment, and in fragments.

In 1964, Giacometti does a portrait of Char that resembles one of Caroline done two years earlier. Char's portrait appears in the *Bibliographie des œuvres de René Char 1929-1963* published by the poet's good friend—and publisher of the majority of his *minuscules*—Pierre-André Benoit. We have no other examples of Giacometti's collaboration with Char, except a series of colored pencil drawings done for the manuscript of «Le Visage nuptial,» presented to Yvonne Zervos in 1963. The sculptor's untimely death in 1966 deprived Char of the only artist who, to my mind, could have given us a portrait—or a statue—of Artine, «la transparence absolue.» «Les figures n'étaient jamais pour moi une masse compacte,» wrote Giacometti, «mais comme une construction transparente» (15). Many of his sculptures are, in fact, skeletons in space, pure transparent constructions that have all the gracefulness, the aeriness, but also the nakedness, and the cruelty of the subject divested, like the heroines of Char, of all human *attaches.* They belong to the realm of the crepuscular («The Palace at 4 a.m.,» or *Les Matinaux*), where they move about almost invisible, and silent.

One of the most prolific of Char's collaborators has been Joan Miró, whom the poet met early in his career, during the Paris surrealist years. However, Miró left France during the war and did not return until 1948. This is the year he does a color lithograph for *Fête des arbres et du chasseur* (G. L. M.) and illustrates, in various media, 32 pages of a Char anthology entitled simply *Poèmes,* presented to Yvonne Zervos. The year 1948 marks the beginning of a long series of collaborative efforts by painter and poet.

Miró has worked on many of Char's *minuscules,* in either manuscript or published form. He did a drawing for *L'Alouette* (G. L. M., 1954), a manuscript illustration of «De moment en moment» for Yvonne, 1957, watercolors and an etching for two different presentations of *Nous avons* (ms 1958, and Broder, 1959). For Christine and Jacques Dupin (Miró's most recent commentator) (16), the painter does a pastel to ac-

---

(15) My quotations from Giacometti are found in *Alberto Giacometti,* with an introduction by Peter Selz and an autobiographical statement by the artist (New York: The Museum of Modern Art, 1965).
(16) It is Jacques Dupin, not Char, who prefaces the catalogue of the last Paris exhibit of Miró's works, held in the Grand Palais, May-October 1974.

company the same text. Jacques Dupin has commented on the collaboration of Miró and Char:

> Il est remarquable de voir, selon les poèmes ou les livres, se modifier le style de Miró, son rythme, sa palette et sa respiration. Allégresse et simplicité rustique de la couleur et de la ligne dans *Fête des arbres et du chasseur.* Mystérieuse évidence du signe, comme d'une écriture mûrie dans le sous-sol et soudainement mise au jour dans *A la Santé du serpent.* Sombre énergie reployée des trois premières gravures de «Nous avons,» magnétisme nocturne que dissipent dans la dernière illustration le jaillissement de deux signes humains formant couple et la lumière d'aurore qui les baigne. Enfin la lente roue noire et l'échelle radieuse qui répondent si exactement aux poèmes criblés du *Chien de cœur.* Miró est ce lecteur impressionnable et ce commentateur bondissant qui demande à la poésie la confirmation de ses audaces et la vérification de ses intuitions, qui lui demande surtout d'être un tremplin vers l'inconnu et l'étincelle du renouvellement (17).

There is a woodcut by Miró in *20 avril 1963,* an homage to the painter, on the occasion of his 70th birthday, by Jacques Dupin, P.-A. Benoit, and René Char. On display during the Maeght exhibit was the book called *13 mai 1962,* texts in honor of Georges Braque (including one by Char), illustrated by Raoul Ubac and Joan Miró. In Char's manuscripts, Miró circles the titles, decorates the margins, fills in the silences, the empty spaces between lines. One of the priceless little books kept in the Bibliothèque Littéraire Jacques Doucet, Paris, is the 12 page *minuscule, Homo poeticus,* published by P.-A. Benoit in 1953. The poetic man described here is not Char, the poet, but Miró, the painter. Miró's drawings are

---

(17) Jacques Dupin, «Avec Miró, les rencontres et le chemin,» Maeght catalogue, 1971.

the poetry of the book, commented upon by Char's text. *Homo poeticus* has never been republished in any of the poet's anthologics. The drawings and the text are so intimately joined here that the poem could not properly stand by itself.

The text opens with an apostrophe to the moon, one of Miró's favorite subjects, but one infrequent in the landscapes of Char:

> —O Lune,
> qu'est-ce qui me brûle les doigts?
>
> —Le
> temps rongé.

Char then gives an account of his meetings with the painter and his art:

> Sur le marché
> de mon petit village
>
> j'ai rencontré Miró
> douze cents treize
> fois.
>   J'ai vu des
> Mirós de tout âge
> qui s'embrassaient;
>
> et de très jeunes qui
> se chamaillaient
>   Cela
> faisait du monde et
> encore
>   un joli dessin.

Char falls in with the tone and subject matter of the painter, giving us a text which, in its playfulness, its light-footed meter and popular ring, is really quite unlike the poet we know. I feel somewhat the same way about *Six patiences pour Miró*, a series of short, sometimes witty and whimsical poems which come to be literally overshadowed by the predominantly black lines and circles used by Miró to punctuate the text.

«A Miró,» Char's 1963 homage to the painter, is retitled «Ban» in *Recherche de la Base et du Sommet*, 1965, where it reads:

> Ses tombeaux vides,
> Le monde qui plane
> Va-t-il retomber?
>
> Miró,
> Du pinceau de sa paupière
> Allume une querelle d'étoiles,
> Loisir d'anniversaire.
>
> Le bel exubérant!
> Ô nuit en amont sans linceul,
> Ton rare fiancé.

Again, Char adopts the short, supple line of the painter, his exuberance and effervescence. The marriage of Miró and Char is concluded at the expense of the poet. It comes off best when the poem is interwoven with or absorbed into the drawing, and the *homo poeticus* is clearly identified as the painter. As an illustrator of Char texts, Miró rarely succeeds. The effect of his lines and colors is overpowering and, in the end, distracting. Perhaps it is the very Protean nature of the painter, praised by Jacques Dupin, which argues against the authenticity of any collaborative effort. As he tries to adapt his art to the poem, it is the painting which stands out from the page, and the poem fades into the background, becoming —through a reversal of roles—the commentary or interpretation demanded of the painter. Char himself may be aware of this danger when he writes:

> Et notre usure s'en empare, en subit l'attrait.
> Narcisse à rebours. Notre lucide pesanteur est
> effacée. L'*homo ludens* mène le jeu. Un autre âge
> se reconstitue tout autour, et sa plénitude est celle
> du premier jour, et son œuvre, la première étincelle
> dans l'enfance du temps. L'avènement n'a pas
> de fin.

When in 1961 the Galerie Maeght sponsored an exhibit
of Miró's work, Char wrote the text «Dansez, montagnes,» as
a catalogue preface. In it, he praises the painter's independence, his non-conformity, and his rhythm: «Miró flambe,
court, nous donne et flambe.» For Miró, Char has written
the longest, and, perhaps, most technical piece of art criticism.
It appeared as the introduction to an album of dry point
etchings published by Maeght in 1964 under the title of
Flux de l'aimant. In the article, Char comments, under
separate headings, on Miró's subject matter, on his lines, colors,
and form. He admires the painter's spontaneity, the lack of
finality, the fluidity of his lines, the freedom and the aeriness,
the tension and suspense of a world «qui plane encore avant
de retomber dans l'ordre étroit, l'instant où la conscience n'a
pas touché terre...» He sees in Miró's sketches «l'état qui
précède la chose,» which is also the true poetic state. And he
compares his lines to the musical line: «... cette ligne continue
de Miró, réversible en durée, toute axée sur la durée, ductile
à souhait, installée dans le temps à la manière, peut-être, de
la musique.» The «bewitching erotic tunes» (18) of Miró's
«Constellations» have captured the imagination of poets and
critics.

Char, like Tzara before him, speaks of «la grande joie dans
la peinture de Miró,» of the almost sensuous pleasure derived
from the interplay of color, line, and form. That form, in
the work of the Spaniard, is seen not as fixed expression, but
as continuous propulsion, revealing the «identité première du
réel d'avant le mot et qu'on nomme poétique.» Again, Char
expressly attributes poetic qualities to the work of the painter
but himself writes the least poetic—and most theoretical—of
all his texts of art criticism. For Miró, says Char, no formulas
exist, no absolutes, no final truths; only eternal beginnings,
perpetual returns to the source, traces, outlines, propulsions,
tensions, intermittant solutions. The following, with a sub-

---

(18) The expression is borrowed from Renée Riese Hubert's
commentary on Breton and Miró (*Yale French Studies*, no. 31).

stitution of names, would be a fitting description of Char himself:

> Miró qui n'énonce pas, Miró qui indique, Miró qui imagine des noces, Miró ne fera que traverser la conquête magnétique, pareil au fauve céleste qui, après panique, une fois la forêt brûlée, s'éloigne par-delà les cendres. Qu'elle agisse enfin, cette forme, entre toutes les formes, apte à demeurer solitaire, comme un filtre qui s'interpose entre nous et la conscience rigide que nous avons du réel, pour que, la magie aboutie, nous soyons la Source aux yeux grands ouverts.

Both Char and Miró pay close attention to insignificant objects, like the blade of grass that can conjure up a whole landscape. «J'obtiens de m'évader dans l'absolu de la nature et mes paysages n'ont rien à voir avec la réalité extérieure,» Miró wrote to Rafols in 1924. «Ils sont néanmoins plus montrogiens que s'ils avaient été faits d'après nature... Je sais que je suis des chemins périlleux, et j'avoue que souvent je suis pris de panique, de cette panique du voyageur qui marche en des chemins inexplorés...» (19). A simple line can propel painter and poet out of what Char has called the «illiterate parentheses of the earth» («Mission et révocation,» *Partage formel*).

Miró in his search for the unknown goes towards an imaginary world beyond the earth. His women are birds, fantastic creatures like the «oiseau lunaire» that join with star, sun, and moon in a perpetual «instant de fête» (Jacques Dupin) celebrated in the sky.

> Celui qui lâche des cerfs-volants
> aux quatre coins de l'azur
> n'a que faire de l'autre face de la lune.
> (Michel Leiris, *Fissures*).

---

(19) My quotations from Miró are contained in the catalogue of the 1974 Paris exhibit.

Char, on the other hand, explores the territory which exists not above, but beneath apparent reality. His «Extravagant,» wanderer of outer space, cannot survive in a lunar landscape. Both painter and poet feel a great attraction for the void. «Tout ce qui est dépouillé m'a beaucoup impressionné,» wrote Miró. But while the latter fills the empty spaces with arabesques of color in perpetual motion, the poet is caught in the black and white silences of the page. Miró and Char both respect the destructive element in creation. Char publishes his poems *En trente-trois morceaux*. Miró speaks of the «assassinat de la peinture» to which his partially burned and slashed canvases of 1973 testify. And yet—even with their partly exposed frames which allow one to see behind the paintings—Miró's works have a certain flatness. They never explore «the other side of the moon.» The mutilated poems of Char add a measure of depth to isolated words, which come together again in *La Parole en archipel*.

Miró's paintings impose themselves upon the viewer as poems in their own right. He, too, has written his «Chanson des voyelles» (an oil of 1966), and, indeed, only Rimbaud could have filled the blanks left by the painter. «Pour collaborer,» wrote Eluard, «peintres et poètes se veulent libres. La dépendance abaisse, empêche de comprendre, d'aimer» («Donner à voir»). The *Homo poeticus* of Char and Miró will stand primarily as a testimony to the painter.

Three of the more recent collaborators of Char are Zao Wou-Ki, Szenes, and Vieira da Silva. The first of these illustrated *Les Compagnons dans le jardin* (Broder, 1957). Szenes did a series of gouaches for *Sur les hauteurs* and manuscript illustrations for «Le Terme épars,» 1966. Vieira da Silva collaborated in *L'Arbre frappé* (P.-A. Benoit, 1961) and in two anthologies called simply «8 Poèmes» (manuscripts presented to Yvonne Zervos) and *Deux Poèmes* (P.-A. Benoit, 1963). Her paintings have the transparency of glass and the deep luminosity of the mediaeval *vitrail*. She has done a beautiful oil called «La Bibliothèque» and a «Bibliothèque de René Char,» seen as blocks of glass that translate the magical windows of Char, «la vitre de l'heureux» and the «verre voué aux tourments» (19a). Vieira da Silva gave us in 1968 what I consider to be the best portrait of Char published to date.

The contact with the poet induced the artist to learn a whole new art. Vieira da Silva did her first dry point etchings for *L'Inclémence lointaine,* published in 1961 (Pierre Berès). By reducing painting to its bare skeleton, and by substituting for the soft impressions of the canvas the harder lines of metal, the painter sought to move closer to the crisp, incisive poem of Char. Dora Vallier, in a recent article, affirms that Vieira da Silva has, in fact, succeeded in becoming the best of Char's living collaborators. She writes:

> L'évidence saute aux yeux. Nulle peinture aujourd'hui n'était si penchée sur la poésie, si la poésie est cette ouverture sur l'inconnu, cette répercussion qui étend le langage; n'était si proche de la poésie de René Char qui pour ouvrir brise, loin de l'épanchement et de sa facile et prévisible extension de pouvoir, toujours sur la pointe d'une tension rebondissant des bords atteints. Cette poésie où les mots deviennent incommensurables avec eux-mêmes, projetés comme ils sont sur une étendue qu'ils attirent, avait tout pour retenir Vieira da Silva. Et avant tout, une affinité avec sa peinture. Qu'un projet de livre ait provoqué leur rencontre, remercions le hasard (20).

In honor of the painter, Char published a series of nine short pieces entitled «Neuf merci pour Vieira da Silva» (*La*

(19a) «Derrière chacune de toutes les fenêtres allumées il y a une présence; et dans cette présence unique, un mystère.» Antoine Terrasse, «Marie-Hélène Vieira da Silva,» *N. R. F.*, no. 276, décembre 1975.
(20) Dora Vallier, «Gravures de Vieira da Silva pour *L'Inclémence lointaine* de René Char,» Maeght catalogue, 1971.

Bibliothèque est en feu, 1957). These texts, ranging from the aphorism to a poem in verse, are not reprinted in *Recherche de la Base et du Sommet,* but some of them reappear, separately, in other Char anthologies. The most important of the «Neuf merci,» for the present study, is the sixth text, which expressly links one of Char's own works with the work of the artist. It is called «Artine dans l'écho» and reads:

> Notre emmêlement somptueux dans le corps de la voie lactée, chambre au sommet pour notre couple qui dans la nuit ailleurs se glacerait.

When the artist's works are exhibited by the Galerie Jeanne Bûcher in 1960, Char again speaks of the luminous quality of Vieira da Silva's paintings, of her warmth and strength:

> L'œuvre de Vieira da Silva surgit et l'aiguillon d'une douce force obstinée, inspirée, replace ce qu'il faut bien nommer l'art, dans le monde solidaire de la terre qui coule et de l'homme qui s'en effraie. Vieira da Silva tient serrée dans sa main, parmi tant de mains ballantes... quelque chose qui est à la fois lumière d'un sol et promesse d'une graine...

Ten years later, Char dedicates to the painter the poem «Prêles de l'entre-rail.»

For one of his earliest painter friends and one of the last great surrealists, Char writes, in 1970, a tribute which is, at the same time, a summing up of the surrealist experience. In the text entitled «Passage de Max Ernst,» Char says:

> Le surréalisme, en sa période ascendante, avait, croyons-nous, un absolu besoin de Max Ernst... Max Ernst, enjambant Hegel, lui a communiqué ce que l'impressionnable et combatif Breton attendait d'un merveilleux—mot usé et retourné—parti du nord, venu de l'est, merveilleux dont les peintures de Cranach et de Grünewald contiennent les prémices sous leur dessin non courtisan et leur apprêt

mercuriel... Qu'on veuille bien se souvenir de son tableau *La Révolution la nuit,* il illustre excellemment ce qu'il n'a pas songé à illustrer: les *Poésies,* qui n'en sont point, d'Isidore Ducasse, Comte de Lautréamont.

Grâce à Max Ernst et à Chirico, *la mort surréaliste,* entre tous les suicides, n'a pas été hideuse. Elle a éclos sur les lèvres d'une jeunesse imputrescible au lieu de finir au bout d'un chemin noirci.

Ernst represents, I think, a manner that the young Char admired but abandoned as early as 1930. The letter addressed to «Chère Artine» is a farewell to a mode, style and technique reminiscent of Max Ernst. Though they knew each other during the early days of *La Révolution Surréaliste,* Char and Ernst did not, so far as I know, collaborate until 1969, when the painter did eleven color lithographs for the publication of *Dent prompte.* Aside from these, there is only an undated series of gouaches for a manuscript version of *Fête des arbres et du chasseur* presented to Yvonne.

The last piece of art criticism recorded in the second edition of *Recherche de la Base et du Sommet,* 1965, is called «Nouvelles-Hébrides, Nouvelle-Guinée.» It was written as the catalogue preface to an exhibit of sculptures from Oceania organized in 1961 by the Jeanne Bûcher galery in Paris. Char uses the occasion to restate his belief in the pluralistic existence of *les dieux* that monotheism tried to destroy. He writes:

Ces sommets sans mains, ces mâts despotiques, ces Hypnos d'archipel, nous découvrent la virginité d'un crépuscule identique à celui dans lequel nous baignons. C'est l'heure de l'appontement.

Dieux, aujourd'hui sans fonction, sans tribu, quel principe nous fait vos captifs? Vous avez cessé de nous protéger et nous nous sommes approchés de vous, vous avez dépensé votre chaleur et notre cœur bat dans votre retranchement, vous êtes devenus silencieux, nous vous entourons de paroles d'océan.

Concurrently with this article on the sculptures of Oceania, Char published *La Parole en archipel* (January 1962), containing evocations of the primitive, virginal age of Hypnos.

*   *   *

On the occasion of the last Picasso exhibit in Avignon which opened just after the painter's death in 1973, a reviewer for *Time* magazine expressed his disapproval not only of the paintings, but of Char's catalogue preface as well. In an article entitled «Picasso's Worst» (*Time,* June 18, 1973), Robert Hughes writes:

> The opening day of Pablo Picasso's last exhibition of new works resembled a French state funeral: a crowd whispering and shuffling beneath the lofty medieval arches of the papal chapel in Avignon, orations, bereaved friends; and afternoon light, the color of dusty honey, sifting in benediction through the lancet windows.
>
> The centerpiece of the summer's Avignon Festival, *L'Exposition Picasso* consists of 201 paintings. They date from September 1970 to June 1972, and may be said to form Picasso's last testament as an artist. The show bears signs of haste. The installation is confused, the catalogue scrappy, and its preface, by René Char, is a tangle of the glutinous verbiage that some French poets exude like silkworms when in the Spanish presence...

We had just returned from the exhibit when we stopped to see Char, in the summer of 1973. I had, of course, read the catalogue preface and was anxious to discuss with the poet my own reactions, mostly negative, to the Spaniard's last testament. While I was still looking for a way to broach the subject, Char handed me a copy of *Picasso sous les vents étésiens,* the catalogue text published separately by G. L. M.

Near the end of that text, Char writes: «Le sorcier abuse, le magicien mesure.» This remark started a conversation centering around the meaning of the words *sorcellerie, magie, mystère.* Every authentic and viable work of art, Char insisted, must be endowed with that inalienable and inexplicable quality we call mystery, magic, or, in Char's poetry, *chimère. Sorcellerie,* on the other hand, is a term applied by the poet—with negative connotations—to some of the experiments of surrealism. It implies a willful and forcible deformation of reality that can be technically or mechanically achieved and measured. In that sense, it comes close to the Bergsonian definition of humor. *Sorcellerie,* Char might say, is something mechanical superimposed on something living. It implies an abuse of—rather than a reverence for—the mystery of life, the gods within us.

Char then recounted how, not long before the Avignon exhibit was to open, Picasso had asked him to do the introductory text. At first, the poet had refused, saying that he could not work under time pressure. Unlike the painter who was able to produce dozens of canvases in a matter of months, Char would require much time for even the shortest of texts. He did, in the end, write a rather lengthy catalogue preface, completed after the painter's death. The article is a tribute to the whole of Picasso's artistic output—a fact which *Time's* reviewer failed to notice—, not a mere appreciation of the last 201 paintings, tortured or comical distortions of the artist himself, caricatures born of witchcraft and haste, that none of the glutinous verbiage («dusty honey»!) of Robert Hughes can damn or redeem.

«Il n'est pas d'œuvre séparatrice dans l'énorme travail de Picasso, il y a, certes, des rameaux survenus par excès de sève,» Char writes. The excessive branches of Picasso's work, hung from the walls of the Papal Chapel in Avignon, left the viewer with a sense of uneasiness or even embarrassment. When, at the end of that summer visit, Char dedicated our copy of his catalogue preface, he called his text a «survol du pays du sorcier évanoui.» And after the meditations of that afternoon, those words said everything about Char's appreciation of the painter.

Although one of the earliest and most prolific of Char's collaborators, Picasso is not, in fact, the poet's best «allié substantiel.» The two men are fundamentally different in tone, temperament and rhythm, color and form. While Picasso appends his ubiquitous bull to *Dépendance de l'adieu,* 1936, and to *Le Marteau sans maître suivi de Moulin premier,* 1945, Char, in search of animals, turns to the anonymous artists of the Périgord, to the «bête innommable» of Lascaux. Not only the world of Char's animals, but his plants, as well, remain strangers to the eye of Picasso, «le maître du tordage, imperméable à l'humidité fertilisante dont rêvent les formes végétales ou mentales libres» (*De La sainte famille au Droit à la paresse,* 1976).

* * *

From this chronological overview of Char's artistic collaborators I have purposely left out, until now, the one painter who, to my mind, best captures the poet's sense of mystery and magic, and whom Char has called «l'anti-Picasso.» He is the only collaborator with whom Char has actually engaged in poetic dialogue. He is the artist who, like the poet, kept a war diary filled with aphoristic reflections on art and life. His *Cahier* and the *Feuillets d'Hypnos* were published the same year. The painter turned to poetry, as Char turned to painting. «Il faut toujours augmenter le trouble,» said the painter. Char writes: «Ce qui vient au monde pour ne rien troubler ne mérite ni égards ni patience.» The painter is Georges Braque, who was among those represented (with 13 works) at the remarkable «Exposition de peintures et sculptures contemporaines» organized by Yvonne and Christian Zervos during the Avignon Festival of 1947. The works of Braque revealed to Char a brother, and a *devancier* on the road he had mapped out for himself. In a text entitled «Georges Braque intra-muros,» Char describes the exhibit:

> J'ai vu, dans un palais surmonté de la tiare, un homme entrer et regarder les murs. Il parcourut

la solitude dolente et se tourna vers la fenêtre. Les
eaux proches du fleuve durent au même instant
tournoyer, puis la beauté qui va d'un couple à une
pierre, puis la poussière des rebelles dans leur
sépulcre de papes.

Les quatre murs majeurs se mirent à porter ses
espoirs, le monde qu'il avait forcé et révélé, la vie
acquiesçant au secret, et ce cœur qui éclate en
couleurs, que chacun fait sien pour le meilleur et
pour le pire...

Later, in a poem written for the painter's 80th birthday, Char
paid to Braque the supreme compliment of calling him «le
seul élu d'Avignon aimé des murs de son palais» («Octantaine
de Braque,» 1962). Braque has remained, for Char, the only
painter worthy of decorating the walls of the Papal Chapel.

Biographical details of the lives of Braque and Char read
like a deliberate exercise in *décalage*. The year the poet was
born at L'Isle-sur-la-Sorgue, Braque, twenty-five years his
senior, was introduced to Picasso by Apollinaire and held his
first important exhibit in Paris, where all of his paintings were
sold. In 1912, Braque follows Picasso to the Midi and sets
up a summer house in Sorgues, near Avignon, where he will
return regularly until 1927. Char, who learned of his early
neighbor only many years later, has recounted the painter's
attraction to the Vaucluse in a text called «Braque, lorsqu'il
peignait,» 1963:

Braque, lorsqu'il peignait à Sorgues en 1912, se
plaisait, après le travail, à pousser une pointe jusqu'à
Avignon. C'est sur les marches du fol escalier extérieur qui introduisent au palais des Papes que
toujours le déposait sa rêverie. Il s'asseyait à même
la pierre, et dévisageait, en la convoitant, la demeure
qui n'était solennelle et au passé que pour d'autres
que lui. Les murs nus des salles intérieures le
fascinaient. «Un tableau accroché là, s'il tient, pen-
sait-il, est vérifié.» Il attendit, pour savoir, l'année

1947, année au cours de laquelle ses œuvres y furent mises en évidence.

While Braque learns—from southern land- and sea-scapes —the secret of primary colors, textured surfaces, flat perspectives and depersonalized subjects, Char, a schoolboy in Avignon, begins to write—under the influence of Baudelaire and Apollinaire—his first tortured verses of introspection. While Braque, in Sorgues, learns new techniques of realism, Char, in Paris, is introduced into the laboratories of dream.

In the Midi, Braque did his first *papiers collés* that evolved from the *collages* perfected by Picasso. He experiments with other mixed media techniques aimed at adding a new dimension or realism to art.

Two painters, discovered by both Braque and Char—though at different moments in their lives and independently of each other—exercised a decisive influence on the art of painter and poet. I am, of course, referring to Courbet and Corot. From the former, both Braque and Char learned that art should not concern itself exclusively with edifying subject matter. When in February 1938 Char sent to Christian Zervos, director of the *Cahiers d'Art,* his first two poems dealing with paintings, he stressed the anti-didactic nature of his work, saying: «J'ai surtout souhaité traduire sans *instruction,* intuitivement puis nécessairement leur relief épais d'émotion dans le sens où les modèles auraient pu se prononcer en s'apercevant à travers le peintre. Complications de la poésie... Simplicité de la peinture...» (21) In «Courbet: Les casseurs de cailloux,» the poem subsequently published in *Dehors la nuit est gouvernée,* 1938, Char paints a landscape that is anything but idyllic or morally edifying. The second stanza of the poem reads:

Nous dévorons la peste du feu gris dans la rocaille.
Quand on intrigue à la commune,

---

(21) The letter is preserved in the Bibliothèque Littéraire Jacques Doucet, Paris.

C'est encore sur les chemins ruinés qu'on
    est le mieux:
Là, les tomates des vergers, l'air nous les porte
    au crépuscule
Avec l'oubli de la méchanceté prochaine
    de nos femmes
Et l'aigreur de la soif tassée aux genoux.

The work which Proudhon called the first socialist picture ever painted may, to be sure, be taken as a satire on industrial civilization. Courbet, however, saw it as a poem of gentle resignation that would respect the individuality of both thing and man, object and subject. Braque and Char learned from Courbet, the painter of Baudelaire, that humble, everyday objects—whether morally elevating or not—have their proper place in art; that there is, ultimately, no «ton juste,» just a motley array of forms and colors all part of life and, therefore, legitimate components of the artistic experience.

Corot was revealed to Braque by the Salon d'Automne of 1909 that exhibited 24 of his figure paintings, a series of women with musical instruments. In a canvas entitled «Souvenir de Corot,» the modern artist recreates, in his own manner, Corot's portrait of Christine Nilsson, done in 1874. Braque, himself an accomplished musician (Apollinaire had compared his painting to the music of Saint Cecilia), was attracted to Corot's mandolins as much as to his portraits. He recreates—though with a substitution of instruments—the mood of Corot: a certain purity, nobility, and serene joy. In 1938, Char published with his commentary on Courbet, in the *Cahiers d'Art,* a poem called «Une Italienne de Corot,» which stresses the humble and palpable realism of Corot's paintings:

Une haie d'érables se rabat chez un peintre qui
    l'ébranche sur la paix de sa toile:
C'est un familier des fermes pauvres,
Affable et chagrin comme un scarabée.

By the time Char moved to Paris to join the surrealists,

Braque—never in support of the movement—had tired of both the Midi and the capital. In 1928, he moves back to Normandy, where his chilhood was spent, and where his first portraits and landscapes had seen the light. He builds his house in Varengeville, near Dieppe, where, beginning in 1947, Char will be a frequent guest. (Already before the outbreak of the war, the poet, too, had become disenchanted with the capital. In 1940, Char went into hiding in Provence, while Braque, who, until then, had sought shelter in the Pyrenees, returned to a secluded Paris studio.)

As though always running away from each other while discovering—independently—many of the same artistic truths, Char and Braque did not meet until 1944, when both had reached artistic maturity. Their very physical similarities— Char, the giant of Provence; Braque, the giant from the North —must have struck those present at their first meeting (22).

Though Char has referred to Braque as «celui qui nous aura mis les mains au-dessus des yeux pour nous apprendre à mieux regarder et nous permettre de voir plus loin» («Songer à ses dettes,» 1963), it is incorrect to speak of cross influences in the work of poet and painter. Rather, Braque and Char came face to face each having shaped his own vision of the world which, by a number of curious coincidences, had focused on many of the same forms, colors, and subjects, people and places. Commenting on the relationship between poet and painter, Georges Blin has talked of the crossroads at which—each man having come by a different route—Braque and Char met, «au carrefour de sa propre route, de celle qui le menait le plus sûrement à lui-même» (23). Their artistic views did not influence each other. They happened to coincide.

---

(22) When I mentioned the apparent physical similarities between Braque and Char, the latter immediately objected that Braque was «much more handsome.» A beautiful photograph of the painter stands on the poet's mantelpiece at Les Busclats.

(23) Georges Blin's text appeared as the preface to the catalogue of the «Exposition Georges Braque—René Char» organized in 1963 by the Bibliothèque Littéraire Jacques Doucet, Paris.

20

One of the first Char manuscripts illustrated by Braque is, fittingly, the poem «Lyre,» published in 1947:

> Lyre sans bornes des poussières,
> Surcroît de notre cœur.

It is Char who paints the musical instrument, and Braque who makes it sing. The first published title sent by Char to Marcelle and Georges Braque is *Fête des arbres et du chasseur,* 1948, with illustrations by Miró. There follow, in 1950, *Les Matinaux* and *Art bref.* The latter contains Char's first homage to the painter, the preface reprinted from the catalogue of Braque's Paris exhibit in June 1947. This text is incorporated into «En vue de Georges Braque,» the article which opens the «Alliés substantiels» series of *Recherche de la Base et du sommet* in 1965. In the article, Char already points to the vibrant quality of the painter's art, to the sense of movement and becoming characteristic of his work. The text also underlines the material beauty of Braque's paintings, endowed with the «frisson des alchimies,» but free from any metaphysical speculation. Char and Braque share an attachment to the earth and all things in it. I know of no better «Portrait analogique» of Char than «Le brabant,» painted by Braque in 1962. It shows a wheelbarrow which—making its way through a desolate landscape—seems suddenly to rise up, making the earth sing. The painting combines Char's definition of the poet given in *L'Action de la Justice...* («le poète solitaire / Grande brouette des marécages») and the illustration of the poet's mission sketched by «Exploit du cylindre à vapeur,» examined earlier. There are other paintings by Braque, like «Les champs,» «Les blés,» or «La charrue,» reminiscent of Char's landscapes.

Poet and painter do not collaborate until 1947, when Braque designs the stage sets for *La Conjuration.* In 1948-49, he does the illustrations for *Le Soleil des eaux,* which inaugurate his subsequent leimotiv of the bird in flight. The play, dedicated to the fishermen of the Vaucluse, unites poet and painter under the sign of Petrarch, and of the sun. Char, the singer of *Le Soleil des eaux,* has found his ally in the painter of Helios, who, in 1949, also projects the sets for *L'Homme qui marchait dans un rayon de soleil.* The master who started as a house painter had an eye for large scale design. In 1923, Diaghilev had commissioned sets for Molière's play *Les Fâcheux.* In 1949, Jouvet invites Braque's collaboration in the production of *Tartuffe.*

Braque, like Char, worked slowly and deliberately. He produced relatively little and destroyed much. His collaboration with Char is restricted primarily to illustrations of manuscripts and single poems published in periodicals, such as the *Cahiers d'Art* or the *Derrière le miroir* collections. Braque also worked on several of the *minuscules* published by P.-A. Benoit. He collaborated in the latter's *Salut à René Char* in 1955, and again in *Né le...,* Benoit's greeting for Char's 50th birthday in 1957. In 1956, Braque illustrated *La Bibliothèque est en feu,* the book dedicated to him. The same year, he worked on one of the poet's favorite *minuscules, Jeanne qu'on brûla verte,* a text dedicated to Joan of Arc. Braque contributed to the catalogue published by Engelberts (Geneva) in 1958, with a text by Char, and supplied the illustration for *5 poésies en hommage à Georges Braque,* published the same year. This collection contains the text of «L'Oiseau spirituel,» which is, I think, the best description Char ever gave of Braque. The poem, later republished in *La Parole en archipel,* reads:

> Ne m'implorez pas, grands yeux; restez à couvert, désirs.
> Je disparais au ciel, étangs privés de seuil.
> Je glisse en liberté au travers des blés mûrs.
> Nulle haleine ne teint le miroir de mon vol.
> Je cours le malheur des humains, le dépulpe
> de son loisir.

In 1960, Braque does a frontispiece for *Le Ruisseau de blé,* containing translations of Pindar by Jean Beaufret.

Their love of Greece is one of the many bonds uniting painter and poet. Braque, we remember, was the painter of Hemera, who hovers—though invisible and unnamed—above the poems of *Les Matinaux*. Herakles, Persephone, Phaeton, the canephorae, and the Theogony are among the painter's subjects.

In 1961, Braque and Char together compose the texts of *Ainsi va l'amitié,* accompanying photographs by P.-A. Benoit and Mariette Lachaud. The *Hommage à Georges Braque* published by Engelberts in 1962 contains texts taken from Apollinaire's *Les Peintres cubistes,* Pierre Reverdy's *Une Aventure méthodique,* and Char's *5 poésies en hommage à Georges Braque.* The volume is illustrated with an original Braque color lithograph. A bird in flight accompanies Char's text «Nous ne jalousons pas les dieux,» 1962, which—perhaps better than any other Char text—shows the respect uniting poet and painter in face of the terrestrial mystery of life. Their work will be dedicated not to any metaphysical God, but to «les dieux» that are within us and whose adventure (*ad-venire*) we perpetuate on earth:

> Nous ne jalousons pas les dieux, nous ne les servons pas, mais au péril de notre vie nous attestons leur existence multiple, et nous nous émouvons d'être de leur élevage aventureux lorsque cesse leur souvenir.

Religion and art are explicitly linked in Char's commentary on «Le Prisonnier,» the Georges de La Tour painting discussed in his war journal, *Feuillets d'Hypnos.* Char writes: «La femme explique. L'emmuré écoute. Les mots qui tombent de la bouche de cette terrestre silhouette d'ange rouge sont des mots essentiels, des mots qui portent immédiatement secours...» Another text of the same collection further identifies the red terrestrial angel as the spirit within us that dictates our words and our silences: «L'intelligence avec l'ange: notre primordial souci. (Ange, ce qui, à l'intérieur de l'homme, tient à l'écart du compromis religieux, la parole du plus haut silence...).»

In an interview with Raymond Jean (*Le Monde,* 11 janvier

1969), Char again speaks of de La Tour: «Pour être celui, non qui édifie, mais qui inspire, il faut se placer dans une vérité que le temps ne cesse de fortifier et de confirmer. Georges de La Tour est cet homme-là. Baudelaire et lui ont des faiblesses mais pas des *manques*. Voilà qui les rend admirables. Georges de La Tour—ne souriez pas—est souvent mon intercesseur auprès du mystère poétique, donc du mystère humain. Il n'y a pas d'auréole d'élu derrière la tête de ses sujets ni sur la sienne. Le peintre *sait*. Le peintre et l'homme...» If the poet opposes organized religion («le compromis religieux»), it is not because it deals with the unknown and the unknowable, but because it would limit, by the «auréole d'élu,» the artist's freedom to probe for himself into the «mystère humain.»

Shortly before his death, Braque collaborated in the publication of *L'Effroi la joie*. The collection ends with a song to earth, and spring, called simply: «Joie»:

> Comme tendrement rit la terre quand la neige s'éveille sur elle! Jour sur jour, gisante embrassée, elle pleure et rit. Le feu qui la fuyait l'épouse, à peine a disparu la neige.

But by far the most important collaborative effort by Braque and Char is the edition of *Lettera amorosa* published by Engelberts in 1963, with 27 color lithographs. This edition was exhibited—along with other Braque illustrations of Char—at the Bibliothèque Littéraire Jacques Doucet, Paris, May 1963. Char had sent Braque the first edition of *Lettera amorosa,* published in 1953. Five years later, work is begun on an illustrated and revised version. At this time, Char carefully specifies the arrangement of his texts on the page, the spacing of lines and the space allotted to the painter. Nothing is left to chance. The men work together for nearly four years. The book, completed in March 1962, will remain, I think, one of the supreme monuments to the art of poet and painter.

Braque's illustrations of *Lettera amorosa* are anything but ornamental or decorative. In fact, they are illustrations in the original sense of that word only, i.e., they illumine the poem. Braque does not give the pictorial equivalents of the literal meanings of words. He interprets, instead, the spirit of the work, respecting its mystery, following its metamorphoses, rhythms and tones, the unwritten message of the text. Thus, for example, the key passage of the poem, which reads:

> Je ris merveilleusement avec toi. Voilà
> la chance unique.

is not represented, by Braque, with a pair of smiling faces. He paints, instead, a flight of green leaves converging on a circle. In his «illumination,» Braque seems to take his cue from another mention of the word *rire* (rare with Char), as it is found in *Feuillets d'Hypnos.* Here the poet had spoken of «un arbre plein de rire et de feuilles.» Braque knows the work of Char. Thus he can paint a word, an image, in all its layers of meaning, and supply to the text of Char the metalanguage that respects the calls—and the silences—of the poet. Char asks:

> Qui n'a pas rêvé, en flânant sur le boulevard des
> villes, d'un monde qui, au lieu de commencer avec
> la parole, débuterait avec les intentions?

Braque alone—among the illustrators of Char—has returned to the beginnings of the poet's world.

Char's is not an ordinary love poem. *Lettera amorosa* is, for one thing, completely devoid of eroticism. And thus Braque's palette, so rich and varied, lacks one color: the color red which, Georges Blin points out, would be far too aggressive for what he calls the «élégie de la solitude» (*op. cit.*). Red is replaced by browns, violets, purple, and pink. The truly active agents of Braque's lithographs—as of the poem—are the yellows and greens, the sun and the flower.

It is, I believe, inaccurate to reduce *Lettera amorosa* to an «elegy.» Let us take it, quite literally, as a letter, the one form of writing suitable to the free combination of various forms, tones, and styles. Char is very adept at «mixed media» technique. The seemingly haphazard mixture of poetic prose, aphorisms, accounts of everyday life, a true verse poem, and dictionary definitions heightens the effect of the letter, underlining the immediacy and the reality of its subject matter. *Lettera amorosa* includes all levels of expression, from the exultation of a Greek 'ΥΜΝΟΣ to the prosaic account of a walk. (The original version of the poem even made reference to a visit to the dentist's: «Hier, après déjeuner, j'ai dû faire le contraire d'une sieste d'une heure chez le dentiste.») The poet shares with his reader concrete details relating to his mental and physical well-being. He starts out his letter with a report on the improved state of his health: «Je n'ai plus de fièvre ce matin.» Later, the writer describes a walk he has just taken: «Je viens de rentrer. J'ai longtemps marché. Tu es la Continuelle. Je fais du feu. Je m'assois dans le fauteuil de panacée.»

Like the poet, Braque strove to achieve contrasts not only of color and form, but of texture, giving to his paintings a new dimension of realism. He added sand, ashes, sawdust, metal filings and even tobacco to his palette of oils. He combined, in a single work, lacquer, which is transparent, with ochre, which is opaque. Shiny and mat surfaces alternate to heighten the effect of his compositions, as poetry and prose succeed each other in the work of Char.

Lettera amorosa is not an elegy, nor is its central theme concerned with solitude. Braque, who has understood the poet better than any critic, begins his illustrations with a woman's head, and ends with two profiles facing each other. For in the seemingly unrelated bits of poetry and prose that make up Char's Letter of Love, one phrase, slipped between the account of two very ordinary acts («J'ai longtemps marché... Je fais du feu»), stands out: «Tu es la Continuelle.» Woman, though unseen, is the unifying theme of Char's Letter. «Tu es partie,» says the writer, «mais tu demeures dans l'inflexion des circonstances...» In her very absence from particularized space and time, the woman of *Lettera amorosa* emerges as the omnipresent, all-pervading, and eternal spirit of love. Like the air in which all things move and all are changed, that spirit transforms both nature and man. Char writes: «C'est alors, en vérité, qu'avec l'aide d'une nature à présent favorable, je m'évade des échardes enfoncées dans ma chair, vieux accidents, âpres tournois.» Like Char, Braque did not aim to portray the physical loveliness of woman. He captures her spiritual beauty in an enormous blue flower, set into a background of blue, that accompanies Char's «profession de foi»: «Tu es la Continuelle.»

Very early in his career, Braque abandoned portraits. Even in his «L'Homme au guitare,» done in 1914, the human figure disappears behind the musical instrument. Braque's canephorae of 1922-25 show much the same interplay of volume and line as the later «Nature morte aux pommes,» 1933, or the «Falaises» painted in 1938. Bathers, apples, and cliffs are but different metamorphic representations of a mood and, in particular, of a certain sensuousness and joy that can be expressed, indifferently, by any object. It is not the apparent subject which matters, but the new reality created by form and movement, volume, line, texture, and color. After 1938-39, Braque removes all human figures from his paintings. At the same time, his empathy with inanimate objects grows, as the «Ateliers» series, 1948-1956, so much admired by Char, shows. In «Sous la verrière,» the poet's imaginary dialogue with the painter recorded in 1950, Char comments on the «Studio» paintings:

> J'aime que dans la suite d'œuvres que vous intitulez *L'Atelier du Peintre,* vous ayez accumulé et comme entassé avec une ingratitude géniale les puissances éminentes et combien usuelles de votre rêverie et de votre travail. Elles se transmettent réciproquement l'essor. Et ce ramier, ce phénix plutôt, tantôt fou de rapidité, tantôt arrondi, soit qu'il parcoure, soit qu'il fixe le ciel floconneux de votre atelier,

dégage un souffle de vent et une présence qui se-
couent toute votre peinture récente.

It was in the second of his «Ateliers» that Braque introduced
the bird-in-flight motif, giving to his painting a feeling of movement and infinite space. The bird and the flower are the
unifying visual elements of *Lettera amorosa*.

«Peindre n'est pas dépeindre,» wrote Braque. «Ecrire
n'est pas décrire.» And Char, the guest of Braque in February
1948, copied from the painter's *Cahier* the following reflection: «Une chose ne peut être à deux places à la fois. On
ne peut pas l'avoir en tête et sous les yeux» (24). Both poet
and painter of *Lettera amorosa* are concerned with attuning
themselves to the world, not with copying it. They paint
not what they see, but what they know to exist, hidden from
the naked eye. They are neither figurative nor non-figurative
artists, but creators of living objects brought forth from the
silence of fountain and stone. When Braque bends the necks of
his guitars towards the viewer, the distortion creates a new
dimension of reality. It lets us see around and behind the
painted object, which in relation to other objects—hidden
behind it—assumes new meaning. In the same manner, the
scattered fragments of Iris (which are united only at the end
of the poem) add space and movement to the poem. As
we pass from the iris of the rainbow to the flower of the
Sorgue, Char's Letter spells out the face of the beloved:
Iris, the woman of Hölderlin, the eternal feminine of all poetry.
It is not an external truth that poet and painter set out to portray. «Les preuves fatiguent la vérité,» wrote Braque. The
only truth of the poem—and of the illustrations accompanying
it—must be internal, testifying to an inner life by which the
object, the word, and the image are verified.

In *Lettera amorosa,* Char and Braque each give fullest

---

(24) This and other quotations from Braque, copied by Char
onto the back of a Braque drawing, are preserved at the Bibliothèque Littéraire Jacques Doucet. For an excellent article on

expression to their metamorphic view of the world in which all things perpetually change color and form, fuse with each other and drift apart, change alliances and come together again. Braque has defined his theory of metamorphosis in a conversation with John Richardson (*The Observer,* 1 December, 1957), stating:

> There are certain mysteries, certain secrets in my own work which even I do not understand, nor do I try to do so. Why bother? The more one probes, the more one deepens the mystery; it's always out of reach. Mysteries have to be respected if they are to retain their power... If there is no mystery then there is no «poetry,» the quality I value above all else in art. What do I mean by «poetry»? It is to a painting what life is to man. But don't ask me to define it; it is something that each artist has to discover for himself through his own intuition. For me it is a matter of harmony, of *rapports,* of rhythm and—most important for my own work—of «metamorphosis.» I will try to explain what I mean by «metamorphosis.» For me no object can be tied down to any one sort of reality. A stone may be part of a wall, a piece of sculpture, a lethal weapon, a pebble on a beach or anything else you like, just as this file in my hand can be metamorphosed into a shoe-horn or a spoon, according to the way in which I use it.

This revelation of the «metamorphic» possibilities of an object came to Braque, he said, during the war. He first applied the insights gained then in his series of billiard tables, painted between 1944 and 1952. Here objects like a chandelier and a hatstand—first sketched separately—ultimately reach up and down to touch each other, to fuse and become one, indis-

---

Lettera amorosa, see Thomas J. Hines, «L'Ouvrage de tous les temps admiré: *Lettera amorosa,* René Char and Georges Braque,» in the *Bulletin du Bibliophile,* no. 1, 1973.

tinguishable in the finished painting. Braque has created a new object, neither figurative nor non-figurative, but as real as its original components, among which the painter has established a new harmony and *rapport*. In much the same manner, the flower and the rainbow of *Lettera amorosa,* the star and the butterfly, reach towards each other and ultimately unite under one sign, one name: Iris. And over all the fragmented visions of that sign there hovers—silently and unseen, but everywhere felt—the Greek divinity, messenger of the gods, spreading her veil, the rainbow, winglike over the world of the poem.

Jean Paulhan has called Braque the «maître des rapports invisibles.» Char has defined the painter's world as «un monde ceinturé d'impossibles» and «un bloc de possibilités.» In *Lettera amorosa* poet and painter explore and discover the secret and invisible relationships between seemingly distant elements. The woman's head placed by Braque among the stars is at once a woman, a goddess, and a bird. Leaves, flowers, birds, faces and stars are painted in pairs to testify to the existence of «la Continuelle,» to punctuate the joy and fullness of life, of which all things inspired by love partake.

Nothing in *Lettera amorosa* is finite. Everything in the poem, transfused with the spirit of the invisible goddess, is continuously transformed. Water, fire, earth and wind contribute to the metamorphoses of the poem and to the birth of «l'homme à tête de nouveau-né... Déjà mi-liquide, mi-fleur.» As nature slowly awakens to the light of spring, so leaves, birds, flowers, stars and faces are moved by wind and sun —effortlessly and gently—towards the «retour du jour sur les vertes avenues libres.» There is a serenity and a tenderness (a word already applied to Braque by Apollinaire) in the work of poet and painter.

This serenity is punctuated, in the Letter of Love, with shouts of joy:

«Amour hélant, l'Amoureuse viendra,
Gloria de l'été, ô fruits!»

As summer comes, Braque's flowers stand as though ready to burst into flame. The birds take flight, and the green leaves dance about the tree. In the imaginary dialogue with Braque recorded by Char in «Sous la verrière,» 1963, the painter gives to the poet the following command: «Tâtez de cette orange au bord de son assiette. Elle n'est pas seulement là pour se lisser les flancs. Portez-lui joie.» As he writes his texts to accompany some of Braque's paintings (the same year Braque finishes the illustrations for *Lettera amorosa*), Char begs his friend's forgiveness for mingling with his work which, being sufficient unto itself, should, he says, be viewed in silence: «Votre œuvre étant un tout nommé et accompli, ce que convient devant elle c'est le silence de la jubilation intérieure que les yeux imperceptiblement accusent» («Lèvres incorrigibles»). Braque himself, in an India ink drawing of his *Cahier,* speaks of the fervor that motivates his work: «Je ne suis pas un peintre révolutionnaire,» he writes. «Je ne cherche pas l'exaltation. La ferveur me suffit.» This fervor, this inner jubilation and joy—derived from the humblest of objects— comes alive in the greens, yellows and violets of *Lettera amorosa* in which poet and painter trace the road of the sun, «un chemin de parélie pour la félicité furtive de la terre des amants.»

In *Lettera amorosa,* Braque and Char have composed a new Song of Songs which, though utterly pagan («Je ne cherche pas l'exaltation. La ferveur me suffit»), expresses nevertheless the sense of paradox, mystery and magic that is a part of every religion. The Song of Solomon is built, like Char's Letter, around an implied dialogue between a visible and an invisible speaker, not always clearly distinguishable. The androgynous quality of the Song, found also in Char's poem, results from the definition of love postulated by the poets. In Solomon's Song as in the Letter of Char, the Lover and the Beloved—though they seemingly go in search of each other—have really become one.

The Song of Songs is, like Char's poem, a hymn to summer:

For, lo, the winter is past, the rain is over
   and gone;
The flowers appear on the earth; the time of the
   singing of birds is come, and the voice of the
   turtle is heard in our land.

Like the woman of Char's poem, the Biblical figure combines
the properties of flower, bird, and fountain. She is the
bundle of myrrh, a cluster of camphire. She has the eyes
of doves. She is the rose and the apple, a garden, a spring,
a fountain, a fountain of gardens, a well of living waters.
The lover stands, like the sun, upon the mountains. The
Biblical bride has a dual habitat: she dwells in the wild,
unprotected regions of nature, and in the secrecy of the house.
«O my dove,» says the Singer, «O my dove, that art in the
clefts of the rock, in the secret places of the stairs.» *Lettera
amorosa* translates the verse into «les marches du monde
concret, la perspective obscure où gesticulent des silhouettes
d'hommes dans les rapines et la discorde. Quelques-unes,
compensantes, règlent le feu de la moisson, s'accordent avec
les nuages.»
   Like *Lettera amorosa,* the Song of Songs speaks of a love
past and future, but seemingly removed from the present.
Both poems go forth about the city in the streets seeking that
absent love, «until the day break and the shadows flee away,»
until the light return «sur les vertes avenues libres.» The poet
and the painter of *Lettera amorosa* believe, like the Biblical
singer, in the return of love, the liberator from death, victori-
ous over time and space. «Je te chéris,» writes Char in the
introduction to his letter. «Tôt dépourvu serait l'ambitieux
qui resterait incroyant en la femme, tel le frelon aux prises
avec son habileté de moins en moins spacieuse. Je te chéris
cependant que dérive la lourde pinasse de la mort.»
   «Who is she,» asked the Song, «that looketh forth as the
morning, fair as the moon, clear as the sun, and terrible as
an army with banners?» She is Iris, answers the Letter,
spreading her veil the rainbow, the banner of peace. She is

the woman and the planet and the butterfly, the red terrestrial angel, «le grand mars changeant,» the messenger of death. She is the iris of the eye, the flower of the river, the Iris of Eros and of *Lettera amorosa.*

The same year that Braque and Char brought out the illustrated edition of *Lettera amorosa,* the poet—describing one of the paintings in Braque's «Guéridons» series—writes: «Nous attendons la réapparition des meilleures parmi les absentes, parmi les aimées. Seulement elles.» The paired flowers, leaves, birds, stars and faces of *Lettera amorosa* bear witness to the perpetual—if silent—presence of the spirit that continues, though unseen, to pass among us.

Who, asked Georges Blin, should speak in favor of the poet? Not the grammarian, not the critic, nor the philosopher or the musician. «Reste, s'il est poète et musicien, le peintre, comme si le silence souverain qu'établit la Parole 'intransitive' ne pouvait être mieux relevé que dans le langage le plus muet, des teintes et des figures» (*op. cit.*). In Braque, Char found the painter who made his lyre sing. But while engaging with the poet in the «conversation souveraine,» Braque also respected the sovereign silences of the «intransitive word,» the eloquence of Orion:

> Et à présent si tu avais pouvoir de dire l'aromate de ton monde profond, tu rappellerais l'armoise. Appel au signe vaut défi. Tu t'établirais dans ta page, sur les bords d'un ruisseau, comme l'ambre gris sur le varech échoué; puis, la nuit montée, tu t'éloignerais des habitants insatisfaits, pour un oubli servant d'étoile. Tu n'entendrais plus geindre tes souliers entrouverts.
>
> («Eloquence d'Orion,» *Aromates chasseurs*) (25).

---

(25) The original discussion of Char and Braque was published as: «René Char and Georges Braque: Poets of Metamorphosis,» in *Kentucky Romance Quarterly,* 1976, no. 2.

4

THRESHOLDS OF PRESENCE: ORION RESURGENT

> L'enfant, le ruisseau, le rebelle ne sont qu'un seul
> et même être qui se modifie suivant les années. Il
> brille et s'éteint tour à tour, au gré de l'événement
> sur les marches de l'horizon.
> («Jouvence des Névons,» *Les Matinaux*, 1950).

> Nous ne sommes plus dans l'incurvé. Ce qui nous
> écartera de l'usage est déjà en chemin. Puis nous
> deviendrons terre, nous deviendrons soif.
> («Aromates chasseurs,» *Aromates chasseurs*, 1975).

> Die Mitteilung der existenzialen Möglichkeiten der
> Befindlichkeit, das heisst das Erschliessen von
> Existenz, kann eigenes Ziel der 'dichtenden' Rede
> werden.
> (Martin Heidegger, *Sein und Zeit*, 1927) (1)

In a 1966 essay called «Le Souhait et le Constat,» René
Char contrasts the roles of philosopher, poet, and physicist,
stating:

> Le philosophe pense et obtient le pays de sa pensée
> à partir d'une œuvre ou d'un concept déjà existant...
> Le philosophe ne divulguera pas le secret suivant
> et ne touchera pas à l'ultime viatique; il en défendra
> l'accès contre toutes les tentations venues d'en finir
> avec eux.

---

(1) All page references are to the 1972 edition of *Sein und Zeit*
(Tübingen: Max Niemeyer Verlag).

Le poète fonde sa parole à partir de quelque embrun, d'un refus vivifiant ou d'un état omnidirectionnel aussitôt digité... D'omission en omission et de soupçon en douleur, le poète est le contraire d'un dynaste; c'est un journalier, de tous le plus irrésolu et distant, et comme éthérisé dans l'implacable; de même qu'apte à se ruer sur le plus enclos des amours.

Le physicien devra prendre scrupule qu'il est le bras droit d'un souverain très temporaire, obtus et probablement criminel...

Lequel des trois aménagera l'espace conquis et les terrasses dévastées? (2).

It is obvious that in the above analysis, Char is referring to systematized philosophy, as illustrated by Aristotle, Descartes, Hegel, etc. But in «La Barque à la proue altérée,» 1967, the poet turns his attention to the «philosophes d'origine,» of whom he says:

Les philosophes d'origine sont les philosophes dont l'existence, l'inspiration, la vue, l'arête et l'expression ne supportent que peu de temps l'intérieur cloisonné de la pensée didactique. Ils sont tirés violemment du dehors pour s'unir sans précaution à l'inconnu des êtres, à leur déroutante anthologie, ainsi qu'aux troubles cycloniques de l'univers. Ils possèdent à leur insu un don de nouveauté inaltérable: ils fécondent en s'étoilant et se fertilisent en se creusant... Ainsi les philosophes et les poètes d'origine possèdent-ils la Maison, mais restent-ils des errants sans atelier ni maison...

---

(2) «Le Souhait et le Constat» is the last critical essay contained in the 1971 edition of *Recherche de la Base et du Sommet.* «La Barque à la proue altérée,» also in this edition, was first published in *L'Endurance de la Pensée. Pour saluer Jean Beaufret* (Paris: Plon, 1968), which also contained Heidegger's «Zeit und Sein,» first given as a lecture in 1962 at the University of Freiburg im Breisgau.

This essay is dedicated to Jean Beaufret, the French philosopher who, in the summer of 1955, brought together in Paris René Char and Martin Heidegger. The meeting marked the beginning of a long and intimate frienship between the German philosopher and the French poet (3).

In the two excerpts given above, Char contrasts Aristotelian logic (and the systems built upon its premises) with the pre-Socratic origins of philosophy and the modern heirs of Heraclitus. Though the latter was among the poet's earliest mentors, it was Heidegger who helped Char gain a deeper understanding of the early Greek philosophers and tragedians, as well as of the German philosopher-poets (Hölderlin, Nietzsche) who, like Char, had looked to ancient Greece in their interrogation of the world.

«If the poet should begin to philosophize,» said Howard Nemerov, «he must needs do so as a beginner, as a pre-Socratic, and think in fragments» (4). There is a formal (as well as an ideological) affinity between Char and the philosopher-poets he studies. In 1936, he turned to the fragments of *Zarathustra* (5); in 1940, he translates fragments of Hölderlin, the «Prométhée saxifrage»; in 1948, he writes the preface to *Fragments* of Heraclitus translated by Yves Battistini (6). The poet's own «Impressions anciennes» (1950, 1952, 1964),

---

(3) Jean Beaufret has recorded the meeting in «L'Entretien sous le marronnier,» *L'Arc*, no. 22, été 1963, pp. 1-7. Before making his visit to Paris, Heidegger had expressed the wish to meet two men: Braque and Char. He subsequently spent many a summer in the Vaucluse, as the poet's guest. In 1958, Heidegger lectured at the Nouvelle Faculté d'Aix-en-Provence on «Hegel et les Grecs.» With Jean Beaufret, he participated in the «Séminaires du Thor.» Proceedings of these meetings have been published, for the participants, with the title: «Dans la proximité de René Char.»

(4) Howard Nemerov, «Poetry, Prophecy, Prediction,» Collected in *Reflexions on Poetry and Poetics* (New Brunswick, N. J.: Rutgers Univ. Press, 1972), p. 210.

(5) For a discussion of Char and Nietzsche, see Paulène Aspel, «René Char et Nietzsche,» in *Liberté*, juillet-août 1968, vol. 10, no. 4.

(6) Yves Battistini, *Héraclite d'Ephèse* (Paris: Editions «Cahiers d'Art,» 1948).

inspired by and dedicated to Martin Heidegger, end on a series of aphorisms (7).

Introduced into the 1930 edition of *Arsenal* by the text «Le Sujet,» (8) and first used extensively in *Moulin premier,* 1936, the aphorism has remained characteristic of Char down to *Le Nu perdu,* 1971, and *Aromates chasseurs,* 1975. In an interview with Edith Mora (9), he explains his predilection for the poetic and philosophic fragment. Though its literary ancestry can be traced to the pre-Socratics and to Nietzsche, the aphorism also is, to Char's mind, a form dictated by the requirements of our age, of which he says: «Dans une époque oppressive où les gens n'ont pas le temps de lire et de réfléchir, il faut leur offrir cette forme brève...» Even more basically, however, the elliptical form of Char's poems relates to the «aphoristic» landscape of his native Vaucluse: «La Provence est toute en paysages aphoristiques,» he explains, «le berceau de Fontaine-de-Vaucluse, les Alpilles: une véritable sentence de la nature... Voyez-vous, c'est là, dans ce pays... qu'est le point de départ de ma forme aphoristique parfois.» Many of the poet's titles make direct reference to the fragmented nature which is, quite literally, part and parcel of his world: «Les Dentelles de Montmirail,» «Le Bulletin des Baux,» «Sept parcelles de Luberon.» Even when they do not name a specific geographic location, Char's works evoke the splintered aspect of his physical surroundings: *Le Poème pulvérisé, La Parole en archipel, L'Age cassant,* «Le Rempart de brindilles,» «Le Terme épars,» «La Frontière en pointillé,» «Mirage des aiguilles» (9a).

---

(7) «Impressions anciennes,» in *Recherche de la Base et du Sommet,* 1971, pp. 149-52. These «Impressions» are introduced by Char as «un hommage de respect, de reconnaissance et d'affection à Martin Heidegger.»

(8) «Le Sujet» appeared first as «Profession de foi du Sujet» in *La Révolution surréaliste,* no. 12, 15 December, 1929.

(9) Edith Mora, «Poésie-sur-Sorgue,» *Les Nouvelles Littéraires,* 16 September, 1965.

(9a) On fragment and aphorism, see Maurice Blanchot, *L'Entretien infini* (Paris: Gallimard, 1969): «Réflexions sur le nihilisme,»

In his essays gathered under the title: *Unterwegs zur Sprache,* Heidegger writes: «Die denkende Zwiesprache mit dem Dichten kann dem Gedicht nur mittelbar dienen. Darum steht sie in der Gefahr, das Sagen des Gedichtes eher zu stören, statt es aus seiner eigenen Ruhe singen zu lassen» (10). In his aphorisms, Char engages in what Plato called the «dialogue aphone» with himself and with the «indicible qui ne peut, par le langage, être complètement porté à la voix, ni proprement à la parole, donc ne se communique ni aux autres, ni même à l'intéressé. C'est sans doute cet 'indicible' qui... constitue pourtant le sol nourricier à chaque fois différent à partir duquel il [le philosophe] s'élève et se renouvelle constamment» (11). However, the poetry of Char's dialogues is not to be confused with Plato's metaphysics. For the system of rigidly conducted inquiries aimed at the revelation of ultimate truth, Char substitutes the question to which none or only temporary answers are given, like the «Réponses interrogatives» made to Martin Heidegger in 1966 (12). «La

---

pp. 227-55, and «L'Athenaeum,» pp. 525-27. In *L'Endurance de la pensée,* the collective volume offered to Jean Beaufret in 1968, Blanchot makes a distinction between fragment and aphorism, the latter, he argues, a term wrongly used when applied to Char:

> Ainsi dit-on de René Char qu'il emploie «la forme aphoristique.» Etrange malentendu. L'aphorisme est fermé et borné: l'horizontal de tout horizon. Or, ce qui est important, important et exaltant, dans la suite de «phrases» presque séparées que tant de ses poèmes nous proposent—texte sans prétexte, sans contexte—, c'est que, interrompues par un blanc, isolées et dissociées au point que l'on ne peut passer de l'une à l'autre ou seulement par un saut et en prenant conscience d'un difficile intervalle, elles portent cependant, dans leur pluralité, le sens d'un arrangement qu'elles confient à un avenir de parole.

(«Parole de fragment,» p. 104).

(10) Martin Heidegger, *Unterwegs zur Sprache* (Pfullingen: Verlag Günther Neske, 1971), p. 39.

(11) Hannah Arendt, «Martin Heidegger à quatre-vingts ans,» in *Critique,* no. 293, octobre 1971.

(12) In *Recherche de la Base et du Sommet,* 1965. The 1930 edition of *Artine* announced the forthcoming publication of a new title by Char, *L'Homme en question,* which never appeared.

réponse interrogative est la réponse de l'être,» Char comments. «Mais la réponse au questionnaire n'est qu'une fascine de la pensée» («La Frontière en pointillé,» *Aromates chasseurs*). Char is not a philosopher-poet in the tradition of Lucretius, or Voltaire, or even Chénier and Vigny. He does not try to elaborate a system of knowledge. What, it has been asked, would remain of the poetic beauty of Heraclitus, if we had his complete works? What remains of Heidegger, turned poet? (13) What of Char's poetry, reduced to metaphysical dialectics?

«La poésie ne peut en *aucune manière* aider à expliquer la science, ou à enseigner la philosophie, la morale, les structures du monde. Quand la poésie est métaphysique ou morale, elle l'est à partir d'elle-même,» wrote Georges Jean (14). It is in his poetic fragments that Char comes closest to the philosopher-poets he has studied. Generally speaking, the early aphorisms (*Moulin premier,* 1936; *Partage formel,* 1945) try to define the role of the poet and the place of poetry in society. In *Le Nu perdu,* 1971, Char gathers the poems, prose poems and aphorisms previously published in *Retour amont,* 1966; *Dans la pluie giboyeuse,* 1968; *Le Chien de cœur, L'Effroi la joie,* 1969, and *Contre une maison sèche,* 1971. The aphorisms of this period deal with the more basic issues of language and meaning. It is here that Char comes closest to the early philosophers (and to Heidegger) for whom the questions of philology and philosophy were intimately related.

In surrealism, wrote J. H. Matthews, «the confident reasoning of Descartes gives way to the anguished uncertainty of Perceval, impelled to advance into the magic forest toward

---

(13) Heidegger has written many poems to Char, among them those published under the title: «Gedachtes» («Pensivement») in the special issue of *L'Herne,* 1971. These poems, inscribed: «Für René Char in freundschaftlichem Gedenken,» frequently read like an *abrégé* of Heidegger's philosophical essays.

(14) Georges Jean, *La Poésie* (Paris: Editions du Seuil, 1966), p. 38.

the possession of the impossible» (15). Could the same not be said of the pre-Socratics, who, for Char, mark not an *aurore,* but a *crépuscule,* the end of an age «où la philosophie côtoyait la poésie»? (16).

«Levé avant son sens, un mot nous éveille, nous prodigue la clarté du jour, un mot qui n'a pas rêvé» (*Contre une maison sèche*). Myth, magic, and the marvelous were an integral part of the pre-Socratic scene where poets and philosophers tried to read the world in words that were without memory, tested against concrete appearances and held accountable for the things they «called» into existence. In the world of Heraclitus, the *signe* and the *signifié* were simultaneously realized. Philology determined the direction of philosophy (βίος βιòς). Philosophers and poets were, quite literally, «Unterwegs zur Sprache.» The world was conascent and consonant with the word. The universe was not a conglomerate of fixed ideas, but an arsenal of possibilities waiting to be named by the terrible and magic words that had the power to kill, and to create. Man read the world by means of visual confrontation, which was forever new: «Le Soleil se renouvelle chaque jour. Il ne cesse pas d'être éternellement nouveau» (Heraclitus, *Fragments,* no. 6).

But whether we consider the *Poem* of Parmenides or the *Fragments* of Heraclitus, the philosophy of being or the theory of becoming, the ancient world is seen to have believed in a universality of existence and a stability of essence lost to the modern age. Though to Heraclitus—as to Char—the world seems, at first glance, an incomprehensible chaos governed by strife (πόλεμος), the early philosopher presumes the universe to be ultimately subject to invariable and inviolable principles of being and becoming which, though invisible, can be known through observation, understood, classified, and used.

---

(15) J. H. Matthews, *Surrealist Poetry in France,* p. 216.
(16) Reported from a private conversation with the poet, July 1973.

Le soleil... est nouveau chaque jour, mais il ne franchit jamais les limites qui lui sont propres, car les Erynnies, gardiennes de justice, ne cessent d'être aux aguets. Si de même le feu devient mer et si la mer devient terre, la mer cesse à son tour de relever de ce dont elle avait pris mesure avant que naisse la terre. Plus radicale que le mouvement est donc la permanence des mesures qui ne cessent de le régir (16a).

Jean Beaufret has shown that the distinction commonly made between the concept of immobility in Parmenides and the doctrine of universal mobility (πάντα 'ρεῖ), attributed to Heraclitus is arbitrary and superficial. Ultimately, the ancient Greek world—whether it believe in the cyclical evolution or the static permanence of being—is a world at rest.

«Certains se confient à une imagination toute ronde,» wrote Char. «Aller me suffit» («La Compagne du vannier,» *Seuls demeurent*, 1945). The pre-Socratic imagination is round. It believes in the orderly return of predictable events. «Le poème, disait Char sous le marronnier, n'a pas de mémoire; ce qu'on me demande, c'est d'aller de l'avant» (17). Heidegger and Char advance further into the magic forest of Perceval, seeking not only—like the surrealists before them—the identification of word and self, but of self and world, born in language.

«Je n'ai retenu personne, sinon l'angle fusant d'une Rencontre» («Biens égaux»). In the beginning, each word—and every idea—is an encounter (*la Rencontre* is one of Char's early key-words), and man's first contact with existence is visual perception. For Parmenides, this perception took the

---

(16a) Jean Beaufret, «Héraclite et Parménide,» an essay first published in *Botteghe Oscure*, no. XXV, Rome, 1960, and dedicated to Char in the special issue of *L'Herne*, 1971.

(17) Reported by Jean Beaufret in «L'Entretien sous le marronnier,» *loc. cit.*

form of purely contemplative vision. Hegelian dialectics and western philosophy in general start, according to Heidegger, with this basic assumption of being, questioned, by the modern philosopher, in *Sein und Zeit*.

«Entends le mot accomplir ce qu'il dit. Sens le mot être à son tour ce que tu es. Son existence devient doublement la tienne,» says Char in «La Scie rêveuse,» a series of aphorisms published in *Dans la pluie giboyeuse*. In every encounter, the poet seeks a rapport, a hitherto veiled and secret relationship between two or more *existants*. This rapport does not depend on any predetermined mechanism, nor can it be deduced from *a priori* assumptions (Hegelian dialectics, destruction and creation by fire in the *Fragments* of Heraclitus). It is based not on a universal *ratio*, but on individual sensory perception and states of being (Heidegger's «Stimmung» and «Befindlich-keit») different, at every moment, for every man. Therefore, it cannot be classified, transmitted, or used to predict the outcome of future encounters. The pagan sense of joy and terror sprang from man's ignorance and the concomitant feeling that the laws of nature—in which he implicitly believed, though he did not comprehend them—worked in dark and mysterious ways for his benefit or destruction. The existential anguish is the ultimate realization of man's freedom to call from the void a world for which he is responsible and which, in turn, is responsive to him. It is by a progression of individually established rapports that Char (like Braque) would try to uncover the nature of existence and essence.

> Nous savons que les Choses arrivent
> Soudainement,
> Sombres ou trop ornées.
> («Le Village vertical,» *Retour amont*).

Though the meeting of two *existants* may be—and often is—a chance encounter, the relationship established between them is never fortuitous. Nor is it limited to pure contemplation. It is not satisfied with rational calculation, but calls for affective participation of an «hyperconscience sensorielle» (18), total individual commitment, which begins, for Char, as the poet sets out on his «marche forcée dans l'indicible, avec, pour tout viatique, les provisions hasardeuses du langage et la manne de l'observation et des pressentiments» («Introduction,» *Dehors la nuit est gouvernée,* 1949) (19). The choice of the directional preposition (*dans*) is interesting. The poet embarks on a journey not towards, but into the unknown. His knowledge of the world will not come—as it did for Descartes—from a simple confrontation of a *res cogitans* with a *res extensa*. Visual contact alone does not reveal the secret relationships of being which the poet must unveil, at the risk of his own life. Man and the world mutually define each other: «En poésie c'est seulement à partir de la communication et de la libre-disposition de la totalité des choses entre elles à travers nous que nous nous trouvons engagés et définis, à même d'obtenir notre forme originale et nos propriétés probatoires» (*Partage formel,* XXI). If language and being are one, then every encounter with language is going to bring about a profound change within us (20). And every creative act will be not a spectacle, but «une naissance dont il [l'esprit créateur] sort lui-même transformé» (21).

«A l'exact opposé de la tentative mallarméenne, l'esprit, pour Char, a pour unique fonction d'adhérer à cet acte par lequel, immédiatement, indubitablement, l'être se risque dans l'existence,» wrote Georges Poulet (22). The poet and the world enter into a *commune présence* to mutually create—or destroy—each other. It is in this sense that every poem is

---

(18) Claude Vigée, *Révolte et Louanges,* p. 113.
(19) *Dehors la nuit est gouvernée,* originally published in 1938, was reissued in 1949 with *Placard pour un chemin des écoliers.* The preface which I quote was added to the work at this time.
(20) Martin Heidegger, *Unterwegs zur Sprache,* p. 159.
(21) Claude Vigée, *op. cit.,* p. 94.
(22) Georges Poulet, «René Char: De la constriction à la dissémination,» in *L'Arc, no. cit.,* p. 33.

an act, and every act, a risk, an act of faith. Though in order to see (and evaluate correctly what he sees) the poet must be free from preconceived ideas, his vision is not an empty glance. It seeks out the «terres émues, des terres propres à émouvoir une nature à nouveau enragée» (*Contre une maison sèche*). Desire and anticipation, unknown to the contemplative gaze of the pre-Socratics, enter into the poem of Char. «La sagesse,» says an aphorism of *Rougeur des Matinaux,* 1949, «est de ne pas s'agglomérer, mais, dans la création et dans la nature communes, de trouver notre nombre, notre réciprocité, nos différences, notre passage, notre vérité, et ce peu de désespoir qui en est l'aiguillon et le mouvant brouillard.»

The poet sets out on his journey of discovery with nothing but the hazardous provisions of language, the manna of observation and his «pressentiments.» The latter, one of Char's earliest *mots-clé,* appears in the title of a poem from *Le Tombeau des secrets,* 1930:

> Bel édifice ou les pressentiments
>
> J'écoute marcher dans mes jambes
> La mer morte vagues par-dessus tête
>
> Des yeux purs dans les bois
> Cherchent la tête habitable

This text was preceded in *Le Tombeau des secrets* by «L'Illusion imitée,» which reads:

> Revenir là où je n'ai jamais été
> En rapporter ce que j'ai déjà vu
> Aux prises avec l'ignorance
>
> La belle inconnue-limite.

The last line was used by Char to end a poem of *Ralentir Travaux,* «Découverte de la terre,» published the same year. When «Bel édifice ou les pressentiments» is reworked for inclusion in *Le Marteau sans maître,* 1934, the ending is changed to read:

> Des yeux purs dans les bois
> Cherchent en pleurant la tête habitable

and a new stanza, incorporating the title of «L'Illusion imitée,» is added:

> J'écoute marcher dans mes jambes
> La mer morte vagues par-dessus tête

> Enfant la jetée-promenade sauvage
> Homme l'illusion imitée

> Des yeux purs dans les bois
> Cherchent en pleurant la tête habitable

The title of the poem undergoes a small but significant change. It now reads: «Bel édifice *et* les pressentiments,» a correction already entered into the copy sent to Eluard in 1931, and more in keeping with the widespread surrealist practice of joining opposites not with the disjunctive *ou,* but by the conjunctive *et.*

A recent American thesis maintains: «In 'Bel édifice ou les pressentiments,' man's illusions hinder his search for truth; the poet seeks to be a 'bel édifice' which will contain this truth, but his 'pressentiments' prevent him from suceeding in this search» (23). Had the author examined the «Introduction» to *Dehors la nuit est gouvernée* which links «les provisions hasardeuses du langage» with «la manne de l'observation et des pressentiments,» she would, I think, have seen that of the either/or alternatives offered by «Bel édifice ou les pressentiments,» the poet, «errant sans atelier ni maison,» will choose the latter in search of his «demeure.»

---

(23) Virginia A. La Charité, *The Poetics and the Poetry of René Char,* p. 47.

For Char, the «pressentiment» is not an obstacle, but the hope interjected by the poet into «le vide horrible,» an «espoir-pressentiment qui ne relève que de nous, et n'est que le prochain état d'extrême poésie et de voyance,» (24) making of the poet the

> Visionnaire adapté aux surprises de la terre
> Malgré l'intimité multiforme du néant
> («Dire aux miens,» *Dehors la nuit est gouvernée*).

It is a premonition which leads poets and philosophers to the astonishment and surprise accompanying the «Découverte de la terre,» «car l'étonnement qui est le début de la philosohie —tout comme la surprise est le début des sciences—vaut pour le quotidien, l'évident, le parfaitement connu et reconnu; cela est aussi la raison pour laquelle il ne peut être réduit par aucune connaissance» (25). The foreboding of which Char speaks is a part of language itself, waiting to be verified—or disproven— by contact with the world: «La parole dépourvue de sens annonce toujours un bouleversement prochain. Nous l'avons appris. Elle en était le miroir anticipé («Couche,» *L'Effroi la joie*).

«L'Illusion imitée» would trace the origins of that antici-pation to prior experience (implying, perhaps, the Jungian archetype) which limits discovery of existence and meaning to that which is already known to exist. What is the «bel édi-fice» or the «belle inconnue-limite» that the poet should make thereof the repository of the truth he seeks? It is a *déjà-vu,* a forgotten certainty, limited by prior knowledge. It is a dead sea, the illusion of an illusion («l'illusion imitée»), without meaning or form. «Déjà en naissant,» says a text of *Aromates chasseurs,* «nous n'étions qu'un souvenir. Il fallut l'emplir d'air et de douleur pour qu'il parvînt à ce présent.»

---

(24) René Char, «Arthur Rimbaud,» in *Recherche de la Base et du Sommet*, 1965, p. 128.

(25) Hannah Arendt, *loc. cit.*

But the new second stanza of «Bel édifice et les pressentiments» introduces a man-made order into the original chaos,
as it invests the child with the power to divide the waters:
«Enfant la jetée-promenade sauvage.» It projects into the
void a new existence by establishing personal contact with
the world, a contact denied to the «Homme l'illusion imitée»
locked in what Heidegger has called «die Verfallenheit an
die Welt.»

The child—and the poet—come into contact with reality
by means of original sensory experience: «J'écoute marcher
dans mes jambes... Des yeux purs dans les bois cherchent...»
The poet listens to the stillness of the world and searches
the void in anticipation of the «bouleversement prochain.»
Hören and Horchen are, for Heidegger, primary prerequisites
for the phenomenological revelation of being. «Das Hören
konstituiert... die primäre und eigentliche Offenheit des
Daseins für sein eigenstes Seinkönnen... Das Dasein hört,
weil es versteht... Nur wer schon versteht, kann zuhören»
(Sein und Zeit, pp. 163, 164). The narrator of Char's
poem hears the sea march in his legs as his head is engulfed
by the waves. His consciousness is drowned as new ontological rapports are established via sensory perceptions not
limited to contemplative vision. It is in moments like these
that the poet comes to know the meaning of true freedom, as
defined in the journal of Hypnos: «Les rares moments de
liberté sont ceux durant lesquels l'inconscient se fait conscient
et le conscient néant (ou verger fou)» (Feuillets d'Hypnos,
no. 170). In order to perceive the independence and true
meaning of things, man must relinquish his power and control,
and his desire to dominate existence. Only in the «verger
fou» of total freedom will he find the «son à l'arbre suspendu»
(«Naissance du jour,» Les Cloches sur le cœur), and the «yeux
purs.»

«L'erreur du surréalisme, en tant que phénoménologie,»
wrote Claude Vigée, «fut de chercher dans les rapports de soi
et des mots la solution d'un problème qui ne peut être trouvée
aujourd'hui que dans les rapports plus essentiels de soi et du

monde. L'identification du mot et du monde, qui est la règle dans une période historique normale, ne convient plus à notre culture éclatée; c'est un héritage trompeur de la vieille 'fable du monde' cartésienne, trop sûre d'elle-même, et le legs du nominalisme philosophique qui substitue, à celui de la créature, 'le mystère d'un nom'.» (26) The meeting with Martin Heidegger signaled, in Char's development, a new direction: a movement away from the magical world of phanton and fable—to which the surrealist experience had led him—and a step forward into the existential void. Char is no longer a poet in the etymological sense, no ποιητής or *homo faber,* rhyming word and world, but a tool assisting in the transformation of matter and itself transformed in the process.

It is in «Le Bois de l'Epte,» one of the *Poèmes des deux années 1953-54,* that Char comes closest to the incarnation of the poetic tool, suggested very early in his career—though with quite different implications—by *Le Marteau sans maître.* «Le Bois de l'Epte» predates Char's personal contact with Heidegger. It was, however, written after the poems of *Les Matinaux* and the first version of *Lettera amorosa,* texts which, to my mind, are the last to celebrate the Heraclitean *Weltanschauung.* Beginning with the *Poèmes des deux années,* Char's canvases become more and more barren, and the collection begins with the quatrain:

> Harpe brève des mélèzes,
> Sur l'éperon de mouse et de dalles en germe
> —Façade des forêts où casse le nuage—,
> Contrepoint du vide auquel je crois.

In «Le Bois de l'Epte» the poet explores the void sketched by the tree and gives most memorable expression to what Heidegger has called «die Mitteilung der existenzialen Möglichkeiten der Befindlichkeit, das heisst das Erschliessen von Existenz...»

---

(26) Claude Vigée, *op. cit.,* p. 22.

Je n'étais ce jour-là que deux jambes qui marchent.
Aussi, le regard sec, le nul au centre du visage,
Je me mis à suivre le ruisseau du vallon.
Bas coureur, ce fade ermite ne s'immisçait pas
Dans l'informe où je m'étendais toujours plus avant.

Venus du mur d'angle d'une ruine laissée jadis par
    l'incendie,
Plongèrent soudain dans l'eau grise
Deux rosiers sauvages pleins d'une douce et inflexible
    volonté.
Il s'y devinait comme un commerce d'êtres disparus,
    à la veille de s'annoncer encore.

Le rauque incarnat d'une rose, en frappant l'eau,
Rétablit la face première du ciel avec l'ivresse des
    questions,
Éveilla au milieu des paroles amoureuses la terre,
Me poussa dans l'avenir comme un outil affamé et
    fiévreux.

Le bois de l'Epte commençait un tournant plus loin.
Mais je n'eus pas à le traverser, le cher grainetier du
    relèvement!
Je humai, sur le talon du demi-tour, le remugle des
    prairies où fondait une bête,
J'entendis glisser la peureuse couleuvre;
De chacun—ne me traitez pas durement— j'accom-
    plissais, je le sus, les souhaits.

Char tells us that this poem was conceived in Saint-Clair-
sur-Epte, a small town midway between Paris and Rouen.
Saint Clair, commonly referred to as «le Saint de la Lumière,»
had fled to the village to escape the amorous advances of a
lady. On the banks of the Epte, in a meadow called «le pré
du Paradis,» he built an hermitage to spend his life in seclusion
and prayer. But the vengeful lady's henchmen found and
killed the hermit. It is told that picking up his head, Saint
Clair threw it into a fountain, and then proceeded to his chapel,
where he lay down to die. A pilgrim's song recounts his
death:

Il meurt... ô prodige
Sa tête en ses mains,
Rose sur sa tige...
Surprend les humains.

To this day, the water of the numerous fountains dedicated
to the saint is said to cure eye ailments and even to restore
sight to the blind. A «cérémonie du Feu» is celebrated in
Saint-Clair-sur-Epte. The feast of the «Saint de la Lumière»
recalls earlier festivals dedicated to Vulcan, God of fire, the
original patron saint of the city, and celebrations of Jupiter,
God of thunder, venerated in a neighboring village.

The city has historic as well as religious significance. It
was on the banks of the Epte that Charles the Simple and
Rollon met in 911. In the church of Saint Clair they concluded a verbal treaty which gave to Rollon the provinces of
Normandy and Brittany. In 1911, the anniversary of the
founding of Normandy was celebrated in Saint-Clair by the
local inhabitants and the descendants of their Nordic invaders.

Char no doubt knew the legend of Saint Clair: the hermit,
the rose, the plunge into the water and subsequent renascence
are part of his scenario. But the poem is more than the
retelling of an old legend. Like the earlier «Bel édifice et les
pressentiments,» it records an original experience of existence,
not tied to any mythical past.

In the beginning, the poet is reduced to two legs that
walk. As he ventures into the amorphous and seemingly inert
world («dans l'informe»), he is without prior knowledge or
experience: «le regard sec, le nul au centre du visage» (27).
Suddenly, however, the phenomenological possibilities of
existence are revealed to him. The «deux rosiers sauvages»
plunging into the water establish, much like the earlier «Enfant
la jetée-promenade sauvage,» a new and meaningful rapport

---

(27) The words *nul, sec,* and *vide* are near synonyms in Char.
They designate the state most propitious to the emergence of an
«espoir-pressentiment» and have, therefore, a positive value.

with the world springing from the «angle fusant d'une Rencontre» («Biens égaux»). The «nul au centre du visage» becomes «la face première du ciel avec l'ivresse des questions... .» Sensory and affective involvement make of the aimless wanderer an «outil affamé et fiévreux,» the hammer of fire.

«Je humai... le remugle des prairies, ... J'entendis glisser la peureuse couleuvre...» The «Correspondances» established by Char are immediate and tangible. They exist only in the «Augenblick» of true presence, perceived with the rapidity of lightning (which the *passés simples* used here help to underline). Char will not cross the symbol-forest of Baudelaire in quest of a «ténébreuse et profonde unité.» He is not going towards any fixed goal that would lie somewhere at the other end of the wood, but remains content in the moment, the flash of lightning, «le rauque incarnat d'une rose,» the incomprehensibly new language emerging from the void, language that is concrete, almost carnal, the red and raw language of existence unpolished by formulaic or conceptual art. Char seeks not the «expansion des choses infinies,» but the ultimate contraction of the *instant.* In *Lettera amorosa,* 1953, he explains: «Il est des parcelles de lieux où l'âme rare subitement exulte. Alentour ce n'est qu'espace indifférent. Du sol glacé elle s'élève, déploie tel un chant sa fourrure, pour protéger ce qui la bouleverse, l'ôter de la vue du froid.»

It is interesting to see Char come back, in «Le Bois de l'Epte,» to one of his early words, *incarnat.* It figured in the original version of the poem «Confronts,» called «A la faveur de la peau,» one of the *Poèmes militants* in the 1934 edition of *Le Marteau sans maître,* reading, in part:

Hypothétique lecteur
Mon confident désœuvré
Qui a partagé ma panique
Quand la bêche s'est refusée à mordre le lin
Puisse un mirage d'abreuvoirs sur l'atlas des déserts
Aggraver ton désir de prendre congé

Les vivants parlent aux morts de médecine salvatrice
    de tireur de hasard à la roue de la raison
Les armées solides sont liquides à la sortie des
    oiseaux après le court exercice de la solitude
L'incarnat accomplit un mouvement de rotation
    autour d'un symbole d'une insignifiance désolante
Les yeux les moins avides
Embrassent à la fois
Le panorama et les ressources de l'île
Plante souple dans un sol rude

Mais voici le progrès
Les mondes en transformation appartiennent aux
    poètes carnassiers
Les distractions meurtrières aux rêveurs qui les
    imaginent
A l'esprit de fonder le pessimisme en dormant
Au temps de la jeunesse du corps
Pour voir grandir
La chair flexible et douce
Au-dessus des couleurs
A travers les cristaux des consciences inflexibles
Au chevet de la violence dilapidée
Dans l'animation de l'amour
Lorsqu'elle passera devant le soleil
Peut-être le dernier simple incarnera la lumière

Like «Le Bois de l'Epte,» the early text sends us back to Baudelaire, whose «Hypocrite lecteur» Char turns into the «Hypothétique lecteur.» «Confronts» is a speculative piece typical of the young Char. It separates mind from matter, «la chair flexible et douce» from «les cristaux des consciences inflexibles.» It is a mirror poem in the symbolist tradition, even if distorted by surrealist ideology. The world is the poet's inner view projected onto an outer screen and reflected back to the viewer, a dead and unfaithful image of reality: «symbole d'une insignifiance désolante.»

Both «Confronts» and «Le Bois de l'Epte» treat the subject of transformation. However, the early poem is, as its title

22

suggests, an ideological confrontation. It stipulates and defines a future existence seen as predictable event, «die Welt als Wille und Vorstellung.» The red color, «l'incarnat,» rotating around a meaningless symbol, is bent to the will of the *poètes carnassiers*. And yet, the poem's last line which names «la médecine salvatrice» in the medicinal plant of «le simple,» also echoes the Biblical word: «Dieu aime les simples.» The poet himself, for all his rebellious energy, returns to the fold. He is trapped in the closed and unbreakable circle of tradition, just as the «fade ermite» of the later poem is bound by the river banks. In «Confronts,» the speaker dreams of a world transformed by human word and will. In «Le Bois de l'Epte,» he is involved in the very act of transformation achieved, in the present, by the free interaction of mind and matter, man and world. It is precisely by *not* crossing «Le Bois de l'Epte» that the poet fulfills the desires of all. Unlike the *poeta vates,* Char does not seek to lead his readers through the *selva oscura* of earth into eternal salvation. There is, for him, no *diritta via smarrita,* only the continual *demi-tour,* the return to the beginning, and the *Retour amont.*

As C. A. Hackett has so well observed, the illumination sought by Char is not a light come from afar, not the «enlightenment» of Valéry or the mirror transparency of Eluard, but «le rayonnement d'une force intérieure,» shared, I would add, by word and world, man and nature, and made visible in the transformations of matter and mind recorded by the poem (28).

> Sans lendemain sensible ni capitale à abréger
> ...
> Sans ces forains tardifs aux bras chargés de lilas
> Sans ces perfections émaciées attirantes comme la
>   rondeur classique
> Messager en sang dans l'émotion du piège expiré
>   le congé d'orage,

---

(28) C. A. Hackett, «La Lumière dans l'œuvre de Char,» in *L'Arc,* no. 22, été 1963.

Je t'étreins sans élan sans passé ô diluvienne
amoureuse indice adulte.
    («Certitude,» *Dehors la nuit est gouvernée*).

«Le prix de René Char est ici,» wrote Georges Mounin,
«c'est un poète philosophe à l'état natif, et dont l'accent
dominant reste mis sur le sens du devenir» (28a).   Char rejects
both history and physical sciences as tools proper to the discovery of truth, or reality. «L'obsession de la moisson et
l'indifférence à l'Histoire sont les deux extrémités de mon arc.
L'ennemi le plus sournois est l'actualité,» the poet writes in
A une sérénité crispée.   And again: «Bien qu'elle affecte
d'avancer à coups d'excès, l'Histoire adore la modération; c'est
pourquoi l'Histoire est trouble, non troublante» (*ibid.*).   In
L'Age cassant, 1965, Char writes: «L'histoire des hommes
est la longue succession des synonymes d'un même vocable.
Y contredire est un devoir.»   He returns to the same theme
in 1972:   «Sortir de l'Histoire se peut.   En dynamisant ses
souterrains.   En ne lui laissant qu'un sentier pour aller» (*La
Nuit talismanique*).   In *Aromates chasseurs,* Char goes back
to prehistoric times, to the paleolithic theme of the hunter
transfixed by the animal he killed.   Of the discoveries of
science, the poet writes, in 1973 (*Argile* I):

> Entre télescope et microscope, c'est là que nous
> sommes, en mer des tempêtes, au centre de l'écart,
> arc-boutés, cruels, opposants, hôtes indésirables.
>   Après ces deux guerres totalisantes, échec de la
> philosophie et de l'art tragique, échec au seul profit
> de la science-action, la metteuse en œuvre, devenue,
> la gueuse à son fait-tout, sous ses visages meurtriers
> et ses travestis, le passeur de notre vie hybridée,
> pour elle affaire triviale.
>
>   («Lombes»).

(28a) Georges Mounin, *La Communication poétique précédé de
Avez-vous lu Char?*, p. 193.

Char is not interested in either past or future, but only in the «présent perpétuel, le passé instantané» («Aux portes d'Aerea,» *Retour amont*), in the moment or *instant* which, while enbracing all time and space, is itself without past or future. «Il y a le présent-passé, le présent-futur, il n'y a rien qui précède et rien qui succède, seulement les offrandes de l'imagination.» Char's aphorism of *Aromates chasseurs* re-states, in its own terms, Heidegger's definition of the «Augen-blick,» the true instant in which ontological possibilities are suddenly perceived. Existence is *freed from* the bondage of the past and the vain illusions of the future and made *free for* the possibility of individual choice in the present. It is in that sense that Char can speak of *delivering* «les mots de l'avenir de soi» («Buveuse,» *Dans la pluie giboyeuse*) and exhort man to «rejeter l'avenir au large de soi pour le maintien d'une endurance, le déploiement d'une fumée» («Maurice Blanchot, ...» *ibid.*).

That which is future-oriented (*avenir*) is founded on igno-rance and motivated by curiosity and fear. It seeks that which is far off and runs away from that which is at hand. It avoids the responsibility of choice. It is characterized by dispersion, uprooting, haste, ambiguity. The act of becoming (*devenir*), on the other hand, requires endurance, patience (an important word in Char and one not unrelated, in its original meaning, to Heidegger's concept of «Sorge»), and «la manne de l'obser-vation.» Antonin Artaud writes (in a letter to a friend dated «Paris, 3 avril 1931»): «C'est la fatigue d'esprit qui crée l'absence de patience, qui pousse l'esprit à *se* rejeter sur un verbalisme hâtif et *d'emprunt,* non vérifié par la sensation intérieure, par un *heurt* authentique du cerveau sur la réa-lité» (29).

The future is constructed on an illusory ideal which negates the freedom of choice and change. The true pre-sence comes

---

(29) Antonin Artaud's letter, addressed «A un ami,» was pub-lished in *L'Ephémère*, no. 10, été 1969. In the same issue, Char published *L'Effroi la joie*.

to terms with the real. In becoming, there is the anguish of individual possibilities of existence suddenly revealed. Anguish is without memory or prophecy. «Nous demandons à l'imprévisible de décevoir l'attendu. Deux étrangers acharnés à se contredire—et à se fondre ensemble si leur rencontre aboutissait!» («Encart,» *Le Chien de cœur*). Anguish respects distances and seeks to comprehend only the «Permanent invisible» (*Dans la pluie giboyeuse*), that which is near in space and time. It seeks the passage through and beyond that which it uncovers («Aliénés,» *L'Effroi la joie*), not into the predictable discoveries of science, but into the uncultivated regions of existence. It is not content to turn «le souhait» into «le constat.»

> Oui, l'ouragan allait bientôt venir;
> Mais cela valait-il la peine que l'on en parlât
>   et qu'on dérangeât l'avenir?
> Là où nous sommes, il n'y a pas de crainte urgente.
>   («Les Inventeurs,» *Les Matinaux*).

Anguish does not tolerate the fear of invisible but predictable future events. It plunges into the void. It accompanies not an *avenir*, a coming towards from without, but a *devenir*, an emergence from within. Heidegger defines the 'ἐκ-στάσις of the moment as follows:

> Die in der eigentlichen Zeitlichkeit gehaltene mithin *eigentliche Gegenwart* nennen wir den *Augenblick*. Dieser Terminus muss im aktiven Sinne als Ekstase verstanden werden. Er meint die entschlossene, aber in der Entschlossenheit *gehaltene* Entrückung des Daseins an das, was in der Situation an besorgbaren Möglichkeiten, Umständen begegnet ... Im Augenblick kann nichts vorkommen, sondern als eigentliche Gegen-wart lässt er *erst begegnen*, was als Zuhandenes oder Vorhandenes «in einer Zeit» sein kann.
>
>   (*Sein und Zeit*, p. 338).

— 341 —

The instant is an encounter in which the word and the world, being and existence establish a rapport and are simultaneously realized in the light of the *éclair*. Time, space, and the contradictions they govern are temporarily abolished:

> L'homme qui naît appartient à l'éclair. Il sera pierre d'éclair aussi longtemps que l'orage empruntera son lit pour s'enfuir.
> Y a-t-il vraiment une plus grande distance entre nous et notre poussière finale qu'entre l'étoile intraitable et le regard vivant qui l'a tenue un instant sans s'y blesser?
> («Excursion au village,» *Aromates chasseurs, in Argile* I, 1973).

The *res cogitans* and the *res extensa* are not just confronted, but fused, momentarily, in the «matière-émotion instantanément reine» (*Moulin premier*). Man and the world become one in what Antonin Artaud has called «un sentiment dans un espace de temps» (30). The instant is the moment of delivery in which being and existence emerge from the void. In this moment, anguish ceases to exist:

> A la seconde où tu m'apparus, mon cœur eut tout le ciel pour l'éclairer. Il fut midi à mon poème. Je sus que l'angoisse dormait.
> («Le Météore du 13 août,» *Fureur et Mystère*).

However, the joy that comes from the cessation of anguish can only be a temporary halt on the poet's journey into the unknown. «S'assurer de ses propres murmures et mener l'action jusqu'à son verbe en fleur. Ne pas tenir ce bref feu de joie pour mémorable,» says a self-given directive of «La Scie rêveuse» (*Dans la pluie giboyeuse*). The poet's «pressentiments» must lead him «de soupçon en douleur,» to the encounter of other *existants* waiting, like «des yeux purs dans les bois»

---

(30) *Op. cit.*

and the «rosiers sauvages,» to be called and delivered from
the seemingly meaningless chaos of darkness and night.

> Au même passé au même avenir
> Agonise un être qui avait faim de vivre
> («Morte saison,» *Les Cloches sur le cœur*).

Like Yeats, Char will leave the familiar and comfortable
labyrinth of legend and fable, casting away the coat «of old
mythologies» to face, in all its nakedness—and beauty—the
birth of his own creation, of which he says: «Te voici nue et
entre toutes la meilleure, seulement aujourd'hui où tu franchis
la sortie d'un hymne raboteux» («Biens égaux,» *Dehors la
nuit est gouvernée*, 1938) (31).   Like «Archiduc,» the partisan,
the poet will walk naked and insecure on the road beyond
happiness and despair, into the void, «Le Nu perdu»:

> Porteront rameaux ceux dont l'endurance sait user
> la nuit noueuse qui précède et suit l'éclair.   Leur
> parole reçoit existence du fruit intermittent qui la
> propage en se dilacérant.   Ils sont les fils incestueux
> de l'entaille et du signe, qui élevèrent aux margelles
> le cercle en fleurs de la jarre du ralliement.   La rage
> des vents les maintient encore dévêtus.   Contre eux
> vole un duvet de nuit noire.
> («Le Nu perdu,» *Retour amont*) (32).

The poet's journey is not a leisurely walk leading back to
the comfort and security of childhood and home, (33) but a
«marche forcée dans l'indicible,» a «marche forcée au terme

---

(31) «Biens égaux» was deleted from the 1949 edition of *Dehors
la nuit est gouvernée*, having been moved, in 1947, to *Le Poème
pulvérisé*.

(32) The prose poem «Le Nu perdu» was included in *Retour
amont*, 1966, and later gave its name to the anthology published
in 1971.

(33) Here my interpretation of Char's recent poetry differs from
that given by the late René Lacôte in his review of *L'Effroi la joie*
in *Les Lettres Françaises*, 23 July, 1969.

épars.» In *La Nuit talismanique,* Char restates his mission thus: «Nous marcherons, nous marcherons, nous exerçant encore à une borne injustifiable à distance heureuse de nous. Nos traces prennent langue» («Dévalant la rocaille aux plantes écarlates»). The poet walks the untrodden ways, going beyond the unjustifiable limits set by the dictionaries of reason. Step by step, he paces out reality, and language, on roads not marked on any map. «Les routes qui ne promettent pas le pays de leur destination sont les routes aimées,» says Char («Encart,» *Le Chien de cœur*). These are the *Holzwege* of Heidegger, «les routes qui ne mènent nulle part,» and which are, nevertheless, the paths of the forest «qui, parce qu'ils ne conduisent pas à un but fixé à l'extérieur de la forêt, et 'se perdent soudain dans le non-frayé,' sont incomparablement mieux à la mesure de celui qui aime la forêt et se sent chez lui en elle que les routes à problèmes soigneusement tracées sur lesquelles se bousculent les recherches des spécialistes en philosophie et en sciences humaines» (34).

The roads traveled by Heidegger and Char lead not to any «bel édifice,» but only «Von Dunkel zu Dunkel,» *Von Schwelle zu Schwelle* (35). For the threshold is the only permanent *séjour* of true pre-sence: «Die Schwelle ist der Grundbalken, der das Tor im ganzen trägt. Er hält die Mitte, in der die Zwei, das Draussen und das Drinnen, einander durchgehen, aus. Die Schwelle trägt das Zwischen. In seine Verlässlichkeit fügt sich, was im Zwischen aus- und ein-geht» (36). The key of this door, «la clé de la demeure» held by the poet, is the word:

Wechselt dein Schlüssel, wechselt das Wort,
das treiben darf mit den Flocken.

---

(34) Hannah Arendt, *loc. cit.*
(35) This 1955 collection by Paul Celan, Char's best German translator, contains an homage to Char called «Argumentum e silentio.»
(36) Martin Heidegger, *Unterwegs zur Sprache,* p. 26.

Je nach dem Wind, der dich fortstösst,
ballt um das Wort sich der Schnee. (37).

For the only home known to the poet—and to the philosopher—is the house of language, «das Haus des Seins.»

Char's *Retour amont* is not a journey into the past, but
a pressing forward and upward, into the unknown: «Amont
éclate. Et en bas le delta verdit. Le chant des frontières
s'étend jusqu'au belvédère d'aval. Content de peu est le pollen
des aulnes» («L'Ouest derrière soi perdu,» *ibid.*). The poet
remains the wanderer, «sans au-delà et sans lignée» («Les
Parages d'Alsace,» *ibid.*), sans «contentement ni désespoir»
(*Contre une maison sèche*).

* * *

Nul n'empêche jamais la lumière exilée
De trouver son élu dans l'inconnu surpris.
Elle franchit d'un bond l'espace et le jaloux,
Et c'est un astre entier de plus.
                    («Corail,» *Les Matinaux*).

The light of the *éclair,* in which meaning and existence
are simultaneously realized, can be neither predicted nor transmitted. The moment of its appearance is without past or
future; it is forever new. In an aphorism of *Contre une
maison sèche,* Char states: «Au séjour supérieur, nul invité,
nul partage: l'urne fondamentale. L'éclair trace le présent,
en balafre le jardin, poursuit, sans assaillir, son extension, ne
cessera de paraître comme d'avoir été.» Since any experience
of being and existence gained by any one man (poet or philosopher) is valid for none but himself, each one must try to
discover for himself the flash of lightning, each man anew
must «frapper le silex à l'aube» (*Aromates chasseurs*). Every-

(37) **Paul Celan,** «Mit wechselndem Schlüssel,» in: *Von Schwelle
zu Schwelle.*

one for himself must read the world, «s'opposer au flot des mots» (*ibid.*) to rescue from chaos the «paroles amoureuses» that divide the waters and make the rose speak.

The texts of *Aromates chasseurs* published in the first issue of *Argile* were preceded, in the journal, by a poem of Martin Heidegger, entitled: «Sprache»:

Wann werden Wörter
wieder Wort?
Wann weilt der Wind weisender Wende?

Wenn die Worte, ferne Spende,
sagen —
        nicht bedeuten durch bezeichnen —
wenn sie zeigend tragen
an den Ort
uralter Eignis, —
        — Sterbliche eignend dem Brauch—
wohin Geläut der Stille ruft,
wo Früh-Gedachtes der Be-Stimmung
sich fügsam klar entgegenstuft.

The world is a call, a sentence, «une phrase un peu plus longue,» which the poet and the philosopher, pilgrims in the void, discover in fragments:

> Nous la lisons en chemin, par fragments, avec des yeux usés ou naissants, et donnons à son sens ce qui nous semble irrésolu et en suspens dans notre propre signification. Ainsi trouvons-nous la nuit différente, hors de sa chair et de la nôtre, enfin solidairement endormie et rayonnante de nos rêves. Ceux-ci s'attendent, se dispersent sans se souffrir enchaînés. Ils ne cessent point de l'être.
> («Possessions extérieures,» *Dans la pluie giboyeuse*).

Though the illuminations perceived along the way are but intermittent flashes of light, isolated in space and time, the meeting of many stars may, in the end, make a constellation: Orion, or the poet's λύρα, «l'image [qui] scintille éternelle, quand elle a dépassé l'être et le temps» (38), *Sein und Zeit.*

(38) *Feuillets d'Hypnos.* An early version of this chapter, entitled: «The Light Within: The Encounter of Word and World in the 'Poem' of Martin Heidegger and René Char» appeared in the *Rivista di Letterature Moderne e Comparate,* vol. XXIX, n. 4, December 1976.

«POSTFACE»

L'inaction ce devoir nous quitte. Les tâches du réveil s'allument distinctes des berges de leur trajectoire. Le présent traité conjointement avec la puberté des ongles ne brime plus l'espoir sur le point de produire. Les formalistes toisent des mœurs invisibles. Au calendrier nos délégués déposent leur mansuétude. Le printemps gronde. Quel goût ont les outils?
«Postface,» Dehors la nuit est gouvernée.

The birth of a book—from private inception to public exorcism—is, as we know, a slow and cumbersome process. Since *Orion Resurgent* reached the proof stage, there have been three important critical studies of Char (1), a special Char issue of *World Literature Today* (2), and the first major English translations of his poetry (3).

Char has followed the songs of Orion with the *Chants de la Balandrane* (Gallimard, 1977): poems, dialogues, aphorisms, prose poems that sing «l'alliance de l'absurde et de l'amour;» winter-songs that celebrate night and dawn, the «froid glacial» and «le bruit de l'allumette,» «la voix et l'écho.»

«Je me voulais événement,» says a text of 1926 resurrected here. The event of Char's poem reaches an ever widening audience, ever more aware. Perhaps, one day, all of us, searching together, may hear «the whisper of stars,» dis-cover the constellations, and perceive the light in the land of Orion «resurgi parmi nous.»

---

(1) Mary Ann Caws, *René Char* (Twayne 1977), and *The Presence of René Char* (Princeton, 1976). James Lawler, *René Char. The Myth and the Poem* (Princeton, 1978).

(2) *World Literature Today*, vol. 51, no. 3, Summer 1977.

(3) Mary Ann Caws and Jonathan Griffin, *Poems of René Char* (Princeton, 1976).

APPENDIX

A. The Works of René Char

Listed below in chronological order are Char's major titles with dates of original publication and subsequent editions. Also given are several individual texts not contained in the major collections.

1924-25: «Toute poésie...» A prose text first published by Georges Mounin in *Les Temps Modernes*, no. 137-138, juillet-août 1957.

1927: «Comparses,» Paris, *Le Rouge et le Noir*, no. 4, oct.-nov. 1927. An essay dealing with the work of André de Richaud.

1928: *Les Cloches sur le cœur* (Paris: Le Rouge et le Noir).

1929: «Ce soir,» Aix-en-Provence, *Le Feu*, avril 1929.
«Mesures pour rien,» Paris, *Le Rouge et le Noir*, no. 8, mars 1929.
Arsenal (Nîmes: Méridiens). Republished with *Le Marteau sans maître, infra*.
«Profession de foi du Sujet,» *La Révolution surréaliste*, no. 12, 15 décembre 1929.

1930: *Le Tombeau des secrets* (Nîmes: Imprimerie Larguier).
«Le Jour et la Nuit de la Liberté,» *Le Surréalisme au Service de la Révolution*, no. 1, juillet, 1930.
«Les Porcs en Liberté,» *Le Surréalisme au Service de la Révolution*, no. 2, octobre 1930.
Artine (Paris: Editions surréalistes).

1931: *L'Action de la Justice est éteinte* (Paris: Editions surréalistes). Republished with *Le Marteau sans maître, infra*.

1934: *Le Marteau sans maître* (Paris: Editions surréalistes). Republished: 1945 (Corti), 1954, 1963, 1970.

1936: *Moulin premier* (Paris: G. L. M.). Republished: 1945, 1954, 1963, 1970, with *Le Marteau sans maître*.

1937: *Placard pour un chemin des écoliers* (Paris: G. L. M.). Republished: 1949, 1971, with *Dehors la nuit est gouvernée, infra*.

1938: *Dehors la nuit est gouvernée* (Paris: G. L. M.). Republished: 1949, 1971, with *Placard pour un chemin des écoliers*.

1945: *Seuls demeurent* (Paris: Gallimard). Republished with *Fureur et Mystère*, *infra*.

1946: *Feuillets d'Hypnos* (Paris: Gallimard). Republished with *Fureur et Mystère*, *infra*.

Premières alluvions (Paris: Fontaine). Republished: 1950 (G. L. M.), with *Art bref*.

«A la Santé du serpent,» Paris, *Fontaine*, no. 56, nov. 1946. Republished: 1954 (G. L. M.).

«La Conjuration,» Paris, *L'Arche*, no. 22, déc. 1946. Republished: 1947, 1967 (in *Trois coups sous les arbres*).

«Le Poème pulvérisé,» Marseille, *Cahiers du Sud*, no. 279, 1946. Republished: 1947 (Fontaine), 1953, 1972 with *Arrière-Histoire du Poème pulvérisé*, *infra*, and with *Fureur et Mystère*, *infra*.

1948: *Fureur et Mystère* (Paris: Gallimard). Republished: 1962, 1967.

Fête des arbres et du chasseur (Paris: G. L. M.). Republished with *Les Matinaux*, *infra*.

1949: «L'Homme qui marchait dans un rayon de soleil,» *Les Temps Modernes*, no. 41, mars 1949. Republished: 1967 (in *Trois coups sous les arbres*).

«Pourquoi ce chemin,» *Imprudence*, no. 3, mars 1949. Republished: 1957, with the title «De moment en moment,» included in *Poèmes et Prose choisis*, 1963, and reprinted as preface to Albert Camus: *La Postérité du Soleil* (Genève: Engelberts, 1965).

Le Soleil des eaux (Paris: H. Matarasso). Republished: 1951, 1967 (in *Trois coups sous les arbres*).

Claire, théâtre de verdure (Paris: Gallimard). Republished: 1967 (in *Trois coups sous les arbres*).

1950: *Les Matinaux* (Paris: Gallimard). Republished: 1964, 1969, with *La Parole en archipel*, *infra*.

«Quatre fascinants,» Marseille, *Cahiers du Sud*, no. 300, 1950. Republished: 1951, 1952 (in *La Paroi et la Prairie*, *infra*).

1951: *A une sérénité crispée* (Paris: Gallimard). Second version: Marseille, *Cahiers du Sud*, no. 373-374, sept.-oct., 1963. Republished: 1965, 1971 (in *Recherche de la Base et du Sommet*, *infra*).

1952: *La Paroi et la prairie* (Paris: G. L. M.). Republished: 1962, 1969 (in *La Parole en archipel*, *infra*).

1953: *Lettera amorosa* (Paris: Gallimard). Republished: 1962 (in *La Parole en archipel*), 1963 (Genève: Engelberts), 1964 (in *Commune Présence*, *infra*. Final version).

Arrière-Histoire du Poème pulvérisé (Paris: Jean Hugues). Republished: 1972.

«Le Rempart de brindilles,» Rome, *Botteghe Oscure*, XI, 1953. Republished: 1953 (Paris: Louis Broder), 1955 (in *Poèmes des deux années*, *infra*).

Homo poeticus (Alès: PAB, 1953).

«L'Abominable homme des neiges,» *N. N. R. F.*, no. 10, octobre 1953. Republished in Cairo, 1957, and 1967 (*Trois coups sous les arbres*).

1954: *Petit Dictionnaire portatif de santé* (Paris: G. L. M.). Introduction by René Char.

1955: *Recherche de la Base et du Sommet suivi de Pauvreté et Privilège* (Paris: Gallimard). Republished: 1965, 1971, considerably augmented.

Poèmes des deux années 1953-1954 (Paris: G. L. M.). Republished: 1962 (in *La Parole en archipel*).

1956: *La Bibliothèque est en feu* (Paris: Louis Broder). Republished: 1957 (*La Bibliothèque est en feu et autres poèmes*), 1962 (*La Parole en archipel*).

En trente-trois morceaux (Paris: G. L. M.).

1957: *Poèmes et prose choisis* (Paris: Gallimard). Republished: 1963.

1958: *Le Dernier Couac* (Paris: G. L. M.).

1962: *La Parole en archipel* (Paris: Gallimard). Republished: 1969 (with *Les Matinaux, supra*).

1964: *Commune Présence* (Paris: Gallimard).

1965: *L'Hôtel-Dieu de L'Isle-sur-Sorgue* (L'Isle-sur-Sorgue, 1965).

L'Age cassant (Paris: José Corti).

La Provence Point Oméga (Paris: Imprimerie Union).

Retour amont (Paris: G. L. M.). Republished: 1966, 1971 (in *Le Nu perdu, infra*).

1967: *Trois coups sous les arbres* (Paris: Gallimard).

1968: *Dans la pluie giboyeuse* (Paris: Gallimard). Republished: 1971 (in *Le Nu perdu, infra*).

1969: *Le Chien de cœur* (Paris: G. L. M.). Republished: 1971 (in *Le Nu perdu, infra*).

L'Effroi la joie (Saint-Paul-de-Vence: Au Vent d'Arles). Republished: 1969 (revue *L'Ephémère*, no. 10), 1971 (Paris: Jean Hugues), 1971 (in *Le Nu perdu, infra*).

1971: *Le Nu perdu* (Paris: Gallimard).

Contre une maison sèche, *L'Herne*, special issue: René Char, 1971. Republished in *Le Nu perdu*.

1972: *La Nuit talismanique* (Paris: Albert Skira, collection «Les sentiers de la création).

1973: «Aromates chasseurs,» *Argile*, no. I, hiver 1973.

1975: *Aromates chasseurs* (Paris: Gallimard).

1977: *Chants de la Balandrane* (Paris: Gallimard).

B. *Collaborative Works*

1930: *Ralentir Travaux* (Paris: Editions suréalistes), with André Breton and Paul Eluard. Republished: 1968 (José Corti).

1937: «Neuve,» «Paliers,» two poems written jointly with Paul Eluard.

1951: *Arthur Rimbaud, boulevard d'enfer* (Paris: Imprimerie Tour-non), with Jacques Dupin. Republished as «Sous un Portrait d'Arthur Rimbaud,» *Soleil*, no. 6, juin 1951.

1960: *Deux Poèmes* (Paris: Jean Hugues). First publication of the 1937 poems listed above.

Selective Bibliography

(Listed below are critical studies devoted wholly or in part to René Char and works of literary criticism of broader scope that may have influenced the foregoing analyses.)

Albérès, R.-M.: *Littérature du XXᵉ siècle* (Paris: Aubier, 1956).

Arendt, Hannah: *Essai sur la Révolution* (Paris: Gallimard, 1967).

Bachelard, Gaston: *La Dialectique de la Durée* (Paris: P. U. F., 1963).
— *La Flamme d'une chandelle* (Paris: P. U. F., 1964).
— *L'Air et les Songes. Essai sur l'imagination du mouvement* (Paris: José Corti, 1943).
— *La Poétique de la Rêverie* (Paris: P. U. F., 1961).
— *La Poétique de l'espace* (Paris: P. U. F., 1961).
— *La Psychanalyse du feu* (Paris: Gallimard, 1949).
— *Lautréamont* (Paris: José Corti, 1965). Nouvelle édition augmentée.
— *La Terre et les Rêveries de la volonté* (Paris: José Corti, 1948).
— *La Terre et les Rêveries du repos* (Paris: José Corti, 1948).
— *L'Eau et les rêves. Essai sur l'imagination de la matière* (Paris: José Corti, 6ᵉ éd., 1964).
— *Le Droit de rêver* (Paris: P. U. F., 1970).

Balakian, Anna: *Surrealism: The Road to the Absolute* (New York: The Noonday Press, 1959).
— *The Literary Origins of Surrealism. A New Mysticism in French Poetry* (New York: New York Univ. Press, 1947).

Barelli, Jacques: *L'Ecriture de René Char* (Paris: La Pensée universelle, 1973).

Barthes, Roland: *Essais critiques* (Paris: Editions du Seuil, 1964).
— *Le degré zéro de l'écriture* (Paris: Editions du Seuil, 1953).
— *Le plaisir du texte* (Paris: Editions du Seuil, 1973).
— *S/Z* (Paris: Editions du Seuil, 1970).

Battistini, Yves: *Héraclite d'Ephèse. Avant-propos de René Char* (Paris: Editions «Cahiers d'Art,» 1948).
— *Trois Présocratiques* (Paris: Gallimard, 1968).

Bayser, Yves de: «Horoscope d'un poète» in *Le Deuil des Névons»* (Bruxelles: Le Cormier, 1954).

Bédouin, Jean-Louis: *La Poésie surréaliste* (Paris: Seghers, 1964).

Béguin, Albert: *Poésie de la Présence de Chrétien de Troyes à Pierre Emmanuel* (Paris: Editions du Seuil, 1957).

Benoit, P.-A.: *Bibliographie des œuvres de René Char de 1928 à 1963* (Ribaute-les-Tavernes: Le Demi-Jour, 1964).

Bense, Max: *Die Realität der Literatur* (Köln: Verlag Kiepenheuer & Witsch, 1971).

Berger, Pierre: *René Char* (Paris: Seghers, collection «Poètes d'aujoud'hui,» 1951).

Bernard, Suzanne: *Le Poème en prose de Baudelaire jusqu'à nos jours* (Paris: Nizet, 1959).

Bersani, Jacques, et al.: *La Littérature en France depuis 1945* (Paris: Bordas, 1970).

Biemel, Walter: *Heidegger* (Hamburg: Rowohlt, 1973).

Blanchot, Maurice: *La Bête de Lascaux* (Paris: G. L. M., 1958).
— *La Part du Feu* (Paris: Gallimard, 1949).
— *L'Entretien infini* (Paris: Gallimard, 1969).
— *Le Livre à venir* (Paris: Gallimard, 1959).

Blin, Georges: *Georges Braque — René Char. Avant-propos au Catalogue de l'Exposition* (Paris: Bibliothèque Littéraire Jacques Doucet, 1963).

Bloom, Harold: *Kabbalah and Criticism* (New York: The Seabury Press, 1975).

Bodkin, Maud: *Archetypal Patterns in Poetry. Psychological Studies of Imagination* (London: Oxford Univ. Press, 1934, 1963).

Bohusch, Otmar, ed.: *Interpretationen moderner Lyrik* (Frankfurt a. Main: Verlag Moritz Diesterweg, 1971).

Boisdeffre, Pierre de: *Une Anthologie vivante de la littérature d'aujourd'hui* (Paris: Librairie Académique Perrin, 1965).

Boudon, Raymond: *A quoi sert la notion de «Structure»?* (Paris: Gallimard, 1968).

Bounoure, Gabriel: *Marelles sur le parvis* (Paris: Plon, 1958).

Breton, André: *Entretiens* (Paris: Gallimard, 1969).
— *Manifestes du Surréalisme* (Paris: Gallimard, 1966).
— *Position politique du Surréalisme* (Paris: Bibliothèque Méditations, 1972).

Brodin, Pierre: *Présences contemporaines* (Paris: Nouvelles Editions Debresse, 1954).

Buch, Hans Christoph: *Ut Pictura Poesis. Die Beschreibungsliteratur und ihre Kritiker von Lessing bis Lukács* (München: Carl Hanser Verlag, 1972).

Caillois, Roger: *Art poétique* (Paris: Gallimard, 1958).
— *La dissymétrie* (Paris: Gallimard, 1973).
— *La pieuvre. Essai sur la logique de l'imaginaire* (Paris: La Table Ronde, 1973).

Camus, Albert: *Carnets. Janvier 1942—Mars 1951* (Paris: Gallimard, 1964).

Caws, Mary Ann, ed.: *About French Poetry from Dada to «Tel Quel»; Text and Theory* (Detroit: Wayne State Univ. Press, 1974).
— *Poems of René Char* translated and annotated by Mary Ann Caws and Jonathan Griffin (Princeton: Princeton University Press, 1976).

— *The Presence of René Char* (Princeton: Princeton University Press, 1976).

— *René Char* (Boston: Twayne World Authors, 1977).

Chapon, François: *Dessin de Poètes. Préface au Catalogue de l'Exposition* (Paris: Galerie Le Bateau Lavoir, 1966).

— *Georges Braque — René Char. Texte du Catalogue de l'Exposition* (Paris: Bibliothèque Littéraire Jacques Doucet, 1963).

Charpier, Jacques et Seghers, Pierre: *L'Art poétique* (Paris: Seghers, 1956).

Chomsky, Noam: *Language and Mind* (New York: Harcourt, Brace & World, 1968).

Claudel, Paul: *Positions et Propositions* (Paris: Gallimard, 1928).

Clébert, Jean-Paul: *Histoires et Légendes de la Provence mystérieuse* (Paris: Claude Tchou, 1968).

Clouard, Henri: *Histoire de la littérature française du symbolisme à nos jours* (Paris: Albin Michel, 1962), 2 vv.

Cranston, Mechthild: *Enfance, mon amour... La Rêverie vers l'enfance dans l'œuvre de Guillaume Apollinaire, Saint-John Perse et René Char* (Paris: Nouvelles Editions Debresse, 1970).

Doubrovsky, Serge: *Pourquoi la Nouvelle Critique. Critique et objectivité* (Paris: Editions Gonthier, 1972).

Ducasse, Isidore: *Œuvres complètes* (Paris: Librairie Générale Française, 1963).

Dufrenne, Mikel: *Le Poétique* (Paris: P. U. F., 1973).

Durand, Gilbert: *Structures anthropologiques de l'imaginaire* (Paris: P. U. F., 1963).

Dutoit, Ernest: *Domaines* (Fribourg: Editions Universitaires, 1960).

Eco, Umberto: *Opera aperta* (Milano: Casa Ed. Valentino Bompiani, 1962).

Eliade, Mircea: *Le Mythe de l'éternel retour. Archétypes et répétition* (Paris: Gallimard, 1949).

— *Méphistophélès et l'androgyne* (Paris: Gallimard, 1962).

Eluard, Paul: *Œuvres complètes* (Paris: Bibliothèque de la Pléiade, 1968).

Empson, William: *7 Types of Ambiguity* (New York: New Directions).

Etiemble: *Hygiène des Lettres IV: Poètes ou faiseurs?* (Paris: Gallimard, 1966).

Fontainas, André: *Tableau de la poésie française d'aujourd'hui* (Paris: La Nouvelle Revue Critique, 1931).

Fraser, John: *Violence in the Arts* (New York: Cambridge Univ. Press, 1974).

Friedrich, Hugo: *Die Struktur der modernen Lyrik. Von Baudelaire bis zur Gegenwart* (Hamburg: Rowohlt, 1956, 1970).

Garelli, Jacques: *La Gravitation poétique* (Paris: Mercure de France, 1966).

Gascht, André: *Charme de René Char* (Bruxelles: Le Thyrse, 1957).

Glissant, Edouard: *L'Intention poétique* (Paris: Editions du Seuil, 1969).

Goldmann, Lucien: *Kultur in der Mediengesellschaft* (Frankfurt a. M.: S. Fischer Verlag, 1973).

Gracq, Julien: *Préférences* (Paris: José Corti, 1961). Nouvelle édition augmentée.

Gros, Léon-Gabriel: *Poètes contemporains* (Marseille: Cahiers du Sud, 1951).

Guerre, Pierre: *René Char* (Paris: Pierre Seghers, 1961). Collection «Poètes d'aujourd'hui.»

Hartley, Anthony, ed.: *The Penguin Book of French Verse, 4: The Twentieth Century* (Baltimore: Penguin Books, 1969), 5th ed.

Hartman, Geoffrey: *The Unmediated Vision* (New York: Harcourt, Brace & World, 1966).

Heidegger, Martin: *Der Satz vom Grund* (Pfullingen: Verlag Günther Neske, 1971).

— *Erläuterungen zu Hölderlins Dichtung* (Frankfurt: Vittorio Klosterman, 1963).

— *Identität und Differenz* (Pfullingen: Verlag Günther Neske, 1957).

— *Platons Lehre von der Wahrheit* (Bern: A. Francke AG, 1954).

— *Sein und Zeit* (Tübingen: Max Niemeyer Verlag, 1972). Neunte Auflage.

— *Unterwegs zur Sprache* (Pfullingen: Verlag Günther Neske, 1971).

Jakobson, Roman: *Questions de poétique* (Paris: Editions du Seuil, 1973).

Jean, Georges: *La Poésie* (Paris: Editions du Seuil, 1966).

Kristeva, Julia: *La Révolution du langage poétique* (Paris: Editions du Seuil, 1974).

Kreuzer, Helmut, und Gunzenhäuser, Rul: *Mathematik und Dichtung* (München: Nymphenburger Verlagshandlung, 1971).

La Charité, Virginia A.: *The Poetics and the Poetry of René Char* (Chapel Hill: The Univ. of North Carolina Press, 1968).

Lalou, René: *Histoire de la littérature française contemporaine* Paris: P. U. F., 1953).

Lawler, James R.: *René Char. The Myth and the Poem* (Princeton: Princeton University Press, 1978).

Lemaitre, Henri: *La Poésie depuis Baudelaire* (Paris: A. Colin, 1965).

Magny, Claude-Edmonde: *Essai sur les limites de la littérature. Les sandales d'Empédocle* (Paris: Petite Bibliothèque Payot, 1968).

Matt, Peter von: *Literaturwissenschaft und Psychoanalyse. Eine Einführung* (Freiburg: Rombach & Co, GmbH, 1972).

Matthews, John H.: *Surrealist Poetry in France* (Syracuse: Syracuse Univ. Press, 1969).

Mayer, Franz: *René Char Dichtung und Poetik* (Salzburg: Fink, 1972).

Ménard, René: *La Condition poétique* (Paris: Gallimard, 1959).

Minder, Robert: *Dichter in der Gesellschaft. Erfahrungen mit deutscher und französischer Literatur* (Frankfurt a. Main: Suhrkamp, 1972).

Mondor, Henri: *Mallarmé lycéen: avec quarante poèmes de jeunesse inédits* (Paris: Gallimard, 1954).

Mounin, Georges: *Avez-vous lu Char?* (Paris: Gallimard, 1947).
— *La Communication poétique précédé de Avez-vous lu Char?* (Paris: Gallimard, 1969).
— *Poésie et Société* (Paris: P. U. F., 1962).
Müller, Hartmut: *Formen moderner deutscher Lyrik* (Paderborn: Ferdinand Schöningh, 1970).
Nadeau, Maurice, and Kanters, Robert: *Anthologie de la Poésie française* (Genève: Editions Rencontre, 1967).
Nadeau, Maurice: *Documents surréalistes* (Paris: Editions du Seuil, 1945).
— *Histoire du surréalisme* (Paris: Editions du Seuil, 1964).
— *Littérature présente* (Paris: Corréa, 1952).
Nelli, René: *Poésie ouverte, Poésie fermée* (Marseille: Cahiers du Sud, 1947).
Onimus, Jean: *La Connaissance poétique* (Paris: Desclée de Brouwer, 1966).
Picon, Gaëtan: *L'Usage de la lecture* (Paris: Mercure de France, 1960), v. 1.
— *Panorama de la Nouvelle Littérature Française* (Paris: Gallimard, 1960).
Podewils, Graf Clemens von und Piontek, Heinz: *Ensemble 4. Internationales Jahrbuch für Literatur* (München: Bayerische Akademie der Schönen Künste, 1973).
Poulet, Georges: *Etudes sur le temps humain* (Paris: Plon, 1961).
— *Le Point de départ* (Paris: Plon, 1964).
— *Les Métamorphoses du cercle* (Paris: Plon, 1961).
Rau, Greta: *René Char ou la poésie accrue* (Paris: José Corti, 1957).
Raymond, Marcel: *De Baudelaire au Surréalisme* (Paris: José Corti, 1952, 1963).
Renard, Jean-Claude: *Notes sur la poésie* (Paris: Aux Editions du Seuil, 1970).
Renéville, Rolland de: *L'Expérience poétique* (Neuchâtel: A la Baconnière, 1948).
Richard, Jean-Pierre: *Onze études sur la poésie moderne* (Paris: Aux Editions du Seuil, 1964).
Rousseaux, André: *Littérature du Vingtième Siècle*, t. III, 1949; t. VII, 1961 (Paris: Albin Michel).
Rousselot, Jean: *Panorama critique des nouveaux poètes français* (Paris: Seghers, 1959).
Roy, Claude: *Descriptions critiques* (Paris: Gallimard, 1949-1958), 4 vv.
Sartre, Jean-Paul: *L'Imaginaire* (Paris: Gallimard, 1960).
Seghers, Anna: *Über Kunstwerk und Wirklichkeit. Die Tendenz in der reinen Kunst* (Berlin: Akademie Verlag, 1970).
Shattuck, Roger: *The Banquet Years. The Origins of the Avant-Garde in France 1885 to World War I* (New York: Doubleday & Co., Inc., 1961).
Simon, Pierre-Henri: *Histoire de la littérature contemporaine* (Paris: A. Colin, 1956).
Sojcher, Jacques: *La Démarche poétique* (Genève: Editions Rencontre, 1969).

Sollers, Philippe: *L'Ecriture et l'expérience des limites* (Paris: Aux Editions du Seuil, 1968).

Staiger, Emil: *Grundbegriffe der Poetik* (Zürich: Atlantis, 1963).

Stein, Peter, ed.: *Theorie der politischen Dichtung* (München: Nymphenburger Verlagshandlung GmbH, 1973).

Stevens, Wallace: *The Necessary Angel. Essays on Reality and the Imagination* (New York: Vintage Books, 1951).

Thomas, Henri: *La Chasse aux trésors* (Paris: Gallimard, 1961).

Todorov, Tzvetan: *Introduction à la littérature fantastique* (Paris: Editions du Seuil, 1970).

— *Littérature et signification* (Paris: Librairie Larousse, 1967).

— *Qu'est-ce que le structuralisme? 2. Poétique* (Paris: Editions du Seuil, 1968).

Tzara, Tristan: *Le Marteau sans maître. Prière d'insérer* (Paris: Editions Surréalistes, 1934).

Valéry, Paul, ed.: *Anthologie des Poètes de la N. R. F.* Préface de Paul Valéry (Paris: Gallimard, 1958).

Valette, Robert D.: *Album Eluard* (Paris: Tchou, 1967).

Vigée, Claude: *Révolte et Louanges. Essais sur la poésie moderne* (Paris: José Corti, 1962).

Weber, Jean-Paul: *Genèse de l'œuvre poétique* (Paris: Gallimard, 1960).

Wellershof, Dieter: *Literatur und Veränderung. Versuche zu einer Metakritik der Literatur* (Köln & Berlin: Verlag Kiepenheuer & Witsch, 1969).

Wimsatt, W. K., Jr.: *The Verbal Icon. Studies in the Meaning of Poetry* (Lexington: The Univ. of Kentucky Press, 1954).

Wise, Susan: *La Notion de Poésie chez André Breton et René Char* (Aix-en-Provence: Publications des Annales de la Faculté des Lettres, Série: Travaux et Mémoires, No. L, 1968).

Wright, James, *et al.*: *René Char's Poetry: Studies by Maurice Blanchot, Gabriel Bounoure, Albert Camus, Georges Mounin, Gaëtan Picon, René Ménard and James Wright* (Rome: Editions De Luca, 1956).

In addition to the book-length studies above, articles published in various journals have dealt with the life and work of René Char. A partial listing of these will be found in the special issue of *L'Herne, infra.*

The titles listed below will be particularly useful to scholars of Char:

Argile I, hiver 1973.
A journal founded in 1973 by Claude Esteban and containing in its first issue Martin Heidegger's poem «Sprache,» René Char's texts called «Aromates chasseurs,» and «Dessins» by Georges Braque.

Botteghe Oscure XIV, 1954.
Contains Jackson Matthews' translations of *Feuillets d'Hypnos* and *Lettera amorosa,* and an essay by René Ménard: «La Responsabilité des poètes modernes.»
Europe, juillet-août 1974.
A special issue devoted to the topic: «La Poésie et la Résistance,» with an article by Raymond Jean, «René Char ou le refus.»
L'Arc, no. 22, été 1963.
An issue devoted exclusively to René Char.
L'Ephémère, no. 10, été 1969.
Contains four letters by Antonin Artaud and René Char's «L'Effroi la joie.»
L'Herne, 1971.
A special issue devoted exclusively to Char and the most important single issue of a French journal dealing with the life and work of the poet.
Liberté, vol. 10, no. 4, juillet-août 1968, Montreal, Canada.
An «Hommage à René Char.»
World Literature Today, vol. 51, no. 3, Summer 1977. The first collection of «hommages» exclusively in English. Edited by Ivar Ivask, with beautiful photographs of Char and his landscapes.
The following catalogues contain texts by or about René Char:
Fondation Maeght: *Exposition René Char,* 1971. Foreword by Jacques Dupin.
Carpentras: *Exposition Denise Esteban,* 1974. Foreword by René Char: «Un droit perpétuel de passage.»
Paris: *Exposition Joan Miró,* 1974. Texts by Breton, Eluard, Char, *et al.*
Avignon, Palais des Papes: *Picasso 1970-1972.* Foreword by René Char.

INDEX

Se terminó de imprimir en
la Ciudad de Madrid el día
17 de Julio de 1979.

stuðia humanitatis

LOUIS MARCELLO LA FAVIA, *Benvenuto Rambaldi da Imola*: *Dantista*. XII-188 pp. US $9.25.

JOHN O'CONNOR, *Balzac's Soluble Fish*. XII-252 pp. US $14.25.

CARLOS GARCÍA, *La desordenada codicia*, edición crítica de Giulio Massano. XII-220 pp. US $11.50.

EVERETT W. HESSE, *Interpretando la Comedia*. XII-184 pp. US $10.00.

LEWIS KAMM, *The Object in Zola's* ROUGON-MACQUART. XII-160 pp. US $9.25.

ANN BUGLIANI, *Women and the Feminine Principle in the Works of Paul Claudel*. XII-144 pp. US $9.25.

CHARLOTTE FRANKEL GERRARD, *Montherlant and Suicide*. XVI-72 pp. US $5.00.

The Two Hesperias. Literary Studies in Honor of Joseph G. Fucilla. Edited by Americo Bugliani. XX-372 pp. US $30.00.

JEAN J. SMOOT, *A Comparison of Plays by John M. Synge and Federico García Lorca: The Poets and Time*. XII-220 pp. US $13.00.

Laclos. Critical Approaches to Les Liaisons dangereuses. Ed. Lloyd R. Free. XII-300 pp. US $17.00.

JULIA CONAWAY BONDANELLA, *Petrarch's Visions and their Renaissance Analogues*. XII-120 pp. US $7.00.

VINCENZO TRIPODI, *Studi su Foscolo e Stern*. XII-216 pp. US $13.00.

LOPE DE VEGA, *El Amor enamorado*, critical edition of John B. Wooldridge, Jr. XII-236 pp. US $13.00.

NANCY DERSOFI, *Arcadia and the Stage: A Study of the Theater of Angelo Beolco* (called *Ruzante*). XII-180 pp. US $10.00.

JOHN A. FREY, *The Aesthetics of the* ROUGON-MACQUART. XVI-356 pp. US $20.00.

CHESTER W. OBUCHOWSKI, *Mars on Trial: War as Seen by French Writers of the Twentieth Century.* XVI-320 pp. US $20.00.

MARIO ASTE, *La narrativa di Luigi Pirandello: Dalle novelle al romanzo «Uno, Nessuno e Centomila».* XVI-200 pp. US $11.00.

MECHTHILD CRANSTON, *Orion Resurgent: René Char, Poet of Presence.* XXIV-376 pp. US $22.50.

FORTHCOMING PUBLICATIONS

El cancionero del Bachiller Jhoan Lopez, edición crítica de Rosalind Gabin.

Studies in Honor of Gerald E. Wade, edited by Sylvia Bowman, Bruno M. Damiani, Janet W. Díaz, E. Michael Gerli, Everett Hesse, John E. Keller, Luis Leal and Russell Sebold.

HELMUT HATZFELD, *Essais sur la littérature flamboyante.*

JOSEPH BARBARINO, *The Latin Intervocalic Stops: A Quantitative and Comparative Study.*

NANCY D'ANTUONO, *Boccaccio's novelle in Lope's theatre.*

ANTONIO PLANELLS, *Cortázar: Metafísica y erotismo.*

Novelistas femeninas de la postguerra española, ed. Janet W. Díaz.

La Discontenta and La Pythia, edition with introduction and notes by Nicholas A. De Mara.

PERO LÓPEZ DE AYALA, *Crónica del Rey Don Pedro I,* edición crítica de Heanon and Constance Wilkins.

ALBERT H. LE MAY, *The Experimental Verse Theater of Valle-Inclán.*

JEREMY T. MEDINA, *Spanish Realism: Theory and Practice of a Concept in the Nineteenth Century.*

Robert H. Miller, ed. *Sir John Harington: A Supplie or Addicion to the «Catalogue of Bishops» to the Yeare 1608.*

María Elisa Ciavarelli, *La fuerza de la sangre en la literatura del Siglo de Oro.*

Mary Lee Bretz, *La evolución novelística de Pío Baroja.*

Dennis M. Kratz, *Mocking Epic.*